# Becoming Rhetorical

## Analyzing and Composing in a Multimedia World

### JODIE NICOTRA

*University of Idaho*

CENGAGE

Australia • Brazil • Mexico • Singapore • United Kingdom • United States

**Becoming Rhetorical:**
**Analyzing and Composing**
**in a Multimedia World**
**Jodie Nicotra**

Product Manager: Laura Ross

Senior Content Developer: Leslie Taggart

Associate Content Developer: Jacqueline Czel

Product Assistant: Shelby Nathanson

Senior Marketing Manager: Kina Lara

Content Project Manager: Rebecca Donahue

Manufacturing Planner: Betsy Donaghey

IP Analyst: Ann Hoffman

IP Project Manager: Betsy Hathaway

Production Service/ Compositor: MPS Limited

Senior Art Director: Marissa Falco

Text Designer: Liz Harasymczuk

Cover Designer: Irene Morris

Cover Image: iStockPhoto .com/Nathanx1

For product information and technology assistance, contact us at **Cengage Customer & Sales Support, 1-800-354-9706**

For permission to use material from this text or product, submit all requests online at **www.cengage.com/permissions.**

Library of Congress Control Number: 2017942435

Student Edition:
ISBN: 978-1-305-95677-3

Loose-leaf Edition:
ISBN: 978-1-337-55416-9

**Cengage**
200 Pier 4 Boulevard
Boston, MA 02210
USA

Cengage is a leading provider of customized learning solutions with employees residing in nearly 40 different countries and sales in more than 125 countries around the world. Find your local representative at: **www.cengage.com.**

To learn more about Cengage platforms and services, register or access your online learning solution, or purchase materials for your course, visit **www.cengage.com.**

Printed at CLDPC, USA, 07-20

# Brief Contents

## PART 1

### What "Becoming Rhetorical" Means                                          1

Introduction   What It Means to Become Rhetorical                             2

1   The Basic Rhetorical Situation                                            8

2   The Expanded Rhetorical Situation                                        26

## PART 2

### Rhetorical Analysis                                                      49

3   Analyzing Textual Rhetoric                                               50

4   Analyzing Visual Rhetoric                                                67

5   Analyzing Multimodal Rhetoric                                           100

## PART 3

### Rhetorical Production                                                   121

6   The Invitation to Rhetoric: Formulating Rhetorical Problems             122

7   Responding to Rhetorical Problems with Arguments                        146

8   Explaining                                                              186

9   Defining                                                                206

10   Evaluating                                                             223

11   Proposing                                                              243

## PART 4

### Tools for Composing                                                     259

12   Research: Composing with Multiple Sources                              260

13   Creating Written Compositions                                          290

14   Creating Visual Compositions                                           321

15   Creating Multimodal Compositions                                       356

# Contents

Readings by Modality      xvii

Preface      xxiii

Using *Becoming Rhetorical* to Meet WPA Outcomes (v3.0):
An Instructor's Guide      xxxi

## PART 1

### What "Becoming Rhetorical" Means      1

#### Introduction
#### What It Means to Become Rhetorical      2

What Is Rhetorical Training?      3
     **MindTap Tiny Lecture 1:** Rhetoric Is a Muscle      4
Why Rhetorical Analysis Is Important      4
Why Rhetorical Action Is Important      5
What It Really Means to Become Rhetorical: Transfer of Skills      6

#### Chapter 1
#### The Basic Rhetorical Situation      8

1a Communicators: How Do They Convince Us of Their Relevance?      8
     Appealing to Audiences through Character:
       How Communicators Build Ethos      9
       Ethos from sources external to the message      10
       Ethos from the message itself      10
1b Message: What Is the Communication About?      14
     Appealing to an Audience through the Strength
       of a Message: Logos      14
1c Audience: Who Is the Communication For?      18
     **MindTap How-To Video 1:** Analyzing an Audience      19
     Appealing to an Audience's Emotions: Pathos      21
     Assignment   Uncover Your Rhetorical Self      22
     For Reflection   Transferable Skills and Concepts      25

Chapter 2
**The Expanded Rhetorical Situation**                                        **26**

2a Context: What Are the Circumstances of Communication?                      27

2b Exigence: What Invites You to Communicate?                                 28
  **MindTap Tiny Lecture 2:** What Is Exigence?                               28
  **Questions to Ask:** Investigating Exigence                                30
  Letter: Mushroom Discrimination                                            31
  Letter: That Third Street Bridge                                           31

2c Purpose: What Does This Communication Want?                                34
  **How to** Determine a Communication's Purpose                             36

2d The Means of Communication (Modality, Medium, Genre, Circulation):
  How Does Communication Physically Happen?                                   38
  **MindTap Tiny Lecture 3:** Thinking about the Means
    of Communication                                                         39
  The Modality of Communication                                              39
  **Questions to Ask:** Thinking about Modality                              40
  The Medium of Communication                                                41
  **Questions to Ask:** Thinking about Medium                                41
  The Genre of Communication                                                 42
  **Questions to Ask:** Thinking about Genre                                 43
  The Circulation of Communication                                           44
  **Questions to Ask:** Thinking about Circulation                           46
  Assignment  Compare Compositions That Have Similar
    Purposes but Different Formats                                           47
  For Reflection  Transferable Skills and Concepts                           47

PART 2

**Rhetorical Analysis**                                                      **49**

Chapter 3
**Analyzing Textual Rhetoric**                                               **50**

3a Thinking Rhetorically about Reading Texts                                 51
  Understanding WHAT Is Said                                                 52
    Preview the piece.                                                       52
    Identify the main point of the text.                                     52
    Identify the text's purpose.                                             53
    Notice how the writer supports that main point.                          53
  Understanding HOW It Is Said                                               53
    Recognize the "big moves" of the piece.                                  53

Use a graphic organizer.                                         53
Identify the "textual structures" in the piece and understand what
     rhetorical work they're doing.                              53
Identify what creates the style and tone of the piece.           54
Finally, read the piece one more time.                           54
**An Annotated Rhetorical Reading:** Why You Should Think Twice
     Before Shaming Anyone on Social Media, by Laura Hudson      55

3b Writing Summaries                                             58
**How to** Write a Summary for an Academic Essay                 58
**An Annotated Academic Summary:** A Summary of "Why You
     Should Think Twice Before Shaming Anyone on Social Media"   59

3c Researching the Rhetorical Situation of a Text                60
**MindTap How-To Video 2:** Analyzing a Written Text             60
**Questions to Ask:** Researching the Rhetorical Situation       60

3d Doing a Rhetorical Analysis of a Written Text                 61
Preparing to Write a Rhetorical Analysis                         61
**Questions to Ask:** Analyzing Written Rhetoric                 62
**An Annotated Rhetorical Analysis Essay:** Shaming as Bullying:
     A Rhetorical Analysis of Laura Hudson's "Why You Should Think
     Twice Before Shaming Anyone on Social Media"                63
Assignments Analyze Op-Ed Pieces and Political Communications    66
For Reflection Transferable Skills and Concepts                  66

# Chapter 4
## Analyzing Visual Rhetoric                                     **67**

4a Thinking Rhetorically about Stand-Alone Images                69
**Questions to Ask:** Analyzing Images                           70
Thinking Rhetorically about an Image's Creator                   70
**Questions to Ask:** Analyzing the Creator of an Image          71
Thinking Rhetorically about the Technologies Used to Produce
     an Image                                                    71
     Photographs                                                 71
     Illustrations                                               73
**Questions to Ask:** Analyzing the Rhetorical Technologies of an Image   73
Images Create a Rhetorical Effect through Formal
     and Social Layers                                           73
**MindTap Tiny Lecture Video 4:** The Formal and Social Layers
     of an Image                                                 73
     The formal layer of images                                 74
     The social layer of images                                 82
**Questions to Ask:** Analyzing the Human Actors in an Image     87
**Questions to Ask:** Analyzing an Image's Objects and Settings  90

4b Thinking Rhetorically about the Placement, Circulation,
     and Distribution of Images                                              90

4c The Rhetorical Work of Images in Texts                                    91
     Analyzing Images Used as Illustrations                                  91
     **How to** Analyze Text and Images in a Composition                     93
     Assignment  Map an Issue through Images                                 94
     Analyzing Print Advertisements                                          95
     **How to** Generate Ideas for a Rhetorical Analysis of a Print Ad       95
     Assignment  Write a Comparative Ad Analysis                             98
     **MindTap How-To Video 4:** Doing a Comparative Ad Analysis             98

     For Reflection  Transferable Skills and Concepts                        99

## Chapter 5
## Analyzing Multimodal Rhetoric                                            **100**

5a Thinking Rhetorically about How Modalities Interact                       101
     **How to** Analyze Multimodal Compositions                              102

5b Applying Multimodal Analysis to Video                                     103
     Analyzing the Verbal Modality of Video                                  103
     **Questions to Ask:** Noticing the Effects of Text in Conjunction
        with Other Modalities                                                103
     Analyzing the Auditory (Sonic) Modality of Video                        105
     **Questions to Ask:** Analyzing the Rhetorical Effects of the
        Auditory Modality                                                    105
     Analyzing the Visual Modality of Videos
        (Still and Moving Images)                                            106
     **Questions to Ask:** Analyzing the Visual Modality of Videos           106
     Putting It All Together: Analyzing How Modalities Interact in Video     109
     **Annotated Example of a Multimodal Analysis:** Fear, Sorrow,
        and Finally, Relief: A Rhetorical Analysis of "Waiting for You to Notice"
        by Shared Hope International                                         109
     Assignment  Do a Multimodal Analysis of a Video                        112

5c Applying Multimodal Analysis to Websites and Apps                         112
     Identify the Basic Type of Site                                         113
     Identify the Site's Owner, Rhetorical Purpose,
        and Target Audience                                                  114
     Examine the Site's Content                                             115
     Study the Site's Interface                                             115
     **MindTap Tiny Lecture 4:** The Rhetorical Effect of Website Layout     117
     Examine the Interplay of All the Various Modalities                     117
     **How to** Analyze and Evaluate Websites                                118

Special Case: Analyzing Apps                                      118
**Questions to Ask:** The Metaphors of an App                     118
Assignments  Analyzing and Evaluating Websites and Apps           119
For Reflection  Transferable Skills and Concepts                  120

## PART 3

## Rhetorical Production                                          121

### Chapter 6
### The Invitation to Rhetoric: Formulating Rhetorical Problems    122

**MindTap Tiny Lecture 5:** Event-Based and Everyday Problems        122
6a Event-Based Problems                                              123
**Questions to Ask:** Event-Based Rhetorical Problems                124
Assignment  Tune in to Event-Based Problems                          125
6b Everyday Problems                                                 126
6c Tasks for Defining Rhetorical Problems                            128
1. Do Research to Deepen Your Understanding of a Problem             129
**MindTap How-To Video 4:** Identifying a Rhetorical Problem         129
Long-Term Assignment  Keep a Research Scrapbook                      129
**MindTap Student Maker Video 1:** Creating a Digital
   Research Scrapbook                                                130
Assignment  Visualize Your Problem                                   130
2. Identify Stakeholders in a Rhetorical Problem
   to Help Define Your Audience                                      131
**Questions to Ask:** Rhetorical Problem: Increase in Use
   of "Ghostwriting" Websites                                        132
3. Define Your Own Ethos in a Problem                                133
4. Describe the Problem and Give It Presence                         133
**How to** Give a Problem Presence                                   134
6d Articulating Rhetorical Problems through Writing:
   The Rhetorical Problem Statement                                  135
Describe the Problem                                                 136
Provide Evidence for the Problem                                     136
Find Your Focus: Write a Problem Analysis Statement                  136
Organize the Statement                                               136
**Example of Writing That Identifies a Rhetorical Problem:**
   The Problem with Little White Girls (and Boys): Why I Stopped
   Being a Voluntourist, by Pippa Biddle                            137

6e Addressing a Rhetorical Problem: Public Awareness Campaigns   140

   Assignment Create a Public Awareness Campaign   141

   For Reflection Transferable Skills and Concepts   145

## Chapter 7
## Responding to Rhetorical Problems with Arguments   146

7a Arguments as Inquiry, Not Fights   147

   Assignment Write an Initial Position Statement on an Issue,
   Then Question It   148

7b Inhabiting an Idea: Arguments as Response   149

   Using Stasis Theory to Clarify the Most Important Question   151

   **MindTap Tiny Lecture Video 7:** Using the Stases to Think
   through an Issue   151

   **Questions to Ask:** The Four Stasis Questions   151

     Questions of fact: Does/did something exist or happen?   152

     Questions of definition: What is it?   152

     Questions of quality: How do we judge it?   153

     Questions of procedure: What should be done about it?   153

   Assignment Use Stasis Theory to Map an Issue   154

   Identifying Your Position   155

     Why is this issue timely?   155

     What is your motive for arguing?   155

     What is your purpose for arguing?   156

     Who is the intended audience for your argument?   156

   **Questions to Ask:** Understanding Your Intended Audience   156

     What are the most appropriate means of communication
     (modality, medium, genre, circulation) for your argument?   157

     What are the outcomes and consequences of your position?   157

     What reasonable objections might there be to your position?   157

   **How to** Identify and Evaluate Counterarguments or Differing Positions   157

   Structuring Your Argument   159

     Claim   159

     Reasons   159

     Evidence   160

7c Written Arguments   161

   Response (Reaction) Papers   161

   **How to** Structure a Response Essay   163

   **An Annotated Academic Response Essay:** You Better Teach Your
   Boys to Cry: A Response to Chitra Ramaswamy, by Martha Mendez   164

   Assignment Write an Academic Response Essay   166

**Editorial:** Readers, Not Censors, Keep Fake News from Spreading,
by the Board, *St. Louis Post-Dispatch* (MO)    166

Responding to Arguments in Public    167

   Letters to the editor    167

   Assignment   Write a Letter to the Editor    172

   Open letters    172

**Example of a Serious Open Letter:** *Slack.com* to Microsoft    173

**Example of a Funny Open Letter:** An Open Letter to Recent College
Grads Who Are Already Paying Their Own Phone Bills, by Jenna Barnett    175

   Assignment   Write an Open Letter    177

   Responding with comments to blogs and news stories    177

   Assignment   Entering the Discussion    178

7d Visual Arguments    178

   **MindTap Student Maker Video 2:** Designing a Logo    179

   Assignment   Create Public Awareness Campaign Posters    180

   Incorporating Images in Your Poster    180

**Questions to Ask:** Choosing Images for Your Public
Awareness Campaign Posters    181

7e Multimodal Arguments    183

   Assignment   Create an Op-Doc    183

   For Reflection   Transferable Skills and Concepts    185


**Chapter 8**
## Explaining    **186**

8a The Booming Business of Explanations    186

8b Explaining as a Rhetorical Activity    189

8c The Elements of Explanations    195

   Understand Your Audience    195

   Have a Specific Purpose for Your Explanation    196

   Organize Your Explanation Logically    197

     Possible scheme for explaining current events    197

     Possible scheme for explaining scientific or technical objects,
concepts, or processes    198

**An Annotated Explanation of a Technical or Scientific Process:**
HowStuffWorks: How Do They Get the Fat Out of Fat-Free Foods?    199

     Possible scheme for explaining cultural phenomena    201

   Decide How to Present Your Explanation    202

   Assignments   Composing Explanations    203

   For Reflection   Transferable Skills and Concepts    205

## Chapter 9
## Defining                                                                    206

9a Definitions within Communities                                              206
   **MindTap Student Maker Video 3:** Defining a Canon            207
9b Making Arguments of Definition                                              208
   **MindTap Tiny Lecture Video 8:** Understanding When a Thing
   or Concept Is Ripe for Redefinition                           208
   Arguments about Genus: How Should the Thing Be Defined?       210
   Arguments about Classification: Should the Thing Be Defined
   as Y or Z?                                                     216
9c Formulating Definition Arguments                                            219
   **An Annotated Written Definition Argument:** Technology Is a Lens,
   Not a Prosthetic                                               219
   Assignments Composing Definitions                              222
   For Reflection Transferable Skills and Concepts                222

## Chapter 10
## Evaluating                                                                  223

10a Everyday Evaluations                                                       223
   **MindTap Student Maker Video 4:** Reviewing a Video           225
10b Establishing and Ranking Criteria: The Heart of an Evaluation              225
   **MindTap Tiny Lecture Video 9:** Identifying and Rating
   Criteria for Evaluation                                        225
   **An Annotated Example of Identifying Criteria:** *Frozen* an Icy Blast
   of Fun from the First Snowflake, by Betsy Sharkey, *Los Angeles
   Times* Film Critic                                             227
10c Using Evidence in Evaluation Arguments to Draw Conclusions about X         230
10d Evaluating Consumer Products                                               233
   Assignment Write a Review of a Local Business, Event, or Attraction   234
10e Composing Multimodal Consumer Reviews                                      234
   Assignment Create a Video Review of a Consumer Product         235
   Assignment Review a Film for Common Sense Media                236
10f Evaluating a Person's Accomplishments                                      236
   Assignment Appreciation or Critique                           238
10g Evaluating Policies                                                        238
   **MindTap How-To Video 5:** How to Evaluate a Policy          238
   Assignment Write an Evaluation of a Policy or Decision         241
   For Reflection Transferable Skills and Concepts                242

## Chapter 11
**Proposing**      **243**

11a The Gold Standard of Persuasion: Action      243

11b Components of Proposal Arguments      244

11c Persuasively Describing a Problem or Need      246
> **Questions to Ask:** Defining Problems      247

11d Making a Compelling Proposal Claim      249

11e Providing Support for Your Proposal      251
> **An Annotated Policy Proposal:** How Should We Deal with
> Plastic Bags? By James MacDonald      252

11f Acknowledging Potential Problems with Your Proposal      254

11g Showing That Your Proposal Will Fix the Problem      255
> Assignments Composing Proposals      255
> For Reflection Transferable Skills and Concepts      257

## PART 4
**Tools for Composing**      **259**

## Chapter 12
**Research: Composing with Multiple Sources**      **260**

12a The Recursive Steps of the Research Process      262
> Formulating Initial Research Questions      262
> Generating Initial Keywords to Help You Conduct a Search      263
> Identifying Initial Sources to Help You Clarify Your Own Position      264
> Establishing a System to Help You Keep Track of Your Sources      264
> Evaluating the Validity and Relative Rhetorical Significance
> of Your Sources      266
> **Questions to Ask:** Thinking Rhetorically about a Research Source      268
> E-Learning: India's Education System Needs to Get Online      269
> Finding Better Sources and Generating Better Keywords
> as Your Position on the Issue Becomes Clearer      271
> Writing "Zero Drafts" to Clarify Your Thinking      271

12b Incorporating Sources into Your Compositions      271
> Summarizing, Paraphrasing, and Quoting to Incorporate
> Texts and Avoid Plagiarism      272
> Indicating use of sources      274
> Citing Sources with Different Citation Styles      276

MLA style                                                             277
   The core elements of a works-cited entry            277
   The elements of an in-text citation                 278
   Formatting the core elements in a works-cited entry 278
   Sample works-cited entries: Books                   280
   Sample works-cited entries: Periodicals             280
   Sample works-cited entries: Other source types      281
APA style                                                             282
   The elements of in-text citations in APA format     282
   Sample references entries: Periodicals              284
   Sample references entries: Books and book chapters  284
   Sample references entries: Other source types       285
Informal Citation in Written, Visual, and Multimodal Compositions     286
   Informal citation in print texts                    286
   Informal citation in Web texts (linking)            286
   Informal citation in infographics                   286
Assignment Write a "Critical Conversation" Essay                      288
For Reflection Transferable Skills and Concepts                       289

## Chapter 13
## Creating Written Compositions                                      **290**

13a Embracing the Messiness of the Writing Process                    291
   Invention: Generating Ideas                         292
     Considering purpose, audience, and the means of communication   293
     Freewriting                             294
     Mind mapping                            294
     Questioning                             295
   Drafting                                            296
   Revising                                            297
     Reverse outlining                       298
   **Annotated First Draft:** You Better Teach Your Boys to Cry   298
13b Writing in Academic Genres                                        302
   Anatomy of Academic Essays                          303
     Titles                                  304
     Introductions                           305
     Paragraphing with PIE (Point, Illustration, Explanation)   308
     Conclusions                             311
   **Questions to Ask:** Drafting a Conclusion         311
   **An Annotated Academic Essay:** Echoes of 1776 in 2011: A Rhetorical
   Analysis of Nicholas Kristof's "Watching Protesters Risk It All"   312

13c Writing for Civic Participation                                     315
    Letters to Legislators                                          315
    Opinion Pieces (Newspaper Op-Eds, Opinion-Based Web Content)    316
    **An Annotated Opinion Column:** Their View: Why Health Insurance
        Isn't a Rolls Royce or a Beater, by Christopher Drummond and Jessica
        Bearman                                                       318
    Fact Sheets                                                    319

## Chapter 14
## Creating Visual Compositions                                        321

14a When to Use Visual Compositions for Rhetorical Purposes             322
    **Questions to Ask:** Using Visuals to Address Rhetorical Problems    323
14b Good Visual Design: Basic Building Blocks                           324
    Contrast: Boldness Creates a Hierarchy of Information          325
        Creating contrast with color                              326
        Creating contrast with size                               329
        Creating contrast with typeface                           331
        Don't overdo it: Use contrast sparingly                   332
    Repetition: Create Meaningful Visual Patterns                  333
        . . . But TOO much repetition is boring                   335
    Alignment: Strong Lines Guide the Viewer's Eye                 336
        Don't center everything                                   336
        Design with a grid to ensure alignment                    338
    Proximity: Keep Related Things Together                        339
        Use white space deliberately                              341
14c How-Tos: Tutorials for Specific Visual Compositions                 341
    Designing Infographics                                         341
        Identifying a subject for your infographic                342
        Identifying an audience for your infographic              342
        Creating your infographic                                 343
    Designing Presentation Slides                                  343
    Designing Posters                                              345
        Designing posters to announce events                      345
        Remember the CRAP principles!                             347
    Assignment Design a Poster Announcing an Event                 348
        Designing posters for presentations                       348
    Designing Brochures                                            350
        Getting started: Using audience to determine a brochure's
            content and format                                    351
        Brochure content                                          352

Brochure format                                                                          352
A word about templates                                                                   354
A good example: "The Chicken Dance Trail" brochure                                       354

## Chapter 15
## Creating Multimodal Compositions                                                      356

**Questions to Ask:** Creating Multimodal Compositions                                   357

### 15a How to Create Videos                                                              358
Planning the Video                                                                        358
  1. Answer the basic rhetorical questions.                                     358
  2. Pitch your idea in a "treatment."                                          359
**Questions to Ask:** The Elements of a Treatment                                         359
  3. Write a script.                                                            360
  4. Plan your shots (brainstorming, sequencing, and storyboarding).            360
  5. Create a storyboard.                                                       361
**How to** Plan the Sequence of Your Video                                                362
  6. Schedule as necessary.                                                     362
Getting Footage for the Video                                                             363
  "Found footage," B-roll, and other elements                                   363
  Shooting your own video                                                       363
  Rhetorical considerations for shooting video                                  363
  Conducting interviews                                                         364
  Technical considerations for shooting video                                   365
Editing Video                                                                             369
Copyright and Fair Use                                                                    371

### 15b How to Create Podcasts                                                            373
Basic Steps for Creating a Podcast                                                        373

### 15c How to Create Websites                                                            376
Rhetorical Considerations for Creating Websites                                           376
**Questions to Ask:** Planning Website Content                                            378
  Example of a student planning website content                                 379
Technical Considerations for Creating Websites                                            380
  A domain name                                                                 380
  Website-building software                                                     380

Glossary                                                                                  382
Bibliography                                                                              384
Credits                                                                                   388
Index                                                                                     391
Assignments by Modality                                                                   406

# Readings by Modality

## ▤ TEXTUAL SELECTIONS

American Diabetes Association, "Healthy Weight Loss" (online article), 1b

Barnett, "An Open Letter to Recent College Grads Who Are Already Paying Their Own Phone Bills" (open letter), 7c

Biddle, "The Problem with Little White Girls (and Boys): Why I Stopped Being a Voluntourist" (online article), 6d

Cassidy, "A Welcome Setback for Donald Trump" (magazine article), 8b

Chaney, "That Third Street Bridge" (letter), 2b

Dinehard, "Teaching Handwriting in Early Childhood: Brain Science Shows Why We Should Rescue This Fading Skill" (online magazine article), 11c

Drummond and Bearman, "Their View: Why Health Insurance Isn't a Rolls Royce or a Beater" (newspaper op-ed), 13c

Florez, "Student Loan Debt: A Problem for All" (article), 10c

French, "Trump's Executive Order on Refugees—Separating Fact from Hysteria" (online article), 8b

*The Hindustan Times*, "E-Learning: India's Education System Needs to Get Online" (newspaper op-ed), 12a

Hudson, "Why You Should Think Twice Before Shaming Anyone on Social Media" (online magazine article), 3a

Jorgensen, "Dancing to Help an Aging Brain" (article excerpt), 12b

Kulik, "Miranda Parks Visualized Her Way to a Better Body" (magazine article), 1b

Lampo, "Why Gay Rights Are Civil Rights—and Simply Right" (newspaper op-ed), 9b

MacDonald, "How Should We Deal with Plastic Bags?" (online magazine article), 11e

Magid, "View of Civil Rights Troubling" (letter to the editor), 7c

Maxwell, "Higher Education Needs Soul" (newspaper op-ed), 9b

Mendez, "Reverse Outline, 'You Better Teach Your Boys to Cry'" (table), 13a

Mendez, "You Better Teach Your Boys to Cry" (student essay), 13a

Mendez, "You Better Teach Your Boys to Cry: A Response to Chitra Ramaswamy," (student essay), 7c

Millenson, "College Rankings Should Account for Binge Drinking" (newspaper op-ed), 1a

Morrongiello, "White House Supports Making Women Register for the Draft" (newspaper article), 2b

"On-Campus 'Carry' Bill" (article), 10g

Parry, "With Gorsuch, Don't Judge the Book by Its Cover" (newspaper op-ed), 7c

Queen, "God's Definition of Marriage" (newspaper op-ed), 9b

*St. Louis Dispatch*, "Editorial: Readers, Not Censors, Keep Fake News from Spreading" (newspaper editorial), 7c

Salaita, How Do They Get the Fat Out of Fat-Free Foods? (article), 8e

Sharkey, "*Frozen:* An Icy Blast of Fun from the First Snowflake" (movie review), 10b

Slack.com, Open Letter to Microsoft (open letter), 7c

USDA, "Protect Your Baby and Yourself from Listeriosis" (fact sheet), 13c

Wellspring, "Steel Cut Oats, a Non-Fancy Superfood" (blog excerpt), 12b

Yake, "Mushroom Discrimination" (letter), 2b

## VISUAL SELECTIONS

Washington Monument (photo), Introduction

NutriGrain Bars (photo), Introduction

*University of Idaho* (website), Introduction

Ronald Reagan (photo), 1a

"Crying Jordan Afghan girl" meme (photo), 1b

"Lose Weight…" (print advertisement), 1b

Branco, "Quick Pick" (cartoon), 1c

Kairos (photo), 2b

Chad Elliott (photo), 2d

Baggage Claim (photo), 4

Subway (photo), 4

Pre- and Post-Digitally Altered Photograph (photo), 4a

Oval Office (photo), 4a

Obama Selfie (photo), 4a

Obama Selfie with Michelle (photo), 4a

Obama and Holder (photo), 4a

Obama Cabinet Meeting (photo), 4a

White House (photo), 4a

Obama in Oval Office (photo), 4a

Marine One (photo), 4a

Junior Ranger Day (photo), 4a

Pig Drawing (infographic), 4a

Sunflowers (photo), 4a

Clarins (print advertisement), 4a

Malarial Parasite (infographic), 4a

Panda (photo), 4a

Doritos Model (photo), 4a

Tupac Shakur (photo), 4a

"We Can Do It!" (print advertisement), 4a

*The Raw Story* (website), 4b

TV News Screen (screen capture), 5

Shared Hope International (website), 5b

*Paper Moon Salon* (website), 5c

*University of Idaho* (website), 5c

Microsoft "Bob" (screen capture), 5c

*US Bank* (website), 5c

iPad Calendar App (screen capture), 5c

Megaload Protest (photo), 6a

*Wikipedia* Black-out Page (website), 6a

*Pinterest* Board (website), 6c

Removing Rocks from Beans (photo), 6d

Tying Friendship Bracelets (photo), 6d

Greenpeace, "Don't Believe the Dirty Lie" (print
advertisement), 6e

*Stand Up 4 Public Schools* (website), 6e

National School Boards Association (print advertisement), 6e

Images of Rain (photo), 7d

World Wildlife Fund, Poster (print advertisement), 7d

Hillary Clinton and Barack Obama (print advertisement), 7d

Meth Project (print advertisement), 7d

"The Marijuana Divide" (video still), 7e

"Ideological Profile of Each Source's Audience" (infographic), 8a

"Shoplifters of the World Unite" (infographic), 8c

Logging (photo), 9a

Snowmobiles (photo), 9a

Forest (photo), 9a

Hot Dog (photo), 9b

Vandalism or Art? (photo), 9b

Jeans (photos), 10a

City Street (photo), 10b

Yelp logo (photo), 10d

*Angie's List* logo (photo), 10d

*Consumer Reports* logo (photo), 10d

"I Lose My Keys All. The. Time." (print advertisement), 11c

Snow-Covered Steps (photo), 11c

Bumper Stickers (photo), 11e

*Google* Searches (website), 12a

*Google* Search: "Effectiveness Online Education" (website), 12a

*LexisNexis* Search: "Effectiveness Online Education" (website), 12a

*LexisNexis* Search: "Effectiveness Online Education, Distance Learning" (website), 12a

Library Database with DOI Number (website), 12b

"Brachiosaurus" Wikipedia Page (website), 12b

"Blogging and Intellectual Property Law" (website), 12b

"A Traveller's Guide to Tap Water" Source List (infographic), 12b

Paragraph PIE (photo), 13b

USDA, "Food Safety Information" (infographic), 13c

John Gotti's Defense Chart (infographic), 14

"Can You See the Forest for the Trees?" (photos), 14b

PowerPoint Color Value Gradient (screen capture), 14b

Saturation Gradient (screen capture), 14b

*ChurchMedia* (website), 14b

*Discover Los Angeles* (website), 14b

*Folk Couture* (website), 14b

"Marshalling Signals" before and after (infographic), 14b

"Booktalks" (brochure), 14b

Somersby Cider (web advertisement), 14b

Somersby Cider (web advertisement), 14b

*Digital Public Library of America* (website), 14b

Wexford Garden Club (print advertisement), 14b

"Violent Crime Duo Caught on Video" (photo), 14b

"Aikido" (flyer), 14c

"Effects of Floral Defenses and Attraction on Flower Insects" (poster), 14c

Project Baseline (poster), 14c

"The Chicken Dance Trail" (brochure), 14c

Inadequate Lighting (video still), 15a

Silhouette (video still), 15a

Three-Point Lighting (photo), 15a

Microphone (photo), 15a

Podcasting Setup (photo), 15b

*Nathaniel A. Rivers Ph.D* (website), 15c

WYSIWYG on *Wix* (website), 15c

Bacterium as Disease-Causing Agent (presentation slide), 14c

Church Street (Burlington, Vermont) Prospective (architect's drawing), 10b

Church Street (Burlington, Vermont) (photo), 10b

## ▷ MULTIMODAL SELECTIONS

*University of Idaho* (website), Introduction

Kulik, "Miranda Parks Visualized Her Way to a Better Body" (article), 1b

"Lose Weight…" (print advertisement), 1b

*Elite Daily* (website), 2c

Chocolate Chip Recipe from *Delish* website (video still), 2d

Chad Elliott (video still), 2d

*The Raw Story* (website), 4b

TV News Screen (screen capture), 5

*Shared Hope International* (website), 5b

*Paper Moon Salon* (website), 5c

*University of Idaho* (website), 5c

Microsoft "Bob" (screen capture), 5c

*US Bank* (website), 5c

iPad Calendar App (screen capture), 5c

*Wikipedia* (website), 6a

*Pinterest Board* (website), 6c

Biddle, "The Problem with Little White Girls (and Boys): Why I
    Stopped Being a Voluntourist" (article), 6d

*Stand Up 4 Public Schools* (website), 6e

"The Marijuana Divide" (video still), 7e

*Google* Searches (website), 12a

*Google* Search: "Effectiveness Online Education" (website), 12a

*LexisNexis* Search: "Effectiveness Online Education" (website), 12a

*LexisNexis* Search: "Effectiveness Online Education, Distance
    Learning" (website), 12a

Wellspring, "Steel Cut Oats, a Non-Fancy Superfood" (blog excerpt), 12b

Library Database with DOI Number (website), 12b

"Brachiosaurus" *Wikipedia* Page (website), 12b

"Blogging and Intellectual Property Law" (webpage), 12b

*ChurchMedia* (website), 14b

*Discover Los Angeles* (website), 14b

*Folk Couture* (website), 14b

Somersby Cider (web advertisement), 14b

*Digital Public Library of America* (website), 14b

Inadequate Lighting (video still), 15a

Silhouette (video still), 15a

*Nathaniel A. Rivers Ph.D* (website), 15c

WYSIWYG on *Wix* (website), 15c

"Should We Eliminate Tobacco on Campus?" (storyboard), 15a

Lakoff, "Trump's Tweets" (visual essay), 4c

USDA, "Protect Your Baby and Yourself from Listeriosis" (fact sheet), 13c

# Preface

*Becoming Rhetorical* aims to give composition students the tools to become more dynamic, powerful communicators who are attuned to the energy and spark of rhetoric and able to direct it skillfully. This project was inspired in part by recent scholarly interest in the classical tradition of *paideia*, or cradle-to-grave rhetorical training. Such a tradition has been compellingly described in David Fleming's article "Rhetoric as a Course of Study," which imagines a revival of *paideia* in which students actively work to make the art of rhetoric "resident" within themselves—or, as he terms it, to become rhetorical. While such a goal may be ambitious for a sixteen- or even thirty-two-week course, it is my hope that once students read this book and practice applying the concepts, they will be better attuned to how rhetoric works in all aspects of their communicating life.

*Becoming Rhetorical* also takes as inspiration the increasing acceptance in composition studies that composition is more than just writing, the traditional focus of composition courses. For instance, Anthony J. Michel, David Michael Sheridan, and Jim Ridolfo, the authors of *The Available Means of Persuasion*, argue that given the variety of means of communication available in this historical moment, instructors are better off helping students learn to recognize opportunities for response and to make informed decisions about the most effective means by which to use those opportunities. In other words, one can imagine a course in which writing isn't always the only or even the most obvious means of responding. By providing instruction about the foundational components of *all* rhetorical action, *Becoming Rhetorical* aims to help students analyze and create a wide variety of written, visual, and multimodal compositions.

## ORGANIZATION OF THE TEXT

*Becoming Rhetorical* is organized into four parts. Instructors and students can move through these in order, or they can carve different pathways through the book, depending on the particular aims of the course.

Part 1, What "Becoming Rhetorical" Means, first introduces students to the reasons that rhetorical analysis and rhetorical production are important and how these complementary activities will help them in their other courses and communicative contexts. Chapters 1 and 2 then describe for students what I call the "basic" and "expanded" rhetorical situations. Chapter 1 walks students through the interactions among communicator, audience, and message. Chapter 2 layers in the other dynamic building blocks that serve as the foundations of all communicative acts: purpose, exigence, and the means of communication (genre, medium, modality, and circulation). Each subsequent chapter of the book refers back to these two foundational chapters.

Part 2, Rhetorical Analysis, teaches students to use these foundational concepts to become more attentive analysts of existing instances of rhetoric, whether written, visual, or multimodal. Chapter 3 on analyzing textual rhetoric focuses on distinguishing what is said from how it is said. After instruction on how to write a summary and questions to ask when researching the rhetorical situation of a text, students write a rhetorical analysis. Two annotated texts—an article about shaming and a rhetorical analysis of it— share with students commentary on rhetorical decisions both writers made. Chapter 4 on analyzing visual rhetoric illustrates with numerous photos and advertisements the concepts of the formal and social layers of images. Chapter 5 on analyzing multimodal rhetoric focuses on video, including textual, auditory, and visual modalities, and on the interplay of modalities on websites and in apps.

Part 3, Rhetorical Production, teaches students to become effective producers of rhetoric. In Chapters 6 and 7, they learn to identify rhetorical problems and respond to them with arguments. Chapter 6 defines two types of rhetorical problems and shares with students the activities that lead to identifying them. Students write a rhetorical problem statement to focus their efforts. Chapter 7 defines argument as a form of inquiry and has students use stasis theory to clarify the most important question they want to address. Chapter 7 includes sections on written, visual, and multimodal argument assignments. In Chapters 8 to 11, students practice common types of rhetorical actions: explaining, defining, evaluating, and proposing. Like Chapter 7, these chapters end with assignments in a range of modalities.

Part 4, Tools for Composing, serves as a toolbox for various forms of academic and public composition. Chapter 12 on research identifies composing with multiple sources as a recursive process, provides examples of search strategies, discusses methods for tracking research, and describes how to incorporate sources, as well as how to use MLA and APA styles of documentation. Chapters 13, 14, and 15 outline the principles and practices of creating textual, visual, and multimodal compositions.

# SPECIAL FEATURES AND PEDAGOGICAL AIDS

## A Nuanced Model of Rhetorical Analysis

*Becoming Rhetorical* helps students move beyond the overly simplified conception of the rhetorical situation as being composed of communicator, audience, and message (or ethos, pathos, and logos). While the "rhetorical triangle" is a helpful place to begin, especially for students without previous rhetorical instruction, it frequently leads to rather rote analyses of rhetorical activity and overlooks the rhetorical effects of modalities other than the written word. After practicing with the analytical tools specific to writing, images, and multimodal forms of composition, students will be able to better identify the rhetorical effects of communicative activity in many different forms.

## Diverse Assignments in Multiple Modalities

Multimodal invention techniques such as mapping an issue using images (Chapter 4) and analyzing a video by storyboarding (Chapter 5) are introduced, as well as assignments that ask students to analyze and compose in different modalities. Some examples are the assignments for analyzing op-ed pieces in Chapter 3, writing a comparative ad analysis in Chapter 4, scoring a written piece in Chapter 5, composing an academic response essay in Chapter 7, and creating a video review of a consumer product in Chapter 10.

There are at least two assignments which (separately or together) could form the trajectory of the entire course. One is the assignment in Chapter 3 for students to imagine they are part of an opposition research team for a political candidate, which requires analyzing how the opposition is talking about a certain issue and making recommendations to the candidate's communications team about the weaknesses in their communication. This assignment has several analytic components; it could also be extended to include producing communications from the composer's candidate. The other assignment, in Chapter 6, is to create a public awareness campaign, which can include not only a campaign brief and a campaign kit, but also a variety of compositions in different genres and modalities such as fact sheets, press releases, posters, brochures, social media campaigns, and public service announcements.

Major assignments are listed by modality on page 406 and inside the back cover of the book.

## Emphasis on the Nitty-Gritty of Composing

Throughout the book, annotated sample texts, short assignments, checklists, and heuristics give students ample practice and advice on applying rhetorical concepts.

- Annotated readings provide a window into the rhetorical choices composers make. The book includes annotated samples of rhetorical analyses of textual and multimodal works; summary; writing that defines a rhetorical problem; academic response essays; and other genres to help students become aware of the many decisions a composer makes to respond to the rhetorical situation.

- "How to" directions guide students in the steps or tasks involved in specific analysis or composing processes.

- "Questions to Ask" help students investigate rhetorical situations, problems, and issues.
- "For Discussion" and "For Homework" questions ask for individual, group, and whole-class responses to ideas and, sometimes, to readings. A list of all the readings in the book appears on pages xvii–xxii.
- "Assignments" ask for major compositions in a variety of modalities and genres.

## Reflections on Transferring Skills and Concepts to Other Contexts

The ability to transfer knowledge out of this course and into other areas of their lives is a key component to students becoming rhetorical. In Parts 1 through 3, chapters end with a "For Reflection" activity that helps students understand how the chapter concepts can be applied to their other courses, at work, and in the world.

## A Flexible Organization

The book is organized to allow for courses that focus on particular modalities or that treat analysis and production in separate parts of the course (or over two courses). To organize the course by modality, Chapters 3 and 13 can be paired in a focus on textual analysis and production, Chapters 4 and 14 discuss rhetorical analysis and production of visuals, and Chapters 5 and 15 examine analysis and production of multimodal texts. Or the chapters of Part 2 can be used to practice analysis in a variety of modalities and those in Part 3 to compose.

## Video Program

The video program for *Becoming Rhetorical* emphasizes rhetorical concepts and composing processes:

- Tiny Lectures are live-action videos in which author Jodie Nicotra explains a major concept.
- How-To's are animated examples of important processes students need to master.
- Student Makers, filmed by students, show students engaged in multimodal composing processes.

The video program is available on the MindTap for *Becoming Rhetorical*.

## Online Program

*MindTap® English for Nicotra, Becoming Rhetorical* is the digital learning solution that powers students from memorization to mastery. It gives you complete control of your course—to provide engaging content, to challenge every individual, and to build their confidence. Empower students to accelerate their progress with MindTap. MindTap: Powered by You.

MindTap gives you complete ownership of your content and learning experience. Customize the interactive assignments, emphasize the most important topics, and add your own material or notes in the eBook.

- Interactive activities on grammar and mechanics promote application to student writing.
- An easy-to-use paper management system helps prevent plagiarism and allows for electronic submission, grading, and peer review.
- A vast database of scholarly sources with video tutorials and examples supports every step of the research process.
- A collection of vetted, curated student writing samples in various modes and documentation styles to use as flexible instructional tools.
- Professional tutoring guides students from rough drafts to polished writing.
- Visual analytics track student progress and engagement.
- Seamless integration into your campus learning management system keeps all your course materials in one place.

MindTap® English comes equipped with the diagnostic-guided JUST IN TIME PLUS learning module for foundational concepts and embedded course support. The module features scaffolded video tutorials, instructional text content, and auto-graded activities designed to address each student's specific needs for practice and support to succeed in college-level composition courses.

The Resources for Teaching folder provides support materials to facilitate an efficient course setup process focused on your instructional goals; the MindTap Planning Guide offers an inventory of MindTap activities correlated to common planning objectives, so that you can quickly determine what you need. The MindTap Syllabus offers an example of how these activities could be incorporated into a 16-week course schedule. The Instructor's Manual provides suggestions for additional activities and assignments.

# Acknowledgments

Thank you to the delightfully energetic and smart Cengage team: Laura Ross, Kina Lara, Vanessa Coloura, Rebecca Donahue, Kori Alexander, Ann Hoffman, and Betsy Hathaway. Extra-special thanks to my mighty and diligent editors: Steph Carpenter, who helped me shape the book in its earlier stages, and Leslie Taggart, who kept the manuscript moving along in its later stages and who made it better in hundreds of ways. I couldn't have done this without your help.

I am also grateful for the feedback and help from those who reviewed the manuscript for *Becoming Rhetorical*:

Brenda Hardin Abbott, *Bay Path University*
Lauryn Angel, *Colin College*
Jennifer Bay, *Purdue University*
Larry Beason, *University of South Alabama*
Catherine Becker, *Northwest Nazarene University*
Paul Beehler, *University of California Riverside*
Allen Brizee, *Loyola University Maryland*
Jen Cellio, *Northern Kentucky University*
Brooke Champagne, *University of Alabama*
Sherry A. Cisler, *Arizona State University*
Gracie Forthun, *University of Idaho*
Michael Franco, *Oklahoma City Community College*
Renea Frey, *Xavier University*
Sean M. George, *Dixie State University*
Anissa Graham, *University of North Alabama*
Leigh Graziano, *University of Arkansas at Monticello*
Brian C. Harrell, *University of Akron*
Dollie Hudspeth, *Northeast Lakeview College*
Peter Huk, *University of California Santa Barbara*
Chad Iwertz, *Ohio State University*
Fayaz Kabani, *Allen University*
Bonnie Lenore Kyburz, *Lewis University*
Nicholas Lakostik, *Columbus State Community College*
Lindsay Lewan, *Arapahoe Community College*
Stephanie Maenhardt, *Salt Lake Community College*
Joyce Malek, *University of Cincinnati*
Bonnie Lini Markowski, *Scranton University*
Stephanie Reese Masson, *Northwestern State University of Louisiana*
M. Sheila McAvey, *Becker College*
Laura Micciche, *University of Cincinnati*
Cara Minardi, *Georgia Gwinnett College*
Tracy Ann Morse, *East Carolina University*
Nolana Nerhan, *San Diego State University*
Sherry Wynn Perdue, *Oakland University*
Thomas Reynolds, *Northwestern State University*
Jennifer Riske, *Northeast Lakeview College*
Chip Rogers, *Middle Georgia State University*
Courtney W. Schoolmaster, *South Louisiana Community College*
Jessica Schreyer, *University of Dubuque*
Shannon Stewart, *Coastal Carolina University*
Shevaun E. Watson, *University of Wisconsin-Milwaukee*
Scott Wible, *University of Maryland*
Lydia Wilkes, *Idaho State University*
Courtney Adams Wooten, *Stephen F. Austin State University*

Thanks, too, to participants in the focus groups held at the College Composition and Communication conferences in 2016 and 2017:

Brenda Hardin Abbott, *Bay Path University*
Christian Aguiar, *University of the District of Columbia Community College*
Jill E. Anderson, *Tennessee State University*
Mary Behrman, *Kennesaw State University*
Jennifer Cunningham, *Kent State University Stark*
Darren DeFrain, *Wichita State University*
Ash Evans, *Pacific University*
Heather Fester, *Naropa University and University of Denver*
Lorrae Fox, *University of Idaho*
Kat Gonso, *Northeastern University*
Kim Haimes-Korn, *Kennesaw State University*
Brian C. Harrell, *University of Akron*
Andrew Howard, *University of the District of Columbia Community College*
Peter Huk, *University of California Santa Barbara*
John Hyman, *American University*
Chad Iwertz, *Ohio State University*
Heather Lettner-Rust, *Longwood University*
Bonnie Lini Markowski, *Scranton University*
Lilian Mina, *Auburn University at Montgomery*
Sylvia Newman, *Weber State University*
Sherry Wynn Perdue, *Oakland University*
Jeff Pruchnic, *Wayne State University*
Martha Webber, *California State University Fullerton*
Marta L. Wilkinson, *Wilmington College*
Cassandra Woody, *University of Oklahoma*

Finally, a special thanks to those who tested part of the manuscript with their students:

Brenda Hardin Abbott, *Bay Path University*
Kristin DeMint Bailey, *University of Wisconsin-Milwaukee*
Catherine Becker, *Northwest Nazarene University*
Ash Evans, *Pacific University*
Gracie Forthun, *University of Idaho*
Renea Frey, *Xavier University*
Bonnie Lini Markowski, *Scranton University*
Deon Martineau, *Idaho State University*
Sherry Wynn Perdue, *Oakland University*
Jennifer Riske, *Northeast Lakeview College*
Shevaun E. Watson, *University of Wisconsin-Milwaukee*
Lydia Wilkes, *Idaho State University*

The manuscript has been much improved thanks to your specific and direct feedback.

The University of Idaho and the Department of English gave me the material and emotional support to complete this project. A sabbatical in 2013–2014, thanks in large part to Gary Williams, provided the time to work through the first and most difficult drafts. Special thanks to Dean Andy Kersten and former and current department chairs David Barber, Kurt Olsson (in memoriam, 1941–2017), and Scott Slovic; also my departmental colleagues Victoria Arthur, Erin James, Mary Ann Judge, Diane Kelly-Riley, Barb Kirchmeier, Jenn Ladino, Tara MacDonald, Alexandra Teague, Gordon Thomas, Karen Thompson, and other compatriots who make it such a delight to work at the university.

This book never could have been written without the brilliance of my first teachers of rhetoric—Rich Doyle, Jack Selzer, Stuart Selber, Susan Squier, and Cheryl Glenn—and without the ongoing inspiration of my rhetoric tribe, among whom are Casey Boyle, Jeremiah Dyehouse, Jess Enoch, Caroline Gottschalk-Druschke, Debbie Hawhee, Jordynn Jack, John Muckelbauer, Jeff Pruchnic, Jeff Rice, Jenny Rice, Thomas Rickert, Nathaniel Rivers, Blake Scott, Marika Seigel, Christa Teston, and Scott Wible (to name just a few of those who help my thinking on a regular basis).

And finally, thanks to my nearest and dearest loves, Randy Teal and Zoe Clyde: You are my best and most constant support and inspiration.

# Using *Becoming Rhetorical* to Meet WPA Outcomes (v3.0):

## An Instructor's Guide

By Shevaun E. Watson
University of Wisconsin-Milwaukee

## Contents

| | |
|---|---|
| Using *Becoming Rhetorical* to Meet WPA Outcomes (v3.0) | xxxii |
| The WPA Outcomes and *Becoming Rhetorical:* A Quick-Start Guide | xxxiii |
| Suggestions for Assessing Rhetorical Knowledge | xxxiii |
| Suggestions for Assessing Critical Thinking, Reading, and Composing | xxxvi |
| Suggestions for Assessing Processes | xxxviii |
| Suggestions for Assessing Knowledge of Conventions | xl |
| Adopting WPA Outcomes for Assessing Your First-Year Writing Course | xliii |
| The Big Picture: An Overview of Outcomes-Based Assessment in Your Course | xliii |
| Taking Action: Using Outcomes as Pedagogy for Lesson Plans | xliv |
| Sample A: Segment Plan and Assignment Sequence | xlv |
| Sample A: Lesson Details | xlix |
| Sample B: Segment Plan and Assignment Sequence | l |
| Sample B: Lesson Details | liii |
| Using WPA Outcomes to Evaluate Student Work | lv |
| E-Portfolios, WPA Outcomes, and *Becoming Rhetorical* | lvii |

# Using *Becoming Rhetorical* to Meet WPA Outcomes (v3.0)

The Council of Writing Program Administrators (WPA) began developing outcomes for first-year writing programs in the late 1990s in response to the growing need for nationally recognized goals for composition courses. Since then these outcomes have undergone several revisions to meet the ever-changing needs and contexts of first-year composition, with the most recent version (3.0) adopted in 2014. Instead of "standards" that define specific levels of competency for certain skills, these guidelines offer learning "outcomes," which give a clear sense of the kinds of "writing knowledge, practices and attitudes" that students should strive to achieve in first-year writing while allowing individual programs and instructors to determine what to emphasize and assess in actual classes.

The purpose of this instructor's manual is to highlight how *Becoming Rhetorical* addresses these outcomes both in content and approach, and to serve as a guide for instructors who are incorporating the WPA outcomes into their day-to-day teaching, assignment design, and course assessment practices. The information that follows details the WPA outcomes and identifies assignments, readings, and class activities in *Becoming Rhetorical* that will help you meet primary course goals and assess student learning. The table below links chapters to specific outcomes to make course planning a bit easier. It is important to note that there is even more overlap of the outcomes throughout the book than indicated here as instructional content, writing assignments, course readings, and in-class activities often pertain to multiple learning objectives.

For a full copy of the current WPA statement, visit: http://wpacouncil.org/positions/outcomes.html.

| WPA Outcomes | Becoming Rhetorical |
|---|---|
| ✓ Rhetorical Knowledge | ✓ Introduction, Chapters 1–5 |
| ✓ Critical Thinking, Reading, and Writing | ✓ Chapters 6–12 |
| ✓ Processes | ✓ Chapters 13–15 |
| ✓ Knowledge of Conventions | ✓ Chapters 7–15 |

# The WPA Outcomes and the *Becoming Rhetorical* Approach: A Quick-Start Guide

## Suggestions for Assessing Rhetorical Knowledge

*Becoming Rhetorical* is unique and valuable in its fundamental design around this first outcome. As the WPA rationale for this outcome states, "Rhetorical knowledge is the basis for composing." *Becoming Rhetorical* takes this assertion seriously and helps students develop this knowledge in multifaceted and flexible ways throughout the entire text. The *Becoming Rhetorical* approach not only helps students gain a more sophisticated understanding of rhetoric to deepen their thinking and writing, it also makes abundantly clear the connections between this outcome and the others. That is, rhetorical knowledge undergirds critical thinking and reading, dynamic composing processes, and facile understandings of writing conventions, as they all become most effective when considered from a rhetorical point of view. *Becoming Rhetorical* goes beyond explaining basic rhetorical concepts to helping students perceive unlimited opportunities for response in the world around them, and to make informed decisions about every aspect of their textual productions.

| Rhetorical Knowledge | *Becoming Rhetorical* |
|---|---|
| By the end of first-year composition, students should | **Introduction** |
| ■ Learn and use key rhetorical concepts through analyzing and composing a variety of texts. | ✓ Three foundational points ground students' learning. First, rhetoric is all around us. Anything that is intentionally crafted to evoke response is rhetorical. Rhetoric is not merely an academic pursuit in first-year composition but something that affects us all. |
| ■ Gain experience reading and composing in several genres to understand how genre conventions shape and are shaped by readers' and writers' practices and purposes. | ✓ Second, rhetoric is like a two-sided coin: It is both analysis and action, dissection and creation, examination and production. Students often struggle to make this connection, typically going through the motions of rhetorical analysis without seeing how this kind of critical thinking lays the groundwork for their own rhetorical decision-making as communicators. To "become rhetorical" is to work across analysis and production, transferring insights from one to the other, and applying rhetorical thinking to an array of texts and contexts in and out of class. "For Reflection: Transferable Skills and |
| ■ Develop facility in responding to a variety of situations and contexts calling for purposeful shifts in voice, tone, level of formality, design, medium, and/or structure. | |
| ■ Understand a variety of technologies to address a range of audiences. | |
| ■ Match the capacities of different environments (e.g., print and electronic) to varying rhetorical situations. | |

Concepts" appears at the end of every chapter in Parts 1 through 3 to facilitate this learning.

✓ Third, becoming rhetorical takes practice. It's not something that can be learned once, understood, and applied. Instead, developing rhetorical knowledge is like building a muscle. Students have to keep working at it with increasingly complex texts and situations.

## Chapters 1–2

✓ Rhetorical situation is the most fundamental concept of rhetoric. The basic elements of any rhetorical situation—the communicator, the message, and the audience—are often referred to as the "rhetorical triangle." These chapters establish the basics and then layer on complexity to move students toward deeper understanding and greater facility. Most other texts just skim the surface of rhetoric, limiting students' practice of these outcomes. The layered approach to rhetorical situation prepares students to engage the outcomes fully, understanding that genres, technologies, and writing environments both create and function within specific contexts that drive communicative choices.

✓ The concepts referenced in these outcomes are usefully expanded in Chapter 2 as component parts of the "means of communication," which include modality, medium, genre, and circulation (see 2d). These terms serve as additional tools to give students more interpretive leverage with texts and reflect the complexity of rhetoric in the digital world.

✓ Detailed examples of all concepts are provided throughout. These can be discussed with students in class, and they can generate their own examples as well.

| | **Chapters 3–5** |
|---|---|
| | ✓ Even though the outcomes explicitly address nonprint texts, rhetorical analysis explanations and assignments typically focus on the presentation of written arguments. Yet we know that various communicative modes and media entail different kinds of rhetorical considerations. These chapters bring the rhetoric outcomes alive, giving students the opportunity to learn and use a wider range of rhetorical terminology and to analyze a variety of texts across genres and media. Students' examinations of diverse texts through a rhetorical lens early in the term will help them produce their own effective, situated texts later on.<br><br>✓ The "For Discussion," "How To," and "Questions to Ask" sections, in addition to the detailed and annotated examples, provide explicit guidance for tackling in-depth and sophisticated rhetorical analyses. |

**Individual Assessment:** Early on, help students understand how broad rhetoric is and how much our culture is saturated with rhetorical texts. A fun way to do this is to invite students to bring a "rhetorical artifact" to class. A rhetorical artifact can be any kind of item or text: buttons, coasters, clothing tags, grocery bags, bookmarks, water bottles, postcards, key chains, magnets, business cards, etc. Encourage students to avoid magazine ads since part of the point is to get them to see how a lot of material beyond ads is rhetorical. Students can work individually or in groups to apply the terms and concepts presented in Chapters 1 and 2 to their artifacts. This could take the form of a short, low-stakes out-of-class writing assignment to prepare for class discussion or an informal in-class writing activity where students brainstorm ideas about the rhetorical situation of an artifact. If working in small groups, students could select one artifact from each group to present to the class, giving you the opportunity to explain and clarify key points. This informal, on-the-go kind of assessment is a valuable way for you to see what students are understanding and where they are getting stuck so that you can prepare the next class(es) accordingly. This activity/assessment can be recycled to use with Chapters 3, 4, or 5 to provide students ways to practice rhetorical analysis together in class.

For more formal assessments of student learning, each chapter provides engaging writing project prompts. The writing assignment in Chapter 1, "Uncover Your Rhetorical Self," offers an excellent way to help students understand that they are already rhetorically active and proficient in some areas of their lives. The rhetorical analysis projects in Chapters 3, 4, and 5 give students opportunities to flex their new rhetorical muscles and demonstrate some progress toward these outcomes. Keep in mind that building rhetorical knowledge takes quite a bit of repetition, so be sure to scaffold these bigger, graded assignments with lots of low-stakes writing and thinking activities that allow students to get ample practice with all of the new terms and concepts.

**Course Level Assessment:** Students can assemble a "unit 1" or preliminary portfolio of their formal (and informal) writing based on Chapters 1 through 5. Have students write a brief writer's memo or reflective essay in which they assess their own learning for each rhetorical knowledge outcome and identify areas they need to work on to gain greater proficiency over the rest of the term. This activity offers an additional kind of course level assessment that complements paper grades, as those do not always accurately reflect students' progress on outcomes. It also gives you a better snapshot of the class's learning as a whole. In addition, since rhetorical knowledge comes full circle throughout the book, where students shift from analysis to rhetorical action, these outcomes can be reassessed at the end of the term. Have students reconsider these outcomes in relation to the projects they create based on Chapters 6 through 11.

## Suggestions for Assessing Critical Thinking, Reading, and Composing

| Critical Thinking, Reading, and Composing | Becoming Rhetorical |
| --- | --- |
| By the end of first-year composition, students should<br><br>■ Use composing and reading for inquiry, learning, critical thinking, and communicating in various rhetorical contexts.<br><br>■ Read a diverse range of texts, attending especially to relationships between assertion and evidence, to patterns of organization, to the interplay between verbal and nonverbal elements, and how these features function for different audiences and situations. | **Chapter 6**<br><br>✓ Rhetoric is carried through as a means to critical thinking, reading, and writing, specifically in relation to defining problems that can be effectively researched and written about.<br><br>✓ Students are guided through ways to define different kinds of rhetorical problems (instead of just picking a current hot topic), as well as how to do preliminary research on them by reading a range of texts and keeping a "research |

- Locate and evaluate (for credibility, sufficiency, accuracy, timeliness, bias, and so on) primary and secondary research materials, including journal articles and essays, books, scholarly and professionally established and maintained databases or archives, and informal electronic networks and Internet sources.

- Use strategies—such as interpretations, synthesis, response, critique, and design/redesign—to compose texts that integrate the writer's ideas with those from appropriate sources.

scrapbook." These, plus the work of identifying stakeholders for a problem, defining one's ethos in relation to it, and crafting problem statements, help students use reading and writing as tools for learning and critical thinking.

## Chapter 7

✓ Argument is presented as a thoughtful, audience-centered response to a rhetorical problem rather than a rote exercise in advocating for one's own views.

✓ Arguments can be written, visual, or multimodal, and students should consider their options of modality, medium, genre, and circulation based on their intended audience and purpose. This approach facilitates critical thinking as students use rhetorical knowledge to move away from standard templates of classical arguments to constructing situated, audience-oriented texts.

✓ Claims, reasons, and evidence are considered rhetorically, helping students see that "what counts" or "what's good" is not based on universal, checklist-type qualities but on highly contextual ones.

## Chapter 8–11

✓ Argument, along with explaining, defining, evaluating, and proposing, give students multiple opportunities to read widely, synthesize and interpret information, and design texts that address real-world problems and audiences.

| | **Chapter 12** |
|---|---|
| | ✓ Research is a rhetorical and recursive process. Students gain experience in finding and using diverse source materials. Summary, paraphrasing, quoting, and avoiding plagiarism are less about rules than context and purpose, pushing students to think critically and independently about how to use others' ideas. |

**Individual Assessment:** Students can keep a research scrapbook as they work on various reading and writing projects (see 6c). As their work continues throughout the term, the research scrapbook could include many other in- or out-of-class assignments, such as visualizing activities (6c), stasis theory maps (7b), organizing guides (8c), definition activities (9b), and so on. Not only do these scrapbooks serve as way for students to generate, collect, and refine their thoughts—practicing ways that reading and writing spur inquiry and discovery—they can also be a way for you and them to assess their progress on these learning outcomes, in addition to the formal projects or papers you assign.

**Course Level Assessment:** The "Critical Conversation" assignment in Chapter 12 highlights the rhetorical nature of research and gets away from "cookie-cutter" research projects, which often don't yield as much practice or insight into various strategies of inquiry as this kind of exploratory writing does. Moreover, this particular assignment invites students to consider the "public dimensions" of their topics, which facilitates deeper critical thinking for various rhetorical contexts. In addition to grading these essays in a traditional way (letter grades or point values), you could also use these outcomes to create a non-graded, qualitative assessment rubric for students' learning (meets, exceeds, developing, etc.).

## Suggestions for Assessing Processes

One of the most unique and valuable aspects of *Becoming Rhetorical* is Part 4: Tools for Composing. These chapters offer in-depth guidance on creating written, visual, and multimodal texts. A big roadblock to undertaking visual and multimodal compositions is students' and instructors' trepidation about how to go about actually tackling these projects. Part 4 not only provides step-by-step support to do this; these chapters also expose students to an incredibly wide range of composing strategies that can help students generate ideas and revisions for any project, regardless of modality. Rhetorical knowledge comes full circle in Part 4 as the rhetorical insights gained from the analysis and modal chapters are applied to an array of dynamic processes for creating all kinds of effective compositions.

| Processes | Becoming Rhetorical |
|---|---|
| By the end of first-year composition, students should<br><br>■ Develop a writing project through multiple drafts.<br><br>■ Develop flexible strategies for reading, drafting, reviewing, collaborating, revising, rewriting, rereading, and editing.<br><br>■ Use composing processes and tools as a means to discover and reconsider ideas.<br><br>■ Experience the collaborative and social aspects of writing processes.<br><br>■ Learn to give and act on productive feedback to works in progress.<br><br>■ Adapt composing processes for a variety of technological modalities.<br><br>■ Reflect on the development of composing practices and how those practices influence their work. | **Chapter 13**<br><br>✓ Written communication has certain affordances and constraints that students need to consider as they work through various writing processes. Print words need voice and presence, for example, in a way that other modalities do not, so students can develop editing strategies to meet that need, among others.<br><br>✓ Writing is necessarily a messy and recursive process, leading writers to as many dead-ends as insights. Students are presented with, and need to try, many different strategies to generate ideas and refine their presentation of them so they develop a broad repertoire of composing practices to deal with any writing situation.<br><br>**Chapter 14**<br><br>✓ It can be difficult to determine the circumstances or rhetorical contexts that call for visual communication. Students are invited to work through these important considerations as part of the larger composing process.<br><br>✓ The basics of visual design need to be integrated into students' overall composing strategies. They can practice and reflect on these design principles through the major project assignments of infographics, presentations, posters, or brochures.<br><br>**Chapter 15**<br><br>✓ The detailed guidance on producing common multimodal texts, videos, podcasts, and websites helps students use different processes to discover new ideas and find new ways to present them. The explicit invention, drafting, and editing stages for these projects reinforces the importance of these processes for other modes of communication. |

**Individual Assessment:** The in-depth coverage of processes provides students with ample opportunities to experiment with new strategies at every stage of the composing process, and across media and modalities. As students try out new approaches, have them reflect on their efficacy: what worked, what didn't, what will they try again, what can they adapt, etc. Urge students to think about different processes that can and cannot be transferred to other composing situations. The goal is for students to be as deliberate about their process as they are about their content and design. These reflections could be informal quickwrites in class or part of more fully developed writers' memos that accompany the final project. Peer review of projects could also include explicit attention to process (in addition to comments on content), such as sharing composing strategies that worked well or brainstorming strategies for each other that could be used to address peers' suggestions.

**Course Level Assessment:** Students can remix their written essays into visual or multimodal texts, which provides an excellent opportunity to assess not only the shift in their content presentation (based on different rhetorical considerations like context, genre, modality, etc.) but also their uses of similar and different composing practices to make those shifts.

## Suggestions for Assessing Knowledge of Conventions

The WPA Outcomes take a rhetorical approach to correctness and form: "Conventions are the formal rules and informal guidelines that define genres, and in so doing, shape readers' and writers' perceptions of correctness and appropriateness. [C]onventions govern such things as mechanics, usage, spelling, and citation practices. But they also influence content, style, organization, graphics, and document design." This nicely matches the focus of *Becoming Rhetorical*.

| Knowledge of Conventions | *Becoming Rhetorical* |
|---|---|
| By the end of first-year composition, students should<br><br>■ Develop knowledge of linguistic structures, including grammar, punctuation, and spelling, through practice in composing and revising.<br><br>■ Understand why genre conventions for structure, paragraphing, tone, and mechanics vary.<br><br>■ Gain experience negotiating variations in genre conventions. | **Chapters 7–11**<br><br>✓ Part 3 of this book teaches students the conventions of written, visual, and multimodal arguments, as well as explaining, defining, evaluating, and proposing genres. Importantly, these guidelines are not presented as hard-and-fast rules but as key considerations for writers to work effectively within genre constraints. Students need to understand how audience, purpose, context, etc. shape readers' expectations and writers' choices. |

- Learn common formats and/or design features for different kinds of texts.

- Explore the concepts of intellectual property (such as fair use and copyright) that motivate documentation conventions.

- Practice applying citation conventions systematically in their own work.

✓ Conventions range from format to tone to design, among many other things, all of which underscore the rhetorical issues of students' ethos (e.g., 6c) and audience awareness (e.g., 7b).

## Chapter 12

✓ Common citation formats in MLA and APA with examples are provided.

✓ Source evaluation and citation are considered rhetorically in terms of authorship, purpose, timeliness, etc.

✓ Summarizing, paraphrasing, and quoting are presented as issues of intellectual property and inquiry instead of rote guidelines for merely avoiding plagiarism.

✓ Students learn key 21st century skills of citing appropriately within nonprint texts.

## Chapters 13–15

✓ Additional information about genre conventions for written, visual, and multimodal texts complements the guidelines in earlier chapters. The "Anatomy of Academic Essays" (13b), "Designing Brochures" (14c), and "Questions to Ask: Planning Website Content" (15c) are all excellent examples of how students can learn to think rhetorically about core conventions and key variations.

✓ Copyright and fair use, additional 21st century concerns, are covered under multimodality but also pertain more broadly.

**Individual Assessment:** For a homework assignment or in-class writing activity, have students reflect upon earlier learning experiences (such as high school English classes) in terms of what was taught about conventions and correctness. How were they graded on these? How important did these issues seem? What was the main message conveyed? Then invite students to consider how differently these issues are presented in *Becoming Rhetorical*. What does knowledge about conventions and correctness have to do with becoming a rhetorical reader and writer? The point is not to castigate former teachers or suggest that the information they learned was wrong, but that now in college they need to move beyond right-or-wrong thinking about conventions toward rhetorical awareness of every aspect of their reading and writing practices.

**Course Level Assessment:** A generally good assessment practice is to discuss grading rubrics or evaluation guidelines explicitly with students, but in the case of conventions, such a discussion might be particularly fruitful (especially perhaps on the heels of the activity above). Build a grading rubric for a major paper or project with students. They can work in small groups to devise initial language and weighting of criteria. How important are these outcomes to them and to this project? How much do they think these things should be worth? How do they want to be evaluated on their knowledge of conventions? How do they think they can best demonstrate deepening learning and growing proficiency in these areas?

# Adopting WPA Outcomes for Assessing Your First-Year Writing Course

## The Big Picture: An Overview of Outcomes-Based Assessment in Your Course

1. **Determine course objectives and main assessments.** Most writing programs or institutions have some kind of outcomes or learning goals already established for composition courses, and often these goals reflect the WPA outcomes. You'll want to be aware of any specific program goals you need work with, as well as the degree to which you can adapt them to your own classes. The same goes for assessment procedures: These may already be determined for all courses in the program (such as required portfolios), or you might have a lot of leeway in deciding what and how to assess. If there is little guidance on learning goals or assessment processes, the WPA outcomes and this instructor's guide are the places to start. In this case, you can either adopt the WPA outcomes wholesale, or you can consider the focus of the course you're teaching and adapt some of the outcomes that fit best. The first step in any course planning is to write the course objectives and determine the primary assessments (major papers/projects, cumulative portfolio, etc.). The main questions you need address at this early stage are: What do you want students to be able to do (better) by the end of your course, and how will they demonstrate their learning to you or others?

2. **Use "backwards design" to scaffold learning experiences.** It may seem counterintuitive, but you don't want to start planning with the beginning of your course. Instead, you want to begin at the end—the end of the term, unit, or major assignment—and work backwards from there. Planning chronologically from day one may cause you to "miss the forest for the trees," so to speak, or lose sight of the key course objectives. Backwards design is an educational concept whereby instructors plan all learning experiences with outcomes and assessments in mind, breaking larger goals and projects into smaller pieces, which can then be delivered as discrete chunks of instructional content in an order that ensures adequate scaffolding (or practice) for learning to happen. Doing this typically results in something like an assignment sequence or unit plan, where each day's activities and assignments are clearly outlined for students in a way that seems both manageable and connected to learning outcomes (see #1 in the next section).

3. **Build in summative and formative assessments.** Plan to use a combination of big (summative) and small (formative) assessments, including major projects that are "high stakes" or count significantly toward the final grade, and others that are "low stakes" opportunities for students to practice new skills and for you to give formative feedback during the learning process. Again, rather than thinking about the course as a series of papers, consider how the different learning outcomes or course objectives you've identified can be realistically accomplished and adequately represented in your assessment mechanisms. For example, if one objective is to help students "gain experience negotiating variations in genre expectations," how

can you foster that learning over the term and see it in action in students' work? What can best capture that outcome? You could use formative assessments along the way to have students track and reflect on their learning of convention variations, as well as a summative project that asks them to choose conventions most appropriate for the genre and medium. Regardless of the outcomes you adopt, be sure to build in a variety of big and small assessments throughout the term.

## Taking Action: Using Outcomes as Pedagogy for Lesson Plans

Now that you've established the core components of the course (objectives, units, assessments), it's time to dive into working out the day-to-day details. Here are some tips for moving from the "big picture" to the "Monday morning" specifics.

1. **Plan in segments or units.** It can be overwhelming to think of the entire term all at once, and in doing so, a lot can get lost as you try to juggle so many things that need to be accounted for (readings, activities, assignments, etc.). Don't start by thinking about the papers you want to assign; instead, using backwards design, identify specific learning goals you want students to achieve. Consider what outcomes you think need to be addressed first, which ones lay the foundation for others, and which ones make sense to work on later in the term. Then divide those outcomes into segments or units to deliver focused instruction and learning experiences. Each segment should build on the other, ensuring that all outcomes will be addressed at least once, if not multiple times. Weekly and daily lesson plans will flow out of your backwards-designed segments. The organization of *Becoming Rhetorical* complements such an approach. For example, here are three different ways (among many) to use the book to organize your course into smaller chunks or units:

   A) Segment 1: Introduction to Rhetoric (3 weeks: *Becoming Rhetorical* Part 1) [See Sample A for a full segment plan, pp. xlv–l.]
   Segment 2: Analyzing Texts (5 weeks: *Becoming Rhetorical* Part 2)
   Segment 3: Producing Texts (7 weeks: *Becoming Rhetorical* Parts 3, 4)

   B) Segment 1: Thinking Rhetorically (2 weeks: *Becoming Rhetorical* Part 1)
   Segment 2: Written Compositions (4 weeks: analysis and production from Parts 2, 3, 4)
   Segment 3: Visual Compositions (4 weeks: analysis and production from Parts 2, 3, 4)
   Segment 4: Multimodal Compositions (5 weeks: analysis and production from Parts 2, 3, 4)

   C) Segment 1: Introduction to Rhetoric (3 weeks: *Becoming Rhetorical* Part 1)
   Segment 2: Rhetorical Problems & Doing Research (3 weeks: Chapters 6, 12)
   Segment 3: Rhetorical Action in Writing (4 weeks: Chapters 3, 7–11, 13)
   Segment 4: Remix: Rhetorical Action in Multimodality (3 weeks: Chapters 5, 7–11, 15)

[See Sample B for a full segment plan, pp. l–liv.]
Segment 5: Reflections (2 weeks: "For Reflection" sections throughout book)

2. **Talk about the course outcomes explicitly with students.** Too often, we think of assessment as something we do outside of class without the students, like grading papers over the weekend or reviewing final portfolios at the end of the term. However, we need to keep in mind that our assessment processes directly affect students, not only in terms of their grades, but more importantly, in terms of their learning. Therefore, students should be well informed about the course outcomes, the assessments you'll use, and how those assessments support the outcomes. This is not information just to trudge through on the first day of class; this is crucial information to talk with your students about explicitly and repeatedly. Too often, students don't see or understand the trajectory of the course, experiencing it instead as a series of random assignments or hoops to jump through to get the grade. To counter this, you'll need to explain and refer to the bigger trajectory of the course throughout the term by clearly tying daily or weekly components of the class to the main goals. For example, if you break your course into segments, you can introduce each new unit by highlighting which outcomes the segment will have students working on. Or when you present a major assignment, be sure to identify the learning objectives it is intended to help students achieve. Or when you introduce a class activity, clarify how it connects to the work of previous or upcoming classes and how it helps students practice specific skills. Being consistent and explicit with students about the outcomes, assessments, and supporting work will go a long way toward making your class seem more objective and relevant to students. Doing so will also force you to be more intentional in your day-to-day teaching, which will only help your students.

3. **Use a variety of methods to deliver content and foster learning.** You don't want to use the exact same teaching format every class period. Not only does the repetition get stale for you and your students, it doesn't account for the ways in which different kinds of content are suited for different kinds of instructional delivery (not to mention that different students learn material in different ways). As you use backwards design to break the learning outcomes into smaller chunks of teaching material, consider (and experiment with) various instructional methods, including mini lectures, free-writes, videos, handouts, Prezis, podcasts, small groups, partners, large group discussions, and so on. The *Becoming Rhetorical* MindTap, and all of the "For Discussion," "How To," "Questions to Ask," and "For Reflection" sections throughout the book, will help you devise diverse and engaging ways to teach concepts, practice skills, and foster students' learning.

## Sample A: Segment Plan and Assignment Sequence

One way to effectively convey outcomes to students is to create segment plans that include a daily assignment sequence. This is illustrated in the following models, Sample A and Sample B.

## Segment One: Introduction to Rhetoric

This first unit of the course will introduce you to key rhetorical terms and concepts that lay the foundation for all of the other segments and work we'll do in this class. Specifically, by focusing on the Introduction and Chapters 1 and 2 of our textbook, *Becoming Rhetorical*, this segment is intended to help you begin to work on the following learning objectives:

### Rhetorical Knowledge

a. Learn and use key rhetorical concepts through analyzing and composing a variety of texts.
b. Gain experience reading and composing in several genres to understand how genre conventions shape and are shaped by readers' and writers' practices and purposes.
c. Develop facility in responding to a variety of situations and contexts calling for purposeful shifts in voice, tone, level of formality, design, medium, and/or structure.
d. Understand a variety of technologies to address a range of audiences.
e. Match the capacities of different environments (e.g., print and electronic) to varying rhetorical situations.

### Segment Project/Main Assessment of Learning Outcomes:

Compare Compositions That Have Similar Purposes but Different Formats (p. 47) Due: Day 10

The learning in this segment will culminate in a short written essay or creative project that will allow you to demonstrate your new rhetorical knowledge by applying some key terms and thinking rhetorically across genres and media. Specific details about this assignment and how it will be evaluated will be provided closer to the due date.

| Week/Day | Objectives | Lesson Plan & Assignment Sequence (see Sample A Lesson Details for some activities as indicated*) |
|---|---|---|
| Week 1: Monday (day 1) | ✓ Learn key rhetorical concepts (outcome a) | **In class:** Introductions, course overview, quick rhetoric activity.* **Due for next class:** Read Introduction, "What It Means to Become Rhetorical." Prepare the "For Discussion" activity on p. 5. Jot down your answers to share in class. |

| Week 1:<br>Wednesday<br>(day 2) | ✓ Learn key rhetorical concepts to prepare for analyzing and composing texts (a) | **In class:** Work through Introduction, using students' prepared notes for the discussion activity to teach concepts, clarify points, and answer questions. Show and discuss Tiny Lecture 1: "Rhetoric Is a Muscle."<br><br>**Due for next class:** Read Ch. 1, pp. 8–13. Prepare the "For Discussion" activity on pp. 12–13. Only do #1 and #3. Bring your prepared notes to share in class. |
|---|---|---|
| Week 1: Friday<br>(day 3) | ✓ Learn and use key rhetorical concepts, focusing on communicators, audiences, messages, and the dynamics between them (a)<br><br>✓ Begin to consider the rhetorical features of a variety texts and different situations (a, b) | **In class:** Teach/discuss/practice concepts from first part of Ch. 1: rhetorical triangle, two kinds of ethos.* Show How-To Video 1: "Analyzing Audiences" to preview the reading. At the end of class, have students jot down a question they still have about any of the terms or concepts discussed so far.<br><br>**Due for next class:** Read Ch. 1, pp. 14–22. Complete the Invention Work for the "Uncover Your Rhetorical Self" assignment (p. 24). |
| Week 2: Monday<br>(day 4) | ✓ Use rhetorical concepts to analyze and compose texts (a)<br><br>✓ Gain experience considering a variety of modes and genres from the writer's and audience's points of view (b)<br><br>✓ Begin to develop understanding of how various modes and genres call for different kinds of tone, design, structure, etc. (c) | **In class:** Start by answering students' questions from last class. Discuss pathos and logos with examples provided plus your own; work through the "For Discussion" activity on pp. 15–18.<br><br>**Due for next class:** Modify the "Uncover" assignment to be an informal writing activity. Have students prepare parts 2 and 3 (p. 24) of the assignment to discuss and share in next class. |

| Week 2: Wednesday (day 5) | ✓ Use rhetorical concepts to analyze and compose texts (a)<br><br>✓ Gain experience considering a variety of modes and genres from the writer's and audience's points of view (b)<br><br>✓ Begin to develop understanding of how various modes and genres call for different kinds of tone, design, structure, etc. (c) | **In class:** Share and discuss students' work on "uncovering their rhetorical selves." Do the rhetorical artifact activity to review concepts and preview Ch. 2.*<br><br>**Due for next class:** Read Ch, 2, pp. 26–37. View Tiny Lecture 2: "What Is Exigence?" that goes along with the two letters on pp. 31–33. |
|---|---|---|
| Week 2: Friday (day 6) | ✓ Learn additional rhetorical concepts (a)<br><br>✓ Read and consider some different genres to understand writers' purposes (b)<br><br>✓ Understand context with greater complexity (c) | **In class:** Break students into groups to have them review and explain the concepts and examples in parts 2a, 2b, 2c. Work through tables, "How To," and "For Discussion" sections as needed or time allows.<br><br>**Due for next class:** Read Ch. 2, pp. 38–46. |
| Week 3: Monday (day 7) | ✓ Learn additional rhetorical concepts (a)<br><br>✓ Begin to understand relationship between technologies and audiences (d)<br><br>✓ Begin to understand how communicators match the capacities of different composing environments to various audiences (e) | **In class:** Discuss rest of Ch. 2, focusing on modality and medium; introduce segment assignment (p. 47); have students jot down any questions.<br><br>**Due for next class:** Begin work on assignment. Find the three texts you want to work with and brainstorm ideas. Bring texts and notes to class. |
| Week 3: Wednesday (day 8) | ✓ Deepen understanding of modality, medium, genre, and circulation (b, d, e) | **In class:** Begin class by having students answer questions from last class. Discuss Ch. 2 focusing on genre and circulation. Review, share, discuss students' preliminary work on projects.<br><br>**Due for next class:** Project drafts. |

| Week 3: Friday (day 9) | ✓ Use rhetorical concepts to understand and compose texts (a) <br><br> ✓ Understand how genre conventions are shaped by writers' contexts, purposes (b) <br><br> ✓ Develop understanding for how different situation and contexts call for different rhetorical strategies (c) <br><br> ✓ Deepen understanding of the rhetorical aspects of technologies and different composing environments for writers and audiences (d, e) | **In class:** Peer review projects. <br><br> **Due for next class:** Revised projects ready to submit for grade/ formal evaluation. Consider having students complete a self-assessment of their progress toward the segment learning outcomes to hand in with their projects. See sample evaluation rubric for this project below (p. 14). |
| --- | --- | --- |

## *Sample A Lesson Details

**Quick Rhetoric Activity (approx. 10 min.):** Have students jot down a definition of rhetoric—what do they think rhetoric is? Also have them jot some adjectives that they think go along with rhetoric—how do they think rhetoric is perceived? Then have students introduce themselves to a neighbor and work in partners to compare notes. Do they have the same ideas or are they different? Share with the whole class, jotting some of their ideas down on the board. Then look at the definition and description of rhetoric provided in *Becoming Rhetorical*, pages 2–3. Highlight what is similar and different.

**Two Kinds of Ethos (approx. 25 min):** Prepare your own example of a politician or other public figure (entertainer, cable show host, etc.) demonstrating both kinds of ethos with a short video clip to show in class. Use the clip to explain how ethos is created both by sources from outside the text and within the text itself. Bring in the examples provided on pages 10–11. Ask students to share the examples they prepared for today ("For Discussion" #1). This could be done in partners, small groups, or as whole class. You could either work through their responses to the editorial (pp. 12–13), or you could bring in an editorial relating to an issue on campus or in the community and consider the same kinds of questions ("For Discussion" #3).

**Rhetorical Artifacts Activity (approx. 25 min; see also page xxix of this instructor's guide):** You can either have the students bring in a rhetorical artifact to class or you can collect your own to use for this activity (or both). A rhetorical artifact can be any kind of item or text: buttons, coasters, clothing tags, grocery bags, bookmarks, water bottles, postcards, key chains, magnets, business cards, etc. Encourage students to avoid magazine ads since part of the point is to get them to see how a lot of material beyond ads is rhetorical and exemplifies these concepts presented in these initial rhetoric chapters. Students can work individually or in groups to apply the terms and concepts presented in Chapters 1 and 2 to their artifacts.

## Sample B: Segment Plan and Assignment Sequence

### Segment Four: Remix—Rhetorical Action in Multimodality

This unit of the course will ask you to apply your research and rhetorical knowledge by shifting a major written project into a different modality. Specifically, by focusing on Chapters 5, 7–11, and 15 of *Becoming Rhetorical*, this segment is intended to advance your learning by bringing many of the course outcomes together.

#### Rhetorical Knowledge

a. Learn and use key rhetorical concepts through analyzing and composing a variety of texts.
b. Gain experience reading and composing in several genres to understand how genre conventions shape and are shaped by readers' and writers' practices and purposes.
c. Develop facility in responding to a variety of situations and contexts calling for purposeful shifts in voice, tone, level of formality, design, medium, and/or structure.
d. Understand a variety of technologies to address a range of audiences.
e. Match the capacities of different environments (e.g., print and electronic) to varying rhetorical situations.

#### Critical Thinking, Reading, and Composing

f. Use strategies—such as interpretations, synthesis, response, critique, and design/redesign—to compose texts that integrate the writer's ideas with those from appropriate sources.
g. Gain experience negotiating variations in genre conventions.
h. Learn common formats and/or design features for different kinds of texts.

#### Processes

i. Adapt composing processes for a variety of technological modalities.

**Knowledge of Conventions**

j. Understand why genre conventions for structure, paragraphing, tone, and mechanics vary.

**Segment Project/Main Assessment of Learning Outcomes:**

Remix a Written Essay into a Video, Podcast, or Website (Ch. 15)
Due: Day 42 (beginning of Week 14)

**NB:** This segment plan assumes that students will have already created a written project based on Chapters 6, 7–11 (one of these), 12, and 13. They will not have time to start a whole new project in terms of a different topic, or need to do a lot of new research or other substantial reading. The point of this segment is production and application, for students to work with existing material and ideas in order to reshape and remix them into a new composition that suits a different rhetorical situation. It would also be helpful if students completed a rhetorical analysis of a visual or multimodal text (Chapters 4 or 5) in an earlier segment. Finally, you'll need to decide ahead of time if you're going to let students choose between a video, podcast, and website (which are the options outlined in Chapter 15), or if you're going to have everyone do the same thing. Either is fine, but generally speaking, the more choices students have, the more rhetorical decision-making they engage in.

| Week/Day | Objectives | Lesson Plan & Assignment Sequence |
|---|---|---|
| Week 11: Monday (day 33) | ✓ Apply key rhetorical concepts through analyzing and composing a variety of texts (a) | **In class:** Segment overview and multimodal project assignment details; review key points from Ch. 5. **Due for next class:** Using the questions in 5a ("How to Analyze Multimodal Compositions"), begin to brainstorm your remix. |
| Week 11: Wednesday (day 34) | ✓ Gain more experience reading in several genres to understand how genre conventions shape and are shaped by readers' and writers' practices and purposes (b) | **In class:** Discuss effective features of example videos, podcasts, and websites, focusing primarily on issues of audience and purpose. Using the questions and example in Chapter 15, p. 357, have students explore and discuss possibilities for their projects. (It is crucial that students identify the audience and purpose for their remix before further planning.) |

| | | |
|---|---|---|
| | ✓ Deepen understanding of how various technologies address a range of audiences (d)<br><br>✓ Match capacities of different composing environments to varying rhetorical situations (e)<br><br>✓ Learn common formats and/or design features for different kinds of texts (g) | **Due for next class:** Compile a list of "Dos and Don'ts" for videos, podcasts, and/or websites. See "For Discussion" in 15a; adapt for a homework assignment. You can give students samples to consider or you can have them select some good and bad ones themselves. |
| Week 11:<br>Friday<br>(day 35) | ✓ Gain more experience reading in several genres to understand how genre conventions shape and are shaped by readers' and writers' practices and purposes (b)<br><br>✓ Deepen understanding of how various technologies address a range of audiences (d)<br><br>✓ Match capacities of different composing environments to varying rhetorical situations (e)<br><br>✓ Learn common formats and/or design features for different kinds of texts (g) | **In class:** Share notes, ideas, insights from "Dos and Don'ts"; audience analysis activity.*<br><br>**Due for next class:** Project plan (or "Treatment;" see page 359) using the "Expanded Rhetorical Situation" (Ch. 2). |
| Week 12:<br>Monday<br>(day 36) | ✓ Use strategies—such as interpretations, synthesis, response, critique, and design/redesign—to compose texts that integrate the writer's ideas with those from appropriate sources (f) | **In class:** Return project plans with comments so students can revise and finalize; finding gaps in research or information.*<br><br>**Due for next class:** Fill in research or knowledge gaps; bring new sources, information, ideas, notes to class to share. |
| Week 12:<br>Wednesday<br>(day 37) | ✓ Adapt composing processes for a variety of technological modalities (i) | **In class:** Experimenting with different composing processes and strategies (what do they need to do differently to produce multimodal texts?); use guidelines, suggestions, and samples from Ch. 15 to show and discuss.<br><br>**Due for next class:** Create storyboard, script, or other structural/ step-by-step plan for composing final project. |

| Week 12: Friday (day 38) | ✓ Respond to a variety of situations and contexts calling for purposeful shifts in voice, tone, level of formality, design, medium, and/or structure (c) ✓ Understand common formats and/or design features for different kinds of texts (h) ✓ Understand why genre conventions for structure vary (j) | **In class:** Thinking about form, structure, and design. **Due for next class:** Working on project. |
|---|---|---|
| Week 13: Monday (day 39) | ✓ Respond to a variety of situations and contexts calling for purposeful shifts in voice, tone, level of formality, design, medium, and/or structure (c) ✓ Understand why genre conventions for tone and mechanics vary (j) | **In class:** Thinking about language, tone, and ethos. **Due for next class:** Working on projects. |
| Week 13: Wednesday (day 40) | ✓ Understand why genre conventions for mechanics vary (j) ✓ Use strategies—such as interpretations, synthesis, response, critique, and design/redesign—to compose texts that integrate the writer's ideas with those from appropriate sources (f) | **In class:** Representing your research in multimodal texts (see "Informal Citations," 12b); considering copyright, fair use, and remixing (15a, p. 371). **Due for next class:** Project drafts. |
| Week 13: Friday (day 41) | ✓ All outcomes (a–j) | **In class:** Peer review projects. **Due for next class:** Revised projects ready to submit for grade/formal evaluation. Consider having students present all or part of their multimodal projects in class. They could discuss their rhetorical decision-making along with the content of the project. |

## *Sample B Lesson Details

**Audience Analysis Activity (15-30+ min., depending on whether or not you have students discuss and practice this in class):** To produce successful multimodal projects that are remixed for nonacademic audiences, purposes, and genres, students first need to understand and envision their intended audience as clearly as possible. One way to help them do this is to show them how laser-focused magazines are about their readerships. Most magazine websites provide advertising or "media kit" links (at the very bottom of their pages) with detailed demographic information about their readers. Two examples you could use are *Time* and *The Atlantic Monthly* (links below), or you can find your own. Show students this information and discuss what various categories of information convey (such as age, income, gender, level of education, and so on). Then have students brainstorm specifics for their intended audience: What do they already know about their intended audience, what can they reasonably assume about this group, and what else could they find out or verify with a bit of online research?

www.timemediakit.com/audience/
www.timemediakit.com/digital-audience/
rethink.theatlantic.com/pdf/TheAtlantic_MediaKit_062017.pdf

**Finding Gaps in Research or Information (approx. 15 min.):** When students shift to composing for a different audience, purpose, or genre, they often need some additional information about their topic/issue and/or their intended audience. Sometimes these are gaps in knowledge or understanding; they need to do some additional research to fill those holes. Other times, they need additional research to establish or bolster their ethos with this new audience. You can help students identify these needs and gaps by assessing what they have and comparing that to what their audience will expect. Once they find some gaps, you can help them strategize how to find the specific kind of information they need, or students can visit the library with these specific research needs (e.g., I need to find more data on X because a visual graph of X suits this different genre and audience). Alternatively, you might have students do some interviews to gather more information and content (footage, quotes, etc.) for their project, as suggested on pages 363–365.

# Using WPA Outcomes to Evaluate Student Work

*Becoming Rhetorical* invites students to produce a range of work across genres, media, and modalities. Evaluating student work can be tricky for several reasons, and both the WPA Outcomes and *Becoming Rhetorical* can help you devise valuable ways to assess and respond to graded projects. One common issue is that students feel like writing quality is highly subjective and liable to instructor bias. A related concern is a lack of clarity and transparency about how work will be evaluated. Students can get easily frustrated and discouraged if assessments of their work seem arbitrary or unfair. In their efforts to be clear, instructors sometimes unwittingly exacerbate these issues by communicating "standards" to students that are in actuality more idiosyncratic than generalizable, such as expectations that come across as personal demands and pet-peeves (usually appearing in bold and accompanied by exclamation points). To make things more complicated, instructors often struggle to shift their well-established evaluations of written work to visual and multimodal genres. Here are some tips to help you avoid these problems and pitfalls.

1. **Use a rubric based on WPA outcomes.** See the following examples. Use the outcomes to communicate consensus-based and disciplinary-oriented expectations of student compositions.
2. **Involve students in creating the rubric.** Use class time to have students develop criteria and input for the rubric. Adapt the language of the outcomes to terms they themselves use.
3. **Emphasize effectiveness over correctness.** *Becoming Rhetorical* teaches students to think rhetorically about the texts they encounter and produce in the world, focusing on audience, purpose, and context rather than rules or right-and-wrong. The same goes for your evaluation of their work: Is it effective in meeting the audience's expectations and achieving its stated purpose?
4. **Have students self-assess.** Using the same rubric you'll employ, invite students to assess their own work. This helps students understand the outcomes better by applying them to their own compositions, and it forces them to find specific evidence in their work that illustrates their learning.

## Basic Rubric—All Outcomes

| Outcomes & Level of Achievement* | exceeds | clearly meets | meets but is inconsistent or uneven | does not meet |
|---|---|---|---|---|
| Rhetorical Knowledge | | | | |
| Critical Thinking, Reading, and Writing | | | | |

| Outcomes & Level of Achievement* | exceeds | clearly meets | meets but is inconsistent or uneven | does not meet |
|---|---|---|---|---|
| Processes | | | | |
| Knowledge of Conventions | | | | |

*You'll need to develop specific language that clearly describes each level or category. You can invite students to help create language they will understand.

## Detailed Rubric—One Outcome (sample for Segment One assignment, p. 47 in *Becoming Rhetorical*)

| Rhetorical Knowledge Components | Comments |
|---|---|
| a. Learn and use key rhetorical concepts through analyzing and composing a variety of texts. | |
| b. Gain experience reading and composing in several genres to understand how genre conventions shape and are shaped by readers' and writers' practices and purposes. | |
| c. Develop facility in responding to a variety of situations and contexts calling for purposeful shifts in voice, tone, level of formality, design, medium, and/or structure. | |
| d. Understand a variety of technologies to address a range of audiences. | |
| e. Match the capacities of different environments to varying rhetorical situations. | |

# E-Portfolios, WPA Outcomes, and *Becoming Rhetorical*

Portfolios are a common assessment mechanism in composition courses, and electronic portfolios are a popular iteration of the traditional paper format. Whether you have your own students assemble portfolios or your writing program requires them of all students, portfolios function in the same way to emphasize process, growth over time, and self-assessment. Portfolios also match rhetorically-oriented approaches to composition, such as *Becoming Rhetorical*, in that they provide students with a real rhetorical situation (e.g., end-of-term final evaluation) to work within in order to assemble and present their work. Moreover, all portfolios should be accompanied by some reflective writing (e.g., cover letter, writer's memo, reflective essay, etc.) wherein students explain their learning in the course based on the outcomes and point to specific moments in their work they feel best demonstrates their achievement. In other words, a portfolio cover letter explains and exemplifies how the student has "become rhetorical."

E-portfolios present several advantages over paper ones. First, as electronic documents, they are much easier to collect, store, manage, share, and review than their print-based counterparts. Just the sheer volume of paper generated by traditional portfolios is usually enough to inspire instructors to use digital formats. Second, more and more campus learning management systems (e.g., Blackboard, Desire to Learn, etc.) include some e-portfolio functionality, at least allowing students to upload their work electronically. Sometimes using the campus system has important advantages, encouraging students to assemble their work throughout college as an e-portfolio and enabling the sharing of work with others on campus for multiple assessment purposes. Additionally, many composition instructors and programs use freeware options like Word Press for students' portfolios.

But the primary benefits of e-portfolios are most apparent when using a text and approach like *Becoming Rhetorical*. The entire book is geared toward getting students to think rhetorically across media, genres, and modalities such that an e-portfolio presents an excellent opportunity for them to do this work and demonstrate their learning. Whereas print-based portfolios, or even exclusively assigning paper-only texts and essays, limit students' ability to think and work across different writing environments, e-portfolios allow for a wide range of compositions as students can upload videos (Ch. 8), infographics (Ch. 14), podcasts (Ch. 15), and more. Not only do e-portfolios accommodate the diversity of compositions students can create in a writing course based on *Becoming Rhetorical*, they also foster exactly the kind of rhetorical thinking and reflection that the book calls for.

# PART 1

# What "Becoming Rhetorical" Means

# Introduction: What It Means to Become Rhetorical

"The goal of rhetorical training is . . . to become a certain kind of person, one who has internalized the art of rhetoric . . . . [Rhetoric] is 'resident' in the educated person, who doesn't so much *learn* rhetoric as '*becomes* rhetorical.'"

—David Fleming

What might it mean to *become rhetorical*, and why would anyone want to do that? After all, the term "rhetoric" tends to be associated with sleazy smooth talkers, able to spout empty political puffery or be generally bombastic. You probably don't need to look far to find an example of these qualities in political debates, on talk shows, or via social media feeds.

So let's clarify this right away: **rhetoric** in the context of this book refers to the wide array of communicative devices humans have at their disposal to create effects on each other. Rhetoric is an ancient art, one of the first disciplines. While it was originally developed to help people make persuasive speeches, rhetoric is still studied for its supreme practicality and adaptability. Popular depictions of rhetoric focus on its more negative qualities: persuasion at all costs (including manipulation, trickery, and browbeating)—the opposite of speaking the truth—but in reality such depictions present a very limited and skewed version of rhetoric. The twentieth-century literary critic Wayne Booth called this kind of manipulative rhetorical practice "rhetrickery," to distinguish it from rhetorical practice as a whole.

**FIGURE 1** What messages and embedded values and beliefs are embodied in the intentionally designed compositions depicted here?

In actuality, *all* intentionally designed communication is rhetorical: not just traditionally persuasive things like advertisements, opinion pieces, and grant proposals, but also instructions, photographs, websites, tweets, documentaries, and posters with restaurant nutritional information. Even aspects of the built environment like the design of cities and parks, stores, hospitals, prisons, schools, and public monuments and memorials embody particular beliefs, values, and attitudes and are intended to have some sort of effect on an audience (Figure 1).

## What Is Rhetorical Training?

The fact that the definition of rhetoric encompasses so much shows how it is different from other kinds of study. Unlike disciplines such as psychology and biology, rhetoric doesn't comprise a body of knowledge that one needs to absorb before one can really become a master. Rather, studying rhetoric is more akin to studying music performance: it involves mastering a set of principles and tools through extensive practice in many different situations. "Becoming rhetorical" means honing your ability to recognize, analyze, and respond appropriately to any situation that involves communication—whether verbal, visual, auditory, or a more complex mix of all of these (a form of composition called **multimodal**).

**EXAMPLE**   Just as everyone has at least some innate musical ability, all people have some measure of rhetorical talent. Through your attention to audience and your awareness of the unwritten rules of what is appropriate and not appropriate to do in particular circumstances, you successfully navigate any number of communication situations. The fact that you're in a college course right now is evidence of this rhetorical ability. At the same time, musicians can become more skilled and accomplished through extensive study and practice, just as people can become better rhetoricians: more attuned to the nuances of audience and situation, more aware of how various forms of communication affect them, and more able to mobilize their own rhetorical skills to appropriately and skillfully communicate.

The goal of rhetorical *training* is first to more consciously develop your rhetorical skills, then to make those skills habitual, or, as the quote from rhetorical

**MindTap°**
View Tiny Lecture 1:
Rhetoric Is a Muscle

scholar and professor David Fleming that begins this chapter puts it, to make rhetorical skill "resident" (think *reside*) in oneself. Becoming rhetorical means being able to effectively diagnose (through *rhetorical analysis*) the dynamics of a communication situation. Developing skills in rhetorical analysis will help you develop a richer, more nuanced understanding of the factors that comprise and affect communication. It will also help sensitize you to how you can produce your own appropriate and skilled responses to situations that require communication. It's the goal of this book to teach you how to do both.

## Why Rhetorical Analysis Is Important

**Rhetorical analysis** refers to the effort to understand how communication (by a variety of means) creates particular effects on people. In situations that they encounter regularly, people perform rhetorical analysis without much conscious effort.

**EXAMPLE**   As a college student you make dozens, if not hundreds, of small decisions every day based on your analysis and assessment of a variety of communication situations. You might assess what's being communicated by someone's outward appearance, as represented by his or her clothing, gestures, and posture. If your history professor always wears a bow tie and begins his meticulously prepared lectures without pleasantries, you may decide to address him politely and formally as "Dear Dr. Smith" when you email to ask for an extension on your assignment. And based on the misspellings and strange syntax in an email you just received, you choose to delete it rather than following its instructions to reset the password for your university account.

Chapters 3, 4, and 5 in this book focus on taking that natural inclination to analyze and assess, and applying it to judging situations that you may encounter less frequently: namely, to deliberately designed messages that are aimed at persuading you to do, change, be, think, or believe something. Of course, you already do this to some extent. Even if you're irritated by certain kinds of messages (perhaps those ubiquitous ads on *Facebook* and other websites inviting you to "click here for one weird old trick to eliminate belly fat"), this irritation indicates that you've quickly analyzed them to some extent, if only to dismiss them. The goal here is to make this process of quick analysis more explicit and deliberate—to be able to articulate precisely how and for whom a message is constructed, what effect it aims to have on its intended audience, and how effective its strategies are.

It's been said that we live in an attention economy, where the most limited resource is our ability to pay attention to the bombardment of messages. If this is the case, then it's possible for many of the messages we see each day to affect us without us realizing it. To be more grounded and attentive thinkers, it's vital to be able to slow down our attention and patiently

notice the particulars of how messages are attempting to
work on us. This is the goal of Part 2 of *Becoming Rhetorical*.

Each chapter of Part 2 addresses a different type of
rhetoric. Since analysis of written texts is still the gold
standard for most introductory writing courses, Chapter 3,
"Analyzing Textual Rhetoric," focuses on discerning arguments and rhetorical tools specific to written and spoken
texts. But because communication these days takes place
in so many other forms, *Becoming Rhetorical* also aims to
help you analyze messages that are not primarily verbal.
Chapter 4, "Analyzing Visual Rhetoric," provides tools for
analyzing rhetoric that relies heavily on static images: photographs, advertisements, visuals that appear in written texts, and new specialty genres such as infographics. And Chapter 5, "Analyzing Multimodal
Rhetoric," teaches you how to analyze more complicated compositions, ones
that might use several different types of communication (videos, podcasts,
or websites that embed video, for instance).

**TEXTUAL**
Chapter 3

**VISUAL**
Chapter 4

**MULTIMODAL**
Chapter 5

---

**FOR DISCUSSION**

To become attuned to your rhetorical environment, think of three intentionally designed messages that you've encountered today. These don't
have to be verbal messages (in fact, it's better if they're not); they can
be visual, auditory, or material messages as well. For each one, jot down
some thoughts about whom they aim to persuade and what kind of
messages they send. What effects do they aim to have on their audience? What messages are more overt, or on the surface? What messages
might be more hidden, or less obvious? Share these with the class as a
means of developing a richer, more nuanced picture of the rhetorical
environment. Which of the examples provided by your classmates was
most surprising to you as an example of rhetoric?

---

# Why Rhetorical Action Is Important

The concepts and vocabulary that you'll work with in Parts 1–2 of this book
serve as the foundation for **rhetorical action** (the focus of Part 3). Rhetorical action means the deliberate shaping of messages for an audience. Part 3
of *Becoming Rhetorical* aims to provide you with techniques to define rhetorical problems and respond to specific kinds of rhetorical situations with
arguments and other rhetorical tools. While it can't possibly cover every
kind of rhetorical problem you might encounter, it aims to highlight those
that you will most likely run into over the course of your career as a college
student and as a citizen: explaining, defining, advocating, evaluating, and

proposing. Each chapter in Part 3 includes assignments for academic writing, for public writing, for visual rhetoric, and for multimodal rhetoric.

Developing skills in rhetorical analysis helps provide a richer, more nuanced sense of the possibilities for responding to situations that involve communication. Here, "rhetorical practice" means producing a *skillful* response to any situation that requires or invites communication. "Skillful" is the operative word here.

**EXAMPLE**  To go back to the musical example, if you've ever played a musical instrument, you know the difference between having a natural "ear" or sense of rhythm and being able to really make music. Making music requires that you play so proficiently that you can forget what your body is doing as you become immersed in the act of playing.

Even if you've never trained enough to get to that point, you probably understand that the difference between the two is *practice*—conscious, diligent, frequent repetition, both of one particular song and many different types of songs. Likewise, skillful rhetorical practice requires that you continually train with the techniques of rhetoric. This book introduces you to a number of tools in rhetorical analysis and rhetorical practice—some are ancient, some only a decade old—with the understanding that only repeated practice with them will help you become rhetorically skillful.

## What It Really Means to Become Rhetorical: Transfer of Skills

Much of educational research in the last several decades has focused on the important question of the transfer of knowledge or skills. **Transfer of knowledge**, or the ability to take understanding, knowledge, skills, or concepts from one field of knowledge and apply it in a different situation, is considered the true measure of learning. However, it has proven to be an elusive goal. People notoriously silo information—that is, they often cannot see connections even among courses in the same major. Learning to communicate, in writing or otherwise, poses the same problem.

**EXAMPLE**  Many people assume that because they learned to write a five-paragraph essay for their high school English classes, they know how to write. This isn't to say that the five-paragraph essay is bad or invaluable; in fact, this form of thesis-driven writing will serve you well on essay exams and certain kinds of academic responses. But learning this model in the sense of trying to repeat it over and over, even in situations where it's inappropriate or flat-out wrong, isn't the kind of learning that many would call useful.

Researchers argue that for knowledge and skills to become transferable, learners must *know what they know*: to apply lessons from one situation to another, they must first recognize those lessons. In writing, for instance, a writer who *knows what she knows* is able to see not just how to write a particular kind of essay but also recognize the elements of the situation in-volved in writing. You've probably heard the expression "if you give a man a fish, he eats for a day; if you teach him to fish, he can eat for a lifetime." Well, this book does give you "fish" in the form of tutorials for composing in many different genres and modes. But more importantly, it also aims to teach you to fish in the sense that practicing with rhetorical concepts such as audience, exigence, and purpose across a wide variety of situations will help you be able to apply them to new situations that aren't covered here (or maybe don't even exist yet).

This is why each chapter concludes with a brief "For Reflection: Trans-ferable Skills and Concepts" assignment. These are designed to help you, the communicator, take stock of the skills and concepts that you've learned in that chapter and think about other situations not mentioned in the chapter to which these might apply.

## FOR DISCUSSION

To better understand the concept of transfer, think of how skills you may have developed in one area have helped you in another, seemingly unrelated area. Choose something that you're skilled at (for instance, playing a musical instrument, language, a team sport, gaming, building things). Now see if you can break this activity down into all the specific skills required to do this thing well. Write these all down, then look over the list of skills. In what other areas of your life have these skills helped you, even if they're totally unrelated? (Learning to read music is said to improve the ease with which you learn languages, for instance.) As a class, make a map of these skills and how they transfer.

# 1

# The Basic Rhetorical Situation

## LEARNING OBJECTIVES

*By working through this chapter, you will be able to...*
- Identify the elements of the rhetorical triangle.
- Understand how communicators create ethos.
- Identify how messages change according to their audience.
- Understand the importance of audience to communication.
- Analyze the needs and concerns of potential audiences.
- Understand how emotional appeals (pathos) can be used to affect audiences.
- Apply these basic rhetorical elements to analyzing your own rhetorical identity.

For many years, rhetoric and writing teachers have identified the elements common to all communication in a graphic called the rhetorical triangle, which aims to help students think both about *analyzing* rhetoric and *composing* it. While Chapter 2 complicates and enriches the traditional rhetorical triangle, it's important to think about the three elements that make it up: a communicator, a message, and an audience for that message (Figure 1.1).

## 1a Communicators: How Do They Convince Us of Their Relevance?

The communicator can be defined most basically as the person or entity responsible for the act of communication.

**EXAMPLES** A communicator might be a single person (like you, when you email a company to complain about a defective product); it could be a group of people, such as a committee (like the Intergovernmental Panel on Climate

Change, which presents reports on the state of climate change science to the international community); and it could be an organization or institution (like the World Wildlife Fund, which produces a number of ads, video spots, and other materials to advocate for environmental issues).

In analyzing communication, we always need to think about why someone might have chosen this moment, this topic, and this way to communicate. When you are analyzing a message, the first step is to identify and describe the communicator(s):

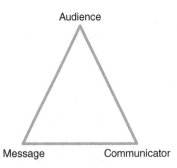

**FIGURE 1.1** Traditional Rhetorical Triangle

- What are the communicator's demographics? Do these provide any clues about the communicator's relation to the subject?
- What does the communicator have to gain or lose as a result of this particular communication?
- What are the communicator's investments in the issue, and how might these affect what the communicator thinks and says about the subject?

Conversely, when *you* are acting as a communicator, you need to consider how your audience will perceive you and your message, something explored in more detail in the section on ethos.

## Appealing to Audiences through Character: How Communicators Build Ethos

Not only do we need to think about the communicator's relation to the topic, we also need to consider how the communicator creates *ethos*. Ethos is one of what Aristotle defined as the "rhetorical appeals," along with *logos* and *pathos* (discussed later in this chapter). Ethos refers to how messages persuade (or "appeal" to an audience) as a result of the communicator's character. Aristotle claimed that ethos was the most important appeal, since if the source of a message isn't trustworthy, then no matter how well-produced the message, it will probably fail to persuade an audience. Ethos, Aristotle claimed, requires that the communicator display three factors:

1. Practical intelligence
2. A virtuous character
3. Good will

When these three qualities seem to be in evidence, Aristotle argued, the audience will be more inclined to accept the communicator's message. The twentieth-century rhetorician Kenneth Burke amplified this idea in his concept of "identification." According to Burke, persuasion isn't so much a matter of changing someone's mind with a given message as getting him or her on your side. If someone identifies with you and your beliefs and ways of being, he or she is much more likely to buy into what you're saying.

How does an author build ethos? Ethos in rhetorical acts comes from two places: from sources external to the message, and from the message itself.

## Ethos from sources external to the message

The external sources of ethos are everything that an audience may already know about a communicator, the topic, and the means by which the audience received the message.

**EXAMPLE**   Through her credentials, the director of a research center on autism will probably gain automatic credibility in an opinion piece about the best ways to educate autistic children.

But just because you're well known doesn't mean that you'll automatically have credibility in the eyes of an audience. When the author is a well-known person, it's important to take into account *how* they're known and how that affects how the audience might perceive them.

**EXAMPLE**   Bono, the lead singer of the band U2, has written a number of op-ed pieces for *The New York Times* about various social problems. While his celebrity arguably helps in that it draws attention to the causes he discusses, it also serves as a point of derision for some. ("What does a rock singer know about hunger in Africa?")

When you don't know very much about a communicator, as a good analyst you need to look for clues that provide an indication of whether you can trust the source.

**EXAMPLE**   You may have never heard of Andrew Jensen, the author of a *New York Times* op-ed piece arguing for a ban on semi-automatic assault weapons. However, you do know that he was published in *The New York Times,* a highly respected national newspaper. The brief note at the end of the piece states that he was an Army infantry officer for five years. So even if you're opposed to gun control, you may be more inclined to read what he has to say, knowing that because of his job he at least has had significant experience with guns (and is not some liberal pansy). The note helps lend Jensen ethos, in other words.

Other external sources of ethos might include the communicator's gestures, dress, facial expressions, and tone of voice.

**EXAMPLE**   Ronald Reagan's warm, reassuring voice, steady gaze, and carefully modulated gestures notoriously made him seem both stately and grandfatherly. If you watch a video of his speech to the nation after the explosion of the space shuttle *Challenger*, for instance, you'll be able to see why he was known as "The Great Communicator." (See Figure 1.2.)

## Ethos from the message itself

Ethos also has to do with the content of the message itself: How does the content of the message convince you that it's trustworthy? This could include things like the tone and style of the message, as well as the points

FIGURE 1.2 Ronald Reagan

that it makes and the evidence it uses to support those points. As with the external sources of ethos, this is always context-dependent: In some cases (as with, say, communications from universities and other organizations) you would expect the message to be formal and informative, and would find it suspicious if it were otherwise; in other cases you would find something scruffier and a little more homegrown to be more trustworthy.

**EXAMPLE** You may find a grainy cell-phone video of police beating a motorist distributed on a *YouTube* video that someone posted on *Facebook* more believable than the official police department press statement about the event, for instance.

**EXAMPLE** After it was alleged that Russia had interfered in the 2016 U.S. election by using paid trolls, scammers, and false news stories, schools across the United States began educating students on how to recognize "fake news." Some of the things experts recommend to watch out for include the means of delivery (they advise ignoring viral news stories and those that arrive as chain mails in email inboxes). Punctuation can also serve as a warning flag, like stories that use multiple exclamation points. And fake news stories often have extremely provocative headlines ("Obama Signs Executive Order Banning Pledge of Allegiance in Schools") but have either outright satirical content or cite bogus sources as "evidence." The writers of these stories bank on readers who pass stories along based on a provocative headline without actually reading the stories.

It's important to note, though, that neither form of ethos is stagnant, an eternally present quality in the message. It changes over time and according to who is listening to the message.

## FOR DISCUSSION

1. To think about how a communicator creates ethos, locate a recent video of a politician at a campaign rally or giving a political speech. Analyze the various ways that the politician attempts to build ethos for his or her audience; consider the content of the speech, as well as gesture, tone, and any props that she or he might use.

2. Find and bring to class some communications that include no writing, or not only writing (for example, you might look at videos, flyers, posters, ads, infographics, podcasts, etc.). What is the difference between the role played by the communicator of the written piece and the communicator of these not-just-written pieces?

3. Read the following editorial and respond to the questions that follow.

### College Rankings Should Account for Binge Drinking

#### BY ELLIOTT MILLENSON

"Right now, private rankings like *U.S. News & World Report* puts out each year . . . it encourages a lot of colleges to focus on ways to—how do we game the numbers?"

This comment from President Obama, its contorted grammar aside, hints at a critical and hidden reality. Many college policies, procedures and practices are designed solely to influence *U.S. News* rankings, not to improve education. Meanwhile, the *U.S. News* rankings fail to take many things into account that profoundly affect education and the overall college experience.

According to the Center for Science in the Public Interest, "college presidents agree that binge drinking is the most serious problem on campus." NIH data underscore the fallout, noting "about 25 percent of college students report academic consequences of their drinking including missing classes, falling behind, doing poorly on exams or papers and receiving lower grades overall."

Almost 2,000 college students die each year from alcohol-related injuries, nearly 700,000 are assaulted by another student who has been drinking, and more than 97,000 are victims of alcohol-related sexual assault or date rape.

At many schools, binge drinking—having five or more drinks for a male and four or more for a female within two hours—is becoming the norm. A Harvard survey at 120 campuses revealed 44 percent of students engaged in binge drinking (known in certain contexts as "pre-gaming") in the previous two weeks. At Princeton, the top *U.S. News* ranked college, university policy "prohibits the consumption and serving of alcoholic beverages by and to persons under 21." Enforcement is another matter, based on a Princeton 2011 survey that revealed 73 percent of students had recently pre-gamed, up from 67 percent in 2008.

A few colleges are actually doing something about this. Following alleged recent sexual misconduct at two fraternities, Brown banned alcoholic events in residential areas, and Dartmouth recently banned liquor with more than 15 percent alcohol from its campus. But the status quo prevails at most universities—albeit with hand-wringing and solemn expressions of serious concern tempered by statements on the difficulty of doing anything meaningful.

But imagine if *U.S. News* changed its criteria to include a metric on alcohol abuse, as well as efforts to reduce its incidence. Is there any doubt universities would address the problem with greater urgency?

For perspective, a September 2014 *Boston Magazine* article described how Northeastern University president Richard Freeland set out to move up in the rankings after realizing "schools ranked highly received increased visibility and prestige, stronger applicants, more alumni giving, and, most important, greater revenue potential . . . This single list, Freeland determined, had the power to make or break a school." He embarked on a path to "recalibrate the school to climb up the ranks . . ."

*U.S. News* Editor and Chief Content Officer Brian Kelly has stated, "It's not up to us to solve problems. We're just putting data out there."

Yet the data *U.S. News* chooses to incorporate are never far from a college president's mind. By not including campus drinking data, *U.S. News* may contribute to the problem. Perhaps mindful of the emphasis the magazine places on retaining students (22.5 percent of total rank), administrators don't wish to risk alienating their charges by curbing drinking.

There is no greater influence on college behavior than *U.S. News*. Yet the influence of drinking on education is ignored. The magazine needs some prodding—from government, public interest groups, parents and even educators to change its criteria. With a gentle nudge from *U.S. News* there is no doubt universities, which are home to some of the greatest minds in America, could develop sound ap- proaches to reducing campus pre-gaming. That's a game that should begin with all deliberate speed.

a. Describe the writer (you might even try Googling him). Who is he, and what's his relation to the topic of the op-ed piece? What kind of persona does he present in the piece through the style, tone, and content? Do you find him believable?

b. In what other ways does the piece create ethos (think about external as well as internal sources of ethos)?

FIGURE 1.3  "Crying Jordan Afghan Girl" Meme Source: Know Your Meme.

# 1b Message: What Is the Communication About?

The **message** of an act of communication refers to its content or gist: What is the audience supposed to take away from the communicative act?

Messages can be relatively simple and straightforward: Your supervisor sends an email informing all employees that they need to start doing things a different way, for instance. But messages can also be quite complex.

**EXAMPLE** Consider the Internet meme "Crying Jordan" in Figure 1.3. To understand the message of this meme, readers would first have to be familiar with the tenacious image of Michael Jordan, emotional upon being inducted into the Hall of Fame in 2009. You would have to know that the image of Jordan has been Photoshopped hundreds of times to indicate or poke fun at someone who is struggling. You would also have to recognize the clothes of the famous green-eyed "Afghan girl" from the 1985 *National Geographic* cover, widely used as an image that shows the horrors of the Soviet war in Afghanistan. So knowing both of these things, we might conclude that the message is something like "We should poke fun of how the media use and recirculate images to elicit feelings in viewers."

## Appealing to an Audience through the Strength of a Message: Logos

Another of Aristotle's rhetorical appeals, logos refers to how the *logic* or content of the message appeals to an audience. It's important to note that "logic" here doesn't necessarily equate to formal philosophical logic, or even good logic.

**EXAMPLES** As many recent public debates have demonstrated (vaccinations, climate change, and evolution), as well as the "fake news" debacle mentioned earlier, facts, even those widely accepted by experts, aren't always enough to persuade many of the truth of something.

It might be most effective, then, to think of logos as how the internal consistency of a message (including the claim, reasons, and unstated assumptions) appeals to an audience. See Chapter 7 for a much more extensive discussion of a message's logos.

FOR DISCUSSION

To identify how a message changes according to its audience, study the following three communicative acts (all having to do with weight loss) and respond to the following questions.

- What is the message?
- Where do you locate the message?
- How do the messages in each piece differ according to communicator, purpose, and audience?
- Why would (or wouldn't) the message of the piece persuade its audience?

## Healthy Weight Loss

### BY THE AMERICAN DIABETES ASSOCIATION

Does this sound familiar? You got tired of hearing your doctor and family bug you about losing weight to prevent or manage type 2 diabetes. So, you got a two-week diet plan from a friend. You started gung-ho. The first few days were great. Then you found there were nights you didn't have time to fix your food and the family dinner. By the weekend your family wanted to have pizza. And the diet went out the door when you left for your favorite pizza place.

Many people try to lose weight, but fewer people lose weight and keep it off. This happens for several reasons. Sometimes people try to lose too much weight too fast. Or they try to follow a food plan that isn't how they can eat long term. Reality is that losing weight in a healthy way and learning how to keep it off is not easy. It takes a new way of thinking. Are you ready?

### SET YOUR GOALS

Set a realistic weight loss goal. Think about losing 5, 10, or 15 pounds. One of your goals should be to lose a few pounds and be able to keep it off for a long time. Here are some tips to help you make goals.

- Choose a time to start when you think life will be as calm and in control as possible.
- Do a self-check on what and when you eat. Keep honest food records for about a week. Write down everything you eat or drink. Use these records to set a few food goals. These food

goals should be small changes you can easily make to your existing food habits.

- Don't look for a magic bullet diet. They don't exist. You'll do best if you base eating habits on what you found out in your self check food records. Do you snack a lot? Instead of chips or a candy bar, could you snack on a piece of fruit, pretzels, or some nuts? Are your portions too large? Do you eat too many sweets?

- Be ready to change your food habits (and perhaps your family's food habits) for good. Say good bye to some of your unhealthy habits and food choices.

- Do a physical activity self-check. How much exercise do you get? How can you work more of it into your day? The tip sheet Be Active, But How can help.

## Miranda Parks Visualized Her Way to a Better Body

### BY CASSANDRA KULIK, *FIT* MAGAZINE

*Weight before:* 183 lbs.

*Weight now:* 125 lbs.

*Age:* 28

*Height:* 5'4"

*Location:* Fayetteville, AK

*Occupation:* Paralegal

*Tip for newbies:* "Just fix your mind on the long haul and go for it!"

Miranda lost almost 60 pounds in two years, and picturing what she'd look like was a big factor in her success. "If I felt like I literally couldn't take another step when I was running intervals, I'd picture Olympic coach Ethan Barletti saying 'Ain't nothing but gliding on a cloud!', and then I'd imagine myself floating through the air," she laughs. "And then I'd go on and finish the interval."

When she wasn't imagining heads of broccoli at the ends of her barbells, she visualized the muscles that were forming underneath her extra weight, and how beautiful they'd look when it melted away. "I'd see a woman with long, lean leg muscles or really nice shoulders, and I'd think 'that's what mine will look like,'" Miranda

Iurii Racenkov/Shutterstock

Iurii Racenkov/Shutterstock

said. "It helped inspire me to keep pushing, even when I didn't feel like it."

Knowing that she could set small goals and achieve them gave her confidence. She says that if she can visualize it, she can achieve it.

## YOU CAN GET FIT LIKE MIRANDA

Miranda works out six days a week. She begins every routine with twenty minutes of cardio (alternating between the elliptical machine and intervals on the treadmill). She then does one of six strength routines:

*Monday:* Chest, triceps, and abs

*Tuesday:* Legs and glutes

*Wednesday:* Back and chest

*Thursday:* Legs

*Friday:* Biceps and shoulders

*Saturday:* Legs and glutes

*Sunday:* Rest

# LOSE WEIGHT USING OUR MEDICALLY-APPROVED, EASY-TO-FOLLOW SYSTEM.

AS SEEN ON OPRAH!

Lose a dress size—or three—with our medically supervised weight loss program! Our low–calorie diet triggers your amygdala to help you burn excess fat while it decreases cravings and hunger. On our program, you won't even need to exercise to see results!

At **Port Washington Nutrition Center**, we follow **Dr. Turpington's** diet prescription protocol for a weight-loss program designed to help you rapidly lose weight. Your own personal medical supervisor will monitor and respond to the physiological changes that happen in your body as you burn the fat, to **help you lose weight in a way that's healthy and safe for you.** And our friendly and knowledgable nutrition staff will educate you on making healthy food choices for your body type, and will motivate you to maintain your weight loss so that **you'll keep the pounds off for good.**

Our program is designed to help you identify and address the underlying physical reasons for why it's hard for you to lose weight. We monitor each patient's weight loss very carefully to make sure that patients are getting the best results from the program. **Our patients typically lose 3.5 to 5 pounds per week!**

We know that losing weight and keeping it off is very difficult, and we hope that our medically trained staff will give you the knowledge and confidence you need to achieve your weight loss goals and to maintain those results for the long term.

**We will be joined in April by the newest member of Port Washington Nutrition Center's community, Dr. Joseph Slickerty!** Dr. Slickerty has been helping patients lose weight with Dr. Turpington's protocol for over 15 years, and we feel very lucky to have him.

**Call** 1-800-999-1212 **today for your free, private consultation with our weight loss staff!**

We look forward to helping you start your journey to a lighter, leaner, healthier life.

**Call us:** 1-800-999-1212 **or visit us at:** pwnc.com

Nina Malyna/Shutterstock

# 1c Audience: Who Is the Communication For?

Audience is a complex concept, but generally speaking, we'll use the term here to refer to the *intended recipient(s) of an act of communication*. Composition scholars identify two different types of audiences for a given message: *addressed audiences* and *invoked audiences*.

- **Addressed audiences** are the people who actually receive a text and interact with it.

  EXAMPLE   The addressed audiences in the Port Washington Nutrition Center weight loss ad would likely include anyone who walked into its office and anyone who visited its website; depending on how Port Washington Nutrition Center chose to advertise, the ad might also pop up on *Facebook* feeds of people living in the area who searched on "weight loss."

- **Invoked audiences** are those imagined by the author. The text itself creates roles and invites the audience to occupy those roles, so it plays a part in creating its own audience. With analysis, it is generally easier to gauge who the communicator imagined as the audience than it is to know who actually received the message because you can study the text for clues.

  **EXAMPLE** In the Port Washington Nutrition Center weight loss ad, we can glean from studying the image and the text of the ad that the center imagines its audience as someone, most likely a woman, who wants to lose weight without a lot of effort and who wants noticeable results fairly quickly.

Good communicators pay attention to the needs of their audience and shape their communication accordingly. Likewise, you can study any type of communication in terms of how it might appeal to a specific audience, and this will help you better understand its rhetorical effects. The following five questions can help you think about the audience's role in communication.

MindTap

View How to Video 1: Analyzing an Audience

How-To Video 1: Analyzing an Audience

1. *As far as you can guess, what does the intended audience know, think, feel, value, or believe to be true about the topic of this communication?* Audiences range from hostile to supportive, depending on the topic. Accordingly, effective communicators must make decisions that take the audience into account. Canny communicators will think hard about what their target audience believes and values, and thus what sorts of things might cause them to be more receptive to the message of a particular communication.

   **EXAMPLE** A letter to the university newspaper protesting cuts to the campus facilities budget might do well to appeal to the readers' (i.e., other members of the university) sense of collective pride by detailing the specific ways that the cuts would detrimentally affect the appearance of the campus. This tactic would probably work better than, say, going on a tirade about incompetent and short-sighted university administrators and state legislators. At best, such an attack would create a feeling of sourness in readers, and at worst it might cause readers to take the side of the people being attacked and hence potentially cause them to resist the message.

2. *What is the audience's purpose in reading (or listening to, or watching, or interacting with) your piece of communication?* Just as a communicator has a purpose for communicating, the audience has a purpose for engaging with particular forms of communication. Sometimes these purposes match up (in which case the communication is arguably successful), and sometimes they don't.

EXAMPLE    Someone reading a placard at a historical monument might genuinely want to find out about the events that happened at that place, or they may simply be killing time as they wait for their friend to come back from buying a souvenir.

3. **What does the audience think of the communicator(s)?** The communicator's position vis-à-vis the audience is very important to how the audience receives the communication. An audience will dismiss or discount communicators whom it suspects of not having the right credentials to communicate about a subject. Of course, a communicator's credibility matters differently to different acts of communication. (Note that this is a different way of talking about ethos; see Section 1a.)

EXAMPLE    As a college student, you may not be qualified to make an authoritative claim about matters of astrophysics to astrophysicists, but you may be able to speak credibly about matters of education or any number of other things you're involved in or feel strongly about. Conversely, sometimes people can successfully transfer credibility or expertise from one realm to another realm where they have less expertise. Hollywood actors and other celebrities are infamous for making this kind of "credibility transfer," as when Madonna got involved with (and then botched) a charity orphanage project in Malawi, and Jenny McCarthy argued loudly and persistently about the ostensible dangers of getting children vaccinated (dangers later proven to be false).

4. **What is at stake for the audience in the topic of this communication? What specifically do they stand to gain or lose as a result of the communication?** Having a clear understanding of the importance or significance placed on a particular topic or argument can significantly affect how you talk about it, or whether you talk about it. It's critical to recognize an audience's investments and design your communication accordingly.

EXAMPLE    In using a set of instructions, what's at stake for the audience is their time and their sanity. Good writers of instructions would not, say, put as a reminder at the end of the instructions something that was critical to know midway through, forcing the reader to have to undo the previous twenty steps and start over. (Not that I'm speaking from bitter personal experience or anything.)

5. **In what circumstances will the audience encounter or use this communication, and how did that influence its format?** A communicator needs to consider not only the most appropriate medium and means of distribution for the message but also how and where the target audience may be encountering it.

EXAMPLES    In the case of the bad instructions referenced previously, a good technical communicator would have known to include the "attention" note in the instructions *before* the steps that it affected, since typically when people attempt to complete a task, they don't sit down and read all the instructions first. Similarly, good websites are designed with the knowledge of how people actually use the Internet, and thus a set of principles for designing good, usable Web pages has gradually developed. For instance, people can't scroll for more than three screens without feeling lost and disoriented, so Web designers recommend limiting the amount of scrolling that users have to do to no more than three screens.

## Appealing to an Audience's Emotions: Pathos

Pathos, the third of Aristotle's rhetorical appeals, refers to how messages persuade by arousing the emotions of the audience. "Arousing the emotions" has varying degrees of subtlety. It can mean using the rhetorical equivalent of an emotional sledgehammer: loaded terms and arguments that make the audience very angry (a favorite tactic of certain radio and television talk show hosts); or shameless ploys to arouse an audience's sense of pity and guilt: advertisements for animal shelters that show lingering close-ups of abused, sad-eyed dogs and cats while stirring music plays in the background, for instance. But remember that there are a lot of other, more subtle emotions: humor, fear, grief, uneasiness, disapproval, bemusement, passion, discouragement, pride, pity, indignation, expectation, insecurity, enchantment, tranquility, and many more.

How can we identify pathos, or appeals to emotion, in a given message? The emotions created by a text come on multiple levels. One level is the *overall* emotion that a particular text is meant to arouse in an audience, something deeply connected to the text's overall purpose. But different emotions may be aroused at various points in the text, through specific words, stories, or passages. These might be connected to the emotions of the overall text, or they might simply serve to get the reader more involved with the text. It's important for you as a rhetorical analyst to keep one eye on the main thing that the text is trying to get its audience to feel, while also paying attention to the particulars of emotional stories, words, and passages.

### FOR DISCUSSION

1. To think more about audience, study the *Twitter* post with the following political cartoon. Then answer the following questions.
   a. As far as you can guess, what does the intended audience know, think, feel, value, or believe to be true about the topic of this communication?
   b. What is the audience's purpose in reading (or listening to, or watching, or interacting with) this piece of communication?
   c. What does the audience think of the communicator(s)?
   d. What is at stake for the audience in the topic of this communication? What specifically do they stand to gain or lose as a result of the communication?

Quick Pick @afbranco #HillarysHealth #HillaryLiesMatter #Crooked Hillary #DontGetFooledAgain #VoteGOP legalinsurrection.com/2016/10/branco…

    e.  In what circumstances will the audience encounter or use this communication, and how does that influence its format?
 2.  Identify and bring in for discussion "communication fails," or examples of communication that do not respond well to audience. Where, specifically, do they fail? What could they have done better?
 3.  Find an example of an op-ed piece, a print/visual PSA (public service advertisement; you can find these online), a radio PSA, and a video PSA all on the same topic. First identify the overall emotional effect each of these aims to create. Then identify the specific tactics each medium uses to arouse this emotion. Did you find the form of pathos in one medium more emotionally gripping than the others?

## ASSIGNMENT

### Uncover Your Rhetorical Self

Being social animals, people are deeply rhetorical. That is, all of us work to craft a persona for ourselves that helps us to appeal to specific groups and gain social standing. We may not consciously think "I'm sharing this photo on *Tumblr* so that I can appeal to a certain audience in order to achieve X purpose," but in the background of all of our actions is an awareness

that others are responding to us (our *audience*) and that we want them to respond in certain ways (our *purpose*). This applies to even our most basic sorts of self-presentation: our personal style, the way we dress, the music we like, the way we inhabit our living space, and so forth.

It's also important to acknowledge that we position ourselves differently in different social groups: how we act in relation to our friends is probably different from how we act with our families or with employers. In other words, our choices may differ according to the effect that we hope to have on varying groups.

This assignment asks you to critically analyze the rhetorical effects of at least one of the following modes of self-presentation:

- Your appearance choices (including clothing, hair, body art, makeup, accessories, etc.)
- The choices you make regarding your living space (decor, furniture, linens, tidiness/cleanliness, wall hangings, etc.)

- Your social media activity ("about" information, photos, posting and sharing activity, commenting activity, etc.)
- Where you shop and the products you buy
- Your behavior in different social groups (including family, close friends, new acquaintances, classmates, professors, people older or younger than you)

### INVENTION WORK FOR THE ASSIGNMENT

- Start by doing some freewriting about how you define yourself and how you hope to be seen by the various social groups in which you are involved. (For more on freewriting, see Chapter 13, "Creating Written Compositions.") Which social group is the most important to you at this moment in time?
- Choose one of the modes of self-presentation listed above, and do your best to objectively catalogue and describe your choices and actions.
- Then do a freewrite about what effect the choices and actions related to this mode have on your own rhetorical identity. You can use one or both of the following questions as a guide:
  - How do my choices and actions help to further my own sense of how I want to define myself?
  - How does my self-presentation help me to position myself socially?
- You might ask some people from several of the different social groups listed above to describe you, and see how their perceptions match your own self-perception.

### FORMAT OF THE ASSIGNMENT

Depending on your instructor's preferences, you can do this assignment in the form of an essay (with photos), a personal profile or dossier, or a short video blog. But whatever format you use to present your rhetorical self-analysis, it should contain the following components:

1. An *introduction* that gives an overview of your rhetorical self: It should explain how you define yourself and how you hope to be seen by the various public groups with which you are affiliated.

2. A *description and analysis* of at least two of the modes of self-presentation above and how these contribute to your rhetorical identity.

3. *Evidence* in the form of photos, screenshots, and so forth.

4. A *conclusion* that discusses what you think are the rhetorical effects of the choices and actions associated with this mode of self-presentation.

**Transferable Skills and Concepts**

This chapter focuses mainly on successful instances of communication. However, there are obviously plenty of cases of communication gone awry, and it may not always be because the communicators didn't consider their audience. Think of an instance where you experienced miscommunication with somebody or where you witnessed an instance of miscommunication (even better if you can actually find an online or email conversation).

In a journal entry, first describe the gist of this miscommunication, and then try to pinpoint exactly what went wrong. Could you apply the principles of audience, message, and communicator described in this chapter to the miscommunication, or was it something beyond that? If it was, what does that tell you about the limitations of the basic elements of rhetoric?

# 2

# The Expanded Rhetorical Situation

*By working through this chapter, you will be able to...*

- Identify the exigence of a communication situation.
- Understand the role of purpose in communication.
- Define the means of communication: modality, medium, genre, and circulation.
- Explain how the means of communication shape a communication's message and purpose.

As you'll recall, Chapter 1 introduced the rhetorical triangle (Figure 2.1), widely acknowledged to be the basic elements of the rhetorical situation.

While the rhetorical triangle is a very useful way of thinking about rhetorical acts, it also leaves a lot out. If you only relied on the rhetorical triangle, you might think that communicative acts happen in a vacuum: Someone simply decides they have something they need to say, they find someone to say it to, and presto—rhetoric!

So while the communicator, message, and audience are critical to understanding rhetorical acts (and to creating your own), it's more accurate to say that acts of communication emerge from a dynamic, shifting stew of various elements. Along with the communicator, message, and audience, these also include:

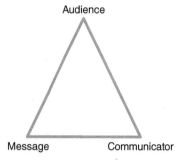

Audience

Message          Communicator

**FIGURE 2.1** Traditional Rhetorical Triangle

- the *context* for the communication;
- an *exigence* that prompts the communication;
- a *purpose* for the communication;
- *the means of communication*, or the material ways by which the communication happens: modality, medium, genre, and circulation.

So a more complicated and true-to-life representation of the rhetorical elements of communication might look more like Figure 2.2 (more like a rhetorical star than a triangle).

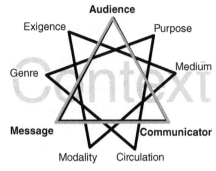

All of these elements need to be considered when analyzing the communicative acts of others and when you are communicating (so I'll be referring to them frequently in subsequent chapters). Each is explored in more detail in the following section.

**FIGURE 2.2** Expanded Rhetorical Situation

# 2a Context: What Are the Circumstances of Communication?

No rhetorical actions take place in a vacuum. If a rhetorical action is to be effective, it must respond to its **context**, which we could define as the *circumstances of communication*. We might distinguish several different levels and types of context:

- *Citational context*. This refers to a rhetorical action's location within a medium; so, for instance, a magazine article might be considered in the context of a particular issue of that magazine, or perhaps in the context of that magazine in general, or perhaps all magazines. Or one might consider an automobile advertisement within the context of where it appears (alongside an article in an online publication, or in a commercial break for a televised NASCAR race), or in the context of other automobile advertisements, or in the context of all advertisements.

- *Geographical context*. This is the physical location of the rhetorical action. What does the rhetorical action have to do with a physical place? For instance, to be effective, lost pet flyers probably need to be posted in the area in which the pet was lost. And professional documents such as project reports refer to things taking place in a location that would be familiar to everyone on the project team.

- *Historical context*. Everything exists in time (no smart comments about Schrödinger's cat, please), so all rhetorical actions have a historical context. When you watch a 30-second public service announcement for emergency preparedness, for instance, you might consider whether it's responding to historical events such as hurricanes or other natural disasters, or in the context of increased fears about terrorist attacks.

- *Sociocultural context*. This is the trickiest contextual category because in many cases sociocultural forces may be difficult to grasp or see. You could think of sociocultural context as all the things that have been said and done about a particular issue or (on perhaps a less over-whelming scale) the state of public feeling about or energy around a particular issue or topic. So if you are planning to communicate about an issue that's currently a hot topic—like abortion, religious freedom, gun control, or privacy—it's important to have an awareness of the sociocultural context.

While all of these levels of context will apply to a given rhetorical action, not all of them may be equally important or influential.

**EXAMPLE** I'm a frequent—some might say avid—reader of my local newspaper's Letters to the Editor section, and the differences between letters that do and don't respond to their various contexts are often all too obvious. The best letters to the editor are written in response either to something that was in the paper (the citational context) or something that's happening in town (the geographical context—appropriate because it's a *local* as opposed to a national paper). It's often very clear when a first-year writing class is doing a Letter to the Editor assignment because suddenly the section is filled with letters about issues that are irrelevant to what's been happening in the paper or to the region. (This serves as a cautionary tale: Read your newspaper before you decide to submit a letter to the editor!)

## 2b Exigence: What Invites You to Communicate?

MindTap®
View Tiny Lecture 2:
What Is Exigence?

Context overlaps significantly with **exigence** (also known as ex-igency), which can be defined as *whatever prompted a rhetorical action*. Exigence refers to whatever situation has invited or made possible some sort of response. In fact, each type of context de-scribed in the previous section can also serve as a kind of exi-gence. Receiving a gift provides the exigence for a thank-you card, for instance. The death of someone culturally important provides the exigence for not only typical rhetorical acts like obituaries and eulogies but also other sorts of public reflections about the person's contributions.

But exigence is often more complex and layered. A pattern of uncivil behavior on campus that you notice can be an exigence—an invitation for response. A polluted stream can be an exigence; so can a natural disaster or a war, a series of controversial decisions made by a city council, or the overdevelopment of a particular area of town that's causing it (you feel) to lose its character. Such situations provide opportunities, or perhaps urgent invitations for response. What they *don't* do is dictate, or even strongly suggest, what that response might be. For this, communica-tors also need to consider the other elements common to all communica-tive acts (Figure 2.3).

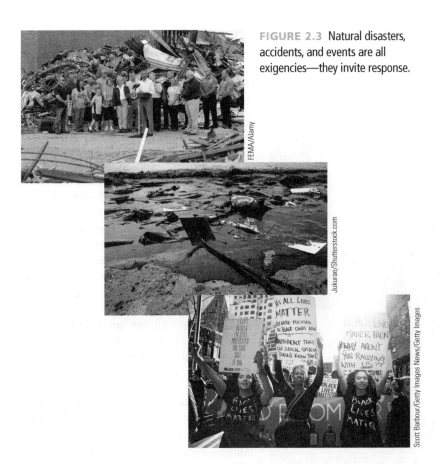

FIGURE 2.3 Natural disasters, accidents, and events are all exigencies—they invite response.

FEMA/Alamy

Jukurae/Shutterstock.com

Scott Barbour/Getty Images News/Getty Images

Underlying exigence is a more complicated notion of timeliness, or the proper moment for communication. You've probably heard the cliché "strike while the iron is hot." This expression, and others like it, evoke the ancient Greek concept of *kairos*. Kairos, actually the Greek god of the "fleeting moment," was typically portrayed with wings on his feet (to suggest that the opportune moment is always fleeting) and with a lock of hair hanging from the front of his head, but none in the back, to signal that those who would seize the moment had to act quickly and decisively or be left in the metaphorical dust (Figure 2.4).

The representation of Kairos is thus an apt image for communicators, a warning that one needs to always be looking for the appropriate time to convey one's message. Waiting for the right moment can apply to everyday acts of rhetoric; for instance, rhetorically savvy children everywhere know to wait until Mom is in a good mood before asking for favors. (And conversely, asking your boss for a raise the day that the company announces a serious loss in profits probably won't get you the desired results.)

Heritage Images/Getty Images

**FIGURE 2.4** Representation of Kairos

In terms of communicating publicly, arguments on particular topics will get much more of a hearing when something happens to put those topics in people's minds; for instance, people are more likely to be receptive to arguments about global climate change during unusual weather events (whether or not these events actually have any causal tie to climate change), less so when the weather is ordinary. These arguments, or at least the feelings behind them, might exist prior to the events in a latent form, but the trigger of particular events provides the opportunity to give them a wider hearing. The tricky thing about kairos is that because it depends on chance, opportunity, and circumstances, it's impossible to predict when an opportunity will arise. All one can do in the meantime is be attuned to the situation and practice with a variety of rhetorical tools so that one can be ready when the moment strikes.

As an example, let's apply these questions to the following two letters to the editor (taken from my small-town local paper, the *Moscow-Pullman Daily News*): "Mushroom Discrimination" and "That Third Street Bridge." See Table 2.1 for notes on the exigence of these two letters.

## QUESTIONS TO ASK  Investigating Exigence

- What event (or series of events) prompted this rhetorical act?
- Is the exigence relatively simple or relatively complex?
- What might this event (or series of events) mean to the audience, and how might that have shaped the format and content of the rhetorical act?

## Letter: Mushroom Discrimination

Oct 5, 2016

Some of you may know me from the Farmers Markets. My name is Josh Yake, and I am the wild mushroom vendor, Gourmet Foragables. I feature other foraged items as well (nettles, fiddleheads, sea beans, etc.) but we are now in the middle of the best time of year for my products: fall mushroom season.

I have not been at the Farmers Market. I have been systematically excluded by Daniel Stewart, market manager, and his direct supervisor Kathleen Burns, city arts director. As a walk-on vendor with agricultural products, I am considered a farmer and am supposed to be given preference over artists for a spot. As the only vendor with wild mushrooms, common sense and fresh product diversity would seem to guarantee me a spot.

In fact, I was present at the market last year when there was record attendance under the previous market manager, and I had a spot. So, what has changed? Simply put, the new market manager has intentionally excluded me and my product from the market. Apparently, he thinks the public would have no interest in chanterelles, lobsters, matsutake, bears tooth, chicken of the woods, honey mushrooms, cauliflower mushrooms and on and on.

Daniel Stewart is discriminating against me. If you would like to share your disapproval with him, he can be reached at dstewart@ci.moscow.id.us. His supervisor, Kathleen Burns, should also be notified of his discriminatory negligence. Kathleen can be reached at kburns@ci.moscow.id.us. They both can be contacted at the Moscow City Arts Department at (208) 883-7036.

I sure hope to return to Moscow soon and see all of your wonderful faces, but if the arts department has its way, I will be excluded for the rest of the season. I hope you can help me to let them know they have made a mistake.

**JOSH YAKE**

**Spokane Valley, Wash**

## Letter: That Third Street Bridge

Oct 1, 2016

Please join Citizens for a Livable Community in urging the Moscow City Council to approve a bicycle-pedestrian bridge across Paradise Creek at Third Street, near East City Park and Lena Whitmore Elementary. The relatively modest investment would generate big returns by improving safety and connectivity for children, bicyclists, walkers, people with disabilities, and anyone who prefers to experience Moscow's beauty and friendliness from a human-scaled, human-paced perspective. It's an especially good idea now as popularity grows for youth recreation facilities along Mountain View Road.

The cost has been estimated at $70,000, a comparative bargain, especially when advocates have already collected more than $16,000. The federal government recently rejected the city's request for $17.6 million for much-needed transportation improvements along Mountain View. The amount would have been matched with $3.2 million from local sources and $3.4 million from the state. An incongruous piece of the failed application proposed constructing a motor vehicle bridge over Paradise Creek at Third to move through-bound traffic faster, estimated to cost $1 million to $2 million.

Recently, East Third Street was redesignated from neighborhood collector to minor arterial to accommodate more vehicles at higher speeds. Moving more traffic more quickly through any neighborhood or the heart of town is contrary to Moscow's oft touted quality of life, including walkability, bikeability, historic charm, safety, uncommonly healthy downtown, close-knit neighborhoods, parks events, well-situated community center, centrally located high school, Safe Routes to School and national Bike Friendly Community accolades.

A bicycle-pedestrian crossing over Paradise Creek on Third Street is fiscally responsible. It would improve safety for youngsters, elders and other vulnerable citizens. It would renew community conversations about how and why we protect what's special about all Moscow neighborhoods, and how the whole of our community is made up of interdependent parts. For more information, see *http://www.livablecommunitymoscow.com/*.

**NANCY CHANEY**

**Moscow**

TABLE 2.1  Notes on Exigence of the Two Letters

| LETTERS (RHETORICAL ACTS) | "MUSHROOM DISCRIMINATION" | "THAT THIRD STREET BRIDGE" |
|---|---|---|
| **What event (or series of events) prompted this rhetorical act?** | The farmer's market wouldn't give the writer a booth to sell his foraged produce. | Continuing arguments for and against installing a traffic bridge that would allow residents from a fairly new development in the outskirts of town to get to the heart of town faster and more directly. |
| **Is the exigence relatively simple or relatively complex?** | Relatively simple (unless one starts probing the city's reasons behind not giving him a booth—then it may be more complicated). | Relatively complex: There are several years' worth of argument and debate about this issue among citizens and in City Council meetings. |

| LETTERS (RHETORICAL ACTS) | "MUSHROOM DISCRIMINATION" | "THAT THIRD STREET BRIDGE" |
|---|---|---|
| What might this event (or series of events) mean to the audience, and how might that have shaped the format and content of the rhetorical act? | He feels that he is being treated unfairly. The local paper is read by a lot of farmer's market customers, and so he may assume that by writing a letter to the editor, he'll be able to generate sympathy and persuade customers to contact the city. | The writer represents a group that opposes the installation of a vehicle bridge (because the road that it would connect goes past a school and a heavily populated area, they fear the effects of increased traffic). As a compromise, they recommend the installation of a pedestrian bridge that would allow walkers and bikes to cross this junction. They chose a letter to the editor because this debate has been carried out for years in the local paper, so readers of the paper are likely familiar with the issue. |

## FOR DISCUSSION

1. Off the top of your head, see if you can write down ten current situations (local, campus, and national) that would count as exigencies—situations that seem to invite communication. Share these with small groups or the class. As a class, choose a few of the exigencies mentioned and discuss in more detail what *kind* of communicative acts could be mobilized in response to them.
2. Read the following short news piece. Discuss how this situation might constitute an exigence. What possible responses might it warrant? (purpose) From whom, and to whom? (audience) How? (means of communication)

### White House Supports Making Women Register for the Draft

**GAB MORRONGIELLO, *THE EXAMINER* (WASHINGTON, D.C.)**

December 1, 2016

The White House on Thursday came out in favor of requiring women to register for the military draft, despite the fact it was stripped from the compromise defense policy bill this week.

"The administration believes our military is strongest when we draw from a pool of all eligible recruits," Ned Price, a spokesman for the

White House National Security Council, said in a statement provided to the *Washington Examiner*.

"Although we remain committed to an all-volunteer force that meets the highest standards of performance, applied equitably to all who serve, universal registration both furthers our commitment to equity and serves to sustain our legacy of public service," Price said.

He added: "As old barriers for military service are being removed, the administration supports—as a logical next step—women registering for the Selective Service."

The Pentagon joined the Obama administration in backing efforts to require women turning 18 on or after Jan. 1, 2018 to register for the draft.

"While [Defense] Secretary Carter strongly supports our all-volunteer approach and does not advocate returning to a draft, as he has said in the past, he thinks it makes sense for women to register for selective service just as men must," Pentagon press secretary Peter Cook said in a statement.

The measure has drawn mixed reactions from conservatives on Capitol Hill.

Arizona Sen. John McCain, who chairs the Senate Armed Services Committee, told *The New York Times* earlier this year that requiring women to register for the draft is "fair" now that the U.S. allows both men and women to serve in combat roles.

Meanwhile, Texas Sen. Ted Cruz called the proposal "immoral" and suggested colleagues of his who support the measure are "nuts."

"The idea that we would draft our daughters to forcibly bring them into the military and put them in close combat, I think, is wrong," the ex-White House hopeful said at a campaign rally in February. "It is immoral. And if I am president, we ain't doing it."

# 2c Purpose: What Does This Communication Want?

The **purpose** of any act of communication is *what the communicator hopes to achieve with this particular rhetorical action*. When we think about the purpose of a piece of communication, then, we think about not just the content of the piece, but what it is *doing*. To understand a communicator's choices—whether they be the layout of a brochure, the background music in a podcast, the vocabulary used in an email, the emoticons in an instant message, the color scheme of a website, or the length of the paragraphs in a textbook—you first need to understand what the communicator ultimately wants this piece of communication to *do* for and/or to its intended audience.

Purpose is often multilayered; that is, any communication typically contains several purposes, some of which are more explicit and/or important than others.

**EXAMPLE**   You might think of the purpose of advertisements as relatively straightforward: to entice viewers to buy the featured product or service. But even the purposes of ads can be relatively complex. An individual ad might be just a part of a larger, more far-reaching marketing scheme that aims to get the consumer to identify in certain ways with the product and to develop a long-term relationship with that brand—to identify as a "Target shopper" or a "Gap person."

The number of purposes for communicating is almost as extensive as the different means by which people can communicate. Table 2.2 lists some common purposes. In the For Discussion prompt that follows, you'll see how many more purposes you can generate as a class.

TABLE 2.2 Different Types of Purposes

| *Purposes of **Informing*** | • To inform people about the existence and purpose of certain events that will enable them to decide whether to attend or not.<br>• To inform them about developments or happenings that affect their well-being.<br>• To inform them about products with the intent of enticing them to buy the product.<br>• To provide information that will help people solve a problem or accomplish a task.<br>• To provide information that will help them make a decision about something.<br>• Other purposes for informing? |
|---|---|
| *Purposes of **Persuasion*** | • To persuade people to adopt a certain position on a topic.<br>• To persuade them to do certain kinds of actions.<br>• To set policy on an issue.<br>• To critique or condemn things or actions.<br>• To provoke comments or a response.<br>• To make people think or feel differently about a topic.<br>• To prompt them to reflect on their own actions.<br>• To compellingly present a problem in the hopes of inciting people to want to solve it.<br>• To persuade a granting agency to give you money.<br>• Other purposes involving persuasion? |

*(continued on next page)*

| *Aesthetic and Literary* *Purposes* | • To make people laugh.<br>• To make them feel differently about something.<br>• To appeal to their sense of wonder, mystery, or fantasy.<br>• To help them understand more deeply a particular person or way of being.<br>• Other aesthetic and literary purposes? |
|---|---|
| *Purposes of* **Scholarly** **Inquiry** | • To present new knowledge to a scientific or scholarly community.<br>• To challenge established views with new evidence or arguments.<br>• Other purposes for academic inquiry? |

How do you determine the purpose of a given piece of communication? Sometimes, especially in technical writing, the purpose of a piece of communication is stated clearly up front, in a purpose statement: "The purpose of this [piece of communication] is to do X …." However, purpose in most communication isn't so explicitly stated. This means that you need to determine the communication's purpose through analysis. To begin to identify the purpose of any intentionally designed piece of communication, you might simply start by asking, "What does this piece of communication seem to *want* from its audience?" Is it asking them to behave or think in particular ways (perhaps differently than they already do)? Does it hope to evoke particular feelings about the topic? If the purpose is not immediately clear, the following steps can help you more readily identify the purpose of any communication.

---

**HOW TO…**    **Determine a Communication's Purpose**

1. ***Note where and when the communication appears.*** Since purpose is so closely linked to context and audience, thinking explicitly about these things can provide excellent clues about the purpose of the communication.

   **EXAMPLE**   If you're in the student health center and see a row of brochures prominently titled with names of various contagious medical conditions, you might guess even without reading them that their purpose is to inform visitors to the health center about the symptoms of these diseases and how they spread so that readers can take steps to prevent sickening others or becoming sick themselves. Since the student health center (by virtue of the professionals who work there and the money that funds it) is invested in maintaining the health of its patients and the campus more generally, this seems like a logical purpose.

2. ***Gather as much information as you can about the communicators.*** Knowing the values, beliefs, identifications, and social positions of the communicators, as well as who is paying them, may give you some clues about their possible purposes. Say in a Web search for articles about genetically modified foods, you come upon one titled "GMOs proven to have few adverse health effects." Clicking the link takes you to Monsanto's website (Monsanto is a well-known producer of genetically modified plants). So you could probably guess that the purpose of the article is to improve public opinion of GMOs. Of course, this is not to say that communication produced by a communicator with something at stake in the issue has no value; however, you would need to very carefully evaluate the evidence presented to support the argument or underlying purpose.

3. ***Look for clues within the communication itself.*** Focus on the choices made by the communicator. Doing so requires you to have some amount of background knowledge to recognize buzzwords and lines of argument that are associated with certain communities, which can be difficult at first. But with practice, and by combining this with steps 1 and 2, you'll be able to identify the investments and likely purposes of an act of communication.

---

## FOR DISCUSSION

1. Reread the lists of common purposes in Table 2.2. For each purpose listed, generate at least one type of communication (in any modality— written, visual, or multimodal) that attempts to achieve this purpose.

2. Brainstorm a list of every type of communication that you've encountered recently (in all modalities). Match each type of communication on your list with the purposes listed. For the types you've brainstormed that don't match any of the given purposes, try to determine their purposes using How to Determine a Communication's Purpose. Keep a list of the new purposes you come up with. As a class, compile them into the categories in Table 2.2 or create new categories.

3. Find a piece of communication—it could be a published piece of writing in any genre, a visual communication, a website, or a song— that you find to have a particularly interesting purpose. Talk about the purpose(s) of the piece of communication and identify specifically how you came to that conclusion.

4. Consider the following screenshot of the *Elite Daily* website. You can also go to the site *elitedaily.com* and click around. What is the purpose of the site? Does it have multiple purposes?

Source: Elite Daily

## 2d The Means of Communication (Modality, Medium, Genre, Circulation): How Does Communication Physically Happen?

**TEXTUAL**
Chapter 3

**VISUAL**
Chapter 4

**MULTIMODAL**
Chapter 5

Chapters 3, 4, and 5 break down in detail how to analyze the rhetorical moves that are specific to various modalities (verbal, visual, and multimodal rhetoric). But before we dig into the specifics, it's important to understand the big picture of what we might call the means of communication.

With the advent of the Internet, and especially what some have called "the participatory Web"—the websites, apps, and platforms that make it possible for large numbers of people to communicate with large numbers of other people—the communication landscape has shifted dramatically. In less than a decade we've gained the ability to share videos and photos, and to post short or long discourses on anything imaginable through tools such as *Twitter*, *Instagram*, *YouTube*, *Facebook*, *Flickr*, and *Snapchat*. The result is a sort of media Wild West: everything is in a fluid process of development, rules have been cobbled together in slapdash fashion, and nobody quite has a handle on the situation. Not only are traditional media venues scrambling to make sense of the new media scene (and in some cases, like many radio stations and newspapers, folding altogether) but regular people are finding celebrity and notoriety via platforms such as *Instagram*, *Twitter*, and *YouTube*.

While we can celebrate the dramatic increase in the means by which it's possible for everyday people to communicate, this shift also means that you need to have all your wits about you. It's critical to develop a keen attention to not only how these new tools work, but also to their rhetorical effects and consequences: Unfortunately, the Internet abounds with cautionary tales about the perils of misusing or simply being unaware of how social media works.

**EXAMPLE** On Halloween 2013, a 23-year-old woman named Alicia Ann Lynch posted a photo of herself dressed in a Boston marathon bombing victim costume to *Twitter*. Some of her followers, outraged, retweeted her photo to their followers, and thanks to the lightning speed with which information can spread through social media, within three days Lynch had become the most infamous person on the Internet. For the conceivable future, anyone who Googles Lynch will undoubtedly turn up links to stories about the scandal; thus, her reputation has more or less been permanently damaged by her inattention to the rhetorical workings and consequences of *Twitter* as a communication tool.

MindTap®
View Tiny Lecture 3: Thinking about the Means of Communication

The means of communication can be broken down into four parts: modality, medium, genre, and circulation. Each of these is described in the following sections, along with questions that will help you think rhetorically about how they work. But while I break them out to describe them separately here, keep in mind that they are always working together in any given communicative act.

## The Modality of Communication

In some ways the most fundamental element of a rhetorical technology, modality refers to the basic sensory means by which communication happens. While the senses of taste, touch, and smell can certainly communicate, here are the modalities that are most frequently referred to and used for deliberate communication purposes:

- The **verbal modality** (words spoken, sung, handwritten, or typed)
- The **auditory modality** (spoken language, song, music, or ambient noise)

- The **visual modality** (still and moving images, color, written text, gestures, or facial expressions)
- The **haptic modality** (involves a sense of touch and where/how the body is positioned in relation to the communication; think of how you interact with videogames, for instance)

Most types of communication involve more than one modality; for instance, a speech combines the verbal modality (spoken language) with visual modalities such as gestures, facial expressions, and other ambient visual cues.

Paying attention to the modalities of an act of communication helps you understand its most basic limits—what can and can't be done.

**EXAMPLE**  Think about the differences between an in-person gathering of neighbors concerned about a proposed development project and a *Facebook* page devoted to the same concern. The modalities at the in-person meeting include speaking, gesture, and facial expressions (and perhaps handouts or PowerPoint). Such modalities lend themselves to things like spontaneous follow-up questions and collective, real-time discussion, which sometimes is the most efficient means for coming to a mutual understanding and making decisions. The modalities of the *Facebook* page, on the other hand, which might include pictures and short texts in the form of linear, chronological posts and comments, lend themselves to a visual record of the conversation among community members. Whoever is the self-appointed leader of the neighborhood group needs to think carefully about which modalities best lend themselves to the group's goal or purpose.

---

**QUESTIONS TO ASK**    **Thinking about Modality**

- In what situations is this modality used? List as many as you can think of.
- In what sorts of communication situations is this modality most effective? What is this modality good for or best at communicating?
- What sorts of skills does one need to have to *effectively* use this modality? ("Effectively" is the operative word here.)
- What feelings does this modality of communication evoke (speech vs. writing, etc.)?
- How comfortable are people with this modality?

---

FOR DISCUSSION

1. At home or in class (if the technology is available), examine a website like *Buzzfeed*. Create an inventory of all of the modalities apparent on that website. What kind of communicative actions does each modality enable and constrain? After considering the overall purpose of the site, discuss how the combination of the modalities on the site might help it achieve that purpose.

2. Imagine that you are part of a student group that wants to implement campus-wide composting in the dining facilities, dormitories, and other campus buildings. What modalities are at your disposal for enacting your purposes, and what do these modalities make possible or limit?

## The Medium of Communication

Media are closely related to modalities but refer more to *the technical means by which communication is disseminated*.

**EXAMPLES** Some examples of media include the printed page (books, newspapers, magazines, brochures, posters, pamphlets), online PDFs, email, television, *YouTube* videos, photos on *Facebook* or *Flickr*, songs, film, cell phone, Web pages, SMS (text messages), social media sites, and so forth.

**QUESTIONS TO ASK** **Thinking about Medium**

- What is the history of this medium?
- What can this medium do that others cannot?
- What modality(s) can be used with this medium?
- Does this medium allow one-to-many communication, many-to-many communication, or something else? What role(s) does this medium make available for its audience? (Many have argued that centrally controlled media like Hollywood-produced films and documentaries, radio broadcasts, TV news, and print newspapers put viewers in a mostly passive role because viewers don't have access to the means of production.)
- What groups does the medium exclude (i.e., who doesn't have access to the medium)?
- How does this medium shape the messages that it conveys? What constraints does it put on the messages?

> ## FOR DISCUSSION
>
> Choose a specific medium (e.g., the Internet, magazines, zines, radio, TV, streaming content services) and research its history as a form of communication (you can start by Googling "history of [the medium you're researching]"). Use your research to answer the following questions:
>
> - When and where did this medium of communication first begin?
> - Why was the medium developed? What social/cultural/technological need did it fulfill?
> - In what contexts and for what purposes is the medium primarily used nowadays?
> - How has the medium changed from its original use or intent?
>
> Then create a four-slide presentation (see Chapter 14 for instructions on how to design presentation slides) that you can give in class (or, alternatively, a slidecast—a presentation with a recorded voiceover—that you can post online) that answers these questions for the rest of the students in the class.

## The Genre of Communication

**Genres** are somewhat stabilized yet flexible forms of communication that have developed over time and in response to all these other rhetorical factors: purpose, audience, context, exigence, modalities, media, and circulation.

**EXAMPLES**   Almost any form of communication you can think of is a genre: letters, obituaries, blog posts, contracts, advertisements, novels, textbooks, landscape photographs, documentaries, horror movies, and so on.

Genres arise from particular needs or patterns of activity.

**EXAMPLE**   The genre of "listicles" (articles in list form, like "7 Ways You Know You Just Drank Too Much Coffee") emerged in full force once the dominance of social media brought people in contact with way too much information to process. Through their format and content, listicles signal to the reader that they are easy to read and accessible, and hence won't take up too much of readers' time and attention.

Genres can enact certain cultural values and beliefs.

**EXAMPLE**   The passive voice in a scientific lab report reinforces the scientific value of objective facts (not subjective humans) speaking for themselves.

Genres can also shape how their users see the world.

**EXAMPLE**   In one academic study, workers in a group home for women with various mental illnesses were ordered to change how they kept track of the residents, from a journal-like daily log of household events to sheets that kept track of individual patients (Writing UP/Writing Down). A genre analysis of the change showed that the individualized sheets had the effect of amplifying various patients' behaviors because it no longer showed the behavior in the general context of the home (other patients' behaviors and material happenings in the general house such as power interruptions).

It's important to note that genres are not fixed: new genres and sub-genres, even in traditional media such as books and film, are continually emerging.

**QUESTIONS TO ASK** **Thinking about Genre**

- Where does the genre appear? In what medium and context?
- What are the features of the genre? What are the things (content, format) that make it recognizable as a genre?
- Who composes using this genre?
- Who is the audience for this genre? In what circumstances do they typically engage with the genre?
- What actions does the genre help make possible? What actions does it constrain?
- How does this genre circulate?

**FOR DISCUSSION**

1. Brainstorm as many nonfiction genres as you can think of. Choose one of these genres and find three examples of it. Analyze these samples using the questions in the previous box. Write down your answers, supporting what you say with evidence from the genres.
2. Movies provide an easy way to get a feel for the conventions of distinct genres, and the materials used to promote the movies have developed genre conventions of their own. For this assignment, go to an online film streaming service such as *Hulu* or *Netflix* and find a link called "Genres." Choose a genre to analyze: romantic comedy, comedy, drama, military/war, Western, horror, sci-fi, etc.
   a. First study the images for the videos and take notes about their various features: the images used, the typefaces, the colors, the juxtaposition of images and text (where the text appears in relation to the picture).

b. Now study the descriptions of the films. Are there any commonalities in the descriptions of the film?

c. Next, find outliers of the genre—images or descriptions that don't seem to fit the conventions of the genre. What's different about these?

d. Write an overview of the features of the promotional materials for this film genre. Make an argument about the cultural values, beliefs, and assumptions that are revealed through these features.

## The Circulation of Communication

Circulation refers to *the physical means by which a message gets distributed*. In an era where most information is digital, it's important to think of how a message has been or can potentially be copied, forwarded, reposted, or appear in a way other than what one initially intended. This doesn't just refer to unfortunate photos from last Friday's party or texts composed at 2 a.m. that you later wish you hadn't sent (though it's important to think about these rhetorical effects!). Whole websites, like *Upworthy* and *Buzzfeed*, are devoted to recirculating content that they find valuable. *Upworthy* pays people specifically to write titles that will get the stories they circulate more clicks in the hope that those viewers in turn will pass the content on through "liking," sharing, and reposting.

Rhetorically savvy communicators need to think about not just what the message is but also *how* messages circulate and the rhetorical effects that might have.

**EXAMPLE**  I've noticed lately that videos created by media organizations like *Mic* and *The Guardian* now include an easy-to-read script (Figure 2.5

Source: Hearst Communications, Inc.

**FIGURE 2.5**  Screenshot of Chocolate Chip Recipe from a *Delish* Video

shows a screenshot of a chocolate chip cookie recipe video from the site *Delish*). Why do this? One reason may be that the creators of these videos expect them to be shared via *Facebook* or *Twitter*. Thanks to the *Facebook* feature that allows videos to play without sound when a user scrolls past them in the feed, a user can get the gist of the video's content without sound (so they can easily do this at work, for instance).

**EXAMPLE**  Consider the following example as a way one person cannily considered the circulation of messages when composing his own.

In February 2011, football player Alex Tanney uploaded a video entitled "Alex Tanney Trick Shot Quarterback—Better than Johnny Mac" showing off his impressively accurate football throwing skills. The video went viral (as of early 2017, it's gotten over 4 million views). The History Channel's show *Stan Lee's Superhumans* noticed Tanney's video and subsequently filmed a segment featuring Tanney, which aired in July 2011. Soon after, Tanney was signed by the NFL and has since gone on to play for several NFL teams.

Tanney's success, which can arguably be attributed at least in part to the notoriety generated by his viral video, did not go unnoticed. In June 2012 (after Tanney had been signed to the Kansas City Chiefs), another NFL hopeful named Chad Elliott uploaded a video named "Chad Elliott Trick Shot Quarterback—Better than Alex Tanney and Johnny Mac" to *YouTube* (Figure 2.6). Elliott's video, which owing to its title comes up in the search results for "Alex Tanney trick shots," is fairly professionally produced. It also has a direct message, to a specific audience: In the beginning of the video, the text "Attention NFL Scouts … Chad Elliott is here!!" flashes on the screen, followed by Elliott's stats and playing history, and the message "Nows [*sic*] your chance. Call or email today!" His email address is posted below the video.

CHAD ELLIOTT TRICK SHOT QUARTERBACK - BETTER THAN ALEX TANNEY AND JOHNNY MAC

**FIGURE 2.6** Screenshot of Chad Elliott's Video

The interesting thing about Elliott's video was that it shows how he was being strategic about not only his message but about rhetorical circulation—that is how he could get the right people to see his message. The comments below the video suggest that the right people (NFL scouts) in fact *did* see it, though it appears that Elliott's overall knowledge of the game and lack of discipline may have ultimately kept him from the NFL. Perhaps he'd be better as a marketing consultant ...

## QUESTIONS TO ASK — Thinking about Circulation

- What resources (technical, education/training, financial, skills, connections, etc.) does one need in order to produce a message in this modality and medium? Does one need to be a specialist?
- What are the physical and technological means by which messages produced in this modality and medium circulate? How do they reach their intended audiences?
- How can messages produced in this modality and medium be reproduced and redistributed? What are the barriers (legal, financial, technical, and otherwise) to recirculating a message produced in this modality and medium? (For example, digital messages can be reproduced very easily, but print documents and photographs can also be scanned, copied, and circulated in a variety of ways.)
- By what means might you best reach a particular audience? What media or modalities do they have cultural and technical access to?
- Which messages circulated by this modality and medium get the most attention?

## FOR DISCUSSION

1. Identify a case where somebody thought rhetorically about circulation and used it to further his or her agenda. Identify another case where someone didn't think about the rhetorical power of circulation, to bad effect.
2. As a class, try to explain the differences in circulation between academic work (that is, compositions that are aimed at other scholars) and compositions that are aimed at the public. What are the features of each meant to aid in the circulation of the composition?

## ASSIGNMENT

### Compare Compositions That Have Similar Purposes but Different Formats

Find three compositions that are similar in content and purpose but are composed using different means of communication (i.e., modalities, media, genre, and circulation). For example, you might compare a recipe found in a print cookbook, a recipe found in a food blog like *Smitten Kitchen*, and a how-to instructional recipe video like the one by *Delish* shown in Figure 2.5.

First, analyze each of these compositions using the terms described in the previous Questions to Ask box. Then create a Prezi, infographic, or other visual composition that analyzes and shows the difference between each of these rhetorical compositions, using at least some of the terms described in the rhetorical star: exigence, audience, purpose, modality(s), medium, genre, and circulation. You should aim to show someone not versed in rhetoric what makes these compositions rhetorically different from each other and why the difference is important or interesting. Be creative with your presentation style.

## FOR REFLECTION

### Transferable Skills and Concepts

In this chapter we learned about the wider set of forces that influences composition and communication: exigence, purpose, and the means of communication. For this reflective journal piece, think about one specific communication platform that you use frequently: paper, email, writing on walls, *Facebook*, *Instagram*, *Twitter*, etc. What does this platform allow you to do, and what limitations with it have you noticed? How are these linked to the platform's technological features?

# PART 2

# Rhetorical Analysis

# 3

# Analyzing Textual Rhetoric

*By working through this chapter, you will be able to...*
- Identify the main point, purpose, rhetorical moves, structure, and tone of a text.
- Accurately summarize a text for an audience.
- Research the rhetorical situation of a text.
- Write a rhetorical analysis of a text.

**ANALYZE AND CREATE**

**Chapter 3**
Analyzing
Textual Rhetoric

**Chapter 13**
Creating
Written
Compositions

Chapter 1 describes rhetorical analysis as the effort to understand how communication creates particular effects on people. Language (whether spoken, written, or sung) is important to these effects. Of course, it's somewhat artificial to separate language from its living context (since things like the sound of voices, the feel and smell of paper, the look of screens, and even the quality of light also affect how we receive messages). We do so here with the understanding that paying attention to language on its own is useful, even if it shows us only part of the picture.

## FOR DISCUSSION

Language, of course, is vitally important to the rhetorical effects of oral communication. However, speech and song have a range of other elements that create rhetorical effects very different from that of written text. This discussion topic asks you to think about the differences between the two.

1. Find a written text on a topic and a song on a similar topic. (For instance, you might read an April 2013 *Daily Mail* article called

"The Infidelity Epidemic" and listen to Beyoncé's "Pray You Catch Me" from *Lemonade*.) Read and listen to these in class.

2. On the board, make a list of the differences between written and spoken (or sung) rhetoric. Think in terms of not only the language itself but also the rhetorical situation of each (as described in Chapters 1 and 2); for instance, how they are accessed by an audience, the context, the means of communication, etc.

3. What difference does it make in rhetorical effects when language is set in the context of music? What is lost? What is gained?

# 3a Thinking Rhetorically about Reading Texts

We read differently for different purposes. For instance, if you read magazines like *Rolling Stone* or *Glamour* the way most people do (not so much reading as flipping through ads and photos, occasionally stopping to glance at a headline or skimming an article), you know that they don't require your full attention. This is why such magazines, and not copies of *Thus Spake Zarathustra*, populate airports and dentists' offices. Conversely, school reading—studying biology textbooks or reading novels for English, for instance—demands more from you in terms of attention. A similar level of attention is required for rhetorical reading. This kind of reading doesn't come naturally—it requires training—and as with other trained skills, it hurts a little at first. You'll need to build up endurance in your rhetorical reading "muscles" through focused practice. Once you do build up this endurance, though, it's easier to sustain this kind of attention, and you'll find that you more easily notice how texts aim to influence their audiences.

This section describes in more detail what rhetorical reading looks like in practice. Although I break it down into steps here as a way of logically describing what to do, the process of reading rhetorically to summarize and analyze texts is actually much less linear. You'll move back and forth through the following steps as necessary when you read the text you're analyzing, first to clarify its main points (in order to write a summary) and then again as you move into your rhetorical analysis. In short, the business of analysis is *not* efficient, especially at first.

Personally, even as an "expert reader," I still need to go back and read a complex text many times—so many, sometimes, that I end up almost memorizing parts of it. Gaining this level of familiarity with a text lightens what psychologists call your cognitive load. That is, when you firmly understand the basics of what a text is *saying*, your mind is freed up to focus on other interesting questions, like how the text is *working*: the heart of analysis. And like everything else, the more you do it, the better you'll get.

So how do we train ourselves to read a piece of writing rhetorically? Rhetorical reading means paying attention to both *what* is said and *how* it's said, as well as paying attention to the structures of the text.

## Understanding WHAT Is Said

The more background knowledge you have about a text, the easier it will be for you to interact with it in more complex ways (for instance, by writing a summary of it, which is the first step in writing a rhetorical analysis essay). So first, pause to gather your thoughts about the topic. What do you already know and feel about it?

### Preview the piece.

But what if the reading is on an unfamiliar topic? While previewing a text typically means skimming it once just to gain a basic understanding of what it's about, if you don't know much about the topic, take twenty minutes or so to do some informational research. A basic Internet search will do.

**EXAMPLE**   For the sample text at the end of this section, "Why You Should Think Twice Before Shaming Anyone on Social Media," I didn't know anything about the incident that the article was responding to, so I Googled some search terms from the article ("Adria Richards PyCon," "Jezebel teen racists," and "public shaming") just to see for myself what these incidents involved and also to see if I agreed with the author's points about them.

Don't be afraid to mark up the piece—if it's physical, with a pen or pencil, and if it's digital, with free tools like Skitch or even the "Insert Comments" function on Microsoft Word. Circle any words you don't know, and look up their definitions. Underlining, bracketing, and writing in the margins show your engagement with the reading. Your physical interaction with the text will also help you feel more comfortable in developing a response to it later.

### Identify the main point of the text.

The main point (or message; see Chapter 1) is what the writer wants you to understand or take away from it. (It's important to note here that what writers mean for audiences to take away doesn't add up to all the effects that a text will have on its audience; however, it's okay as a starting point.)

Sometimes the main point is explicitly stated as a thesis, and sometimes an audience needs to infer it. While finding the main point of a text can be quite challenging, the advantage you have is that typically writers *want* their audience to understand their main point. If you don't, then the text has essentially failed in its purpose. For this reason, texts have certain key clues that can help you identify the most important points:

- **Structural clues:** The conventions of Western composition typically assign the beginning or the end (of a sentence, of a paragraph, of a whole text) as the most important position. Thus, often (but not always) you'll find the most important point at the beginning of a paragraph or perhaps at the end of the entire text. Headings and subheadings often also contain clues as to important points.

- **Textual clues:** Certain key words act like flashing arrows to signal important information in the text. An author might simply say the word "important" or "central" in reference to a point he or she is making.

- **Repetition:** If a key phrase, idea, or point appears more than once in the text, pay attention: This can signal a theme or something that the writer sees as important.

### Identify the text's purpose.

What does it seem that the writer wants the audience to do, think, or feel after reading the piece? (See Section 2c for more on discerning purpose.)

### Notice how the writer supports that main point.

Once you've identified the main point of the piece, notice how the writer attempts to persuade the audience of this point. What reasons does the writer provide for his or her point? What evidence does he or she rely on? Personal anecdotes? Case studies or stories about individuals? Lots of facts and statistics? Circle anything that strikes you as important or interesting to making the case.

## Understanding HOW It Is Said

Now that you better understand the content of the piece, turn your attention to the rhetorical moves that it's making using the following steps.

### Recognize the "big moves" of the piece.

Take it paragraph by paragraph. Briefly summarize for yourself not only what each paragraph is *saying* (the topic) but also what the author is *doing* in the paragraph. That is, what is its function in the context of the larger piece? Note big turning points in the text—these are usually marked by words such as "however," "but," and "although." Table 3.1 offers ways to talk about a writer's moves, and the rhetorical reading example later in this section demonstrates this step.

### Use a graphic organizer.

Graphic organizers such as bubble maps, cluster diagrams, and main idea/ details charts can visually represent the text. This helps you to understand the text better by breaking up its linear structure. Do a Web search for "free interactive graphic organizers" that you can download and fill in.

### Identify the "textual structures" in the piece and understand what rhetorical work they're doing.

Expository (i.e., nonnarrative) texts typically have one or more recognizable textual structures. Common ones include description, sequence, compare/ contrast, cause/effect, and problem/solution. Each of these structures has certain key words that can be identified through attentive reading. Look at Table 3.1 for some of the signal words that indicate the existence of one

| TEXT STRUCTURE | SIGNAL WORDS | RHETORICAL EFFECT |
|---|---|---|
| **Sequence:** Presents narratives, information, or arguments as a chronological or logical chain of events. | First, before, preceding, then, after, following, next, finally, last | Draws attention to the event, thing, or process by helping the audience better picture it in their heads. |
| **Comparison/Contrast:** Describes how something is like or different from something else. | Like, similarly, as well as, unlike, in contrast, opposed to, instead of, different from, while, instead of, either/or, however | Calls the audience's attention to the qualities of a thing by comparing it to something they might be more familiar with. |
| **Description:** Provides more detailed information about something. | For example, in particular, for instance, such as, most importantly, another | Calls attention to the details of something, perhaps to persuade the audience to form stronger connections to it. |
| **Cause/Effect:** Lays out a logical chain of consequences; might talk about what made something happen or the results of a particular occurrence. | Because, thus, due to, therefore, as a result, the effects of, the reason being, caused, for these reasons, if X then Y | Attempts to persuade the audience to accept the author's view of reality. |
| **Problem/Solution:** Identifies a challenge (a departure from how things should be); may also provide ways to address that challenge. | The problem is, the challenge, if X then Y, therefore, difficult, but | Makes an implicit appeal to the audience about how things should be, aims to persuade them that something isn't right and that it should/could be made right. |

TABLE 3.1  Signal Words for Different Text Structures

of these text structures. Of course, it's not enough just to identify these textual structures; you also need to ask *why* they're there or what kind of work they're doing for the text. How do they support the author's purpose?

Identify what creates the style and tone of the piece.

Look carefully at the language of the piece itself. Generally speaking, how would you characterize the tone? Is it impassioned, sarcastic, earnest, humorous, casual, sad? Circle the specific words and phrases that help to create that tone.

Finally, read the piece one more time.

Write a brief reflection on what point the author was making with the piece and how he or she made it. Write a second paragraph about your reactions to the piece and why you had those reactions.

## An Annotated Rhetorical Reading

### Why You Should Think Twice Before Shaming Anyone on Social Media

#### BY LAURA HUDSON

Earlier this year, at a tech conference called PyCon, the consultant Adria Richards overheard some indelicate puns — involving the terms "dongles" and "forking" — from a couple of male attendees sitting behind her. The jokes made Richards uncomfortable, so in the heat of the moment she decided to register her displeasure by tweeting a picture of the two guys, calling their behavior "not cool."

In the context of a tech culture that often fails to make women feel welcome, it's easy to see why Richards, sitting there in the (roughly 80 percent male) PyCon audience, felt like she wasn't the one with the power in that room.

But online it was a different story. The two men were social-media nobodies, whereas Richards had more than 9,000 *Twitter* followers, some highly connected in the tech world. Her grievance quickly received more than 100 retweets and press coverage that stretched from *The Washington Post* to MSNBC.

PyCon soon responded — sympathetically — to her complaint, but the damage was done. One of the men was recognized by his employer and lost his job. The backlash against his firing then triggered a massive onslaught of online abuse against Richards, who also got fired. No one emerged happy. "I have three kids, and I really liked that job," wrote the newly unemployed jokester. "Let this serve as a message to everyone, our actions and words, big or small, can have a serious impact." Later, Richards made a similar assessment: "I don't think anyone who was part of what happened at PyCon that day could possibly have imagined how this issue would have exploded into the public consciousness ... I certainly did not, and now ... the severest of consequences have manifested."

Shaming, it seems, has become a core competency of the Internet, and it's one that can destroy both lives and livelihoods. But the question of who's responsible for the destruction — the person engaging in the behavior or the person revealing it — depends on whom you ask. At its best, social media has given a voice to the disenfranchised, allowing them to bypass the gatekeepers of power and publicize injustices that might otherwise

---

**Annotations:**

The title does rhetorical work by telling readers the topic of the story and hinting at the position that the article takes.

Signal word (along with "soon," and "later" in the next several paragraphs) that indicates a sequence-based text structure (the article opens with an anecdote, which helps to ground the argument that the author makes later in the article).

She names Adria Richards, but not the two men. Why? (Because her point was that Richards is well known, and the two men were not?)

This seems like a fairly nonjudgmental description of the situation, as compared to say, "dirty jokes" or "sophomoric humor."

The "but" indicates a turn in the text here.

Begins with a relevant anecdote about how powerful social media can be. The way the story is told is relatively neutral—the author doesn't seem to care to take sides in the case.

Here we get to the primary topic of the story (which was just illustrated in the above anecdote). This paragraph makes claims about the power of social media: It gives a voice to the disenfranchised but also can be a "weapon of mass reputation destruction."

remain invisible. At its worst, it's a weapon of mass reputation destruction, capable of amplifying slander, bullying, and casual idiocy on a scale never before possible.

The fundamental problem is that many shamers, like Richards, don't fully grasp the power of the medium. It's a problem that lots of us need to reckon with: There are millions of *Twitter* accounts with more than 1,000 followers, and millions on *Facebook* with more than 500 friends. The owners of those accounts might think they're just regular people, whispering to a small social circle. But in fact they're talking through megaphones that can easily be turned up to a volume the entire world can hear.

Increasingly, our failure to grasp our online power has become a liability — personally, professionally, and morally. We need to think twice before we unleash it.

## WHEN DOES SHAMING BECOME BULLYING?

Consider a form of shaming that a lot of us might want to get behind: calling out people who say indefensibly terrible things online. Numerous *Tumblr* and *Twitter* accounts have cropped up to document racist and sexist remarks on social media. Following a feed like @EverydaySexism or @YesYoureRacist can be a powerful experience; after a while, the shocking ugliness fades to a dull, steady ache, an emotional corrosion that simulates how the dehumanization of prejudice can become almost mundane. These feeds shame the jerks they highlight by broadcasting their ignorance far beyond their typically small, like-minded audiences to tens of thousands of people.

When the website *Jezebel* cataloged a series of racist tweets by high school students about President Obama, it not only published their names but also called their high schools and notified the principals about their tweets. In some cases, Jezebel listed the hobbies and activities of the students, essentially "SEO-shaming" them to potential colleges. Most of the kids have since deleted their *Twitter* accounts, but search any of their names on *Google* and you'll likely find references to their racist tweets within the first few results.

Yes, what these kids wrote was reprehensible. But does a 16-year-old making crude comments to his friends deserve to be pilloried with a doggedness we typically reserve for politicians and public figures — or, at the very least, for adults?

We despise racism and sexism because they bully the less powerful, but at what point do the shamers become the bullies? After all, the hallmark of bullying isn't just being mean. It also involves a power differential: The bully is the one who's punching down.

And this is precisely the differential that so many of us fail to grasp when our friends and followers are just abstract numbers on a social-media profile. Indeed, the online elite don't always wield the same sort of social power and influence in their offline lives and jobs; many have been victims of bullying themselves.

> An important reason for her argument. The assumption that underpins it: Internet power is different from "offline" or "IRL" (in real life) power.

When Mike "Gabe" Krahulik, the artist behind the popular webcomic *Penny Arcade,* heard that an unprofessional PR rep for a game controller had been insulting and taunting one of his readers, he gleefully posted the damning emails to his website, along with the man's *Twitter* name, for the express purpose of unleashing the Internet kraken.

> Interesting metaphor. "Kraken" are giant sea monsters of legend. The metaphor makes it sound like they're actually lurking online somewhere, ready to spring up at any point and eat whoever offends them.

"I have a real problem with bullies," Krahulik wrote, after the marketer was deluged with hate mail. "I spent my childhood moving from school to school and I got made fun of every place I landed. I feel like he is a bully and maybe that's why I have no sympathy here. Someday every bully meets an even bigger bully, and maybe that's me in this case."

> Hudson calls those who use social media to shame other people "bullies."

But even if you think your bullying is serving a greater good, the fact remains that you're still just a bully.

Internet speech can be cruder and crueler than our real-life interactions, in large part due to our literal distance from the people we're talking to and their reactions. That detachment can sometimes be liberating, and it's often a good thing that people speak bluntly online, especially against injustice that they see around them. But a sense of proportion is crucial. These days, too many Internet shame campaigns dole out punishment that is too brutal for the crime. Using an influential social media account to call out individuals, as Richards did, isn't simply saying something is "not cool"; it's a request to have someone put in the digital stocks, where a potentially unlimited number of people can throw digital stones at them. And it turns out to have real-life consequences for everyone involved.

> The analogy here likens using social media as a shaming mechanism to the old Puritan practice of putting sinners in stocks for punishment.

That's why starting a shaming campaign is not a decision to be taken lightly — especially because the Internet doesn't do takebacks if you change your mind later. The bigger the so-called Donglegate story became, the more disproportionate and unfair Richards' original tweet seemed, even if that level of exposure was never her intent. As Krahulik wrote after the PR bully pleaded with him to make the abuse stop, "Once I had posted the emails I didn't have the power anymore. The Internet had it now, and nothing I said or did was going to change that."

> Another interesting metaphor to describe the power of online shaming: It's a door that you can open, but not close (akin to Pandora's box).

Online shaming is a door that swings only one way: You may have the power to open it, but you don't have the power to close it. And sometimes what rushes through that door can engulf you too.

# 3b Writing Summaries

Writing a summary—a condensed version of a text that focuses on its main points—is an important part of doing a rhetorical analysis and an academic skill that will prove useful for many other purposes. A summary serves as a kind of contract between you and your reader. First, it serves as proof that you've read and sufficiently understood the text, and second, it helps a reader who hasn't read the original piece get the gist of it (enough to be able to understand and form a judgment about your analysis). And you will produce different summaries for different types of audiences (for instance, you'd probably have a much briefer, more informal summary if your friend asked you what you were reading than if you had to compose one as part of a rhetorical analysis essay for your English professor).

Contrary to what you might think, writing a summary of a text for an academic essay—especially an expository one like Laura Hudson's article in the previous section—is a notoriously difficult task. You might think "Well, how hard can it be? All I'm doing is restating what the original article said." But to write a *good* summary—that is, one that contains the important information from the article, is succinct, and is written in one's own words— you must first have gone through the steps in the "Reading Rhetorically" section. Then follow the steps below.

## HOW TO...    Write a Summary for an Academic Essay

1.  Write down the identifying information of the article: author, title, publication, date.
2.  Identify the main point of the piece (it may not be a single sentence), and put it in your own words. You can even use the following template to begin your summary: "In ["Article Title"], published in [*Magazine* or *Website*] in [publication date], [Author's Name] argues that [main point of article]."
3.  Identify the main ways the author uses to support this piece, and (briefly) describe them.
4.  Include any other information that provides a representative picture of the original piece.
5.  Go back through and make sure to eliminate any biased language or opinions about the article. Make sure that you use active verbs, such as those used in the sample formal summary that follows.

Good summaries have these characteristics:

- They represent the original piece accurately and fairly. That is, they use neutral language and do not include the summarizer's opinion of the original piece. In a summary, you basically read generously, taking the author's side even if you don't agree with the article.

- They are significantly shorter than the original piece (the general rule of thumb is that a summary should be at most a quarter of the length of the original).

- They include identifying information: the author, title, date of publication, and place of publication (i.e., the journal, website, or newspaper) of the original piece.

- They focus on the main points of the thing being summarized.

- They are written using your own words.

- They are written in the present tense, using active verbs to describe what the author is doing in the text (for example *argues*, *explains*, *mentions*, *points out*, *includes*, etc.).

- They contain few, if any, direct quotations.

Below is an example of an academic summary of Hudson's article, written with the characteristics of good academic summaries in mind.

## An Annotated Academic Summary

### A Summary of "Why You Should Think Twice Before Shaming Anyone on Social Media"

In her July 2013 *Wired* article "Why You Should Think Twice Before Shaming Anyone on Social Media," senior *Wired* editor Laura Hudson argues that social media users, especially those who are highly visible, should be aware that their actions on social media can have disproportionately large effects. Hudson uses as her main cautionary example a well-known episode from a tech industry conference in which Adria Richards, a highly influential woman in the tech industry, who, offended by the comments of two male conference-goers sitting behind her in a presentation, tweeted her annoyance, along with a picture of the two men to her 9,000-plus followers on *Twitter*. Because Richards was so visible a social media figure, Hudson explains, the picture and comment received undue notoriety and generated outrage on all sides, ultimately leading to one of the men and Richards herself getting fired from their jobs. Hudson, a self-described feminist, uses two other examples—one in which the website *Jezebel* calls out teenagers for their racist tweets, and another where a well-known webcomic artist uses his social media power to call out someone who was harassing one of his readers. Hudson argues that social media shaming when one is very influential is tantamount to bullying, and that moreover it can have effects on the shamer/bullier as well: She analogizes shaming on social media as a door that swings open one way, warning potential shamers that "sometimes what rushes through that door can engulf you too."

*Annotations (right margin):*

Includes all identifying information for the article.

Sums up article's main point.

Highlighted throughout the summary: use of active verbs to show what Hudson *does* in her article.

Summarizes Donglegate example.

Mentions (briefly) Hudson's two other examples.

Identifies other main rhetorical tactic of Hudson's article: an analogy between shaming and bullying.

Restates main point, using a snippet of a quotation from the article.

## FOR DISCUSSION

Below is an example of a not-very-good academic summary of Hudson's article. What are the problems with it, according to the characteristics of good academic summaries previously listed?

> This article shows the problem with feminists at a tech conference. Adria Richards posted a picture on *Twitter* of two men who were making bad jokes about dongles and forking repos. She ended up getting one of the men fired, which is unfair, since they were having a private conversation. Luckily, she got fired as well. Hudson also talks about how the website *Jezebel* called up the high schools of teenagers who posted racist things on *Twitter* and tried to get them in trouble. It also posted their real names on *Jezebel,* which is going to cause trouble for the teens when they try to apply to colleges or get a job. Shaming people on social media is a bad thing, especially when you have a lot of followers. "Online shaming is a door that swings only one way: You may have the power to open it, but you don't have the power to close it. And sometimes what rushes through that door can engulf you too."

# 3c Researching the Rhetorical Situation of a Text

**MindTap**
View How to Video 2: Analyzing a Written Text

As Chapters 1 and 2 explained, a critical part of understanding communication involves thinking about the elements common to all communication: the communicator, message, audience, exigence, purpose, and means of communication (mode, medium, genre, and circulation). Without having a better sense of the original shaming incidents that Laura Hudson discusses in her article, for instance, as well as the idea of shaming itself, you might understand the basic gist of the article, but your analysis would lack depth—you'd miss a lot of the article's subtext. Thus, it's critical to research the circumstances in which the text was produced, both for the sake of your own analysis and to help your audience understand the text's significance.

## QUESTIONS TO ASK    Researching the Rhetorical Situation

See Chapters 1 and 2 for an explanation of these terms.

- Who are the communicator(s)? What is their interest in the thing being discussed? What's at stake for them; that is, do they have anything to gain or lose? What makes them qualified to speak about it?

- What is the message of the text?
- Who is the audience for the text?
- What is the exigence for the text?
- What is the text's purpose? What does it hope to achieve?
- What is the text's material means of communication?

It's important to understand that research might look very different depending on what you're researching. If I were researching the context of a historical speech, for instance, I'd need to do a lot more research on specific historical circumstances.

# 3d Doing a Rhetorical Analysis of a Written Text

Why would one want to write out a rhetorical analysis? Except for perhaps in news analyses (*The New York Times* publishes these about once a week) or in bits and pieces by bloggers and satirical talk show hosts like Trevor Noah, it's a genre not seen very often outside academia.

However, as we'll see in later chapters, rhetorical analysis is valuable as a means to an end. The kind of deep, sustained analysis we do here will help us to understand the conventions of genres that we'll be writing in. It also serves practical purposes; for instance, public relations consultants typically analyze the marketing and communication materials of clients to understand how they perceive their audience and help them make better, more appropriate appeals. Most importantly, it gives us a richer sense of the possibilities for how we might rhetorically intervene.

When you're doing a rhetorical analysis of any sort, it's not enough to just point out an instance of a rhetorical appeal. You have to create what we might call an **analytical circle** by linking your observations back to the text's purpose. The following steps walk you through how to do this.

## Preparing to Write a Rhetorical Analysis

1. Read the text closely and attentively, using the steps outlined in Section 3a.
2. Research the rhetorical situation using the steps outlined in Section 3c. Imagine that you are writing for an audience who, even if they're familiar with the text or the communicator, probably don't know that much about the background. It's your job here to help them understand not only the basics about the communicator and exigence for the speech, but to clarify the exigence: why this text may have appeared at this specific time and what it hoped to accomplish given its specific circumstances.

3. State the rhetorical purpose of the text in your own words. You can use the following as a rough template for this statement:

> X wants to persuade his/her audience [you can elaborate on who this audience is] of this major point: [summarize the purpose].
>
> OR, you might state it like this:
>
> X wants his/her audience to do/believe X as a result of his/her text.

4. Complete the following chart as a separate document. These questions will help you generate material for your analysis and identify the primary way(s) that the text attempts to achieve its purpose.

## QUESTIONS TO ASK   Analyzing Written Rhetoric

| | |
|---|---|
| What is the main point? How does the communicator support this point or make it convincing? | How do these attempts to support the main point further the communicator's purpose? |
| What sort of character does the communicator create through the text? What are all the ways in which he or she builds credibility? (ethos)<br><br>List the attempts to build credibility on a separate sheet of paper. | How do the communicator's attempts to build credibility further his or her purpose? |
| How, specifically, does the communicator attempt to appeal to the audience's emotions (pathos)? Which emotions?<br><br>List the emotional appeals on a separate sheet of paper. | How do these emotional appeals further his or her purpose? |
| What tone and style does the writer use? Is the language informal or formal? What do you notice about word choice and the arrangement of the ideas? Are certain words repeated?<br><br>List specific examples of tone and style on a separate sheet of paper. | Why does the communicator use this tone and style? What effects does it create? How does it further his or her purpose? |

5. Find a focus for your essay. Which of the strategies in the previous chart do you think is the MOST significant or important for achieving the purpose of the text? This will likely be the focus of your rhetorical analysis essay. This focus might be expressed in the form of a statement like the following:

> By doing these specific things [list specifically the main rhetorical devices used by the text], [the communicator] aims to accomplish [restate main purpose of text].

6. Use the rest of the essay to support your focus statement (i.e., the one that you came up with in step 5). You can use some of the relevant material you produced using the Analytical Circle chart. Remember that to complete the analytical circle, you need to follow this pattern: Describe what the text does, explain how it attempts to fulfill its purpose, and explain how that supports the main point of your essay.

See the following sample rhetorical analysis essay.

## An Annotated Rhetorical Analysis Essay

### Shaming as Bullying: A Rhetorical Analysis of Laura Hudson's "Why You Should Think Twice Before Shaming Anyone on Social Media"

The title of the essay does rhetorical work: The first part (before the colon) gives readers a sense of the argument; the second part (after the colon) tells readers the purpose of the essay.

Lately it seems like certain Internet sites have made a kind of sport out of public shaming. *BuzzFeed* and *Gawker*, for instance, seem to have discovered that posting pictures of dumb or shocking things that people have done and the outraged responses to them is a surefire way to get people to click on the story (thus generating more attention and advertising revenue for the site). For instance, in October 2013, *Buzzfeed* posted a story about a woman who, after tweeting a picture of herself dressed for Halloween as a Boston marathon bombing victim, had gotten a hailstorm of enraged reactions, including threats of rape and death against her and her family and friends. In less than a week, the *Buzzfeed* story had gotten over two million views and 1,100 comments. It seems that people delight in seeing (and judging) the socially questionable behaviors of their fellow humans, and social media makes it even easier to do that.

The introduction is meant to engage the reader and establish the general topic (public shaming on social media) that the article to be analyzed discusses.

Partly in response to this phenomenon of using media to publicly condemn socially questionable acts, senior *Wired* editor Laura Hudson wrote an article for *Wired* magazine's online site called "Why You Should Think Twice Before Shaming Anyone on Social Media." While the immediate exigence for Hudson's article was an instance of public shaming that occurred at a conference for the

Brief summary of Hudson's article

tech industry, Hudson uses the incident to argue a larger point: that those who wield social media influence (i.e., who have lots of *Twitter* followers or *Facebook* friends) should be wary of using that media to shame others. Hudson likens online public shaming to a door that only opens one way: Once it's open, she writes, "sometimes what rushes through that door can engulf you too."

Hudson demonstrates her rhetorical savvy in the article by presenting a well-balanced argument that thoughtfully considers why public shaming might seem like an attractive option. However, the article's main persuasive device is an emotional appeal in the form of an analogy: By likening public shaming to bullying, Hudson draws on the powerful negative emotions that have been generated by the large amount of current media coverage devoted to bullying.

> Here is the main point or thesis that the essay goes on to develop and support. The thesis statement is found at the end of the introduction, a traditional place for it in the academic essay genre.

Hudson begins the article by recounting a recent incident of public shaming in the tech industry, in which many *Wired* readers are employed. Adria Richards, who had over 9,000 followers on *Twitter*, tweeted a picture of two male "nobodies," as Hudson called them, who were making inappropriate jokes at a tech conference. The tweet prompted a barrage of responses, with people variously defending and condemning the men's and Richards' actions. Ultimately, one of the men and Richards herself lost their jobs over the incident.

> This paragraph simply recounts the incident that provided the exigence for Hudson's article.

Hudson's position as a senior editor at *Wired* provides her with some amount of ethos in the situation. However, since (as many other articles about the same incident Hudson discusses point out) feminism is a touchy subject in the tech industry, since the incident she discusses has a feminist dimension, since Hudson herself is a woman, and since the incident in question was so volatile (and remained so at the time Hudson wrote her article, judging from the number of heated comments that follow the article), it would be very important for Hudson to appear to be fairly neutral on the issue. Otherwise, she would risk infuriating either supporters of Richards or supporters of the two men who Richards publicly shamed, and the point of her article would likely be lost. And indeed, Hudson takes pains to fairly represent the incident, condemning neither the two men's nor Richards' actions. Hudson is also careful to avoid language that would suggest an overtly feminist angle: She refers to the two men's sexually themed jokes as "indelicate puns" rather than "sexually offensive jokes," for instance. But Hudson also takes care to acknowledge what Richards may have been feeling in the situation. Thus she puts herself in the shoes of all the actors in the incident, which makes her seem like a thoughtful and fair commenter on the events. What's more,

> This paragraph discusses how Hudson rhetorically positions herself to appear credible to readers (her ethos).

later in the article, Hudson acknowledges why public shaming may seem like an attractive option. She specifically refers to the powerful effect of *Twitter* feeds like @EverydaySexism or @YesYoureRacist in creating the desire to publicly shame people who propound questionable positions. These concessions help pacify readers who might be potentially hostile to Hudson's main argument that social media should ultimately not be used as a public shaming device.

The central rhetorical device in Hudson's article, though, is an analogy of public shaming via social media to bullying. She writes, "We despise racism and sexism because they bully the less powerful, but at what point do the shamers become the bullies?" Though this is a rhetorical question, as Hudson's next anecdote reveals, it's clear that she believes that highly connected people who use their social media power to shame others are acting like bullies. She argues that Mike Krahulik, the author of a popular webcomic who used his social media power to shame a "PR bully," ultimately became a bully himself. "But even if you think your bullying is serving a greater good, the fact remains that you're still just a bully," Hudson writes.

> This paragraph (which refers back to my thesis statement above) presents my argument and provides evidence from Hudson's article that the central rhetorical device is an equation between shaming and bullying. The evidence comes in the form of direct quotations from Hudson.

Why does the term "bullying" serve as such a potent emotional appeal in Hudson's article? Partly it's because of the amount of attention bullying has been getting in the media in the past few years. After a number of highly publicized incidents of teens committing suicide as a result of real-life and cyberbullying, "bullying" became a very prominent, emotional hot-button term. In fact, many have argued that the term is now being overused, so that any story about the use or misuse of power is being rewritten as a bullying story. But the fact remains that the idea of bullying taps deeply into American values of fairness and justice, and so it brings with it a high amount of emotional reaction. Nobody supports a bully. And so, by equating those who publicly shame others via social media (no matter how deserved such shaming may seem) with bullies, Hudson presents a powerful, if implicit, argument against such practice that would resonate with her readers (many of whom, if the stereotype of "geeks" in the tech industry holds true, might have been bullied themselves as children). Hudson invites them to see acts of public shaming in the same light as they would see a mean older kid picking on a poor younger kid at a playground.

> This paragraph makes an argument about why the term "bullying" packs such an emotional punch.

> This closes the analytical circle by arguing why bullying might be such a powerful emotional appeal to *Wired* readers in particular.

The human desire to have the upper hand being what it is, it's unlikely that people will be able to resist taking revenge on those they feel deserve it by whatever tools they have at their disposal, including social media. But with her powerful emotional equation of shaming to bullying, Hudson at least tries to show why this might not be such a great idea.

## ASSIGNMENTS

### Analyze Op-Ed Pieces and Political Communications

1. Referring to "Shaming as Bullying: A Rhetorical Analysis of Laura Hudson's 'Why You Should Think Twice Before Shaming Anyone on Social Media'" as an example, write a rhetorical analysis essay on an op-ed piece published in the last two weeks.

2. Imagine that you are part of an oppositions research team for a political candidate (you can decide the political party and candidate). Your job is to analyze how the opposition is talking about a certain issue and to make recommendations to your candidate's communications team about the weaknesses in their communication.

   a. With the help of your instructor, identify a list of sources that reflect the opposite political ideology of your candidate, and do a search within those sources on the topic you wish to explore.

   b. Choose two or three different pieces to analyze.

   c. Do a rhetorical analysis of each piece using the questions articulated in "Questions to Ask: Analyzing Written Rhetoric."

   d. For your audience (the political candidate for whom you're campaigning), summarize the main points and rhetorical strategies used in the pieces.

   e. Finally, can you find weaknesses in the rhetorical strategies that you identified and make suggestions about other strategies your candidate might try instead?

## FOR REFLECTION

### Transferable Skills and Concepts

Most of the examples in this chapter have to do with rhetorically analyzing overtly opinion-based texts. Now see if these skills work for non-opinion-based texts—documents that you encounter in your everyday life. Choose any document that came in the mail this past week, and apply the rhetorical analysis skills you learned in Chapter 3: Rhetorically read the text, summarize it, and study its rhetorical situation. Write your results in a journal, and answer the question: What did you learn from doing a rhetorical analysis on this everyday document?

# Analyzing Visual Rhetoric

*By working through this chapter, you will be able to...*

- Recognize the prevalence of visual messages in our culture.
- Identify the purpose, message, likely audience, compositional features, placement, and circulation of an image.
- Explain the implications of the technologies used to create an image.
- Distinguish between the "formal" and "social" layers of an image.
- Analyze the formal layer of an image, including emphasis, framing, point of view, degree of focus, distance from subject, lighting and contrast, and color.
- Analyze the social layer of an image, especially the social significance of its shapes, actors, actions, objects, and settings.
- Discuss the rhetorical role of images within texts.

You're probably already conscious of the fact that we live in what has been described as "an aggressively visual culture" (George 15), in which deliberately designed visual messages of all sorts compete for our attention.

Take advertisements, for instance, responsible for at least half of the visual messages encountered daily by the average American (Figure 4.1). To make up for their inability to reach consumers at home (thanks to changes in consumer reading and viewing habits), advertisers have in recent years turned their attention to public spaces, placing advertisements on every conceivable surface, from sidewalks and toilet doors to subway turnstiles and even eggs. One well-known 2007 marketing research study estimates that

ANALYZE
AND CREATE

**Chapter 4**
Analyzing Visual
Rhetoric

**Chapter 14**
Creating Visual
Rhetoric

Roberto Machado Noa/LightRocket/Getty Images

**FIGURE 4.1** Advertisements account for a large percentage of the visual messages we encounter daily.

Richard Levine/AGE Fotostock

Americans who live in cities are exposed to around 5,000 ads per day. And that's not even counting other kinds of visual messages: photographs in news stories, signs, posters, menus, company logos, bus schedules, Web pages, charts, tables, graphs, and so forth. Even the page design of textbooks like this one is designed to persuade you to interact with the material a certain way.

The prevalence of visual messages in Western culture is only logical given that of all the senses, vision arguably dominates the way people who are sighted interact with the world. A well-known psychological concept called the "picture superiority effect" (identified by Douglas Nelson, Valerie Reed, and John Walling) suggests that people have a much easier time making meaning from and remembering pictures than they do information presented in words alone. Research has demonstrated that when people hear (verbal) information, three days later they remember only 10 percent of that information. But when they are shown a picture in addition to hearing the information, their retention increases to 65 percent. As you might imagine, marketers, consultants for political campaigns, and others who stand to gain by helping people remember things are keenly aware of the pictorial superiority effect.

Because the sense of vision is so fundamental to helping those with sight navigate the world, understanding how and why visual messages work is a critical skill. This chapter aims to provide you with tools to analyze static or still images (we'll look at moving images in the chapters on multimodal rhetoric). The images discussed here include photographs and drawn, inked, or painted representational illustrations; these might be included in advertisements, charts, tables, graphs, Web pages, posters, and brochures. They might be used to support an argument or illustrate a story, as in essays or newspaper and magazine stories. They also serve multiple roles in websites, posters, brochures, advertisements, comics, and political cartoons.

## FOR HOMEWORK

To begin the process of *seeing* visual messages, it will first help to get a general sense for how many and what kinds of messages you encounter in your daily life (perhaps without consciously realizing it).

For some period of time designated by your instructor, record all of the deliberately designed visual messages that you see as well as where you saw them. Visual messages might include road and traffic signs, posters, ads, brand logos, photos, and illustrations. While they might include words, they shouldn't be *only* words—that is, they should have some visual design.

When the time period is over, go through your list and count up each of the different kinds of messages. Which did you see most? Choose three of these visual messages and answer the following questions:

- Why was the message in that particular place?
- Who produced the message?
- What is the actual message? (What does it aim to make viewers think, do, or feel?)
- Who is the target audience for this message?
- What elements of the message's design might particularly influence its audience?

# 4a Thinking Rhetorically about Stand-Alone Images

Learning to see images *rhetorically* (in terms of how they aim to create effects on people) requires a great deal of training in consciously analyzing images and thinking about how they work. Understanding the rhetorical effects of images requires us to ask questions similar to those we asked of texts. We need to think about things like:

- who produced the image and what their agenda(s) might be;
- the purpose of the image (what it wants its intended viewers to do, think, or feel as a result of seeing it);
- the intended audience of the image;
- where the image appears;
- the messages the image itself conveys;
- how the image circulates or is distributed.

Just as we analyzed rhetorical features that are specific to texts in Chapter 3, so here we can analyze features specific to images. Following is a list of questions designed to help you think rhetorically about images. The following sections discuss many of these questions in more detail.

---

**QUESTIONS TO ASK**   **Analyzing Images**

- Who created the image? What was their purpose for producing the image?
- What technologies were used to create the image? What are the rhetorical effects of these technologies?
- What is the purpose of the image? What is its message? What does it want its viewers to think, do, or feel?
- How do the compositional features of the visual message contribute to its purpose?
- Is there a specific audience to whom the image is designed to appeal? How might this image be received differently by different groups of people?
- Where does the image appear? Who is likely to encounter it, and in what circumstances? Was it placed strategically? Was it designed with recirculation in mind?

---

## Thinking Rhetorically about an Image's Creator

As with any message, to begin to understand images rhetorically, it's critical to understand who produced them and why. However, images operate differently from texts in terms of the "who": most images that you encounter are produced by *entities*, not individuals.

**EXAMPLE**   Associated Press photographs were certainly taken by individuals who have names and political views and families, but by the time the photograph is selected by an editor and put in a newspaper or on a Web page, it's no longer important who took the photo. As a viewer, you encounter it as a "press photo," and its content is reliable (or not) because of the publication in which it appears.

**EXAMPLE**   The same goes for photographs and illustrations that appear in advertisements. The image of the model wearing Maybelline lipstick is for all intents and purposes produced by Maybelline—the name of the person who actually did the photography is irrelevant to the advertisement's effect.

The main exceptions to this rule are images produced for the sake of being images (for example, as art under the name of the creator in a gallery or other space) or, perhaps, as comics or political cartoons.

Generally speaking, then, with images it's important to think about *what entity* produced the image, what interests that entity has, and how those interests might affect the content or presentation of the image.

**EXAMPLE**   One example of the importance of considering who produces images and for what purpose was the controversy over the policy of President Obama's administration of preventing independent and press journalists from photographing the workings of the president and his administration, even at routine events. In fact, media outlets were so incensed by what one conservative magazine called the administration's "monopolistic propaganda" that in late 2013 a number of U.S. news outlets banded together to boycott the official White House images, refusing to include them in news stories about the president and his administration. (The section "Images Create a Rhetorical Effect through Formal and Social Layers" analyzes some of these official Obama administration photographs.)

---

**QUESTIONS TO ASK**   **Analyzing the Creator of an Image**

- Who created this image? Was it an individual or an entity (a corporation, news agency, nonprofit organization, government, etc.)?
- What prior reputation does the individual or entity have? What would the viewers of the image associate with this individual or entity?
- Why did the individual (or entity) create this image?
- What is at stake for them in its creation? What do they stand to gain or lose?
- How might those interests affect the content and/or presentation of the image?

---

## Thinking Rhetorically about the Technologies Used to Produce an Image

*All* compositions, whether speeches, texts, images, films, Web pages, or sound recordings, are produced with technologies. Moreover, as Chapter 2 explains, these technologies are more than neutral tools that serve only to create a message—they have cultural meanings and effects on audiences in and of themselves. So it's important to consider not only by what means an image has been produced, but also the effect of the rhetorical technology used to produce that image.

### Photographs

Photos create perhaps the most powerful rhetorical effect of any type of image because they *appear* to represent or capture reality "as it really is." As cultural critic Susan Sontag put it, "Photographed images do not seem to be statements about the world so much as pieces of it, miniatures of reality that anyone can make or acquire" (174). But what photographs actually do is isolate and frame specific, carefully chosen representations of reality.

Because photos are very good at creating what we might think of as a "truth effect," we need to pay special attention to their artifice, or the specific strategies they use to appear "real" or "true." We can't know what a photograph leaves out, or how the photographer selected this particular bit of reality, of course. However, we can analyze the various ways that photographs create rhetorical effects.

Most people are aware of the potential to alter digital photographs with programs such as Photoshop. This practice is especially insidious because the photos still appear to represent reality; they still *look real*. Such alterations of reality can be innocuous—like cropping a photo in order to focus in on a subject—but they can also create unrealistic perceptions.

**EXAMPLE**  Cultural critics have especially attacked the heavy use of Photoshop by magazines and advertisers of products to women to make their photographed female subjects appear more glamorous (see Figure 4.2). These critics argue that digital alteration of photography is unethical not least because it creates unrealistic expectations about body and appearance. Certain politically oriented websites, like *Jezebel*, have made a game of trying to expose the use of digital alteration, and some celebrities like Kim Kardashian have released pre- and post-digitally altered images of themselves.

**EXAMPLE**  On the other end of the spectrum, perhaps in response to the increasing awareness of how photographs and images can be manipulated, the desire for photographs that show "real," untouched versions of reality is evident in the tabloid magazine photo spreads that show celebrities without makeup or in mundane, everyday situations ("Celebrities: They're Just Like Us!").

FIGURE 4.2  Pre- and Post-Digitally Altered Photograph

## Illustrations

Most typically, the word "illustration" is applied to a drawing or painting that accompanies a text. They might be representational drawings to illustrate an essay, drawings in a technical manual, graphic corporate logos, diagrams, or anatomical drawings for a textbook. They can be drawn in pencil or inked, black and white or colored. Illustrations are more obviously artificial and stylized, and so they don't aim for the same "truth effects" as do photographs. The rhetorically important considerations about illustrations are the mood they aim to invoke through their style, tone, color, and placement within the text.

---

**QUESTIONS TO ASK** | **Analyzing the Rhetorical Technologies of an Image**

- What technologies were used to create the image?
- How do these technological processes affect how an audience receives or understands the image?
- How do the technological processes used to create the image hide or reveal the means by which the image was produced? What effect does this have on the audience?

---

## Images Create a Rhetorical Effect through Formal and Social Layers

Truly understanding the rhetorical effects of an image means that we need to understand things that we might have initially considered external to the image: who produced it, the technologies used to create it, in what context it appears, its intended viewers, and the means by which it was distributed. But it would be impossible to really grasp its rhetorical effects without a careful analysis of *the image itself.*

This section provides a set of tools to analyze representational images, including photographs, realistic paintings, drawings, and illustrations—that is, those that attempt to represent the world in some concrete way. The rhetorical effects of these representational images are discussed here separately as layers.

The first "layer" is what we'll call the *formal* qualities of the image, or its basic visual features. The second "layer" is called here the *social* level, the cultural narratives and references that inform the image's content. As the quotation marks around the word "layer" suggest, breaking down the rhetorical effects of representational images this way is more than a little artificial.

MindTap°

View Tiny Lecture Video 4: The Formal and Social Layers of an Image

It's important to keep in mind that this is just a convenient way to talk about the effects of representational images. In actuality, it's impossible to separate the way a photographer has chosen to frame a photograph, for example, from the image's social and cultural elements.

### The formal layer of images

The **formal layer** refers to the structural features of photographs: things like framing, emphasis, camera angle (point of view), focus, distance from subject, lighting and contrast, and color. In other words, the formal layer encompasses everything that affects the viewer on a basic visual level.

To illustrate each of the features of the formal layer, I use different photos of Barack Obama from *whitehouse.gov* along with their original captions. Presidential administrations always have a specific agenda in mind, which means, in part, that they want to control which images are used. As discussed earlier, President Obama's administration was particularly savvy about image use.

***Emphasis.*** The point of emphasis in the photo is the thing that the viewer is supposed to focus on or notice—usually, it's where viewers' eyes are drawn when they first look at the photograph. The point of emphasis provides an important cue for what the viewer is supposed to understand or take away from the photograph.

EXAMPLE    Figure 4.3 has a rather unusual point of emphasis given its subject matter. Though according to the caption, it captures a meeting between President Obama and his senior advisors, only one face is incidentally shown.

White House Photo/Alamy

**FIGURE 4.3** Original caption: President Barack Obama meets with senior advisors in the Oval Office, Jan. 27, 2014.

The point of emphasis in the photo is the basket of apples sitting on the coffee table. The unexpected emphasis (and the cheery look of the bright apples amid the otherwise drab colors) draws the eye into the center of the photo and makes the surrounding scene seem even busier by comparison: a jumble of limbs, an exchange of paper, and a man's shoe placed prominently in the foreground.

***Framing.*** Framing literally means what has been included within the boundaries of the image, but it also refers to how the creators of the image direct attention to the subject of the picture. What is in the image besides the subject, and how does that affect how you view the subject?

Framing is the first, basic way that an image creates a rhetorical effect because it literally governs what the viewers can and can't see.

**EXAMPLE** I can take a lovely photo of a flower, and, just by pointing my camera the right way, avoid showing the toxic waste dump next to which it's growing. Taking a photo that shows the flower in the context of the toxic waste dump would send an entirely different rhetorical message.

While the flower/toxic waste dump example might make framing seem slightly sinister, remember that owing to the basic limits of photography (which, after all, requires that one present an image in a little square box), one can't *help* but frame. But as an attentive viewer of a photograph, it's important to maintain an awareness of what is shown and potentially not shown—and, more importantly, the rhetorical effects of what's actually in the frame.

**EXAMPLE** To take one recent example that shows the difference framing can make, here are two separate photos of an infamous selfie that Obama took with two other heads of state at a memorial service for Nelson Mandela. Figure 4.4 shows the Danish prime minister between Obama and the British prime minister, taking a photo of the three with a smartphone.

FIGURE 4.4 Close-Up of President Barack Obama Posing for a Selfie

Roberto Schmidt/Getty Images

**FIGURE 4.5** Wider Frame of President Barack Obama Posing for the Selfie

In Figure 4.5, the camera is pulled back slightly to show an unsmiling Michelle Obama, clearly not participating in the fun.

It's a small difference in framing that ultimately made a big difference in the stories that came out about the event. The first photo (of just the three heads of state taking a selfie) was initially picked up by media outlets and used in stories about inappropriate behavior at a serious function by people who ought to know better (like goofing off in church).

But the second photo (with Michelle) got much more airtime; it was broadcast in stories that appeared later that same day under headlines like *The New York Post's* "Michelle not amused by Obama's memorial selfie," and, in fact, spawned a host of rumors about the Obamas' marriage being "on the rocks." Ultimately, one of the photographers who snapped a photo showing Michelle felt compelled to publish a statement explaining that Michelle was actually not annoyed by her husband's behavior, and had been joking with the Danish Prime Minister herself just a moment before the photo was snapped.

***Point of view.*** Point of view refers to the angle from which the subject is portrayed or represented in an image: above, below, head-on, from the side, obliquely?

Since the viewer unconsciously adopts the point of view of the camera or the illustrator when looking at images, point of view is very important in creating rhetorical effects. Different points of view invite viewers to take on different kinds of relationships with the image's subject. For instance, photos in which the camera takes a "worm's-eye view," looking up at the subject, puts the viewer in an inferior position and perhaps invites us to admire or marvel at the subject of the photograph. As with all of the other formal aspects of photographs, the effect of particular camera angles isn't

White House Photo/Alamy

**FIGURE 4.6** Original Caption: President Barack Obama, with Attorney General Eric H. Holder, Jr., holds a meeting with intelligence community leaders in the Situation Room of the White House, Jan. 8, 2014.

absolute and doesn't have the same effect every time—it depends on the purpose of the photo, the subject, and a host of other things.

EXAMPLE   In Figure 4.6, the camera angle is just slightly below Obama, so that we get the impression of looking up at his face, which looks serious and unlikely to be distracted (especially not by pesky photographers). The focus literally is on Obama. The viewers' eye is drawn first to Obama's face, then to his outstretched hand and the slightly defocused face of the attorney general. We get the sense at being present (if not an equal participant) in this apparently important meeting.

***Degree of focus.*** "Degree of focus" refers to the crispness of the image. Different kinds of focus create differing effects.

"Soft focus," for instance, where the subject is ever so slightly blurred, is often used to create a nostalgic or romantic feeling (often to cheesy effect). Blurring the background of a photo serves to create a sense of the subject as dynamic, moving quickly through space.

EXAMPLE   As you can see in Figure 4.7, Obama is the only figure in the room who's totally in focus; all of the Cabinet members are blurred. This, plus the fact that Obama is leaning forward, creates Obama as the emphasis point within the photo. The effect (reinforced by his intense expression and the way he's pointing his pen) is to suggest that Obama is dealing with very tense, serious things and that he's a leader who's very much in control (perhaps even a bit demanding). It leads the viewer to wonder what is happening in the meeting: Perhaps Obama is wrestling with a policy issue or problem that he's been publicly quiet about, for instance.

White House Photo/Alamy

**FIGURE 4.7** Original Caption: President Barack Obama holds a Cabinet meeting in the Cabinet Room of the White House, Jan. 14, 2014.

***Distance from subject.*** How far is the camera from its subject? Again, remembering that the photograph implicitly invites the viewer to take the position of the camera, the distance from or closeness to a subject contains subtle messages about how we're supposed to view it.

Typically, when a camera is close to its subject, we're being asked to directly relate in some way to that subject—though depending on the purpose of the photo, it could be relation by way of condemnation, sympathy, admiration, disgust, or pity.

By contrast, when a camera is very far from its subject, we get more of an overview effect. Perhaps we're not being asked to relate to a particular person (or plant, or animal, or rock) so much as getting more of an intellectualized, depersonalized view of a particular thing.

However, it isn't always the case that distance creates emotional detachment. Seeing Earth from space, a "lonely speck in the great enveloping cosmic dark"(xvi), impressed upon astronomer Carl Sagan the silliness of human self-importance and made him appreciate among other things the responsibility humans have to care for each other. As with other formal aspects of representational images, while distance from subject gives you some information, you need to use other clues in the photograph to ascertain its meaning or intended effect.

**EXAMPLE**  In the black and white Figure 4.8, the primary focus is on the building, which (we find out from reading the caption) is the White House Residence, where Obama is walking after "a day of meetings." It's only after we look at the house that we see two small, dark figures walking up the path.

White House Photo/Alamy

**FIGURE 4.8** Original caption: President Barack Obama walks to the White House residence with Chief of Staff Denis McDonough, after a day of meetings in the West Wing of the White House, Jan. 21, 2014.

The lack of color, darkness, distance from the people, and the snowy bushes in the foreground create a somewhat lonely effect.

***Lighting and contrast.*** Contrast, which can be created through light and color, also directs attention.

When a photograph contains a lot of dark tones or low light, it's called "low key"; photographs shot in a low-key tone tend to create a sense of mystery, gloom, or dread. When a photo contains a lot of light and/or lighter tones, it's called "high key"—high-key photos create feelings of delicacy, softness, and lightness (imagine a photo of a young girl playing in a field of daisies or a couple dressed in light-colored clothing walking on the beach).

**EXAMPLE** Consider Figure 4.9 of President Obama working in the Oval Office. It's quite a low-key photograph, the colors primarily dark. The only light is artificial light illuminating the trees outside and shining in on President Obama, working alone at his desk. The lighting works here both to direct viewers' eyes to Obama and to tell a story. Though we have no way of knowing what time it is, the effect is of a tireless president, staying up late or getting up early to do the work of leading the country.

***Color.*** Consider how color is used in the photo and what effect it has on you as a viewer. Are the colors light and bright, as in a high-key photo, or dim and dark, or something else? Is one color emphasized over others, or are the colors balanced?

White House Photo/Alamy

**FIGURE 4.9** Original caption: President Barack Obama works at the Resolute Desk in the Oval Office, Oct. 18, 2013.

In one sense, color operates on a sheerly affective level: Colors have different "energies" that produce noticeably different effects on a viewer. In the United States, the color blue tends to have calming and/ or depressing effects (which is why it tends to get used in the "before" photos of many antidepressant ads). As the color typically associated with masculinity, blue also invokes confidence and strength, so it's used as the primary color in promotional material for many financial companies and banks.

But these effects aren't universal—that is, colors don't just mean one thing across all cultures. Rather, the effects of color are also mitigated by cultural factors, so colors that have one effect in one society might have quite a different effect in another. So when you think about how color is working in a photographic image (or any image, really), it's important to consider these cultural factors.

When analyzing the use of color in photos, also notice the amount of saturation, a term that refers to the intensity of color. Highly saturated images tend to create an amped-up, "hyper-real" feeling; washed-out images evoke nostalgia (many filters on *Instagram* are meant to wash photos out to give them a retro feel—like the event happened in the 1970s).

**EXAMPLE**  Figure 4.10 uses color to interesting effect. On first viewing, the eye is immediately drawn to the riot of brightly colored flowers at the bottom of the frame. It's only then that one notices the helicopter in the background, a somewhat startling contrast. It has the effect of a visual joke, provoking a small, surprised reaction in the viewer.

White House Photo/Alamy

**FIGURE 4.10** Original caption: Marine One departs the South Lawn of the White House at the start of President Barack Obama's trip to Boston, Mass., Oct. 30, 2013.

Analyzing the formal layer of a photograph requires training yourself to see it with a relaxed, yet attentive eye:

1. Soften your gaze and allow your eyes to just take in the photograph. Where are your eyes naturally drawn first (emphasis)?

2. Next, notice what's in the photograph (framing), how the elements are arranged (composition), and where the camera is positioned in relation to its subject (camera angle and distance from subject). How does the photograph invite you to relate to the subject? Let the lighting, color, and contrasts strike your eyes, and try to identify the feelings that these create.

## FOR DISCUSSION

1. For class, find a photo with a deliberate visual message (a photo accompanying a news or feature story, or one used in an advertisement, for instance). Identify the message and the formal features that give it this message, and bring it to class for a discussion and cataloguing of the different kinds of rhetorical effects of various formal elements of photographs.

2. Describe Figure 4.11 in terms of the "formal layer" characteristics explained earlier. Avoid using interpretive language—stick to simply describing things like emphasis, framing, color, etc.

National Park Service

**FIGURE 4.11** National Junior Ranger Day

## The social layer of images

As the section on the formal layer shows, viewers of an image will be affected by its basic physical features.  But that's not the only thing that creates a rhetorical effect—there's also the *content* of the image to consider. We might call this the *social layer*.

The **social layer** refers to the cultural meanings of the images in the image: things like historical contexts, cultural references, visual tropes, narratives, jokes, and so forth. And, if the image contains human subjects, we would think about things like the social meanings associated with bodies (age, gender, race and ethnicity, hair, size, looks), pose, manner, props, and settings (Dyer 1982). Note that while you may also have *personal* associations with particular images, you may need to separate these (for the sake of analysis) from the broader social or cultural associations.

We can analyze the social layer of images using a method called visual semiotics. Visual semiotics treats images like texts that have a grammar (a set of rules or patterns), which can be studied for meaningful patterns. As Gunther Kress and Theo von Leeuwen explain in their book *Reading Images*, certain visual patterns have been established as conventions over the course of Western history, and these patterns can be studied to explain how they make meaning. Developing an understanding of these rules— becoming what they and others call "visually literate"—they say, will soon be "a matter of survival, especially in the workplace" (3).

While the grammar of visual images is quite complex, we'll focus on a few of the aspects that are most fundamental to creating a rhetorical effect: dominant shapes in an image, the narratives (actors and actions), objects, and settings.

**The significance of dominant shapes in an image.** If you ever took a beginning painting or drawing class, you probably learned that on an abstract level, any image is made up of a series of basic shapes: circles, squares, and triangles. Such shapes may be basic, but they're not neutral. Over thousands of years of human history, they've developed socially powerful meanings and associations. And so if a certain shape is prominent in an image, it can create a rhetorical effect (Figure 4.12).

*Circles,* curves, and ovals can be found in natural forms: the moon, the sun, the curves of hills, human faces and bodies, pregnant bellies, and so forth. An image dominated by circles thus tends to evoke cyclical, organic nature. As you might guess, advertisements that want to create such associations with a product might rely on circle-heavy images.

**EXAMPLE** Consider Figure 4.13. The first image is a noncommercial photo of sunflowers with the sun in the distance. While not ALL photos of nature are circle-heavy (think of jagged mountainscapes), this one certainly is. A quick glance at the Clarins ad beside it shows the same reliance on circles (water bubbles) to create an organic feel. The text within the ad furthers the connection to nature through its reference to "Nature's own internal moisturizing mechanism."

*Squares* (and *rectangles*) don't exist in nature, and hence are associated with human construction and mechanical order. Thus, images dominated by squares and rectangles would tend to impress upon viewers a sense of order and rationality and the cultural associations that go along with that: honesty or coldness, depending on one's perspective.

*Triangles,* because they literally can point at things (especially when they're tilted), tend to introduce a dynamic element into an image, one of processes and movement. Thus, images that distinctively incorporate triangles might seem exciting and action-filled.

**The rhetorical effect of narratives in an image.** Many images have a narrative element—that is, they depict culturally familiar stories. As a product of a culture, you are familiar with a vast number of its narratives. To put yourself in mind of some of the most recognizable narratives of Western culture, just think of the plots of many Hollywood blockbusters, boiled down to their most basic form:

- Bad person makes good (or good person is forced by circumstances to become bad).
- Two friends go traveling and have adventures.
- Someone sacrifices her- or himself for others or the greater good.
- A person triumphs over hardships.
- Someone learns something about him- or herself through meeting challenges.

**FIGURE 4.12**  Any image is made up of a series of basic shapes.

PhotographyByMK/Shutterstock.com

The advertising archives

Multi-level moisture for thirsty skin.

NEW

*HydraQuench Cream*

When skin gets thirsty, it isn't only on the surface. Katafray extract and Hyaluronic acid infuse the different levels of the skin to help stimulate Nature's own internal moisturizing mechanism*. Discover new levels of long-lasting comfort and healthy dewy vitality. Essential daily care for all skin types. HydraQuench Cream reveals your deep inner beauty. Clarins. No.1 in UK Premium Skin Care*. *In clinically test note. *Source: The NPD Group 2012.

*Official online store: www.clarins.com*

CLARINS

**FIGURE 4.13** The ad on the right uses shapes found in nature to make a subtle point.

These are some of the stock narratives of Western culture, and some have been around for thousands of years (for instance, the sacrifice story); some are more recent. Not all narratives that inform images will be so complete—a narrative can be as simple as "the girl goes to the store for her mother." But the narratives that stick around are the most culturally resonant ones. They tend to reveal a culture's *ideologies*, or the norms and assumptions that drive it. Thus, narratives are powerful rhetorical devices.

Narratives in textual form have a beginning, middle, and end—they incorporate time, in other words. So how do you know if an image (which, of course, is two-dimensional and static) contains a narrative? In its most basic form, a **narrative** could be rephrased as "something is happening (or has happened)." Other variations include "someone is doing something" or "someone is doing something to someone/something else." So to identify the narratives in an image, look for *action* and *actors*.

The **action** of a narrative is what is happening or what happened. As in language, action suggests a verb, or something being done. To identify the action, you could trace imaginary arrows that follow the movement in the image. The arrow, which after all is a triangle on a line, signifies a dynamic process—something that's happening.

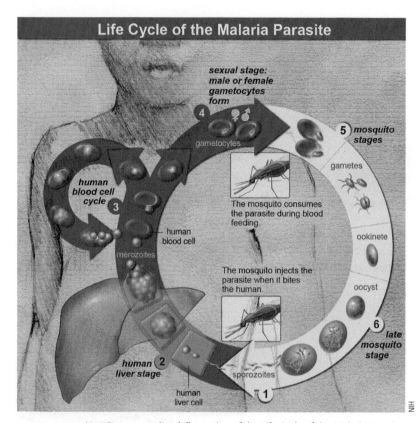

FIGURE 4.14 Non-Representational Illustration of the Life Cycle of the Malaria Parasite

**EXAMPLE** In non-representational illustrations like the one of the life cycle of the malaria parasite in Figure 4.14, sometimes you'll find an actual arrow. The narrative in this illustration is the literal life story of the parasite, one that involves the parasite acting on (and being acted on by) multiple actors.

**Actors** are who or what does the action in the image. Actors could be distinguishable by their size, their placement in the composition, or something else that makes them visually conspicuous. Actors don't need to be human. In Figure 4.15, for instance, the panda is the actor in a story that we might call "the panda waits in his cage for food."

**EXAMPLE** More than just identifying the actors, you need to think about the social significance of the particular actor. The panda, for instance, is clearly a zoo animal, and so the image of the panda unavoidably brings with it an unarticulated series of conversations, moral judgments, and stories about the history of animals in zoos, whether zoos actually protect wild animals from extinction or ultimately do a disservice, the arguments against animals as commodities for human enjoyment, and so on. (Figure 4.15). You might not consciously think of all of these debates when you look at the

BurningWell

**FIGURE 4.15**  Photo of a Panda Bear Waiting for Food

image of a panda, but they are there, and they bring an unavoidable "charge" or electricity to the image to which viewers will react.

Human actors also are raced, gendered, and show signs of economic class, all of which carry their own set of deeply embedded, unavoidable assumptions about social roles and hierarchies. In an analysis, these things need to be fleshed out (so to speak).

---

**QUESTIONS TO ASK**   **Analyzing the Human Actors in an Image**

1. What do the bodies in the image signify?
   - *Gender.* Are the people male, female, or other? Are they portrayed according to typical or traditional gender roles?
   - *Age.* How old are the people in the image, and what do their ages tend to culturally convey?
   - *Race and Ethnicity.* Of what races or ethnicities are the people in the image? Are they being portrayed according to stereotyped social roles (e.g., black man as thug or athlete)?
   - *Weight.* What weight are the people in the image, and what are the connotations of that weight? Does the image show the entire body, or just parts?
   - *Looks.* Are the people conventionally good looking or not? What do their looks signify in the context of the image?

2. What facial expressions are shown?
3. Who is looking at whom, and how? How are the various gazes acting to convey social power in the image? (For example, an image may show women looking jealously at another woman with great shoes, suggesting a power differential in terms of sexual desirability; or a man might look straight at the camera, making a direct challenge, or appeal, to the viewer of the image.)
4. If there are multiple actors, who is active in the image, and who isn't?
5. What is the spatial arrangement of the people in the image? Who is positioned as superior, and who inferior? Are there indications of intimacy among any of the actors?

---

The real question behind all of these is *what difference does the outward identity and appearance make to the message of the image?* Before you too-hastily say "none," or "everyone is equal" or "stereotyping and prejudice are so twentieth century," stop to think about what difference it would make if a different kind of body (different in terms of race, gender, class, nationality, ability, sexuality, etc.) occupied the image instead.

EXAMPLE   As an example of the difference that specific bodies make in images, consider the photograph in Figure 4.16, in which a female model is replaced with a male one. How does replacing the sexualized woman with a man reveal our own cultural assumptions about who is the "proper" object of a gaze and who is not?

FIGURE 4.16  From the Video "This is What Happens When You Replace the Women in Ads with Men"

***Social meanings of objects and settings in an image.*** Along with the actors and actions in an image, look carefully at what objects appear, as well as where the image is set. These things will also be socially significant.

Objects are not neutral, but are charged with significance.

**EXAMPLES** Think about the various social meanings attached to men's white tank tops, a copy of Jack Kerouac's *On the Road*, or a pair of Jimmy Choo heels, for instance. Even different objects in the same category have very different significations. For instance, though Cadillac Escalade SUVs, Rolls Royces, and Lamborghinis are all expensive vehicles and are hence associated with wealth and status, the particular *kinds* of wealth and status they connote are very different.

**EXAMPLES** *All* objects have rhetorical effects, because all objects carry with them the memory of all the situations and contexts in which they have been used, and all the potential ways they *might* be used in the future. When I think of the humble bandana, for instance, a plethora of images and memories immediately comes to mind—among them, images of Rosie the Riveter, biceps flexed, with a bandana on her head (associations of wartime female empowerment); a more personal memory of my father, who has a drawer full of bandanas that he uses as handkerchiefs; a vague visual of 1960's commune dwellers, their hair pulled back in bandanas; an image of a farmer or a cowboy wiping his face with the bandana around his neck; Hell's Angels types wearing cap-style bandanas; Tupac Shakur with a bandana worn street-style, the knot in front of his head (Figure 4.17).

FIGURE 4.17 The bandana has various meanings attached to it.

The bandana holds all these visual memories at once, and as such can be a powerful object of signification, depending on how it is used in an image. The same goes for settings: deserts, American Western landscapes, Brazilian slums, city streets, white sand beaches, the Hollywood hills—all of these places have powerful connotations and associations, and they can't help but evoke these in the context of an image.

One critical thing to keep in mind: objects and settings *mean different things to different groups of people.*

**EXAMPLE**    As a non-New-Yorker, I likely have a very different set of associations with Times Square than someone who lives in midtown Manhattan. Our sets of associations may overlap, but the shades of meaning and connotation will be very different. So as a rhetorical analyst of images, you must consider how the social meanings of objects or settings in an image might change with different viewers.

---

**QUESTIONS TO ASK**    **Analyzing an Image's Objects and Settings**

*Objects*
- What objects are present in the image?
- What social memories, images, and associations do these things have?
- How might these affect the meaning or rhetorical effect of the image? How do they add to the narrative (if there is one)?
- How might these memories, images, and associations be different for different audiences?

*Settings*
- Does the image have an obvious setting?
- What sorts of social memories, images, and associations does this kind of setting evoke? Brainstorm a list of as many associations as you can come up with.
- What is the role of the setting in the image? What difference would it make if the action were taking place somewhere else?

---

# 4b Thinking Rhetorically about the Placement, Circulation, and Distribution of Images

We don't see images in a vacuum—they always come to us by way of a specific medium, which has its own rhetorical effects. Thus, we need to think about not only the image itself but also how and where we encounter it, and what difference this makes to how we understand and respond to the message. To think about the rhetorical effects of the placement, circulation, and distribution of images, consider the following questions:

Where does the image appear? Is it part of a larger visual composition? What information accompanies it? (For more on the conjunction of texts and images, see Section 4c.)

What is its purpose within this context?

- Is it meant to identify and provide a personal feel to a piece of writing (as with the headshots of columnists that appear regularly in newspapers and magazines)?

- If it appears online, is it click-bait? (Study the images that appear with ads on *Facebook*, or those that accompany stories on sites like *Slate*, *Buzzfeed*, and *Upworthy*. What tactics are they employing to try to get you to click on that story? Keep in mind that the more people click on a story, the more ad revenue sites will earn, so it's in their interests to use a really interesting image.)

How has the image *circulated*, and how has that affected its meaning, or how audiences might receive it? (Think, for example, of memes like that of the University of California at Davis pepper-spraying cop, or the many remixes of Shepard Fairy's Obama "Hope" campaign poster.)

## 4c The Rhetorical Work of Images in Texts

Though most of the chapter until this point has focused on the rhetorical effects of stand-alone images, in reality it's almost impossible to find an image that isn't accompanied by some form of text. Even in art galleries, online photo albums, and "Photo of the Day" sections on websites, images at least have titles, captions, and accompanying explanations. Thus, it's important to think about the work that images do in conjunction with text—how together they create a rhetorical effect.

Though there are many we could look at, in this section we'll consider three instances of visuals integrated with texts: as illustrations in news and magazines stories; in print advertisements, posters, and brochures; and on Web pages. I chose these specifically because they are all cases of communication that aim to persuade or influence an audience in some way.

### Analyzing Images Used as Illustrations

It's easy to overlook or take for granted images that appear in texts, or to treat them as just "prettying up" or adding visual interest to text. However, images—whether photos or illustrations—communicate a great deal of information themselves, and hence can add layers of meaning to written compositions.

Images accompanying newspaper or magazine stories are generally chosen by the editor, not the writer. Writers do the raw work of producing the story—it's the editor who decides how to "package" the story via headlines, images, and position within the magazine, newspaper, or website. Thus, the images in a story can often (though not always) provide clues about the most important element or takeaway message from the story.

Images used as illustrations in stories serve one or more of the following purposes:

- **They can convey editorial judgment about the people in the story.** Tabloids are especially notorious for doing this.

  EXAMPLE   If it's a story that aims to stir up speculation about a celebrity couple on the brink of divorce, say, the editor will lead the story with a portrait of the couple together appearing to look tense, or individual photos of the two individuals looking angry and/or teary. In most cases, though, those photos came from an event or situation that had nothing to do with the couple's relationship. The photo serves as a kind of shorthand for what the editor wants readers to believe about the situation.

- **They can serve as visual evidence for what the writer is talking about.** Especially if the story is about a visually important thing (say, fashion or somebody's looks), images can serve as proof, a way for readers to check the validity of what the writer is saying.

  EXAMPLE   A story about a protest that caused a great deal of damage will generally include photos of the damage so that readers can see for themselves.

- **They can highlight or accentuate certain aspects of the story.**

  EXAMPLE   A January 2014 *New Yorker* story brilliantly shows the power of images to subtly underscore points in an accompanying story. The story showed up in my *Facebook* feed as a headline accompanied by a photo of the controversial politician Michelle Bachmann. The photo caught my attention in the context of my *Facebook* feed just for the fact that Bachmann appears so prominently in it. Bachmann, who wears heavy makeup for the cameras, appears centered in the foreground and is the obvious emphasis point in the photo. Her mouth is open, presumably to speak into the microphone that appears just below her.

  The photo by itself isn't all that remarkable—Bachmann looks slightly too made up, and she looks as silly as anyone with an open mouth would. But the photo in conjunction with the headline ("Stephen Hawking on Black Holes Shows Danger of Listening to Scientists, Says Bachmann") reveals a satire that is unclear from the photo on its own. *The New Yorker*, which targets itself to highly educated, urban readers, clearly would look down on any anti-scientific positions. Though the headline represents itself as straight news, the fact that it's published in *The New Yorker* subtly hints at its condemnation of Bachmann's position. Thus, in the context of the headline Bachmann's facial expression suddenly appears vapid and silly, the prominence of her face in the photo seemingly making a point about the ill-informed yapping of politicians.

- **They can serve to deepen readers' connection to the people in the story.**

  **EXAMPLE**   A recent *New York Times* five-part feature story called "Invisible Child: Dasani's Homeless Life," for example, is an extensive portrait of an eleven-year-old girl named Dasani who lives in a New York City homeless shelter with her family, and is accompanied by many photos of Dasani in various situations described by the article. The photos, like the article, are clearly meant to inspire readers' sympathy for Dasani's desperate situation.

Determining the rhetorical effect of visual compositions of text and images will require you to use all the steps you've learned thus far for doing rhetorical analysis of both texts and images.

---

## HOW TO... Analyze Text and Images in a Composition

**First, you'll need to do a rhetorical analysis of the text:**

1. Read the piece attentively, using the steps described in Section 3a of Chapter 3. Notice where the images are placed in the text.
2. Research the rhetorical situation of the text, using the steps described in Section 3c in Chapter 3.
3. Think about how rhetorical appeals are being used in the text, using the steps described in Section 3d in Chapter 3.

**Next, you'll need to rhetorically analyze the images:**

4. Analyze the formal and social layers of each image, using the tools described in Section 4a.

**And finally, think about how the images and the text work together:**

5. Do they have similar messages? What aspects of the text do the images call the readers' attention to?
6. Do the images actually serve to subtly undermine the message of the text, or add an interpretation or layer of meaning that the text doesn't explicitly address?

---

**EXAMPLE**   To see how images might complicate the meaning of a text, consider the following news item published on the website *The Raw Story*. *The Raw Story*, with the tagline "Celebrating 10 Years of Independent Journalism," has an overtly liberal bent—its "About" statement reads,

Orgur Coskun/Shutterstock; Source: Raw Story Media, Inc.

**FIGURE 4.18** Screenshot of News Item at *The Raw Story*

"*Raw Story* is a progressive news site that focuses on stories often ignored in the mainstream media."

The news item, with the headline "South Carolina mass murder-suicide leaves 6 dead after 'edgy' gunman calls 911," is accompanied by a large photograph of a balding, goateed middle-aged white man in a black t-shirt holding a handgun (see Figure 4.18). The image is striking because the barrel of the gun, and the man's hand, is the closest thing to the camera—so close that the gun is out of focus. The point of emphasis in the photo is the man's face, his mouth set and eyebrow arched with a look of determination. The photo has no setting, just a white background. A closer look reveals that the photo is (unsurprisingly) not of the actual gunman who committed the murders, but is a stock photo that the magazine purchased from *Shutterstock*.

The strange combination of the lurid news headline and the striking stock photo was enough to make me stop to read the story. Stock photos are by definition meant to represent generic situations: the *Shutterstock* title for this photo, for instance, is "Angry man points handgun." It doesn't actually matter who the "angry man" is—it's just meant to provide a representation of what an angry man with a gun might look like.

Typically, such stock photos would be found in "soft news" stories about rising trends, issues, how-to pieces, and so forth, in which specific people or events are unimportant. But the title of the *Raw Story* article is clearly a hard-news headline—it's reporting a gruesome event that took place. Such stories conventionally might include images of the victims, the scene where the murder took place, or a photo of the *actual* gunman. The stock photo "Angry man points handgun" provides a clue that although *The Raw Story* is ostensibly presenting this story as news, really the site is attempting to provoke conversation about something more generic. And indeed, the comments after the story reveal that the real interest of the site in publishing this story is to make a not-so-subtle commentary about gun violence. The "angry gunman" stock photo was included to inspire fear and to advocate for gun control.

## ASSIGNMENT

### Map an Issue through Images

For this assignment, you will be analyzing the visual representation of a specific issue. To do so, you'll first need to identify a national issue—something about which people disagree. Do a search to find a significant number of stories on the issue, ideally from clashing perspectives (see Chapter 12, "Research: Composing with Multiple Sources," for tips on how to conduct research). These stories should appear across a number of different publications, and they must be illustrated with images, or the assignment won't work.

First, read the stories to get a gist for the main purpose and argument and audience. Next, study the images that accompany each story, using the analytical tools described in Section 4c. Make comparisons in the functions the images serve for the stories in which they appear. Can you identify any patterns in the way the stories are illustrated? What do these patterns suggest about the cultural beliefs about this topic?

You can present your findings in the form of a presentation or visual essay, in which you combine images with text to demonstrate the patterns you discovered in the way stories are illustrated. For a good example of such a visual comparison, see George Lakoff's taxonomy of Donald Trump's tweets.

## Analyzing Print Advertisements

If you're like most twenty-first century Westerners, print advertisements are likely the visual arguments you see most regularly. Print ads are typically confined to one or two pages, and make sometimes startlingly creative use of images, graphics, and the visual properties of text. They also have a simple message (that often contains a lot of subtext), and are exquisitely conscious of audience. For these reasons, print ads make excellent subjects for rhetorical analysis.

Most advertisements (for consumer products and services) in essence make proposal arguments: "You should buy this brand, product, or service." If we think of advertisements as an enthymeme, though, it's what comes after the "because"—as in "You should buy this brand, product, or service BECAUSE..."—that makes their arguments unique.

| HOW TO... | Generate Ideas for a Rhetorical Analysis of a Print Ad |

The following steps will help you generate ideas for a rhetorical analysis of a print advertisement. Note: these are part of the invention work for writing—they may not appear in exactly this order if you write an academic rhetorical analysis essay.

1. **Define the ad's target audience.** As with rhetorical analysis of texts, before you can analyze how an ad is working, you first need to understand who it's targeting. To figure out an ad's target

## A Taxonomy of
# TRUMP TWEETS

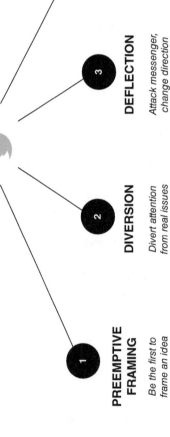

**1**

### PREEMPTIVE FRAMING

*Be the first to frame an idea*

**EXAMPLE:** The hacking of the DNC was the DNC's fault and Democrats lost by a wide margin (when in fact it was one of the narrowest margins in US history).

🐦 **JAN 7**

**@realDonaldTrump**
Only reason the hacking of the poorly defended DNC is discussed is that the loss by the Dems was so big that they are totally embarrassed!

**2**

### DIVERSION

*Divert attention from real issues*

**EXAMPLE:** Divert attention away from real issues around conflicts of interest and Russian hacking and toward Meryl Streep's speech at Golden Globe Awards.

🐦 **JAN 9**

**@realDonaldTrump**
Meryl Streep, one of the most overrated actresses in Hollywood, doesn't know me but attacked last night at the Golden Globes. She is a.....

**3**

### DEFLECTION

*Attack messenger, change direction*

**EXAMPLE:** Attack media in an attempt to erode public trust. Reframe story as "fake news" and establish Trump administration as source of truth.

🐦 **JAN 11**

**@realDonaldTrump**
Intelligence agencies should never have allowed this fake news to "leak" into the public. One last shot at me. Are we living in Nazi Germany?

**4**

### TRIAL BALLOON

*Test public reaction*

**EXAMPLE:** Test public reaction to nuclear arms escalation.

🐦 **DEC 22**

**@realDonaldTrump**
The United States must greatly strengthen and expand its nuclear capability until such time as the world comes to its senses regarding nukes.

audience, first look at the context in which the ad appears. If it's posted in a public place, consider the demographic most likely to frequent that place.

**EXAMPLES**  Ads posted above urinals in sports bars, for instance, are most likely aimed at a young male sports-and-beer demographic. Ads posted on the inside of buses are aimed at urban commuters— the ads make a bet that the bus riders are either (a) concerned with the environment, and on public transport because of that, or (b) can't afford to own a car, or at least can't afford to drive it to work.

**EXAMPLES**  If the ad is in a magazine, you can make an even more precise guess about the audience. Some magazine brands will even tell you their target audience up front. For instance, Hearst National Magazine Company, which owns among others *Cosmopolitan, Elle, Harper's Bazaar, Men's Health, Good Housekeeping,* and *Runner's World,* has a Web page on "Our Brands," which describes, sometimes in explicit detail, the general purpose and audience for their magazines. For instance, "the Cosmo reader" is described as

> a family girl who loves men but she doesn't live through them. She's obsessed with fashion and beauty and the smartest ways to make them work for her. She's proud of her relationship with her friends, and her hard-earned career. She might not always feel 100% confident—about her body, her relationships or her life— but that's where Cosmo comes in.

Knowing that this is who *Cosmopolitan* editors, writers, and photographers see themselves as will give you a better understanding of how the ads work. But not all magazines have mission statements; also, a general description or mission statement is not uniformly indicative of an institution's actions or content. So you also need to look carefully at the particulars of a magazine when doing a rhetorical analysis of an ad—things like the cover, the other ads that are included, the stories, the magazine's ratio of images to words, etc.

2. **Describe and analyze the formal features of the ad's images.** Just as with stand-alone images, it's important in ads to consider how the formal features of the image—framing, composition, distance from subject, color, etc.—create a rhetorical effect. (See Section 4a for specifics.)

3. **Describe and analyze the social features of the ad's images.** The social features of the ad, as explained in Section 4a, include things like the dominant shapes of the image, potential narratives, and the social significance of the human bodies and nonhuman objects that appear within the image.

4. **Explain how the text works with the images.** As in Section 4c, think about what relationship the text has with the images. Do they have similar messages? What aspects of the text do the images call the readers' attention to? Do the images add an interpretation or layer of meaning that the text doesn't explicitly address?

---

## ASSIGNMENT

MindTap°
View How to
Video 4: Doing a
Comparative Ad
Analysis

### Write a Comparative Ad Analysis

Write an essay comparing two different advertisements that are advertising similar products for different audiences. To make a fair comparison, the products advertised should be as similar as possible—for example, if you find an ad for a truck in, say, *Field and Stream*, you'll want to compare it to another ad for a truck in a different magazine—not an ad for a hybrid car. Once you find the product, it's a good idea to find audiences that are very different. This will make for a more interesting comparison. Use the following "Invention Work—Comparing Advertisements" chart to generate as much analytical material as possible. Then, after you've thoroughly analyzed and compared the ads, write your essay. The thesis should make a claim that summarizes the main differences in the way the product is advertised to the two different audiences. The body of the essay should provide information about the target audience and context of each ad, as well as description and analysis of the ads. The conclusion should summarize what one might learn (about audiences, about the way a particular product is sold, etc.) from comparing the two ads.

| CATEGORY FOR ANALYSIS | AD 1 (NAME PRODUCT/BRAND) | AD 2 (NAME PRODUCT/BRAND) |
|---|---|---|
| Target audience | | |
| Formal features of images | | |
| Social features of images | | |
| Relationship of images to ad text | | |

Invention Work—Comparing Advertisements

FOR REFLECTION

**Transferable Skills and Concepts**

Do a *Google* image search on the subject of a major you are considering (for instance, if you were an English Lit major, you'd Google "English literature"). Apply the skills in analyzing visual rhetoric you learned in Chapter 4 to the first few rows of images you see. Write a journal entry about how these images do or don't represent what you understand about people in this major (or the careers that people in your major typically get). What's missing? How would you represent your major differently?

# 5

# Analyzing Multimodal Rhetoric

*By working through this chapter, you will be able to...*

- Define the four modalities: textual, visual, auditory, and haptic.
- Recognize all of the modalities operating in a given piece of communication.
- Identify the rhetorical effects of each modality.
- Describe the rhetorical effects of interacting modalities in a piece of communication.
- Identify the unique rhetorical effects of each modality in videos, websites, and apps.
- Do a comprehensive rhetorical analysis of a multimodal composition like a video, website, or app.

As Chapter 2 explains, the "modality" of communication refers to the basic sensory means by which communication happens:

- The **verbal modality** (words spoken or sung or typed or handwritten on a piece of paper or screen)
- The **visual modality** (live images, still images, or images moving on a screen)
- The **auditory modality** (spoken words, sung words, nonverbal music, or noise)
- The **haptic modality** (touch)

If you think about it, *all* forms of communication involve multiple modalities. A speech, for instance, includes the verbal modality (spoken words), the auditory modality (the pitch and tone of the speaker's voice), and visual modalities (the speaker's appearance, gestures, facial expressions, and perhaps slides, if the speaker is giving a PowerPoint presentation). Video games use haptic, auditory, and visual modalities. Even reading the printed page encompasses verbal, visual, auditory (the sound of pages turning), and haptic (the feel of the pages turning) modalities.

So the term "multimodal rhetoric" is a little mushy. But whereas in Chapter 3 we focused strictly on the verbal modality and in Chapter 4 we focused on the visual modality, here we'll analyze compositions that involve all of these modalities. This chapter gives you the tools to analyze multimodal compositions, including genres like websites, video games, films, songs, and podcasts.

**ANALYZE & CREATE**

**Chapter 5**
Analyzing Multimodal Rhetoric

**Chapter 15**
Creating Multimodal Rhetoric

## FOR DISCUSSION

1. Consider the image below: a screen shot of a typical TV news layout. How many modalities are included? (Obviously, this is a static image, so imagine that this is an actual TV news program.) Why do you think so many different modalities exist here, and what is the overall effect? Talk about your experience watching TV news (if you do). How is your experience watching it different from, say, watching a film?

Craig Stephen/Alamy Stock Photo

2. As a class, brainstorm as many different examples of multimodal communication as you can. Take one of these examples and, together as a class, identify all the modalities it includes. Where does this kind of communication most commonly appear, and how do users typically interact with it?

# 5a Thinking Rhetorically about How Modalities Interact

In the two previous chapters, we considered how two modalities (the verbal and the visual) create rhetorical effects. Now we need to analyze how multimodal compositions, with their layered, interacting modalities, create such effects.

### HOW TO...   Analyze Multimodal Compositions

1. First, identify the communicator, message, audience, and purpose of the piece, as well as its medium, genre, and circulation (see Chapter 2 for a more thorough explanation of how to do this).
2. Then identify all the modalities in the piece, thinking about the rhetorical effects of each modality. How do the various multimodal components contribute to this effect?

   - Does it use spoken or written language? Where and why is language used? How would you characterize it? (Use Chapter 3 to help with rhetorical analysis of text.)
   - Does it use still or static images? (Chapter 4 shows how to analyze visuals.) How are these images arranged?
   - Does it use moving images? What sequence do these images follow, and why? How are they edited?
   - Does it use sound? What kind(s): interview, voice narration, music without words, music with words, other kinds of sounds? How would you characterize these sounds? How are the sounds edited and layered?
   - How do users physically interact with it? Do they turn pages, do they listen to it while walking around or driving, do they click links, touch a screen, or use controllers?

3. Finally, you need to consider the piece of multimodal communication holistically: How do all these rhetorical elements work together to create an overall effect?

### FOR HOMEWORK

1. Search *YouTube* for a video clip produced by BroScienceLife called "Do You Even Lift?" As you watch, write down the different modalities at work in the clip. (The questions in the second step of "How to Analyze Multimodal Compositions" will help you identify the modalities.) Then discuss: What is the overall effect of the video? How does each modality contribute to this overall effect?
2. Choose one of the genres of multimodal communication listed at the beginning of this chapter (websites, films, songs, podcasts, video games). Gather three to five examples and analyze them using the questions listed above. Then generate a list of criteria that you might use to evaluate the form of communication. What makes an excellent video game? A website? A film? (Note: This can serve later as the evaluation sheet for when you produce your own multimodal project.)

# 5b Applying Multimodal Analysis to Video

We've already learned a great deal about visual composition by analyzing images in Chapter 4. Analyzing video is all the more challenging because not only do the images move, but these compositions also include textual components (dialogue, voiceover, song) and various auditory (sonic) components. (Note: While feature films provide a rich source of multimodal analysis, for the sake of simplicity we'll focus our analysis in this chapter on nonfictional forms of video, including documentaries.)

Videos have multiple layers or modalities, all of which operate at once to create an overall rhetorical effect:

- Verbal modality: script, dialogue, narration, on-screen text
- Visual modality: composition of each frame, movement of actors and graphics
- Auditory modality: speech, music, and ambient or incidental sounds

For the sake of analysis—which, again, means "pulling things apart"— we'll examine the effect of each of these individually before we put them back together to figure out the overall effect.

## Analyzing the Verbal Modality of Video

Videos typically incorporate language in spoken, written, and sometimes sung forms. Spoken forms of language might include dialogue, voiceover, direct narration (where the narrator speaks to the camera), and direct/indirect interview (the interviewer is either present or not present). Written text likely plays a lesser role than speech, but it appears in the form of graphics onscreen: titles, logos, explanations (e.g., those that appear on a black screen), and even live shots of text messages and other forms of written communication.

---

**QUESTIONS TO ASK** — **Noticing the Effects of Text in Conjunction with Other Modalities**

- If the video uses dialogue, how, when, where, and why do the people talk to each other in the video? How does this affect your perception of the video's content?
- If the video uses voiceover narration, why do you think the creator chose to do this?
- Where else does text appear in the video (in written form, for instance)? How does that add to the spoken text?
- How do the pitch, tone, accent, etc. of various characters' voices (including the narrator, if there is one) affect how you perceive them?
- Do the other elements (modalities) of the video support what's being said or do they undermine it?

---

Source: Shared Hope International

**FIGURE 5.1** Screenshots from "Waiting for You to Notice" Shared Hope International Video

Source: Shared Hope International

**EXAMPLE** Consider the short promotional video called "Waiting for You to Notice" by Shared Hope International, an organization that aims to end human trafficking. As you can see from Figure 5.1, the video is animated. It includes a voiceover by a female narrator that tells the story of a young girl who becomes a victim of human trafficking. The narrator then presents an alternative reality where Shared Hope stops this from happening through educating the public on how to recognize trafficking, training law enforcement on how to deal with it, and providing services and shelter to trafficking victims. If you were to shut your eyes and listen only to this story, you would recognize (using the concepts you learned in Chapters 2 and 3) that the story relies on pathos, appealing to the audience's sense of care and concern that young, innocent girls don't get used for terrible purposes, desire to help the young girl and others like her, and also hope because there is an organization designed to help.

If you were to watch the video, you'd see that as the narrative continues, single words appear occasionally on the screen. These help to underscore the main narrative: It begins with positive words like "family" and "friends," changes to phrases with a darker tone like "and she's waiting for you to notice" and "for sex," and finally concludes with "Shared Hope International." The written text at the very end of the video takes further advantage of the visual modality: The words "Education," "Training," "Shelter," and "Services" (things that Shared Hope offers) are piled one at a time on the word "Trafficking," eventually squashing it off the screen.

## FOR DISCUSSION

Go to *Vox.com*, *Mic.com*, a news site, or any other website that regularly features videos, and choose one that seems particularly interesting. Identify the foundational rhetorical elements of the video (communicator, audience, message, purpose, and exigence) first. Then listen to the video with your eyes closed, focusing only on the spoken text. Watch it a second time and pay attention to the written text, if there is any. Then answer the questions in the previous "Questions to Ask" box.

## Analyzing the Auditory (Sonic) Modality of Video

The auditory modality is critical to the effect of a video. From the dialogue to the ambient sounds (which can be deliberately heightened or muted) to the music of the film score, sound is critical to creating a mood, directing our attention, and underscoring what we should be feeling about a particular scene.

**EXAMPLES**   For iconic examples, think of the ominous music in *Jaws* that indicates the approach of the shark, for instance, or the song "Gonna Fly Now" that accompanies Rocky Balboa on his run up the Philadelphia Museum of Art steps.

To analyze the effect of the sound, you might try closing your eyes and just focusing on the effects created by the audio.

---

**QUESTIONS TO ASK**   **Analyzing the Rhetorical Effects of the Auditory Modality**

- Is there music?
- Is the sound mostly from natural sources (the ambient sounds of the city or of nature, depending on the setting)?
- Is there a pattern of unusual sounds?
- What kind of mood do the sounds as a whole attempt to create: a sense of peace, or anxiety, or intensity, sadness, etc.?
- How do the sounds within the film combine with the other modalities to create an effect?
- How do they add to the action or to the message and purpose of the video?
- How does it affect the characters or indicate their frame of mind?

---

**EXAMPLE**   Take the sounds in the Shared Hope International video described earlier. From a strictly auditory point of view, the voice of the narrator underscores the textual modality. It starts out sounding relatively neutral, becomes more concerned and ominous as it describes the young girl's plight, then takes a happier, lighter tone when it describes what Shared Hope International does. The emotional, sometimes intense music and ambient sounds like water, growling, faint screams, and murmuring voices help lend the video atmosphere and underscore its main point: that trafficking is a serious problem for young girls and can be stopped by organizations like Shared Hope International.

### FOR DISCUSSION

Listen to a video with the projector/screen turned off or your eyes closed. What mood is created by the sound of the video, and how does that support (or perhaps undermine) the message?

**FOR HOMEWORK**

Choose a short story or article and "score" it; that is, imagine that you're going to film it, and create a soundtrack—including music, ambient sounds, and other sound effects—that would fit it. (The short story would translate as a narrative film, and the article would translate as a documentary film.)

1. First, break down the article or short story into individual scenes (you can even create it as a storyboard, including a description of the shots, lighting, and camera work).
2. Next, find songs, musical compositions, or ambient sounds that would fit the mood and desired effect of your potential film.
3. Annotate the article or short story, either by hand or digitally (you might copy and paste the article to a Word document or Google Doc) to indicate where the sonic components should go. A free online program called *SoundCloud* allows you to upload and edit digital music files for your soundtrack. (Your instructor might ask you to submit the actual music/composition along with the annotated article, perhaps as a list of links to *YouTube* videos or as a *SoundCloud* file.)
4. Write a separate memo to your instructor explaining your choices and the rhetorical effect you attempted to create.

## Analyzing the Visual Modality of Videos (Still and Moving Images)

"Composition" refers to the overall look and feel of the video, an effect created by the sum of the camera work (framing), positioning of people and objects, the color, lighting, and *movement*. Because you've learned to analyze still images in Chapter 3, you already have a good start to analyzing the composition of videos, whether they're live or animated.

To effectively analyze a video, you need to think about how its visual composition and the way the images move relate to its overall rhetorical purpose.

 **Analyzing the Visual Modality of Videos**

**Framing:** Where is the camera positioned in relation to the actors or action, and what effect does that have on our feelings about or understanding of what's happening in the video?

- Is the camera at a long distance from the action (long shot), at a neutral distance (medium shot), or close up (focused on objects or faces)?

- Is the camera mounted (as on a tripod, dolly, or crane), or hand-held? Videos created with hand-held cameras convey the effect of action happening in the moment, as with home videos or live news coverage.
- Does the camera move a lot, or does it stay fairly still? How often does it cut to new action?
- How is the camera angled in relation to the action: level, angled upward, or downward?

*Color:* Is the video in black and white or color? Is there a special or deliberate color scheme? How would you describe the effect it has?

*Lighting:* Is the lighting dim, bright, or neutral? How does it create a mood? How is it used to emphasize certain kinds of things and de-emphasize others? Do you notice anything unusual about the lighting?

*People:* How would you characterize the people in the video: what they look like, how they act, etc.?

*Movement:*  How is the movement created within the scene? Do the people or things move, or does the camera?

- If the people move, who or what is emphasized (by closeness to the camera, for instance)?
- If the camera moves, how does it move? What messages are conveyed by the movement of the camera in relation to the people and things being portrayed?

---

**EXAMPLE**  Consider the visuals in the Shared Hope International video. First, the style of the animation itself creates a specific feel: The animated characters are neither too cutesy (which would make them funny) or whimsical, and the color scheme tends to be dark, especially in the part of the narrative where the young girl is in danger. What is most distinctive about the animation style is the constant movement: Even when the images are relatively still, they are still subtly pulsing. The images frequently morph into one another, and they are framed so that the viewer takes the perspective as a third-party observer to the plight of this young girl who, by virtue of her placement continually at a distance from the viewer, seems small, fragile, and vulnerable, in need of protection. The viewer watches helplessly as she is consumed by monstrous jaws, is chased by black shadows, and (shown from above) curls on a bed in a cell, as shadowy hands reach down for her (Figure 5.2). Thus, the visual style supports the purpose and message of the video's narrative.

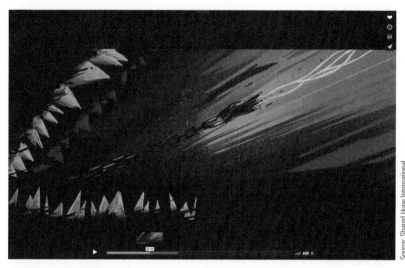

Source: Shared Hope International

**FIGURE 5.2** Screenshot from "Waiting for You to Notice" Shared Hope International Video

## FOR DISCUSSION

The film scholar Jonathan Walley suggests that the "talking head plus B-roll" format of many documentaries (i.e., filmed interviews of people relevant to the topic—the talking heads—followed by a cut to secondary footage—the B-roll—that serves to illustrate what the interviewee is discussing) fails to take advantage of everything the modality of moving images allows, and instead relies too heavily on the textual modality. Documentaries that use this format, he argues, "function as mere audio-visual recording devices." Do you agree with Walley's point? Go to the site "Short of the Week." Choose a few documentaries to watch. Using the questions in the previous "Questions to Ask" box, keep track of the techniques used by the documentaries and formulate an opinion about whether or not and how they could make better use of the multimodal video medium. Prepare to discuss it with your classmates.

## FOR HOMEWORK

Find a short video (5 minutes or less) that overtly aims to persuade viewers of something (you could search under "video editorial" to find one of these). Watch it carefully, twice. Then, in a notebook, do the following things:

1. Describe and analyze (that is, provide a statement about the rhetorical effects of) each of the following elements of the composition: framing, color, lighting, people, and movement. You can do this as a bulleted list: First describe (the *what*), then analyze (the *how* and *why*) of the video's visual modality.
2. Prepare to talk about your video and analysis in class.

**FOR HOMEWORK**

Find a video and "storyboard" two minutes of it. For examples of story-boards of popular films, visit the site *screencrush.com*, or you can just search online for "sample storyboard video."

To create your storyboard, first sketch out all the individual cuts in the video. The sketches can be stick figures; that is, you don't need to be a great artist to create a storyboard, but the activity of reverse-engineering a storyboard from an existing video will help you to pay closer attention to each of its elements.

After you've identified all these elements, make an argument about the overall rhetorical effect of this video on the film's viewer. Your argument should consist of a claim about the video's rhetorical effect, and the evidence you gathered about the individual cuts should help support and provide evidence for that claim.

## Putting It All Together: Analyzing How Modalities Interact in Video

Once you've pulled apart and examined the layers of modalities in a video, it's time to put them all together to come up with a coherent analysis. How do the modalities, working together, create an overall rhetorical effect?

Following is an example of my multimodal analysis of the Shared Hope International anti-trafficking video. To prepare to do this analysis, I watched the video several times: once to understand the overall message, purpose, audience, and exigence; once to pay attention to the text (both written and spoken); once, with my eyes closed, to listen to the sounds; and once to pay attention to the visuals. Notice that I was able to use much of what I wrote earlier, with slight modifications, in the body of my analysis essay.

## Annotated Example of a Multimodal Analysis

### Fear, Sorrow, and Finally, Relief: A Rhetorical Analysis of "Waiting for You to Notice" by Shared Hope International

Shared Hope International describes itself as an organization founded in 1998 by U.S. Congresswoman Linda Smith after she travelled to Mumbai and witnessed the "brutal exploitation and sexual slavery of women and children" (*About/sharedhope .org*). The organization aims to "[bring] an end to sex trafficking

> The first section describes Shared Hope and the promotional video.

through [a] three-pronged approach—prevent, restore, and bring justice" (*What We Do/sharedhope.org*).

In October 2015, Shared Hope released a two-minute promotional video on its website and on *Vimeo* that explains the problem of sex trafficking. Through a narrative about a young girl who gets tricked into sex trafficking and then is rescued by Shared Hope International, the video aims not only to call attention to the problem of sex trafficking, but also to show what Shared Hope as an organization does: It educates the public about sex trafficking, provides training to law enforcement, and offers shelter and other services to victims of trafficking.

This section identifies the basic rhetorical aspects of the video: purpose and audience. The end of the paragraph contains a thesis statement that makes a claim about how the modalities in the video work rhetorically to further its purpose.

One could identify several purposes for the video: first, to call the public's attention to the problem of trafficking and to indicate that there is an organization (Shared Hope) that is working to combat the problem; second, to persuade viewers to go to the organization's website, which has much more information on sex trafficking and Shared Hope's efforts to combat it; and third, to encourage viewers to support the efforts of Shared Hope by donating money (the *"DONATE"* link is the most prominent one in the navigation bar at the top of the site). The video supports these purposes through the use of sympathetic voiceover narration about the plight of a young victim of trafficking, emotional music, and animated visuals that highlight the young girl's vulnerability and provide a compelling visual metaphor for trafficking and how to combat it.

This section discusses the textual modality of the video and its rhetorical effects.

The video uses voiceover narrative to tell a story and make its case. The story relies heavily on pathos, appealing to the audience's sense of care and concern that young, innocent girls don't get used for terrible purposes, desire to help the young girl and others like her, and also hope because there is an organization designed to help (which can be supported with donations from viewers). As the narrative continues, single words appear occasionally on the screen. These help to underscore the main narrative: They begin with words like "family" and "friends" and later to darker things like "and she's waiting for you to notice," "for sex," and, finally, "Shared Hope International." The written text at the very end of the video also takes advantage of the visual modality: The words "Education," "Training," "Shelter," and "Services" (things that Shared Hope offers) are piled one at a time on the word "Trafficking," eventually squashing it off the screen.

From a strictly auditory point of view, the voice of the narrator underscores the textual modality. It starts out sounding relatively neutral, becomes more concerned and ominous as it describes the young girl's plight, and then takes a happier, lighter tone when it describes what Shared Hope International does. The emotional, sometimes intense music and ambient sounds like water, growling, faint screams, and murmuring voices help lend the video atmosphere and underscore its main point: that trafficking is a serious problem for young girls and can be stopped by organizations like Shared Hope International.

> This section discusses the auditory modality of the video and its rhetorical effects.

The visual style of the video also supports the purpose and message of its narrative. The visual story is organized around the metaphor of a young girl who is tricked and then consumed by a monster, where she is batted around helplessly by shadows. The style of the animation creates a specific feel: The animated characters are not too cutesy or whimsical, and the color scheme tends to be dark, especially in the part of the narrative where the young girl is in danger. The images in the video are framed so that the viewer takes the perspective of an observer at a distance of the plight of this young girl who, by virtue of her placement continually at a distance from the viewer, seems small, fragile, and vulnerable, in need of protection. The viewer watches helplessly as the girl is consumed by monstrous jaws, is chased by black shadows, and (shown from above) curls on a bed in a cell as shadowy hands reach down for her.  What is most distinctive about the video's animation style is how the images morph into one another: For instance, as the young girl accepts flowers from a young boy, he turns into a monster that drags the young girl into darkness. These constantly morphing images create a sense of urgency, a sense that what seems stable isn't necessarily so. This in turn supports the narrative's point that many people don't recognize signs of trafficking—though they may trust what they see on the surface, in actuality wicked things are happening. As the narrator talks about what Shared Hope does, the color scheme turns from dark to light, and finally ends with white words on a light blue screen, creating a feeling of lightness and hope that something can be done.

> This section discusses the visual modality of the video and its rhetorical effects.

Together, the modalities work together in the video to create a coherent feeling and rhetorical effect: The voiceover, animated visuals, music, and ambient sounds work on different sensory levels to create fear and sorrow (for young victims of human trafficking) and relief that an organization (Shared Hope International) is there to help.

## ASSIGNMENT

### Do a Multimodal Analysis of a Video

Using the previous example as a model ("Fear, Sorrow, and Finally, Relief: A Rhetorical Analysis of 'Waiting for You to Notice' by Shared Hope International"), write a multimodal analysis essay of a video that is designed to be persuasive. For instance, you might choose to analyze a video that's part of a public advocacy campaign, one that aims to explain some policy (like the kind you'd find on *Vox.com*), or an "Op-Doc" from *The New York Times*.

# 5c Applying Multimodal Analysis to Websites and Apps

Websites are especially interesting forms of rhetorical communication because of the level of active involvement they elicit from their audiences—so much so that audiences for websites are more accurately referred to as "users." Like film, speech, and print media, websites encompass textual and visual modalities; they may also include auditory modalities (if they have sound) and moving images (if they include video). But websites rely most heavily on the *haptic* modality. The haptic modality involves the user's body through touch and movement through space. In the case of mobile websites and applications, or apps, users literally touch their way through their smartphones and tablet computers; in regular desktop computers and laptops, users interact with the website by means of a mouse. But either way, websites require a high level of physical interaction. And the higher level of involvement on the part of the user, the less likely the user is to recognize how the site is working on them rhetorically. Because of this, it's even more vital to learn to consciously recognize how websites and apps work on users.

There are two primary reasons for analyzing websites:

1. To assess how effectively the site works for its intended users; that is, do all the components of the site work well to help users achieve their goals for visiting the site? Most sites, especially those whose primary purpose is to sell products or services, do usability testing to assess how well the site works for its intended audience. (A poorly designed site risks alienating customers and losing potential business.)

2. To understand how the various components of the site work on users to convey or reinforce particular attitudes, feelings, and beliefs about the subject of the website. This type of analysis is intended more for cultural critique.

Regardless of the purpose of analysis, the following steps serve to analyze the individual aspects of websites.

## Identify the Basic Type of Site

Recognizing the physical architecture of the website provides the first clue to its rhetorical purpose. Does it promote interaction from users in the form of comments or even the creation of content, or is it simply meant to serve as an informational resource? Is it designed to entice users to buy products?

- *Static* websites remain the same over time. Similar to printed books, static websites contain a body of information that is relatively stable (Figure 5.3). Many business and organizational websites are relatively static, though they may have some dynamic content (such as the home page of a university website that regularly features different stories about its faculty research and student projects, for instance).

- *Dynamic* websites have content that frequently changes. The websites for all major newspapers and online magazines like *Slate*, *Salon*, and *BuzzFeed* are dynamic websites. The goal of dynamic websites is to entice users to visit the site repeatedly. Among other things, the more visitors the site gets, the more ad revenue is generated. It's in these sites' interest to continually update their content and create headlines that users will be unable to resist clicking.

- *Online stores*, like brick-and-mortar stores, aim to entice users to buy products or services. Online stores aim to display their wares in a way that makes it easiest and most intuitive for their target audience to browse and purchase.

- *Blogs* are websites that organize content in chronological order (with the most recent first). Many individuals have personal blogs that function as online diaries for a small group of readers. Blogs with larger reader populations typically have many contributing authors and publish commentary on specific topics.

FIGURE 5.3  An Example of a Static Website

**EXAMPLES** Among the most popular blogs for 2014 were *The Huffington Post* (news and political commentary, 110 million unique monthly visitors), *TMZ* (gossip, 30 million unique monthly visitors), *Business Insider* (business, 25 million visitors), and *Tech Crunch* (technology, 15 million visitors).

- *Wikis* (from the Hawaiian "wiki wiki," or "quick") are websites that anyone can edit.

**EXAMPLE** *Wikipedia* is undoubtedly the most famous of these; while the site in recent years has limited access to some pages that have contentious information, generally speaking any user can get on and create a page, or add or correct information on already existing information. This makes *Wikipedia* an extremely valuable resource, on the principles that many sets of eyes are better than one, and that many hands make light work. However, for the same reason, the information provided on the site may not be extremely reliable.

To identify the basic type of website, pay attention to what it allows you as a user to do. Can you interact with other users (e.g., via a comment board or by more extensive means)? Can you leave public comments? Can you buy things using an online shopping cart/bag and secure checkout? Can you click through various pages and read information?

## Identify the Site's Owner, Rhetorical Purpose, and Target Audience

Purpose and audience for websites are (as with all communicative acts) intimately linked. All websites aim to get a certain group of people to do, think, or feel something. Identifying the purpose and audience of the site will give you a means of understanding the site's design choices (and vice versa—analyzing the design choices will help you identify the purpose and audience).

Understanding who owns the site might begin to give you a clue about the site's intended purpose.

To identify the site's rhetorical purpose, you might start by asking what problem the site aims to solve for its audience. What does the audience want or need that the site provides?

- To buy something?
- To find a date?
- To be entertained?
- To feel like part of a community?
- News or gossip?
- Information about a product, service, event, or phenomenon?
- To store photos online?

- To waste time at work?
- Something else?

Problems (and websites that grow in response to them) are always changing and are deeply dependent on ever-evolving contexts, including both cultural events and the development of technologies.

**EXAMPLES** A website like *CrimeReports*, which places local police data on local maps, would have been unthinkable before the existence of *Google Maps*. Sites like *10 Minute Mail*, which provides users with an email address that lasts ten minutes, was created in response to the ever-growing prevalence of spammers. And *Persona*, which scans users' social media sites for photos and posts that might be objectionable to employers and other powers that be, was created in response to the growth of social media and the various ways by which people could ruin their chances for employment.

## Examine the Site's Content

What kind of subject matter does the site include? What topics does it *not* include? Paying close attention to what's there and not there will also provide excellent clues about the site's purpose and audience. You can use the techniques for textual analysis presented in Chapter 3 to understand how the site attempts to build credibility with its users (ethos) and how it attempts to appeal to them emotionally (pathos) and intellectually (logos). Among other things, you might consider the site's opinions, propositions, descriptions, stylistic features like register, lexicon, forms of address, use of first, second, or third person, use of metaphor or other rhetorical figures, gendered statements, temporal orientation, humor, and value statements (Pauwels).

## Study the Site's Interface

The interface is the aspect of websites that users interact with. It can be defined as the visual organization of the site, everything from the icons and color scheme used to how users are invited to move through the site. The design choices made in the interface are very important in clearly conveying a sense of the site's purpose, and providing cues about its users and how those users are supposed to interact with the site.

The following are elements of a site's interface:

- *Navigation.* Navigation is unique to websites. Because users have no way of knowing before they click where the hyperlinks in a website will take them, websites have to provide multiple cues to help users understand their organization or structure. To analyze the navigation, consider the various means by which the site attempts to guide users through its structure.

   **EXAMPLES** Many sites use visual metaphors in an attempt to give their users a familiar, intuitive way to move around. Some of these are

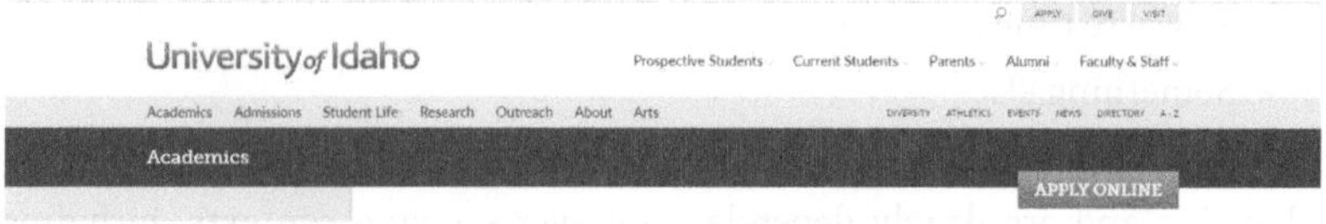

University*of* Idaho

**FIGURE 5.4** A Common Navigation Metaphor: Tab Dividers in a Folder

so common that you may not even recognize them as metaphors, including buttons that users push in order to perform some sort of action on the website, and folders that often include tab dividers, used to create major divisions of information on a site (see Figure 5.4). As the *Yale Web Style Guide* cautions, metaphors that are too "creative" often fail because users aren't familiar with the structure they provide.

**EXAMPLE**  One of the most notorious examples of a failed interface metaphor was "Bob," Microsoft's 1995 attempt to make a "friendly" user interface based around the metaphor of a home, rather than the more familiar metaphor of an office (see Figure 5.5). Though it failed partly because it had a number of clunky features, users also found the cutesy guides patronizing and the home metaphor unintuitive.

- *Links.* An implicit part of a site's navigation is hyperlinks, which take users to different parts of the site and outside the site. Part of the usability assessment for the site would include testing out many of the

**FIGURE 5.5** Metaphors that are too peculiar or creative make navigation more difficult, as Microsoft "Bob" demonstrated.

links to see if they're still live (dead links will lead to a 404 "Page Not Found" error). It might also involve performing searches (if the site has an internal search function) to assess the currency of the information provided on the site.

MindTap®
View Tiny
Lecture 4: The
Rhetorical Effect of
Website Layout

- *Layout.* How much white space does the site include? Is it designed using a grid? Does the page feel busy or calm, sophisticated or fun? How is the user invited to interact with it?

- *Color scheme.* See the discussion of the psychology of colors in Chapter 4. How do the colors of the site support or detract from the site's purpose?

    **EXAMPLE** Many corporate sites use blue, for instance, a color that suggests calm confidence and stability (and is thus intended to inspire trust in the customers who come to the company's site). See Figure 5.6.

- *Typography.* All sites (except the most poorly designed ones) should pay very close attention to the readability of text on the screen. But pay close attention to the mood created by the specific set of typography styles that the site uses. Most sites have a specific feel that they're going for.

## Examine the Interplay of All the Various Modalities

Does the site include video or audio components? What is the relationship between the text, navigation, the visuals, and the sound? How do these, along with the typography, layout and design elements, textual content, visual representations, and sound, contribute to the quality that one author refers to as "point(s) of view or voice" (Pauwels 257).

USbank.com

**FIGURE 5.6** Like most business sites, the U.S. Bank site uses a blue color scheme to convey an image of trustworthiness and stability.

**HOW TO...**  Analyze and Evaluate Websites

1. Identify the basic type of site.
2. Identify the site's owner, rhetorical purpose, and target audience.
3. Examine the site's content.
4. Study the site's interface (navigation, layout, color scheme, typography).
5. Examine the interplay of all the various modalities included in the site.

## Special Case: Analyzing Apps

Media experts contend that more computing now happens on mobile devices such as smartphones and tablet computers (such as iPads) than on traditional desktop or laptop computers. Mobile devices use two main forms of computing: mobile websites, or traditional websites designed to be read and navigated on a smaller screen, and applications, more commonly known as apps. Apps are pieces of software designed to allow the user to fulfill specific functions from their mobile devices: play games (e.g., Super Mario Run, Candy Crush Saga), conduct banking transactions, take and instantly share photos, message groups or individuals, check social media, find a date, look at restaurant reviews, and almost everything else imaginable.

Most of the questions above about website analysis apply to apps as well, with one significant difference: with mobile computing, users literally touch their way through the interface. Metaphors are important in apps, too, though they have a different set of considerations than websites because users navigate them through direct touch. Thus, experience with the real world affects a users' understanding of how apps operate.

**EXAMPLE**   If an app relies on a book metaphor, the user would expect to operate the app as if it were a real book, swiping left on the right-hand page to "turn" the page. The 2011 iPad Calendar app was called out for violating expectations of this real-world book metaphor. Though presented on the screen as a book, users couldn't actually turn the page by swiping in the expected way (see Figure 5.7). Instead, they needed to tap the tiny arrows on the bottom of the page. Worse was the iPad's Contacts app. It also used the book metaphor, but if users did swipe left, they risked deleting content. Both apps were instances of poor design on Apple's part because they defied users' intuitive, embodied habits of interaction with books.

**QUESTIONS TO ASK**  The Metaphors of an App

- What is the metaphor?
- If it's based on a physical object (a camera, a book, a bookshelf), does the app's metaphor support or violate users' experience of interacting with this real-world object?

**FIGURE 5.7** Violation of Intuitive User Expectations in the iPad Calendar App's Interface Metaphor

## ASSIGNMENTS

### Analyzing and Evaluating Websites and Apps

1. **Analyze the rhetorical tactics of a controversial site.** Using the earlier questions, analyze the website of a company that's recently been in the news in a negative way. Examples might include oil and gas companies (BP, Exxon), big banking companies, news sites and blogs with a distinctive political leaning (*Fox News* or *Breitbart* for the conservative side, the *Huffington Post* on the liberal side), organizations that promote controversial ideas (the National Rifle Association, Planned Parenthood), and controversial products (Monsanto, fast food companies like McDonalds or KFC, pharmaceutical companies, producers of high-fructose corn syrup).

   In writing your analysis, first search for recent news and opinion articles about the company and provide a summary of the main issues identified. Then answer these questions:

   - How does the site acknowledge the controversy, either overtly through its content or less explicitly through its interface?
   - What is the site's primary message, and how does this correspond to what's been said about the company in the news?
   - How does the company attempt to manage its reputation or reframe the issue through its website?

2. **Do a comparative analysis of competing websites**. Visit the
   websites of two groups with opposing views on the same topic (the
   most obvious example of this would be the websites of a Democratic
   and Republican candidate for the same political position). How does
   each construct its ethos differently? Using the framework for analysis
   above, consider the intended user and purpose of the site in light of its
   interface and the interplay of the various modalities. Write a brief essay
   explaining the differences in the sites.

3. **Evaluate the effectiveness of a website or app**. Imagine that you
   are a consultant charged with analyzing the effectiveness of a website or
   app. Using the earlier "Questions to Ask", first determine the intended
   audience and purpose of the site or app, and then evaluate its effectiveness in enabling the intended audience to achieve its purposes. Assess
   the content, the interface, and the interplay of the various modalities.
   Present the conclusions of your analysis and evaluation in a memo to
   the leader of the company or organization, along with recommendations for improving the site (or commendations for how well it meets
   the needs of its target audience).

   You might also recommend other audiences that the company
   might want to consider and provide suggestions for how the current
   site might be revised to meet the needs of these new audiences.

---

FOR REFLECTION

**Transferable Skills and Concepts**
How could you apply these concepts to multimodal compositions outside
the few types mentioned here (videos, websites, and apps)? For instance,
you might think about video or board games. What modalities are the
most important in games, and what sort of effect do they produce in
players? Write a journal entry analyzing a specific instance of a game or
another kind of multimodal composition.

## PART 3

# Rhetorical Production

# 6

# The Invitation to Rhetoric: Formulating Rhetorical Problems

## LEARNING OBJECTIVES

*By working through this chapter, you will be able to...*

- Understand why defining problems is an important rhetorical skill.
- Use the recursive process of noticing an "itch," questioning, and researching to identify everyday problems.
- Identify stakeholders and potential audiences for problems.
- Articulate your own ethos in relation to a problem.
- Describe a problem and give it presence.

MindTap®
View Tiny Lecture 5:
Event-Based and
Everyday Problems

Though it's likely apocryphal, Albert Einstein was supposed to have said, "If I had one hour to save the world, I would spend 55 minutes defining the problem and only 5 minutes finding the solution." This statement might seem counterintuitive at first—how could defining a problem (an extremely pressing one, if the fate of the world were at stake) be eleven times as important as solving it? On further reflection, though, it makes pretty good sense: What good is a solution if it's the solution to the *wrong problem*?

Although the word "problem" usually implies something negative or serious, for our purposes we might think of "rhetorical problems" more as *something that invites a response*. As with other invitations, you can always decline to participate, but at the very least it's important to recognize when you're being invited.

How do you know if a problem is ripe for rhetorical response? It can help to think of rhetorical problems in two categories: *event-based problems* and *everyday problems*.

# 6a Event-Based Problems

Sometimes the need for a response is quite obvious and pressing.

**EXAMPLES**

- As the maid of honor or best man, you're expected to give a toast at your friend's wedding.
- Your boss has asked you to write up a report of an incident that happened last week at work.
- As part of your grade for your environmental geography course, you're expected to write a paper about an international environmental problem.

As the name suggests, event-based problems arise from events: Something has happened or will happen that seems to call for some sort of communication. The wedding, work issue, and environmental geography course project mentioned above are all examples of event-based problems that arise from concerns that may be quite close to you personally.

Other event-based problems that seem to invite rhetorical action are more social and public in nature.

**EXAMPLE**  The state of Idaho recently passed a bill allowing "megaloads," trucks carrying huge 600,000-pound loads of oil-drilling equipment, to go on a winding highway through an environmentally sensitive area. The passing of the bill and later each megaload itself served as events that spurred protests and other types of rhetorical action from those concerned about the environmental impact, along with people living in the area through which the megaloads passed (Figure 6.1).

An event-based problem can also refer to an upcoming event, like an imminent decision about legislation.

FIGURE 6.1 A Megaload Protest

Wikipedia

**FIGURE 6.2**  Anti-SOPA Screenshot from *Wikipedia*

**EXAMPLE**  The Stop Online Piracy Act (commonly known as SOPA) was a bill introduced in 2011 by U.S. Representative Lamar Smith of Texas, designed to protect intellectual property on the Internet. The imminent vote on the bill prompted a wide range of rhetorical actions by opponents who contended that the bill threatened free speech and innovation. These included, most notably, a twenty-four-hour *Wikipedia* blackout: Users who tried to access *Wikipedia* during that time found only a screen with the message "Imagine a World without Free Knowledge," an explanation of why the site was protesting SOPA, and links where the users could go to register their objection to the legislation (Figure 6.2).

While event-based rhetorical problems typically are connected to singular events, often these events have roots in deeper rhetorical issues. The events themselves, though, provide a flashpoint and an obvious issue to organize rhetorical action around. (Think of how recent mass shootings in America provided a platform to discuss issues of the Second Amendment and mental illness diagnosis and care, for instance.)

 **QUESTIONS TO ASK**    **Event-Based Rhetorical Problems**

The following list of questions will help you to more specifically identify and articulate event-based rhetorical problems and will also help you generate ideas about a particular problem that may not be obvious at first glance. Note that not all the questions will be relevant to every event-based problem, but at least some should serve to spur your thinking about the rhetorical effects of the event.

- What is the event? Describe it in as much detail as possible, using the six journalistic questions: Who? What? When? Where? Why? How?
- Who are the stakeholders connected with the event, and what is at stake for them?
- What deeper, more wide-ranging issues are connected with the event?
- What negative effects could possibly result from the event?
- How has the problem been defined so far? Are the ways the problem has been defined shortsighted or wrong? In what way?
- Why do I find this problem interesting?
- What is my personal connection to the problem?

## ASSIGNMENT

### Tune in to Event-Based Problems

Many students struggle with what writing teachers call the "invention" part of composing, that is, coming up with topics to communicate about as well as things to say about those topics. Because they aren't brimming with ideas (especially for big projects that involve potentially lots of writing), students tend to panic and grasp at the first hot-button issue that they can think of. In Idaho, where I teach, these topics tend to be wolves (and their effects on hunting and ranching in the state), states' rights, gun control, and perhaps gay marriage, abortion, or immigration. Obviously, these are big, sticky, hard-to-deal-with issues, and they've been talked about to death—and for those reasons, they actually *don't* make the best topics for communication. Though there are still interesting angles one can take on these hot-button issues (for instance, if you have personal experiences that contradict a lot of the received wisdom and opinions out there), for the most part the argumentative ground is too well trampled, so students tend to end up simply repeating the arguments and positions of others. And that is boring, both for the communicator and for his or her intended audience.

Filling your metaphorical well (of ideas) requires becoming attuned to the number of events (and the differing interpretations of those events) that happen every day, everywhere. One way to do this is to start becoming a regular reader (or at least a skimmer of headlines) of local and national newspapers and some of the plethora of Web-based magazines and blogs that report on and editorialize about the events of the day.

Below is a list of the most popular online newspapers and news magazines:

- *The New York Times*
- *The Washington Post*
- *The LA Times*
- *The Wall Street Journal*
- *The Boston Globe*
- *The Chicago Tribune*

- *The Guardian*
- *Mail Online*
- *NBC News*
- *Yahoo! News*
- *Google News*
- *HuffingtonPost*
- *CNN*
- *BBC News*
- *MSNBC*
- *Fox News*
- *Slate*

Every day for one week, skim through three of the sites in the previous list, along with your college or university newspaper. On a designated page in your notebook, write down at least five examples per day of event-based rhetorical problems. The point of the assignment is to take a bit of time each day to acquaint yourself with the current state of affairs.

Once the week is up, bring to class a list of the ten most interesting event-based rhetorical problems you found. Share your list with a small group of classmates, listen to their lists, and compile the top five rhetorical problems (i.e., those that seem most ripe for response). Report the list that came from your group to the class as a whole. (Someone in the class should compile the problems on the board or as a separate list.)

Then, on your own, choose one of these problems (ideally, the one you'd like to work with more deeply) and answer the questions in the previous "Questions to Ask: Event-Based Rhetorical Problems" box.

## 6b Everyday Problems

Not all rhetorical problems arise from singular events. Many problems are subtler, recurring things that only become recognizable as problems over long periods of time. We might call these "everyday problems," to distinguish them from event-based problems.

Everyday problems require a special kind of rhetorical attunement and action. Noticing a problem is often, strangely enough, the hardest step. Partly this is due to human nature—people can live for a long time with bothersome things, especially if the cost of paying attention to and thinking about how to solve the problem seems too high. Problems come to you like a slight itch; they linger around the edges of your consciousness, becoming more persistent at times, fading away at others. The itch might be something that bothers you or a question that arises.

EXAMPLE   Maybe you've started noticing that being on *Facebook* a lot leaves you feeling kind of depressed. "Feeling depressed" would be the problem here, and close on its heels comes a question: "What is it about being on *Facebook* that leaves me feeling depressed, exactly?"

When you turn more direct attention to an itch or a problem, you'll find that there are questions behind this problem. These questions are valuable, because they can serve to guide you into a more formal process of addressing the problem through research. This in turn can refine your question and your sense of the rhetorical problem that you're attempting to articulate. In other words, defining problems is not a linear process, but a *recursive* one, as illustrated by Figure 6.3.

Because everyday problems tend to be subtler than event-based problems, identifying and articulating them might require more time and research. But you can help the process along by systematically considering all the aspects of your own "everyday" for the interesting problems that exist there. The first thing to do is categorize the different aspects of your life. Such a list might look like Table 6.1 (most of the problems listed here came from newspaper stories).

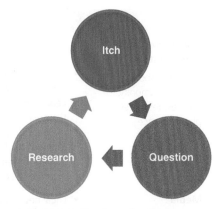

**FIGURE 6.3** The Recursive Process of Articulating Everyday Rhetorical Problems

**TABLE 6.1** Everyday Problem Catalogue

| GENERAL CATEGORY | EXAMPLE PROBLEMS |
| --- | --- |
| **School**<br><br>Academics, classroom issues, campus issues (student etiquette and behavior, faculty and administrator etiquette and behavior, rules and regulations, academic programs, infrastructure of physical campus) | • Incivility among students and toward teachers is on the rise.<br>• There is an increase in students using essay-writing services and other forms of cheating.<br>• Pay of administrators and coaches is high relative to that of faculty.<br>• Alcohol-related incidents in Greek organizations (e.g., sexual assaults, drunk students falling out of windows) have increased.<br>• There is a lack of recycling facilities on campus.<br>• Too many people are smoking near buildings on campus, and people who work in those buildings are complaining.<br>• The school has a consistently terrible football team.<br>• A steady decline in student enrollment forces schools to make decisions about which programs (academic or otherwise) to cut. |
| **Workplace**<br><br>Problems specific to your workplace and more general to the kind of work you do | • Students entering the workplace have unrealistic ideas about work.<br>• The minimum wage hasn't increased in ten years in your state, and this is negatively affecting many in your community.<br>• College students consistently undertip servers.<br>• You've noticed an increase in workplace bullying among women especially.<br>• The large chain restaurant you work for forces employees to deep clean with harsh chemicals. |

*(continued on next page)*

| GENERAL CATEGORY | EXAMPLE PROBLEMS |
|---|---|
| **Hometown/Local Community**<br><br>Concerns about quality of life, community, services, resources, physical space | • The city lacks bike lanes, and drivers are aggressive toward or unaware of cyclists.<br>• Your town has a serious meth problem, and it's beginning to spread to kids.<br>• People have parties in the woods and leave trash, damaging the area.<br>• A local factory is seriously hurting the local air quality.<br>• Many of the businesses in your neighborhood have gone out of business, and the street is full of empty windows with "For Sale" signs. |
| **Media**<br><br>Problems with the way news is reported, what is considered news, behavior on social media, etc. | • Local news wastes time on human-interest stories and weather, not "serious" enough.<br>• Ostensibly unbiased news source presents biased view of [choose your topic].<br>• Online behavior (e.g., increase in the number of "selfies" posted) indicates narcissistic behavior among your peers.<br>• You've recently noticed a lot of rude behavior online.<br>• The way that information is distributed and spread makes it difficult to get a solid, unbiased understanding of an issue. |
| **National** | • It feels like people with differing political views just talk past each other, with no hope of having a conversation.<br>• The United States has mediocre rankings in worldwide educational performance. |

## FOR DISCUSSION

The line between event-based and everyday problems can sometimes seem rather blurry. For instance, the water crisis story in Flint, Michigan (where levels of lead in the city water were at dangerously high levels), was picked up by the media in April 2014. But presumably the problems associated with lead poisoning had been evident for some time. So when did the everyday problem turn into an event-based problem? Brainstorm some instances of local everyday problems that then became events, and try to pinpoint when and how this shift happened.

## 6c Tasks for Defining Rhetorical Problems

Although these are numbered, think about them not as steps you need to follow one by one, but as tasks you need to do.

# 1. Do Research to Deepen Your Understanding of a Problem

MindTap®

View How to Video 4: Identifying a Rhetorical Problem

Identifying a Rhetorical Problem

Including research as a separate step misrepresents to an extent how recursive the process of research is. "Research" as it's usually talked about and practiced in college writing classes suggests one or two days in the university library looking up a combination of books, print articles, and Web-based articles, extracting quotes from them, then never looking back. But research as I'm talking about it here is a much more fluid, ongoing process. It's something that starts even before you've fully identified the problem, and it's a process that will continue while you're composing.

The assignment below will help you to compile and keep track of your research about a problem. In addition, you can also watch MindTap "Student Maker Video 1: Creating a Digital Research Scrapbook" for an example of the research process for one project. See Chapter 12 for more specifics about how to conduct research and integrate sources while composing.

## LONG-TERM ASSIGNMENT

### Keep a Research Scrapbook

Once you've identified a problem that you want to investigate in more depth, start a digital or physical scrapbook of everything you can find about your problem. This might include images, news stories, scholarly articles, public service announcements, analysis or feature stories, videos, *Facebook* conversations (you can take screen shots of these; you can also clip them with tools like Evernote), cartoons, podcasts, and anything else you can find on your topic. (See "The Recursive Steps of the Research Process" in Section 12a for some tips on how to find sources.) For digital scrapbooks, you might use a free tool like Evernote or a social media site like *Pinterest* or *Tumblr* to gather your sources. The image of the *Pinterest* board below (on the 2015 Volkswagen emissions scandal) shows what such a scrapbook might look like.

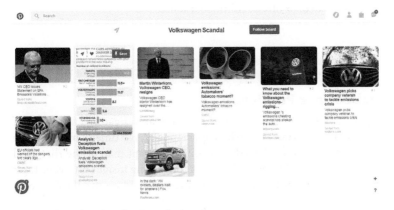

*Pinterest* board with collection of related sources.

If you have limited computer or Internet access, you can do the same thing with an actual scrapbook. Devote a notebook (or, if you want to get fancy, a scrapbook of the sort they sell in craft stores) to your issue. Print stories, images, cartoons, and whatever else you come across and tape them into the scrapbook. Make sure you leave room on the page to write a summary or brief reflection.

**MindTap**
View Student Maker Video 1: Creating a Digital Research Scrapbook

You'll need a way to categorize and organize sources in your scrapbook. Most blog sites and *Pinterest* allow you to tag your items (if you're already a *Twitter* user, you know that you can categorize items by #hashtags). Tags are keywords you can add to anything you post that help you to categorize and organize your sources. You can search through your sources with tags, and you can even create a "tag cloud" that lets you see all of your tags at once (this is a great way to get an overview of your subject). If you're using a paper scrapbook, you can physically tag pages with sticky notes or color-coded file tags.

You will need to collect a fair number of resources in your scrapbook before you start seeing patterns and useful ways to categorize the information you've found. But eventually, you want to develop a consistent way of tagging certain things so that you can go back and find those things when you need to.

**EXAMPLE** If you name a certain cuddly animal "koala" one time and "bear" another, a search on one term might not locate all the instances that you've collected.

Once you've gotten a better sense for what you're looking for, you can always go back and recategorize your information or just add more tags to meet your new organizational scheme. Tags are important not just for organizational purposes; they also give you a meta sense for the issue, which will help you with the next part of the assignment.

You should also comment on your sources as a way to help you better digest the material you're gathering. Comments might consist of a very brief summary and some key ideas if it's a text source or your thoughts about it if it's an image, video, or other multimodal source.

## ASSIGNMENT

### Visualize Your Problem

Once you've collected, tagged, commented on, and organized a number of different sources in your research blog/scrapbook, it's time to interact with them in a different way. You'll be creating a concept map of the rhetorical terrain of your issue. This is critical work for gaining insight into your topic and deciding where and how you might intervene. More specifically, you'll be delving into the sources you've collected and making maps of the following things:

- Topics
- Recurring themes and images
- Recurring terms or ways of talking about the issue
- Stories about the issue
- Feelings evoked in the sources that discuss the issue

Representing the problem visually can help you to see possibilities for intervention that you may have missed. There are many, many kinds of graphic organizers that can help you visualize a problem, including timelines, outlines, mind maps, and concept maps (for everything from mapping the impact of an event, technology, or individual, to analyzing a document). Concept mapping is a good way to provide a broad overview of a problem and to start spinning out possibilities for intervention. You'll be adding to this map later, so the important thing is that you leave room for expansion.

If you want to do a digital version of the rhetorical concept map, you can use an actual concept mapping program (there are several free versions out there, such as *bubbl.us*—you can find others by searching for "free concept mapping software"). You might also use the presentation software Prezi, which is intuitive and easily allows you to present information spatially. For an analog version, it would help to start with a large piece of sturdy paper, like poster board or watercolor paper.

## 2. Identify Stakeholders in a Rhetorical Problem to Help Define Your Audience

One basic question in diagnosing rhetorical problems (both event-based and everyday problems) is "who is this a problem *for*?" It's important to identify the **stakeholders**—all people and groups who have something to gain or lose—in a given problem. Identifying everyone who is affected by a given problem serves two purposes:

1. It helps you get a better sense of the problem's scope;
2. It helps you identify possible *audiences* to address in response to the problem.

To understand how identifying stakeholders helps provide a sense of a problem's scope, let's take an example from the earlier everyday problems list: the increasing numbers of students who pay for papers from Web-based essay-writing services. Thousands of these "ghostwriting" services exist (suggesting that business is booming), and newspaper articles exposing the sites have shown that even doctoral students will pay for someone else to write their dissertations.

## QUESTIONS TO ASK — Rhetorical Problem: Increase in Use of "Ghostwriting" Websites

| Who are some of the stakeholders in this problem? → | What is at stake in this issue for them? |
| --- | --- |
| The students who pay for essays to be written → | Their grades in the course are at stake—depending on their writing ability, they may get a better grade with a ghost-written essay. Their writing ability is also at stake, since they've lost the opportunity to practice writing. |
| Other students (who are writing their own essays) → | The fairness of the grading is at stake, as well as their perception of fairness if they find out that other students aren't doing the same work. |
| Professors → | At stake also is the professors' sense of how well the students are learning the course material, or whether they are meeting the outcomes for the course. |
| University administrators → | At stake is the perception of the outside world of the ethics and general academic quality of the university and, linked to this, the potential losses of funds and gifts by alumni and others. (For example, when a widespread cheating scandal was uncovered at Harvard, the university got a lot of negative media attention.) |
| Future employers of the students who paid someone else to write for them → | At stake is the ability of employees to successfully communicate, which not only affects the quality of the business overall but also requires extra time to train the employee to write effectively. |
| The ghostwriters and the owners of the sites who employ them. → | The writers themselves stand to make a lot of money from students who don't want to or can't write their own assignments. |

Just listing the people affected by the rhetorical problem of ghostwriting provides a clearer sense of who stands to gain and who stands to lose when students use these services.

**EXAMPLE**  You might choose to focus on the future employers of the students who used these services, arguing perhaps that they are the ones being cheated when they hire students who don't know how to write. Or perhaps you might find, through doing more research, that cheating is actually teaching these students skills that are valuable in today's business environment.

> ### FOR DISCUSSION
>
> With a partner, choose one rhetorical problem from Table 6.1 or use one of your own. Identify all the stakeholders and explain what's at stake for them in the issue.

## 3. Define Your Own Ethos in a Problem

Part of the process of articulating a rhetorical problem that seems ripe for some sort of intervention involves identifying the means that you have for responding to it. There are many, many possibilities for rhetorical intervention in any given rhetorical problem, but not all of us have access to these at any given time. "Access" means several different things. First, it refers to the networks of people you know and who know you. Access also refers to one's cultural position and the power that comes with that vis-à-vis a given rhetorical problem.

**EXAMPLE**  If you are a traditional college student (between 18 and 24 years of age), you may not have the worldly standing (in terms of job status, money, position in life) to speak believably to certain groups of people. However, you may have developed expertise and experience in other areas that would resonate with other groups of people. Planning effective rhetorical intervention requires thinking strategically about whom you might reasonably aim to influence and how you might most effectively do this.

Study the stakeholders in the rhetorical problem that you identified in the Discussion prompt above: the various people affected by this problem who also have some means to influence it.

Answer the following questions to help develop a sense of your rhetorical agency vis-à-vis the rhetorical problem that you've identified.

- What connection do I have with each of these groups? How do they view me?
- What experience and expertise could I mobilize to build credibility (ethos; see Chapter 1) with these groups?
- Given my cultural position relative to these groups, what might it be possible to accomplish on the rhetorical problem I've articulated?

It's important to keep an open mind and let your understanding of the problem evolve as you gather more information. What you initially thought were the worst effects of the problem might change as you discover more about it. You will also likely discover different groups of people who are affected by this problem.

The good news is that once you become skilled at identifying and articulating problems (and communicating about them), you become more attuned to other problems. Developing this attentiveness to problems is the beginning of what we might call "rhetorical consciousness."

## 4. Describe the Problem and Give It Presence

Convincing people that there is a problem that needs to be addressed (and that this problem is important to them in some way) is at the heart of a great deal of persuasive communication. Problem statements appear in some fashion in grant proposals, technical reports, opinion pieces, and professional presentations. Problems, really, are what engage readers and listeners, and when there is no problem in evidence, an audience might rightly think "why am I reading/listening to this?"

Simply through the process of gathering and categorizing sources for your research scrapbook, you've already begun to define a rhetorical problem. Even by seeing the juxtaposition of the titles of the various stories about the issue, as well as the point of view conveyed through the images and multimodal things that go along with the topic, you can start to get a sense for what's at stake (and for whom). Seeing and interacting with all this material will also start to give you a richer sense for how you think about the problem—what it is, and what sorts of rhetorical actions it might warrant. However, actually writing about the problem in a systematic and coherent way is the best way not only to think through a problem yourself but to convince your audience that it's a problem worth their attention as well.

To illustrate the need for an argument to have what he calls presence, the rhetorical scholars Chaïm Perelman and L. Olbrechts-Tyteca bring up a Chinese story about a king, who, seeing an ox on its way to be sacrificed, ordered that a sheep be used in its place. When questioned about his actions later, the king said that it was because he could see the ox and not the sheep—the ox was physically present in all its oxness, whereas the sheep at that point was an abstract idea to the king. With this story, Perelman points to the importance of consciously using techniques to help a reader visualize or feel a particular problem (similar to what Aristotle termed pathos). Such techniques are especially important for the mode of writing, which can have a distancing or abstracting effect.

How do you give a problem presence? As the word suggests, one critical element is to literally make problems present by calling things to a reader's attention—potentially a difficult task in an age of information overload, where attention is in short supply. As with the king and the ox, if readers don't see the problem clearly enough, it won't affect them. The next section gives you some ways to literally visualize your problem (through images and other sensory modes), but here we're focusing specifically on what you can do with what Perelman calls "verbal magic" to give your problem presence. The following Presence Generator will help you generate and organize your ideas.

Use the sources that you've already found to generate responses to the prompts. You might also use these questions as a guide for finding more information about your problem.

**HOW TO...**    **Give a Problem Presence**

1. Gather concrete, sensory evidence of the problem—as much as you can. Of course, not all of this will work for the audience you may intend it for, but it will at least help you get a more well rounded sense of the scope of

the problem. What are the visible manifestations of the problem? Where can you see the effects of the problem? On the physical environment or landscape? On human health or well-being? Does it have social effects? On education and schools, the ability of people to get or keep jobs? Look for anecdotes as well as statistics. Remember the ox!

2. Who is affected by the problem? Think of people, communities, places, things. How, specifically, are they affected?
3. When and where does the problem occur?
4. What are the short-term and long-term effects of the problem?
5. What does the world look like without the problem? What should it be like?
6. Why is it important that the problem be fixed? What would happen if we didn't solve the problem?

Now take a step back. Given the specific rhetorical stakeholders you've identified, why does this problem require immediate attention and action from them?

# 6d Articulating Rhetorical Problems through Writing: The Rhetorical Problem Statement

Writing that articulates problems can be an end in itself. For instance, a very common technical and professional writing task is a problem statement, used to clarify for all team members working on a project what exactly they are trying to solve. One business consultant, writing about why problem statements are necessary for businesses, asserts that most projects that fail have poorly written problem statements. Problem statements help put everyone on the same page. Even if the problem statement is directed at an audience external to a particular team working on a project, it serves to help both the reader and the writer clarify what is being talked about.

The problem statement that you'll be writing will serve to clarify a specific problem. However, here we'll be talking about analyzing a problem as a means to an end. It will be a stand-alone written statement, but it's meant to also serve as important invention work for future compositions. Once you've satisfactorily clarified what, for whom, and why something is a problem, you have an excellent basis for understanding better how one might intervene in the problem or work toward solving it.

Note that you are not arguing for how to *solve* the problem here—this is a problem *analysis* statement, not a problem-*solution* statement. However, writing it will help set you up for doing rhetorical intervention or arguing for particular solutions in subsequent assignments.

Think of the following not so much as steps that you need to follow in linear fashion but more as tasks that you need to work through and work through again in order to effectively define a rhetorical problem.

## Describe the Problem

To effectively describe problems, first start by answering for yourself the basic journalistic questions:

- For *whom* is it a problem?
- *What* exactly is the problem?
- *Why* is it a problem?
- *When* is it a problem?
- *Where* is it a problem?

It also helps to think of the situation in negative terms: For whom is this *not* a problem?

## Provide Evidence for the Problem

How do you know that a problem actually exists? Gather evidence that shows that the problem is *significant*, that it has negative effects on various stakeholders. These effects might be financial; they might involve a loss of mental or physical health, or even cause death. They might create bad feelings or in some other way affect the quality of life of these stakeholders. Use the "Keep a Research Scrapbook" and "Visualize Your Problem" assignments in Section 6c as a means of gaining a deeper understanding of the extent of the problem.

## Find Your Focus: Write a Problem Analysis Statement

An important task is to boil down the problem to one or two sentences (otherwise known as a thesis statement). A common technique used in technical or professional problem statements is to posit the difference between the world without the problem (i.e., your answer to #5 in the "How to Give a Problem Presence" box) and the world with the problem. Such a statement would read, "Things should be like X. Instead, they are like Y." The rest of the problem statement would be devoted to explaining what Y is and how it got that way. It should articulate what the problem is, for whom it is a problem, and why.

**EXAMPLES**  The thesis for your problem statement might take one of the following forms:

- X typically is not thought of as a problem. But here's why it is...
- X is generally considered to be a problem that affects this group of people (or this material thing). However, it actually affects (this other group of people or thing) far more interestingly...
- Everyone knows that X is a problem for this reason. But more interestingly, it's a problem for these reasons as well...

## Organize the Statement

You could use the questions in the previous "How to Give a Problem Presence" box to organize your problem statement. You might start with a vivid description of one manifestation or effect of the problem, present your thesis, enumerate the reasons and evidence for why it's a problem, and conclude by explaining how the world would be better if this problem were addressed.

As a specific example of how writers can add presence to arguments, examine how 21-year-old blogger Pippa Biddle defines the rhetorical problem of "voluntourism." Read the essay as an analyst—that is, not for whether you agree or disagree with her statements about voluntourism (you'll get a chance to do that in Chapter 7, "Responding to Rhetorical Problems with Arguments"), but rather for how she defines a specific problem and gives it presence. As you read, try to identify the effects that the post has on you as a reader.

## Example of Writing That Identifies a Rhetorical Problem

### The Problem with Little White Girls (and Boys): Why I Stopped Being a Voluntourist

#### BY PIPPA BIDDLE

White people aren't told that the color of their skin is a problem very often. We sail through police check points, don't garner sideways glances in affluent neighborhoods, and are generally understood to be predispositioned for success based on a physical characteristic (the color of our skin) we have little control over beyond sunscreen and tanning oil.

After six years of working in and traveling through a number of different countries where white people are in the numerical minority, I've come to realize that there is one place being white is not only a hindrance, but negative—most of the developing world.

Removing rocks from buckets of beans in Tanzania.

Pippa Biddle

In high school, I travelled to Tanzania as part of a school trip. There were 14 white girls, 1 black girl who, to her frustration, was called white by almost everyone we met in Tanzania, and a few teachers/chaperones. $3000 bought us a week at an orphanage, a half built library, and a few pickup soccer games, followed by a week long safari.

Our mission while at the orphanage was to build a library. Turns out that we, a group of highly educated private boarding school students were so bad at the most basic construction work that each night the men had to take down the structurally unsound bricks we had laid and rebuild the structure so that, when we woke up in the morning, we would be unaware of our failure. It is likely that this was a daily ritual. Us mixing cement and laying bricks for 6+ hours, them undoing our work after the sun set, re-laying the bricks, and then acting as if nothing had happened so that the cycle could continue.

Basically, we failed at the sole purpose of our being there. It would have been more cost effective, stimulative of the local economy, and efficient for the orphanage to take our money and hire locals to do the work, but there we were trying to build straight walls without a level.

Tying friendship bracelets during my first trip to the Dominican Republic in 2009

That same summer, I started working in the Dominican Republic at a summer camp I helped organize for HIV+ children. Within days, it was obvious that my rudimentary Spanish set me so far apart from the local Dominican staff that I might as well have been an alien. Try caring for children who have a serious medical condition, and are not inclined to listen, in a language that you barely speak. It isn't easy. Now, 6 years later, I am much better at Spanish and am still highly involved with the camp programing, fundraising, and leadership. However, I have stopped attending, having finally accepting that my presence is not the godsend I was coached by nonprofits, documentaries, and service programs to believe it would be.

You see, the work we were doing in both the DR and Tanzania was good. The orphanage needed a library so that they could be accredited to a higher level as a school, and the camp in the DR needed funding and supplies so that it could provide HIV+ children with programs integral to their mental and physical health. It wasn't the work that was bad. It was me being there.

It turns out that I, a little white girl, am good at a lot of things. I am good at raising money, training volunteers, collecting items, coordinating programs, and telling stories. I am flexible, creative, and able to think on my feet. On paper I am, by most people's standards, highly qualified to do international aid. But I shouldn't be.

I am not a teacher, a doctor, a carpenter, a scientist, an engineer, or any other professional that could provide concrete support and long-term solutions to communities in developing countries. I am a 5' 4" white girl who can carry bags of moderately heavy stuff, horse around with kids, attempt to teach a class, tell the story of how I found myself (with accompanying PowerPoint) to a few thousand people and not much else.

Some might say that that's enough. That as long as I go to X country with an open mind and a good heart I'll leave at least one child so uplifted and emboldened by my short stay that they will, for years, think of me every morning.

I don't want a little girl in Ghana, or Sri Lanka, or Indonesia to think of me when she wakes up each morning. I don't want her to thank me for her education or medical care or new clothes. Even if I am providing the funds to get the ball rolling, I want her to think about her teacher, community leader, or mother. I want her to have a hero who she can relate to—who looks like her, is part of her culture, speaks her language, and who she might bump into on the way to school one morning.

After my first trip to the Dominican Republic, I pledged to myself that we would, one day, have a camp run and executed by Dominicans. Now, about seven years later, the camp director, program leaders and all but a handful of counselors are Dominican. Each year we bring in a few Peace Corps Volunteers and highly-skilled volunteers from the USA who add value to our program, but they are not the ones in charge. I think we're finally doing aid right, and I'm not there.

Before you sign up for a volunteer trip anywhere in the world this summer, consider whether you possess the skill set necessary for that trip to be successful. If yes, awesome. If not, it might be a good idea to reconsider your trip. Sadly, taking part in international aid where you aren't particularly helpful is not benign. It's detrimental. It slows down positive growth and perpetuates the "white savior" complex that, for hundreds of years, has haunted both the countries we are trying to "save" and our (more recently) own psyches. Be smart about traveling and strive to be informed and culturally aware. It's only through an understanding of the problems communities are facing, and the continued development of skills within that community, that long-term solutions will be created.

# 6e Addressing a Rhetorical Problem: Public Awareness Campaigns

**Public awareness campaigns**, as the name suggests, aim to build awareness in the public for an issue that's unknown or misunderstood, but important. Public awareness campaigns aim to address rhetorical problems without advocating for a specific policy; for instance, they might want to stop people from texting while driving or promote parents reading to their children. As the name suggests, public awareness *campaigns* typically consist of rhetorical actions that occur on a number of different fronts.

**EXAMPLE** Consider Greenpeace's 2010 "Dirty Lie" campaign (Figure 6.4), aimed at informing the public about misinformation spread by the fossil fuel industry about the potential for alternative energy sources.

The "Dirty Lie" campaign is part of Greenpeace's larger "Global Warming and Energy" campaign. On the "Don't Believe the Dirty Lie" Web page, along with an explanation of the focus and purpose of the campaign, are several specific rhetorical actions aimed at raising public awareness:

- A 30-second public service announcement video.
- A poster (the one shown in Figure 6.4).
- A "Dirty Lie Factsheet" aimed at helping the target audience recognize the "dirty lie" when they hear it.
- A link to a social media campaign called "Help Call Out the Dirty Lie." This part of the campaign directly elicits audience participation. When participants see misinformation in the form defined by Greenpeace's "Dirty Lie" factsheet and other

**FIGURE 6.4** A Poster from Greenpeace's "Don't Believe the Dirty Lie" Campaign

campaign materials, they are supposed to repost the link via *Facebook*, *Twitter*, or the social bookmarking site *Delicious* with the hashtag or keyword "dirtylie." This sort of public awareness and action is intended to create a compilation of such stories. This not only confirms the prevalence of what Greenpeace has defined as "dirty lies" or deliberate misinformation but also makes the ostensible misinformation more visible for people to condemn or otherwise act upon.

- The opportunity to sign up for an RSS (Really Simple Syndication) feed that posts news and calls for action. Users can add RSS feeds to one central place (for example, a newsreader like MyYahoo, Bloglines, Feedly, or Digg) in order to read Web content from a number of different sites.

## ASSIGNMENT

### Create a Public Awareness Campaign

To create a public awareness campaign, first you need to adequately articulate a public problem that needs to be solved (this might be the problem you focused on earlier in your problem statement). An awareness campaign consists of these three things:

- A **campaign brief** that spells out the problem, audience, goals, message, and methods for evaluating your campaign.
- A **campaign kit** that describes in detail the specific campaign materials (typically 4–6 different types) and rhetorical actions that will be a part of your campaign.
- The **campaign materials** themselves.

This also could make an excellent group assignment, where a group writes a campaign brief together and then develops the materials for the campaign kit separately.

#### CLARIFY THE RHETORICAL PURPOSE OF YOUR CAMPAIGN: WRITING A CAMPAIGN BRIEF

Campaign briefs mainly serve as internal documents for organizations. They help to put everyone in the organization on the same page about the purpose, objectives, message, and audience, and provide a concrete document to refer to.

As the name suggests, campaign briefs are relatively brief (typically no more than three single-spaced pages). Along with an introduction that *identifies and articulates the problem* that the public awareness campaign will address (Sections 6c and 6d), they should contain sections, separated by headings, that answer these questions:

1. *Who is the target audience for your campaign?*

   Finding the appropriate audience for your campaign is essential. If you try to appeal to too broad an audience, your message will become diluted, and you'll waste time and resources. To find a focused audience, start by identifying all of the rhetorical stakeholders in the issue. As described above, the stakeholders include everyone who is affected by the issue in some way: those responsible for *causing* the rhetorical problem, those who are the *victims* of the problem, or those who must deal with the fallout of the problem in some capacity. Which of these groups of stakeholders is your real audience? Clearly identifying them will help focus your message. What current behaviors, thoughts, or feelings of this audience need to be changed? What are their main concerns and issues? What appeals might they be most responsive to?

2. *What are the measurable objectives of your campaign? How will you know if and when these objectives have been achieved?*

   Campaigns should not simply be scattershot attempts to address a problem. They should have specific, measurable objectives decided on beforehand.

   **EXAMPLES**   You might want to reduce the number of STDs reported on campus by 25 percent, or generate 250 new visitors to a website disseminating information about the problems with binge drinking, or increase the number of aluminum cans and glass bottles recycled by 15 percent, or raise awareness of the location and services of the campus Career Services office among students to 90 percent.

   Attaching a measurable objective to the campaign can help to focus your thinking about the best way to address the rhetorical problem. Of course, having a measurable objective suggests that you will actually need to *measure* your campaign's effectiveness in the evaluation stage of your campaign. So in your campaign brief you will need to incorporate plans for how to measure the effectiveness of your campaign.

3. *What is the specific message of your campaign?*

   The message should be short, simple, and memorable. It should be relevant to your audience, and it should provide clear actions for them to take.

   **EXAMPLES**   Here are messages from recent public awareness campaigns:

   - "Every year, tens of millions of sharks are killed." (Shark Alliance)
   - "He got life before he was even born." (The Sheriffs' and Recorder's Fund, about children born to convicted fathers)
   - "You don't have to be a celebrity to make a difference." (Unicef's TAP project, to provide clean drinking water for children)
   - "Travelling fruits cause pollution." (Friends of the Earth)
   - "Does he know about birds and bees?" (campaign to prevent uncontrolled breeding of cats and dogs)

4. *What credibility do you (or the institution whom you are representing) have regarding the topic of the campaign?*

This is a question of good old-fashioned ethos. (See Chapter 1.) What previous experience do you, the organization that you represent, and your partners have with the issue, and how will that affect how your audience perceives the materials?

**5.** *How will you evaluate the success of your campaign?*

Evaluating the success of your campaign is directly linked to the objectives section (see Question 2): You set measurable objectives, and then, after the campaign, you measure them. Typical evaluation measures include counting the number of requests for further information or tracking the increased traffic on the website associated with the campaign. You might also do a brief survey to assess changed attitudes or knowledge on the part of the intended audience for your campaign.

## CREATE A CAMPAIGN KIT: AN OVERVIEW OF RHETORICAL ACTION

A campaign kit is a detailed description of the actual materials of the campaign. It can be considered part of the campaign brief, that is, an internal document. Some organizations that are organized around advocacy purposes (Focus on the Family, Greenpeace, the World Wildlife Fund, Citizens United) collect awareness campaign materials on their websites. The kinds of materials included in a public awareness campaign kit depend heavily on the audience and topic, but some examples follow. Note that while I don't tell you how to develop each of the following campaign genres here, many of these are described elsewhere in the book. (See the associated chapters and page numbers for specifics.)

Along with events like press conferences and fundraising occasions, public awareness campaign kits might include any of the following genres:

 TEXTUAL GENRES (CHAPTERS 3 AND 13)
- Fact sheets
- Petitions
- Op-ed pieces
- Press releases

 VISUAL GENRES (CHAPTERS 4 AND 14)
- Poster campaigns
- Brochures
- Infographics
- Print advertisements

 **MULTIMODAL GENRES (CHAPTERS 5 AND 15)**
- Social media campaigns (*Facebook, Twitter,* etc.)
- Public service announcements: 30- or 60-second video or radio messages

- Websites that serve as resources to raise public awareness on an issue
- Public challenges/contests

To create your campaign kit, you need to think carefully about what rhetorical actions would reach the audiences you identified in the campaign brief. If one group of rhetorical stakeholders for your campaign is unlikely to have access to the Internet, for instance, you might consider focusing your attention on creating radio ads. Then, you'll create a document that details (typically with visuals) the materials that will be used in the campaign.

**EXAMPLE**  Many campaign kits, like the "Stand Up 4 Public Schools" example, are Web pages that contain links to the campaign materials.

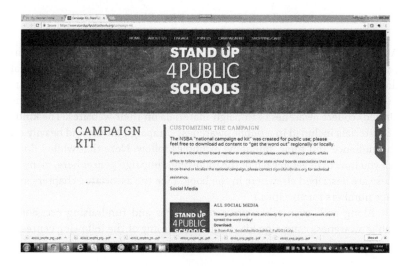

## DEVELOP YOUR CAMPAIGN MATERIALS

Once you've decided on a set of materials that will be the focus of your public awareness campaign, the next step is to actually create those materials (note: this may also be a semester-long assignment). The important thing to remember in developing a set of campaign materials is that they need to appear *unified*, both in message and in visual elements.

**EXAMPLE**  The "Stand Up 4 Public Schools" campaign has three different categories of campaign materials: a social media category, which includes downloadable *Facebook* and *Twitter* profile pictures, cover photos, and easily shareable campaign images; suites of ads featuring Magic Johnson, Montel Williams, Sal Khan, and Barbara Morgan; and online banner ads.

The ads all have unifying visual elements in the form of font, layout, and the National School Boards Association logo running across the bottom; the social media category uses a consistent and recognizable logo.

See Chapter 14, "Creating Visual Compositions," to understand how to create unified thematic visual elements in your campaign materials.

The "Stand Up 4 Public Schools" campaign ads have consistent messages and unifying visual elements.

## FOR REFLECTION

### Transferable Skills and Concepts

This chapter has focused mainly on problems that are important to the public. But how can you apply a rhetorical approach to other-than-public problems? Think about problems that are happening right now in your own life, for instance: with friends and family, or with questions about your beliefs, identity, religion, values, etc. How might you apply the tools discussed in this chapter to these very personal problems? Write a journal entry detailing a personal problem and think about whether or not the concepts discussed here (like "Questions to Ask: Event-Based Rhetorical Problems" in Section 6a, or "How to Give a Problem Presence" in Section 6c) help you develop ways to think through nonpublic problems.

# 7

# Responding to Rhetorical Problems with Arguments

**LEARNING OBJECTIVES**

*By working through this chapter, you will be able to...*

- Articulate the difference between the popular notion of "argument" and argument as a thoughtful, audience-centered response to a rhetorical problem.
- Explain the four stasis questions: fact, definition, value, and procedure.
- Show which stasis question is most important to an issue.
- Explain your motives for making an argument.
- Articulate the audience, purpose, and desirable outcomes for your argument.
- Be able to identify the most appropriate means (modality, medium, genre, circulation) for your argument.
- Make a claim that is well supported by reasons and evidence.
- Practice making written, visual, and multimodal arguments.

In June 2014, the gossip site *Deadspin* posted a story detailing an extreme, though regrettably all-too-familiar example of the current state of public discourse. An Australian radio station had posted a recipe for an impressive-looking, complicated "Amazing Rainbow Tie-Dye Number Surprise Cake" on its website. A commenter asked an innocent question about part of the procedure for baking the cake ("How long should I freeze the numbers?"), which provoked a slightly snarky comment from someone else ("till they are FROZEN"); which provoked an insult from another commenter ("If you were a real baker, you wouldn't be so rude"); and from there, it quickly devolved into what *Deadspin*, in recounting the thread, called a "comment apocalypse," in which commenters called others stupid (and worse), attempted to school each other on the meaning of the word "liberal," and accused other commenters of being fascists.

The cake fight may be an extreme example, but you've probably wit-nessed similar exchanges on yours or others' *Facebook* pages: A friend posts something inflammatory, another indignantly responds, and before you know it, someone has called someone else a Nazi. In everyday speech, exchanges like this are known as "arguments." However, these discursive abominations partake in a very narrow sense of argument, one likely to conjure up images of the late-night yelling of parents, endless bickering of antagonistic friends, or pigheaded politicians trading insults on a television "news" program. The linguist Deborah Tannen refers to this state of affairs as the "argument culture," an unpleasant place where every issue has only two sides, and public discourse often takes the form of participants on opposite sides shouting each other down with logical fallacies and other troublesome tactics. Argument as it's thought of in these situations is mainly about competitive debate, one-upmanship, or winning. Given these examples, it's no wonder that most people would rather confine their public discourse to talking about the weather or posting cat memes on *Facebook*.

# 7a Arguments as Inquiry, Not Fights

While polemics have their place, there are other, perhaps more productive ways to engage in public or academic discussions about serious topics. The way we're talking about argument in this chapter means something dif-ferent than ranting or shouting at each other from entrenched positions. In keeping with the language of the previous chapter, we might define **argument** as *using a process of inquiry to develop a response to a rhetori-cal problem*. Arguments in this sense aim less to win over or persuade an audience of a particular point than to arrive with that audience at a deeper understanding about an issue, one that will enable better decisions and stronger resolutions. Such an approach helps to create a richer, more com-plex view of any issue, one that's ultimately more productive for moving issues forward in a helpful way.

It's a bit misleading to have a separate chapter devoted to argument since all of the chapters in this textbook also have to do with argument. You make an argument (to an academic audience) about how a particular piece of communication is working when you do a rhetorical analysis; likewise, evaluations and proposals (discussed in Chapters 10 and 11) are among the most common types of arguments. Even functions like explaining and de-fining (discussed in Chapters 8 and 9), typically not thought of as argumen-tative tasks, rely on a wealth of different argumentative strategies. In this chapter, we'll focus on the *process* of developing an argument in response to a particular issue or rhetorical problem. Instead of coming up with a position first and then defending it against all comers, this chapter will give you the tools and procedures to take a more organic, audience-centered approach to building effective written, visual, and multimodal arguments.

## FOR DISCUSSION

Find a recent example on social media (on your own or a friend's page) where the discussion got so heated that people began calling each other names. Take a screenshot of the thread; then, with your neighbor or as a class, identify exactly where the discussion broke down.

## ASSIGNMENT

### Write an Initial Position Statement on an Issue, Then Question It

In Chapter 6, you defined a rhetorical problem, a process that described the problem and the rhetorical stakeholders in the issue. This involved, for the most part, keeping your own opinions on the matter out of it.

You might begin by graphically mapping out the issue for yourself with pencil and a big sheet of blank newsprint. Include in your map the different possible positions, the stakeholders who tend to hold those positions, and what reasons they may have for holding them.

#### PART 1

For this initial assignment, you will first clarify what *you* think about an issue by responding to the following questions:

- What do you already know about the issue?
- What personal experiences have shaped how you feel about the issue?
- Based on the above two questions, what opinions do you have about the issue?
- Why is this issue important to you?
- What else would you like to find out about this issue?

Then write your statement in the form of a paragraph that briefly introduces and explains the issue, states what you think about it, and explains why.

#### PART 2

But successful inquiry also requires that you see an issue from perspectives other than your own. So the second part of this assignment requires you to write a second statement that questions your initial position by trying to understand why others might disagree with you. To question your initial position, answer the following questions:

- How do people think differently from me about this issue? What other positions do people take?
- Why do they take these positions?
- How might my initial position on this issue be shortsighted? What might I not be considering?

- What about others' experiences might be different from my own, and how might this lead us to different conclusions on the issue?

Then write a statement that sympathetically explains one position on the issue that is different from yours (and with which you disagree). Explain the position, and explain who tends to hold this position. Explain (to the best of your ability and without critiquing) why they tend to hold this position and why, from their perspective, they are right and you are wrong.

Doing this exercise may feel awkward; in fact, it's supposed to. It will, however, enrich your perspective on the issue and really help you sympathetically inhabit someone else's point of view. It will also give you good ideas for counterarguments or other perspectives that you'll need to address.

# 7b Inhabiting an Idea: Arguments as Response

Many school assignments that ask students to take a position on an issue operate on the predominant notion of argument as war described earlier. To complete such assignments, students typically first decide what they want to say about a particular issue and then confine their required "research" to hunting for quotations from experts and other evidence that supports their position. They may ignore or suppress claims and evidence that disagree with their own position on the mistaken perception that it will weaken their argument. But there are two problems with this approach. First, students fail to develop a richer and more complex understanding of an issue because they spend all their time defending their position from the argumentative equivalent of a foxhole. Second, their arguments tend to be weak since the arguers hold blindly to one position without acknowledging its limitations. Not only would any audience with a better understanding of the matter fail to be persuaded by obviously one-sided arguments, but the arguer would have learned nothing from making the argument. The opportunities for a richer, deeper understanding of an issue would be lost.

To avoid this problem of arguing in a vacuum, it helps to think of arguments as always appearing in *response* to something else. For a truly effective rhetorical argument—one that builds identification with an audience rather than simply trumpeting views you already hold—you'll need to build your argument inductively, from the ground up. This begins with developing an understanding of the current conversation about an issue, or the rich social context from which arguments arise. Chapter 12, "Research: Composing with Multiple Sources," provides a process for identifying and researching the rich conversations out of which arguments arise. Figure 7.1 illustrates the steps involved in using arguments to respond to rhetorical problems.

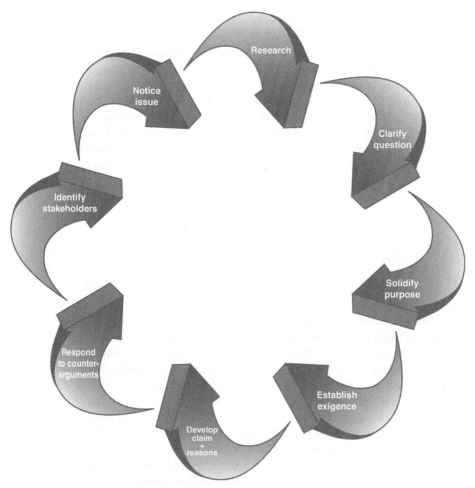

**FIGURE 7.1**  Steps to Responding to Rhetorical Problems with Arguments

## FOR DISCUSSION

News sites and magazines that allow comments after their stories are often valuable places to understand a multitude of perspectives on a given issue, including things you may have never considered.

Before class, go online to *The New York Times* or another website that your instructor recommends. Choose a recent story that strikes you as interesting, read it, and read through comments that appear after the story until you've identified at least five differing perspectives on the story or the issue it discusses. Ignore the comments from obvious trolls (these would include ad hominem attacks, name calling, or other attempts to provoke other readers; you may notice that smart readers will often call out trolls as trolls but refuse to engage with them). Write down the main point of the original story and at least five of these themes (you might even screenshot some of the comments that best represent those themes). What did these comments teach you about the issue? Did they change your perspective, and if so, how? Prepare to discuss your findings with the rest of the class.

## Using Stasis Theory to Clarify the Most Important Question

Even the most rabid, polemical arguments have a question at their heart. So the first thing to do is identify exactly which question your argument comes from. This in itself is not a cut-and-dried task. Sometimes the issue will arise from a very clear question. But sometimes in arguments, people talk past each other because they disagree over which question is being asked.

MindTap
View Tiny Lecture
Video 7: Using the
Stases to Think
through an Issue

**EXAMPLE**  Many lawmakers won't be persuaded by arguments for how to address the problem of climate change because they don't believe that climate change is real or that it can be addressed by human actions.

**Stasis theory** is a time-tested (i.e., 2000-year-old) strategy for helping to clarify which questions are most important to an issue. You might recognize the term "stasis" as the root of the term "static," meaning "to come to a standstill." And this is just what stasis theory refers to: the place where discussion of a topic gets stuck because no agreement can be reached. Stasis theory can be used both as a heuristic (a strategy for generating questions about a topic) and a framework to categorize what's already been said about an issue.

**QUESTIONS TO ASK**     **The Four Stasis Questions**

Stasis theory identifies four basic types of questions:

- Questions of **fact** (what happened?)
- Questions of **definition** (how can we classify it?)
- Questions of **quality** (how do we judge it?)
- Questions of **procedure** (what should be done about it?)

These questions build on each other. As Figure 7.2 shows, answers to the simpler questions must be agreed upon before more complicated questions can be addressed.

**EXAMPLE**  To take the example of climate change mentioned earlier, questions at the stasis of fact (is climate change actually happening?) must have

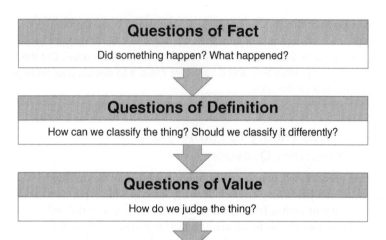

**FIGURE 7.2** Questions to Ask about an Issue Using Stasis Theory

satisfactory answers before questions of procedure (what should we do about it?) can be adequately addressed.

Each question-generating stasis is described in more detail below. To clarify how the stases relate to each other, we'll use them to examine a burning issue, one that affects the daily lives of many people at the university: the quality of snacks in campus vending machines.

### Questions of fact: Does/did something exist or happen?

Questions of fact attempt to establish whether something exists or whether something happens. Not surprisingly, many scientific arguments are arguments of fact (think of the arduous efforts of some scientists to prove the existence of global warming, and the equally arduous efforts of other scientists to provide evidence for the opposite). Arguments attempting to establish facts typically rely on empirical evidence.

**EXAMPLE** For our vending machine example, questions of fact would involve establishing answers to questions like: How many vending machines are on campus? What kinds of snacks do campus vending machines currently sell?

### Questions of definition: What is it?

Building from questions of fact, questions of definition ask "what is it?" or "how can it be classified?"

**EXAMPLE** For our vending machine example, questions of definition would include: What qualifies as a healthy snack?

## Questions of quality: How do we judge it?

Settling questions of quality requires evaluation arguments, which are discussed more in Chapter 10. But suffice it to say here that "quality" goes beyond good and bad. We can determine if a thing is desirable or undesirable, better than something else, reasonable or unreasonable, or a variety of other kinds of qualities—anything that necessitates a judgment.

**EXAMPLE**  For our vending-machine snack issue, questions of quality might include the following: If it's decided that the snacks in vending machines are unhealthy, is that really a problem? People might argue that the food in vending machines was never meant to be used as replacements for actual meals, for instance, and therefore the relative nutritional quality shouldn't matter as much. Others might argue that unhealthy snacks are bad because they cause sugar crashes and ultimately hurt people's productivity.

## Questions of procedure: What should be done about it?

Questions of procedure are where the figurative rubber hits the road. The unstated assumption (or warrant) of procedural arguments is that questions of quality have already been settled. Those involved have already evaluated the thing or event and have moved on to making decisions about the best way to respond to it.

**EXAMPLE**  If we decide that (a) the snacks are unhealthy and (b) that having so many unhealthy snacks available is a problem, then what should we do about this? (Questions of procedure in this case are probably less interesting, as the only reasonable course of action would be for the vending company to include healthier snacks.)

While the stases are good for generating questions, they can also serve as a framework for gathering evidence for your argument.

**EXAMPLE**  To argue that the vendor should include more healthy snacks, for instance, you will need to establish the percentage of healthy versus unhealthy snacks currently available in machines across campus (fact), define what makes a snack healthy (definition), evaluate the current quality of snacks in vending machines and establish why the lack of healthy snacks is a problem (quality), and argue for the vending company to change its selection (procedure).

However, note that the point of viewing an issue through the lens of stasis theory is ultimately to understand which question is most at issue. Thus, while it's useful to examine an issue using all the stasis points to generate questions and evidence, you'll likely find that one stasis in particular is the sticking point for that issue, that is, the one that needs the most careful attention and argument.

**EXAMPLE**  The most relevant point for our vending machine problem is probably that of quality. One can imagine arguments that people on campus aren't supposed to be getting nutrition from vending machines, but rather that the machines should be full of fun snacks that can serve as a welcome distraction from studying, teaching, or working. And likewise, counterarguments could be made that because there are no stores within easy walking distance of campus, vending machines are obligated to have things other than specialty snacks for students, faculty, and staff who don't want to eat in the cafeteria.

## FOR DISCUSSION

As a class, choose one of the following topics (all contemporary college issues) and use the four stasis questions to generate as many questions as possible about the issue. Decide which of the questions you generated seems to be the most important or contentious, requiring deeper investigation. If you have time, you might begin brainstorming what sorts of research might be required to answer the question.

Issues (you can use one of these or generate your own as a class):

- Cheating (plagiarism) among students at your university
- The increasing prevalence of campus carry laws
- Hazing in Greek organizations
- Student debt and predatory loan companies
- The ethics of unpaid student internships
- The lack of female students in STEM (science, technology, engineering, and math) majors
- The lack of parking on campus
- Mental health issues (e.g., depression, anxiety, self-esteem problems) among students on campus
- The lack of diversity on campus, or the lack of understanding about what constitutes diversity
- The so-called hook-up culture among college students, which accepts and encourages casual sexual relationships
- Grade inflation on campus

## ASSIGNMENT

### Use Stasis Theory to Map an Issue

This can be either an analog (paper-based) or a digital assignment.

For the analog version, get a piece of poster board, or paper of a similar size, and write on it "fact," "definition," "quality," and "procedure" at well-spaced-out positions. Read each of the sources you've collected in your research scrapbook (see Chapter 6) and/or from initial research on the issue, and decide which stasis seems most relevant. Under the appropriate stasis category on the poster board, write down some brief details of the argument and the name of the source.

For the digital version, you can add tags ("fact," "definition," "quality," and "procedure") to your sources on *Evernote* or *Pinterest* (whichever tool you're using for your research scrapbook).

After you've done this for at least a dozen sources, it should be clear at which stasis (or multiple stases) the arguments seem to be collecting.

Then write answers to the following questions:

- Which stasis point seems most relevant to the issue? Where do the arguments about the issue seem most intense?

- Are those who are arguing at this particular stasis missing something important at one of the other stasis points? Perhaps others think the question is settled at a particular stasis point, but you see it differently (for instance, maybe most arguments about the issue are arguments about procedure, but you think the issue needs to be *defined* differently).

- Which positions on the issue do you find most compelling or believable? How do these positions conflict with other positions?

## Identifying Your Position

Once you've clarified the question that seems to be the most relevant to the conversation about an issue, you'll need to begin thinking more carefully about the audience and purpose of your argument. This will in turn help you begin to plan your claim and reasons and gather appropriate evidence for your argument. Begin staking out your position by answering the following questions.

### Why is this issue timely?

Why is it necessary or relevant to engage in dialogue about this issue right now? Like many people, you probably feel very strongly about certain topics. But if you were to indiscriminately make arguments about them—even strong, compelling arguments—to anyone who will listen, at any point in time, people would probably start to avoid eye contact and duck into buildings when they saw you coming. We have words for those who rant, spout off about, and beat the dead horse of their pet issue no matter the circumstance, among them "bore," "pedant," and "buzzkill." To avoid being one of these people—and to hone your rhetorical skill—it's critical to be attuned to *when* and *where* arguments about a given issue may be appropriate.

### What is your motive for arguing?

What is at stake for you in making an argument about this issue? What has led you to care about this issue? How is it congruent with your personal beliefs and experiences? What do you have to gain or lose? Why does it matter to you?

## What is your purpose for arguing?

What do you hope to accomplish in making this argument? What is your goal? Purpose is deeply related to motives, but motive has more to do with your motivations (what prompted you to be interested in the topic in the first place), whereas purpose has more to do with your end goals, or what you hope to accomplish in making the argument.

In the previous chapter, you worked on defining a specific problem as significant, which is itself a kind of rhetorical argument. Now you're going to take that argument one step further in order to not just show its significance but also to *transform* the situation in some way.

**EXAMPLES**

- To address people's faulty beliefs about the situation
- To convince them of the limitations of the status quo
- To posit positions that haven't been thought of (or at least that haven't been widely circulated) about the problem
- To redefine the problem, or change how it's typically seen or understood
- To make a judgment about some aspect of the problem and encourage others to accept your way of seeing it
- To prompt people to take some sort of action on the problem

## Who is the intended audience for your argument?

Who do you hope will respond to your argument? Who are you talking to, and what are *their* narratives, experiences, and beliefs that may be different from your own? In Chapter 6 you worked on defining the stakeholders for a specific event-based or everyday rhetorical problem (Section 6c). Now, you need to think more specifically about which of these stakeholder groups you'd like to engage in a deeper discussion. This will be the audience for your argument.

Audiences are typically grouped according to whether they'll be resistant, supportive, or neutral toward your position. Though this may be a rather blunt instrument, it will at least help you think about how you'll select material for your argument and how you'll organize that material. To ascertain your specific kind of audience, work through the following questions.

---

**QUESTIONS TO ASK**   **Understanding Your Intended Audience**

- What might the audience already know, think, and feel about the rhetorical problem?
- How would the achievement of your purpose for arguing affect them? What do they have to gain or lose? What beliefs, experiences, and narratives might they have that might make them resist your understanding of the situation?
- What common ground do you already have?

---

## What are the most appropriate means of communication (modality, medium, genre, circulation) for your argument?

There have always been venues for arguments available to the ordinary citizen, but now for those with an Internet connection, the options have increased exponentially: Arguments can be made not only textually, but also visually and multimodally. Part of the process for entering a conversation is deciding by what means one should do so. This depends not only on your own individual talents and proclivities, but also on how and where the conversation seems to be taking place, and how you might best reach your desired audience. (See Chapter 2 for more about the means of communication.)

## What are the outcomes and consequences of your position?

What sorts of actions would or could follow from your position? Are those actions possible? Are they desirable?

## What reasonable objections might there be to your position?

As rhetorician Richard Fulkerson explains, on any complex issue, those who have differing positions are bound to have some good arguments. The job of a good arguer is to show that even though these positions are valid, they don't negate the arguer's own claim. "The purpose of argumentation in a free society," Fulkerson argues, "is to reach the best conclusion possible at the time" (43). Acknowledging and graciously addressing other positions does not weaken your own position; rather, it actually strengthens your argument in the eyes of your audience, for several reasons:

- It shows that you've done your research and that you have a broader perspective on the issue than if you only knew what you thought about it.
- It shows both big-mindedness and confidence in your own position. Taking other positions seriously and writing sympathetically about them, even if you later argue that they're an insufficient way to consider the topic, is bound to draw your listeners closer, even if they resist your position.

### HOW TO... Identify and Evaluate Counterarguments or Differing Positions

- Identify reasonable objections to your position. Describe these positions as neutrally and fairly as you can. Demonstrate in what contexts these positions might be valid.
- If you disagree with these objections, explain their shortcomings as neutrally and objectively as possible, and why your own position is valid (and in what contexts).
- Explain what your positions might have in common.

| Issue | | Sample issue: the lack of healthy snacks in vending machines |
| --- | --- | --- |
| Timeliness of issue | → | It's the start of the school year, so students, faculty, and staff are suddenly on campus much more often than before. Since 65% of them frequently don't anticipate their hunger, they don't bring food from home and so are forced to rely on food provided on campus, like that in vending machines. |
| Motive for arguing | → | I want better, healthier snacks to be provided in the vending machines because I've been persuaded by information saying that eating processed foods that are full of fat and sugar is bad for me. |
| Purpose of argument | → | To convince members of the campus community to recognize the problem and email the vending machine company to request better snacks. |
| Intended audience | → | Members of the campus community and the people in charge of corresponding with the vending machine company. |
| Appropriate format | → | Probably a simple email to University Housing (or whoever is in charge of the vending machine contracts) would suffice. If that doesn't work, a letter to the editor of the campus paper urging students and others to contact the vending machine people to request better snacks. |
| Outcomes and consequences | → | To have healthier, more nutritious snacks available to the campus community. |
| Reasonable objections and counterarguments | → | Food in vending machines isn't meant to replace meals. Individuals who don't approve of the choices available should bring their own food from home instead of trying to dictate what appears in the machines. |

## FOR DISCUSSION

Once you've decided on an initial position you want to take on an argument, use your classmates to help you identify potential positions that differ from yours. Pitch your idea to a partner or to the whole class; their job is to come up with as many reasonable objections as possible. Write these all down, then decide together what would be an appropriate acknowledgment and response.

## Structuring Your Argument

Once you've clarified the most important question at issue in a conversation and done more work to stake out a position by fleshing out the motive, purpose, audience, consequences, and reasonable objections and counter-arguments to your position, it's time to begin working on actually building your argument.

All good arguments consist of some basic elements:

- A *claim*,
- good *reasons*, and
- *evidence* to support those reasons.

### Claim

A **claim** is a very condensed version of your overall argument, the basic message (see Chapter 1) that you want to convince your audience of. You might think of the claim as the answer to the question you arrived at through thinking about stasis theory.

**EXAMPLES**

- *Claim of fact*: Ninety-five percent of the snacks in the campus vending machines are highly processed and high in sugar and fat.
- *Claim of definition*: The snacks in the vending machines are mostly junk food.
- *Claim of quality*: It's wrong to have only junk food available in the campus vending machines.
- *Claim of procedure:* There should be healthier snacks available in campus vending machines.

All of the claims in this group are arguable, meaning that people could reasonably disagree with them (except, perhaps, for the claim of fact). For this particular case, they also build on each other. If you were to make a proposal claim (arguing that your audience should take action on this issue), implicitly or explicitly you may have made a claim of quality, definition, and fact as well.

### Reasons

If the claim asserts a position, **reasons** explain why an audience should believe this assertion. A claim says, basically, "You should believe this thing I'm saying," and reasons say "because of these valid, persuasive things that I'm saying." Reasons serve as assertions or proof that the claim made is true.

Reasons logically follow the claim and a "because" statement (even if the "because" is implied): "The vending machines should have healthier snacks *because* junk food isn't good for students, and because students who live on campus often rely on these vending machines since there are no convenience stores close by."

The reasons you provide must be acceptable to your audience.

EXAMPLE  A vending machine company, in reading your reason that junk food isn't good for students, might respond with indifference since it only matters to the vendor whether students buy the snacks or not. A more persuasive reason for this audience would be to suggest that more people would buy snacks from vending machine if they could get food that was healthier.

## Evidence

Arguments live and die based on whether the evidence provided is acceptable to the audience. If a claim and reasons are the basic structure of an argument (say, the "bricks"), evidence is the mortar that holds the structure together. If an audience sees the evidence you provide as weak or irrelevant, your argument won't be persuasive.

There are two basic types of evidence: primary and secondary. **Primary evidence** refers to information gathered directly about the topic through observation, interview, experiment, questionnaires/surveys; it can also include newspaper accounts of an event. **Secondary evidence** provides interpretations of primary evidence through scholarly articles, newspaper analyses, and op-ed columns, all of which analyze and provide particular points of views about the event or topic.

Evidence works differently depending on the mode, genre, and circulation of the argument. But generally speaking, all evidence can be judged on the basis of three criteria:

1. The evidence is *sufficient*. The more complex and contentious the subject of your argument, the more your audience will expect to see proof that you've read deeply and thought through all possible angles of your subject. This includes evidence in the form of the inclusion of counterarguments. Also, all of your evidence should come from a source that doesn't stand to gain from the argument you make.

2. The evidence is *relevant*. In the course of your research, you'll undoubtedly find many things that strike you as interesting or important. However, they may not have much to do with the overall point of your argument or what your audience will accept.

3. The evidence is *accurate*. Your evidence should come from sources that would be best equipped to provide the information.

EXAMPLE  The claim that campus vending machines should include healthy snacks is not particularly complex; nonetheless, the audience will expect to see adequate support for your claim. To convince a vending machine company that its machines should include more healthy snacks, you might demonstrate that most of the snacks in the machines are unhealthy by counting them and reporting on their nutritional content (primary evidence). You might cite reliable, unbiased sources that outline the negative effects of eating processed foods on concentration and academic performance (secondary evidence). Reliable sources in this case would include scientific studies by professional nutritionists, reports by the National Institute of Health, and other neutral sources. You should avoid sources written by natural food companies or other sources that gain by people not eating processed foods. You might do a simple poll of everyone who uses that building to find out what kind of snacks they prefer (primary evidence), and also cite evidence that while they have the reputation of not paying much attention to their health, college students today are more focused on eating well (secondary evidence).

It should be said here that there are many, many bad and silly arguments out there, rife with logical fallacies, confirmation bias, questionable evidence, and references to Hitler and Nazis. (See the wonderful *An Illustrated Book of Bad Arguments* for a compendium of these, complete with funny pictures.) Though it's good to be aware of the many ways arguments can go wrong, if you follow the inductive process of making and responding to arguments detailed in this section, you're less likely to make these sorts of bad arguments and more likely to argue in ways that draw your audience closer, even if they may initially resist your position.

# 7c Written Arguments

In academic settings, written arguments are by far the most familiar forms you've likely encountered and produced. Your literary analysis, history paper, and organic chem lab report are all examples of written academic arguments (albeit with very different conventions). Written arguments, of course, rely on the linguistic modality as the primary one; they require that you spell out in language all aspects of your claim, reasons, and evidence. This section discusses some common academic and public arguments you're likely to encounter both in college and out of it.

## Response (Reaction) Papers

The response paper, sometimes called a reaction paper, is a genre used in almost all academic disciplines, as well as in public. Response papers draw on multiple skills and abilities that are highly valued in academia:

- The ability to read a text closely and attentively
- The ability to fairly and accurately summarize someone else's position

- The ability to gracefully integrate someone else's ideas and words with your own
- The ability to identify what's interesting or valuable about a text
- The ability to formulate a response that sheds new light (and potentially therefore generates new knowledge) about the original text's topic or argument

Generally speaking, people who respond to texts in real-world or public situations already know what they think about the text they're responding to, so their response comes rather easily (though, judging from the quality of many responses, sometimes it would have been better for them to think in more depth about their response or to take some time to understand better what the original piece was saying). However, often in academic contexts, you're put in the somewhat unusual rhetorical situation of being asked to write a response to a text that discusses an issue you don't know much about or that you may not have strong opinions on (yet). In fact, doing the work required to produce a good response often helps you understand more about what's at stake in a particular issue about which your professor is asking you to develop an opinion.

Characteristics of rhetorically savvy responses include the following:

- They are careful to respond to what the original piece is actually saying, and not to something that the responder unfairly reads into it.
- They respond to what's important about the piece, not to a tangential or seemingly trivial detail; or, they attempt to convince their audience why what might initially seem like an unimportant detail actually deserves attention.
- They add something *new* to our understanding of the original piece. They can do this in *several* ways:
  - They can show that the original argument is flawed because of something that the piece ignores or fails to consider.
  - They can show that the assumptions of the original piece are wrong.
  - They can show flaws in the argument of the original piece.
  - They can enlarge the scope of the original piece by showing how the author's point also applies to situations outside of the context or examples he/she provides.
  - They can show that the piece is important or argue that it needs more attention because it contradicts most people's beliefs about the matter.

The grounds for a response come from knowledge of the topic or of something related to the topic. Thus, especially if it's a topic you're unfamiliar with, doing some preliminary research by searching on the topic (or, in the case of an online article, clicking on the links provided) would help. Of course, if you've done a rhetorical analysis and the summary of the article, you'll already have done this.

Because the response essay is such a familiar genre in academia, the genre has stabilized into fairly conventional organization. The following box describes the elements that are typically included in these kinds of essays.

## HOW TO...   Structure a Response Essay

The structure below (especially the title) is meant for academic essays specifically, but a slightly modified version can be used in all forms of responses.

1. A two-part title with a colon. The part before the colon should be written to catch a reader's attention and to convey a sense of the argument. The part after the colon should help a reader understand the purpose of the essay. Since you're writing a response essay, the logical second part would be "A Response to [the author's name, or the title of the article, or the author's name AND the title of the article]."

2. An introduction. Like all introductions, this should engage the reader with a clear sense of the rhetorical problem that the essay addresses. You can do this in several ways:

   • Provide an interesting anecdote or a startling fact about the topic of the essay you're responding to (as long as it's related to the response you plan to make).

   • The direct approach. Start immediately with your response to the article: "Laura Hudson's article about social media shaming provides some interesting examples, but the way she thinks about how people behave on social media is problematic."

3. Because written responses (especially academic ones) are usually fairly brief and focused, the introductory paragraph usually includes a thesis statement. (See Chapter 13 for an explanation of how to write a thesis statement.) The thesis statement should acknowledge the original article's argument, make a claim about that argument—whether it is accurate, shortsighted, wrong in some way, insufficient, etc.—and provide reasons for why.

4. A summary of the article. (See Chapter 3 for an explanation of how to write a summary.)

5. Your response to the article. This is the body of the paper, which will articulate the reasons and evidence.

6. A conclusion that asserts what/how we should think about the article.

# An Annotated Academic Response Essay

The title clearly indicates the writer's point, as well as the document's genre (a response).

## You Better Teach Your Boys to Cry: A Response to Chitra Ramaswamy

### BY MARTHA MENDEZ (STUDENT, UNIVERSITY OF IDAHO)

In the intro, the writer starts with a saying that all readers would know, followed by a surprising (and sassy!) reversal. This acts as a good hook to keep people reading.

"Sugar and spice and everything nice." Excuse me, but no. I'm a 5'4" woman who has a lot more than just sugar in my personality. If you want sugar, go bake some cookies.

Here the writer clearly follows up on her first paragraph by stating her take on gender stereotypes; she also gives the point of the paper in a thesis statement (highlighted).

Note that the writer clearly states the author and title of the article she's responding to.

Gender stereotypes make my blood boil. Men are men, and women are women, but both are human. Chitra Ramaswamy's recent article "How a Sexist T-Shirt Harms Us All" demonstrates how gender stereotypes are both common and harmful to everyone. While I support Ramaswamy's conclusion, I would like to extend her argument by taking the time to examine the effects that one specific gender stereotype has had on men specifically.

In these two paragraphs, the writer summarizes the original article.

In her article, Ramaswamy, who is British, discusses the pervasiveness of gender stereotypes in Western culture. She talks about an advertisement for Gap t-shirts, in which a girl is displayed as a social butterfly while a boy is portrayed as a future genius. In contrast, she points out other companies, that, unlike Gap, are making appropriate accommodations to avoid gender discrimination: Sainsbury, for instance, has stopped labeling costumes for a specific gender, and Hamleys is leaving behind its pink and blue signs.

But Ramaswamy also discusses how gender stereotyping happens beyond the media: For instance, she recalls a specific experience where she had gone to the store to buy a little stroller for her son, as a tool to help him learn to walk. The saleswoman commented that she had never seen a boy with a stroller before. Through sharing her frustration with this situation, Ramaswamy also acknowledges that everyday individuals living everyday lives are guilty of discriminating based on gender as well.

The writer identifies specifically what she wants to respond to (what was lacking in the original article), and how she wants to respond to it.

This and the next paragraph provide evidence of the harmful effects of gender stereotyping on men, which the original article doesn't discuss.

However, Ramaswamy doesn't adequately discuss the effects of this pervasive gender stereotyping on men specifically, and so I've found several examples from other articles that extend her point. For instance, Andrew Reiner, author of "Teaching Men to Be Emotionally Honest," recalled seeing a video clip of a boy toddler getting his first vaccination. In the video, when the young boy begins to cry, the father responds by telling his son, "'Don't cry!... Aw, big boy! High five, high five! Say you're a man: 'I'm a man!'"" (Reiner). After watching this video, the author acknowledged "how boys are taught, sometimes with the best of intentions, to mutate their emotional suffering into anger" (Reiner).  Reiner concluded by stating that when we mislead boys into believing that they must block out their emotions, there are unfortunate repercussions that follow.

Likewise, in her article "Here's How (and Why) to Help Boys Feel All the Feels," Lena Aburdene Derhally, a psychotherapist, shares how she has seen this specific stereotype cause a lot of damage in her own patients:

> What stands out to me when counseling men is that much of their struggle with anxiety, depression, and relational trouble has a connection to the inability to understand and process their feelings. This is largely to do with the messages that start in childhood, not only from the family but often from peers and the community. Issues of rage, anxiety, depression, and unhealthy coping mechanisms like heavy drinking often manifest when men don't understand their feelings or don't give themselves permission to have them.

The argument that stereotypes are harmful to our society is reinforced when Derhally shares that "suicide rates are four times higher in men than in women." How absolutely devastating is that? Our men are killing themselves because we as a society have burned the stereotype that men are not supposed to be emotional into their skin. By telling our boys that they cannot cry, we are teaching them that we would rather have them kill themselves and bleed blood than show their emotions.

Chitra Ramaswamy was correct in her original argument: Gender stereotypes are prevalent today and the stereotypes hurt all genders. But this is especially true for men. The truth is this: When we tell men they cannot cry, we restrict their outlets for emotions. Without this outlet, their coping mechanisms are limited to unhealthy drinking habits or suicide. Therefore, if we want our boys to live, we need to tell our boys to cry.

*In this concluding paragraph, the writer summarizes her response to the original article, and ends with a pithy restatement of her main point.*

## WORKS CITED

*Because this is an academic response paper, the writer uses a common academic citation format.*

Derhally, Lena Aburdene. "Here's How and Why) to Help Boys Feel All the Feels." *The Washington Post*, 1 Oct. 2015, *www.washingtonpost.com*. Accessed 26 Oct. 2016.

Ramaswamy, Chitra. "How a Sexist T-shirt Harms Us All." *The Guardian*, 2 Aug. 2016, *www.theguardian.com*. Accessed 17 Oct. 2016.

Reiner, Andrew. "Teaching Men to Be Emotionally Honest." *The New York Times*, 4 Apr. 2016, *www.nytimes.com*. Accessed 26 Oct. 2016.

## ASSIGNMENT

### Write an Academic Response Essay

1. Read the following argument, an editorial from the *St. Louis Dispatch* about fake news. Write a formal response to it in the form of an academic response essay as described and demonstrated earlier in this section. **Note:** if you don't want to respond to this, you can also find your own written argument to respond to; this could be a blog post, an op-ed piece, or an article in a scholarly journal. It could also be an argument related to the topic of your research scrapbook (as described in Chapter 6).

## Editorial: Readers, Not Censors, Keep Fake News from Spreading

### By the Board, St. Louis Post-Dispatch (MO)

Fake news is disruptive, disturbing and confusing, but that doesn't mean it should be censored. The duty of separating fact from fiction, opinion from observation, news from nonsense lies with the news consumer, not some corporate or government word-police force.

The dissemination of false information became an issue during the presidential campaign, with President Barack Obama saying it was a threat to democracy and liberals contending that Donald Trump, now the president-elect, was the main beneficiary of its distribution.

On Monday, a man was arrested in Washington, D.C., for firing an assault rifle in a pizza restaurant. He apparently was acting on fake news reports that the restaurant was operating a child abuse ring led by Hillary Clinton and a top campaign aide.

Fake news is an equal-opportunity menace. Liberals and conservatives alike are misled by it, and people on both sides have distributed it. Readers are the only ones who can prevent it from gaining credibility and artificially skewing public opinion.

Experienced news consumers usually can spot fake news easily. But items often gain acceptance as fact because humans are hardwired to seek agreement and embrace literature that confirms biases. It's often assumed that if something is posted on the Internet or circulated in email groups, it must be true.

Consuming news in the Internet age requires heightened discipline and a different set of tools. It means seeking out different points of view and relying on verified information from credible news outlets.

Much fake news gains circulation via social media, particularly *Facebook* and *Google*. The Internet giants, concerned that their platforms are used to spread lies, are making some changes. That's good, but a slippery slope could lie ahead if filtering turns into censorship.

*Google* plans to ban websites that host fake news from using its online advertising service. That helpful approach would remove the profit motive that often drives fake-news purveyors.

The problem is hardly new. Sensationalized reporting known as "yellow journalism" became part of the newspaper-circulation wars in the late 1900s between Joseph Pulitzer, the founder of this newspaper who later went on to buy the *New York World*, and his rival, *New York Journal* publisher William Randolph Hearst.

A more modern example is the *National Enquirer*.

Professional journalists get things wrong, but rarely intentionally. Reputable news organizations promptly run corrections when errors are found. Multiple layers of editors help ensure that personal biases are filtered out of news reports. The professional journalist's goal is to present only the facts to news consumers. It's a firing offense for any professional journalist to intentionally falsify news.

The information environment is overwhelmed with options, including bad sources that have no business being taken seriously. News consumers who share fake news, without verifying the source, only help multiply the misinformation problem.

---

## Responding to Arguments in Public

While academic response writing is something you're likely to encounter at some point in your college career, as a citizen you also have a number of tools available for response to more public issues that are close to your heart and interests. Whether it's leaving a comment on a news story (perhaps to defend the original article against what you see as a misinterpretation by another commenter) or writing a letter to the editor of your college or home-town newspaper to support, correct, clarify, or disagree with something published by that newspaper, it's important as with any sort of communicative act to stop and think about what the problem is, who you're writing to, your purpose in writing, and how the audience might see you.

### Letters to the editor

Letters to the editor are one of the most easily accessible forms of civic participation. There's a long-established, mature mechanism for publishing letters that's fairly easy for average citizens to participate in, and there's a built-in audience for the letters in the form of the newspaper readership.

Writing a letter to the editor of a journal or magazine to respond to a particular story published by that journal or magazine is a time-tested, familiar means of public writing, one that has existed long before the Internet. In fact, prior to the existence of the Internet and social media, letters from readers were one of the few places people could make their opinions known in a public forum.

Because the letter to the editor is such a familiar genre, it's easy to forget how rhetorically interesting it is. There are two basic types of (good) letters to the editor: letters that respond to something that recently appeared in the paper, and letters that make a point about something that's happening in the town, region, or state that directly relates to readers. However, successful or good examples of letters to the editor also demonstrate awareness of a broader rhetorical situation—while they are responding to a specific text, they also aim to persuade readers. (Open letters, which are discussed later in this chapter, embrace this rhetorical purpose even more explicitly.)

Letters to the editor are short—typically a max of 250 words for local and regional papers, and a max of 150 for larger papers. Longer is not better, in this case.

Following are tips for writing letters to the editor.

- The most important thing is to *read the paper*. As the Chapter 2 discussion of context mentions, I can always tell when the local university English students are doing Letter to the Editor assignments because suddenly there will be multiple letters on topics that haven't been recently discussed in the paper and are irrelevant (or not clearly relevant) to what's happening locally. Your invention process for writing a letter to the editor for a local paper should include reading that paper for several weeks beforehand and getting a sense for what issues are discussed and important to the community. You should also read the paper to get a sense for the format of the typical letter to the editor of that publication.

- The next most important thing is to *focus*. You should have a very clear reason or exigence for writing, and you should make only one point per letter. Otherwise you may end up producing what I think of (not very kindly, I admit) as "crazy cat lady" or "local character" letters, which throw an entire grab bag of problems at readers ("And here's another problem with the Republicans!" "And here's another reason you need to read your Bible!") but present no clear reason for writing other than to spout off.

- Be concise, and use only verified facts to support your point.

- Write to the literacy level and style of that publication (this goes back to the first tip). Be polite and civil, and avoid overstating your point.

## FOR DISCUSSION

1. Read the following article and the letter to the editor that responds to it. What aspects of the article did the letter respond to? Which did it ignore? Do you think the response was reasonable?

## *Philadelphia Inquirer* Opinion Piece and Letter to the Editor

### Commentary: With Gorsuch, Don't Judge the Book by Its Cover

**BY GEORGE PARRY**

*George Parry is a former federal and state prosecutor who practices law in Philadelphia.*

"The biggest damn fool mistake I ever made." So said President Dwight Eisenhower of his decision to appoint Earl Warren chief justice of the United States.

In the 1930s, Warren had been the tough district attorney of Alameda County, Calif. In 1938, after campaigning against Franklin Roosevelt's New Deal, Warren was elected California's attorney general. There followed three consecutive terms as that state's Republican governor.

Significantly, in the immediate aftermath of the Pearl Harbor attack, Attorney General Warren had been instrumental in the internment of his state's peaceful, law-abiding, and industrious Japanese American population. In 1942, as these American citizens of Japanese descent were being arrested and robbed by the government of their businesses, bank accounts, and homes, Warren publicly condemned them as "the Achilles heel" of law enforcement's efforts to prevent alien subversion and sabotage. He explained that "when we are dealing with the Caucasian race, we have methods that will test [their] loyalty," but not so the inscrutable Japanese Americans who, in Warren's estimation, could not be trusted.

In 1943, then-Gov. Warren vociferously opposed the parole of any internees since, "if the Japs are released, no one will be able to tell a saboteur from any other Jap. . . . We don't want to have a second Pearl Harbor in California. We don't propose to have the Japs back in California during this war if there is any lawful means of preventing it."

In 1948, Warren ran for vice president of the United States on the Republican ticket led by former Manhattan District Attorney and New York Gov. Thomas Dewey. They lost to Harry Truman in a stunning upset of Trumpian proportions. But by 1953, Dewey, acting on behalf of President Eisenhower, was vetting candidates for federal judgeships. So it was that Dewey, the racket-busting prosecutor, recommended to Eisenhower the appointment of Warren, another tough law man, to be chief justice of the United States.

Poor Ike. Neither he, Dewey, nor anyone else saw it coming. For inexplicably, despite his well-established law-and-order credentials, once he became chief justice, Warren built and led the coalition of justices who radically transformed the Supreme Court into an activist liberal super legislature that championed the rights of criminal defendants, ignited the civil rights revolution, and paved the way for the judicially created progressive social engineering that has followed.

Most notably, in the 1954 case of *Brown v. Board of Education*, Warren prevailed upon his colleagues to render a unanimous decision declaring an end to racial segregation in public schools. Even Justice Hugo Black, a former member of the Ku Klux Klan, joined in this decision.

*Brown* set off a firestorm of outrage and civil disobedience throughout the segregated South and put Eisenhower in the disagreeable position of having to enforce a legal mandate with which he personally disagreed. But when Gov. Orval Faubus and the Arkansas National Guard barred the entry of nine black students into Little Rock's Central High, Eisenhower sent the 101st Airborne Division to push aside the Guardsmen and integrate the school, literally at bayonet point.

Warren's unpredictable reincarnation and Eisenhower's resulting consternation are not unique in our history. After Abraham Lincoln appointed Salmon Chase to the court, the new justice found unconstitutional the law by which Lincoln was financing the ongoing Civil War. Not only was this a vexing ruling in time of war, it was truly astounding given that Chase, as secretary of the treasury, had helped write the very law that he then declared illegal.

Similarly, Theodore Roosevelt came to deride his court appointee Oliver Wendell Holmes as having a backbone weaker than a "banana." Harry Truman concluded that his appointee Tom Clark was "a dumb son of a bitch." Ronald Reagan appointed Justices Sandra Day O'Connor and Anthony Kennedy, who, to put it mildly, failed to perform as advertised. A nominee of Franklin Roosevelt, the liberal law professor Felix Frankfurter, migrated to the right once he was on the court. Most recently, Chief Justice John Roberts stunned conservatives by saving Obamacare from legal oblivion.

The list goes on, but you get the idea.

Now President Trump has nominated Neil Gorsuch to membership on the court. He appears to be a reliably conservative jurist, and odds are that he will remain so as a justice of the court.

At his confirmation hearing, we can expect the usual anguished parsing of his written legal opinions, school records, public and private utterances, and exploration of his background and resume. Given the distemper of the times, there undoubtedly will be the usual rancorous psycho drama that attends such proceedings, including the standard semihysterical predictions of societal collapse should he be confirmed.

But all of the senatorial blather both pro and con about the nominee will be nothing more than a theoretical discussion of how he might vote once he is on the court. Interesting, no doubt, but until the nominee is facing an actual case with specific facts and real legal issues presented by able advocates, there is no way to even remotely approximate which way he or any other member of the court will decide any given dispute.

For as Warren and so many others have demonstrated, when it comes to Supreme Court nominees, sometimes what you see isn't what you get. We may think we know how a Justice Gorsuch will rule, but, if Eisenhower, Reagan, Lincoln, both Roosevelts, and any number of other dead presidents were here, they might well beg to differ.

### Letters: Writer revealed his bias in calling civil rights laws "social engineering"

#### VIEW OF CIVIL RIGHTS TROUBLING

George Parry's statement regarding the decisions that enabled the Civil Rights Act and the Voting Rights Act as "progressive social engineering" tells you all you need to know about his perspective on judicial appointments ("When new justices defy expectations," Feb. 5). It used to be a totally bipartisan, extremely centrist tenet that these accomplishments were long overdue and essential to the country moving forward to fulfill its full promise, but the center has been blown up by the far-right takeover of the Republican Party.

Judge Neil Gorsuch's rulings on multiple well-known cases leave no doubt that he will realize his self-characterization as a Scalia clone. In light of the theft of this Supreme Court seat from President Obama and Merrick Garland, an actual centrist judge, there is similarly no doubt that his nomination should have been rejected not only by each and every Democrat, but also by those few supposedly centrist Republicans who meekly acquiesced to the thievery.

**JOE MAGID, WYNEWOOD**

2. Find the Letters to the Editor/From Readers section of your local print newspaper (usually located in the Opinion section), print magazine, or an online newspaper like *The New York Times* or *Washington Post*. Choose one letter to the editor that is responding to an article, and find the article that it's responding to. Read both, and make some notes about the features you notice about the letter-to-the-editor genre, using the questions about genre in Section 2d. Bring the letter and the article to class, and prepare to categorize the different rhetorical purposes that readers have for composing letters to the editor. (Or your instructor might ask you to do this as an out-of-class activity instead.)

## ASSIGNMENT

### Write a Letter to the Editor

Write a letter to the editor in response to an article from your research blog/ scrapbook. (You can respond to either an opinion article or a news story, perhaps one that you think misrepresents the problem in some way.) If you're having trouble formulating a response, consult the list of rhetorical purposes for composing letters to the editor that your class generated in the discussion prompt earlier. Your letter to the editor needs to be directed at the editor of the source from which the original article came. Make sure you follow the guidelines for letters to the editor set by that publication—these are usually on the same page as the actual published letters. Everyone in the class should read each other's letters and decide which are the best three and why—these letters should be submitted for publication.

#### Open letters

The genre of the open letter has been around for a long time. The Pauline epistles in the Bible are some of the earliest examples of open letters. Open letters are kind of like letters to the editor on steroids. They are similarly addressed to one person (though lately open letters have been addressed to groups of people or even objects), and they draw on the conventions of letter writing, like directly addressing the ostensible recipient. But they flout the circulation conventions of traditional letters or their digital counterpart the email—both of which are delivered to a single person—by being published in a public forum. Thus, they serve as a form of public response to that person's (or group's, or object's) actions, characteristics, or ideas.

Perhaps the most famous serious open letter of the twentieth century was Dr. Martin Luther King, Jr.'s "Letter from Birmingham Jail." King wrote "Letter from Birmingham Jail" in response to an open letter directed in part at *him* by eight white clergymen in Birmingham, Alabama. The clergymen's letter, called "A Call to Unity," argued against King's and his followers' tactics of civil action, arguing that instead of street protests that could potentially incite "hatred and violence," Negroes should argue for their civil rights through the court and legal systems. King's response, published in several places a month or so after the clergymen's letter, is a masterful example of the open letter form. He responds directly to each of the points made by the clergymen's letter, but uses that as a jumping-off point for more complete and eloquent statements (to an audience widely understood to be white moderates of the time) about the need for civil rights.

Thus, one main rhetorical function of the open letter is to make arguments to a wider public under the guise of response to a specific entity. Recent notable examples fulfilling this rhetorical function include an open letter by *Google* to the public arguing for the importance of net neutrality, and Michael Pollan's (author of *The Omnivore's Dilemma*) open letter to "the next Farmer in Chief" that argued for better national agriculture policy. The example of the following letter, written to Microsoft by the start-up *Slack .com*, which bills itself as a "messaging app for teams," is really aimed at reassuring Slack's customer base, which Microsoft, by releasing competing software, is presumably trying to poach.

Perhaps because of the new ease in publishing, the open letter has gained in popularity—so much so that the site *The Morning News* felt obliged to publish a cheeky "Open Letter to Writers of Open Letters" making fun of the genre. ("We need to have a talk, under the illusion of its taking place in private but actually for anyone to read. Also, the talk will be unilateral and you will never respond to it. Ready? It doesn't matter, because I'm not listening to you!")

## Example of a Serious Open Letter: *Slack.com* to Microsoft

### Dear Microsoft,

Wow. Big news! Congratulations on today's announcements. We're genuinely excited to have some competition.

We realized a few years ago that the value of switching to Slack was so obvious and the advantages so overwhelming that every business would be using Slack, or "something just like it," within the decade. It's validating to see you've come around to the same way of thinking. And even though—being honest here—it's a little scary, we know it will bring a better future forward faster.

However, all this is harder than it looks. So, as you set out to build "something just like it," we want to give you some friendly advice.

First, and most importantly, it's not the features that matter. You're not going to create something people really love by making a big list of Slack's features and simply checking those boxes. The revolution that has led to millions of people flocking to Slack has been, and continues to be, driven by something much deeper.

Building a product that allows for significant improvements in how people communicate requires a degree of thoughtfulness and craftsmanship that is not common in the development of enterprise software. How far you go in helping companies truly transform to take advantage of this shift in working is even more important than the individual software features you are duplicating.

*Communication is hard, yet it is the most fundamental thing we do as human beings.* We've spent tens of thousands of hours talking to customers and adapting Slack to find the grooves that match all those human quirks. The internal transparency and sense of shared purpose that Slack-using teams discover is not an accident. Tiny details make big differences.

Second, an open platform is essential. Communication is just one part of what humans do on the job. The modern knowledge worker relies on dozens of different products for their daily work, and that number is constantly expanding. These critical business processes and workflows demand the best tools, regardless of vendor.

That's why we work so hard to find elegant and creative ways to weave third-party software workflows right into Slack. And that's why there are 750 apps in the Slack App Directory for everything from marketing automation, customer support, and analytics, to project management, CRM, and developer tools. Together with the thousands of applications developed by customers, more than six million apps have been installed on Slack teams so far.

*We are deeply committed to making our customers' experience of their existing tools even better, no matter who makes them.* We know that playing nice with others isn't exactly your MO, but if you can't offer people an open platform that brings everything together into one place and makes their lives dramatically simpler, it's just not going to work.

Third, you've got to do this with love. You'll need to take a radically different approach to supporting and partnering with customers to help them adjust to new and better ways of working.

When we push a same-day fix in response to a customer's tweet, agonize over the best way to slip some humor into release notes, run design sprints with other software vendors to ensure our products work together seamlessly, or achieve a 100-minute average turnaround time for a thoughtful, human response to each support inquiry, that's not "going above and beyond." It's not "us being clever." That's how we do. That's who we are.

We love our work, and when we say *our mission is to make people's working lives simpler, more pleasant, and more productive,* we're not simply mouthing the words. If you want customers to switch to your product, you're going to have to match our commitment to their success and take the same amount of delight in their happiness.

One final point: Slack is here to stay. We are where work happens for millions of people around the world. You can see Slack at work in nearly every newsroom and every technology company across the country. Slack powers the businesses of architects and filmmakers and construction material manufacturers and lawyers and creative agencies and research labs. It's the only tool preferred by both late night comedy writers and risk & compliance officers. *It is in some of the world's largest enterprises as well as tens of thousands of businesses on the main streets of towns and cities all over the planet.* And we're just getting started.

So welcome, Microsoft, to the revolution. We're glad you're going to be helping us define this new product category. We admire many of your achievements and know you'll be a worthy competitor. We're sure you're going to come up with a couple of new ideas on your own too. And we'll be right there, ready.

**— YOUR FRIENDS AT SLACK**

As the "Open Letter to Writers of Open Letters" exemplifies, open letters can also be used to entertain. The literary journal *McSweeney's* has a whole catalogue of funny open letters ("Open Letters to People or Entities Who Are Unlikely To Respond"), including "An Open Letter to People Who Judge My Single, Post-College Lifestyle," "An Open Letter to People Who Take Pictures of Food with Instagram," "An Open Letter to the Leader of the Ant Nation," and "An Open Letter to Pumpkin-Flavored Seasonal Treats."

## Example of a Funny Open Letter

### An Open Letter to Recent College Grads Who Are Already Paying Their Own Phone Bills

**BY JENNA BARNETT**

Dear financially independent recent grad,

You inspire and shame me with your financial autonomy. The Internet, which must know that your parents do not pay for your phone bill, should reward you for your 4G independence.

I hope you post throwback photos on Wednesdays with no social media pushback. I hope Taylor Swift gives you random, wise advice on *Tumblr*, and that you never forget to cancel your *Amazon Prime* free trial before they charge you for the whole year. I even hope you use the Hefe filter for an *Instagram* of an old barn outside of Austin with the caption "#NoFilter" and get away with it—you deserve it.

You deserve so much. Maybe you don't come from a middle-class background that allows for privileged millennial dependency. Maybe you majored in something practical in college like accounting or computer programming (but if you started a lucrative porn site that further promotes and fetishizes the patriarchy, I'm excluding you from this letter). Maybe you even went to a liberal arts school and majored in film studies or creative writing but you gave up on your dreams just in time to pay your first phone bill.

Perhaps you don't even have a smartphone because they are too expensive. (How expensive? Don't ask me.) If you are in fact a dumbphone user, I hope it is not the sliding kind—or worse, the touch-screen kind that gives the mere illusion of Internet access.

Let it be a flip phone.

Let the satisfying, resounding click that your flip phone makes as you end each tele-conversation sound like a door closing on your adolescent parasitism. I hope the smallness of your phone in your pocket leaves room for layers upon layers of dollar bills.

But most of all, I hope you revel in this flip phone's durability—that you literally throw it into the air, over the heads of your friends who are living below the taxable income, above the dining room router that you're not taking advantage of, right up next to the ceiling where your financial stability and moral superiority rightfully reside.

**IN AWE,**

**JENNA**

P.S. You registered for Obamacare without even calling your parents for help, didn't you? Didn't you?

## FOR DISCUSSION

Compare the serious and the funny open letters in this section (or find your own). Jot down notes about the features of the open letter genre (use the Genre Analysis questions in Section 2d to generate ideas). Discuss your findings with your instructor and classmates. As a class, compile a list of the genre features of open letters.

## ASSIGNMENT

### Write an Open Letter

Write an open letter on the topic of your research blog/scrapbook to someone or something related to the rhetorical problem you're investigating. Use it as an opportunity to respond to someone or something specifically while also schooling your readers about something related to your topic. Use the list of genre features generated by the class discussion to help you with the structure, style, and content of your letter. Your open letter might be addressed to one of the following entities:

- A famous (or infamous) person (An Open Letter to Angelina Jolie, Pope Francis, that guy at the grocery store who takes up two parking spots, etc.)
- A group or type/categorization of people (An Open Letter to People Who Wear Axe Body Spray, to club bouncers, to mustache wearers, etc.)
- An idea or concept (An Open Letter to Adulthood, to long-distance relationships, etc.)
- An object or thing (An Open Letter to Times New Roman, to the spider in my bedroom, etc.)

### Responding with comments to blogs and news stories

It's become a truism that the comments sections after news stories and blog posts (on sites that allow them, which are many) are often much more interesting, funny, and lively—albeit also potentially infuriating and offensive—than the story or post itself. Some sites, like *Jezebel*, *Lifehacker*, and *Gizmodo*, along with *Reddit*, *Slate*, and *Daily Kos* explicitly acknowledge the comments as part of the story itself, so that the story and its attending comments feel much more like a conversation than a traditional one-way delivery of media content. Commenters on these sites can earn top or respected commenter badges by the frequency with which they comment and earn "likes" from the site's other commenters and readers. These badges and the commenting activity with which they earned them boosts their credibility and visibility among readers on the site, thereby garnering a kind of fame. With the number of unique visitors to such sites (over 36 million a month, according to some estimates), it's easy to see why people would want to earn such credibility.

Actually engaging in these lively conversations by adding your own comments can be somewhat intimidating, though. Many of the commenters on these sites, especially the top ones, are not only very smart, but also appear to view conversation as something of a blood sport (especially when it's around sensitive topics like race and hot-button issues like gun control), and can hence be somewhat ruthless. Before you actually engage in commenting, then, you'll want to understand the written and (usually) unwritten rules of engagement in this community. Understanding these requires more than anything else simply spending some time on the site, reading comments on different stories.

## FOR DISCUSSION

Go onto *Reddit, Slate, Jezebel, Lifehacker*, or *Deadspin*. Choose several recent stories and read the stories and all the comments that appear after them. Approach these stories as though you're an anthropologist studying a group that you don't know much about. As you read the comments, think about the following questions:

- What is acceptable and not acceptable in conversation? (You might see some unfamiliar terminology, for example, "concern trolling." If you run across what seem to be insulting terms with which you're unfamiliar, Google them.)
- Which comments get the most likes (or stars, or recommendations, or whatever means the site uses to promote comments)? What about these comments seems to be favorable? Do the comments that get the most likes have anything in common?
- Which comments get the most negative response? Which are simply dismissed? (By the logic of how most of these sites' technology works, these comments would end up near the bottom.)

## ASSIGNMENT

### Entering the Discussion

This assignment is split into two parts: first, you will provide a summary and analysis of an original news story or blog post and the reader comments that follow it. Second, you will write and post your own comment in response to the post.

First you'll need to find a story that you want to focus on. Read the story and the comments after it. Write a very brief summary of the story, then provide a rough categorization of the various comment themes and explain what you've learned about what's appropriate or acceptable (you can do this part by answering the questions in the "For Discussion" prompt above).

Second, prepare to enter the discussion by commenting on the story yourself. Keep in mind what are considered to be acceptable approaches and topics. Post the comment, and keep track of the reactions it gets! Take a screenshot of the posted comment for your instructor.

## 7d Visual Arguments

Visual arguments no less than written ones pervade modern life: From graphics (photos and drawings) that underscore points in written texts (as Chapter 4 discusses), to advertisements on the Web, in magazines, and on billboards, visual arguments are everywhere. But they function very differently from written arguments in several ways:

1. Visual arguments aren't linear. For written arguments, audiences are obliged to read from left to right, top to bottom, to absorb the argumentative moves being made. But visual arguments affect the viewer in a more spatially dispersed fashion. The viewer's eye may be drawn to a particular image or part of the image, then move around to other images or parts of the image in order to make sense of what message the image is attempting to convey.

MindTap®
Student Maker
Video 2: Designing
a Logo

2. Visual images convey meaning through a *semiotic* dimension: That is, images are laden with culturally specific social meanings and significations (though as media theorists Gunther Kress and Theo van Leeuwen argue, the "dominant visual language" is now heavily influenced by the globalization of Western mass media).

## FOR DISCUSSION

1. Look at the three images below (generated from typing "rain" into the site *Shutterstock.com*). What are each of the photos saying about rain? What judgment about rain is each of them implicitly making?

azem/Shutterstock

Niyom Napalai/Shutterstock

Derek Croucher/Photographer's Choice/Getty Images

2. Come up with your own list of terms; these might be emotions (fear, anger, happiness), or abstract concepts like patriotism or pride, or concrete things like streets or dogs. Go to *Shutterstock.com*, and type in five of the items from your list. See if you can identify particular *tropes*, or ways of representing the thing being discussed. What commonalities can you spot in the way that the thing is presented, and what arguments are implicitly or explicitly being made about the thing; that is, what is the photo conveying about "rain-ness," "dog-ness," or "patriotism"?

## ASSIGNMENT

### Create Public Awareness Campaign Posters

Public awareness campaign posters aim to create simple but powerful and memorable visual arguments. Since they are designed to reach people on the move, they need to be effective in capturing an audience's attention and drawing their awareness to specific problems.

For instance, a city's public health association running an awareness campaign to decrease the number of sexually transmitted diseases might put posters everywhere from buses to city buildings to community health centers. Poster campaigns can also be location-specific; for instance, an awareness campaign meant to decrease the number of accidents in the workplace might include placing posters in work areas to continually remind workers what behaviors are safe and unsafe.

To develop a set of posters for an awareness campaign, first you need to clarify their rhetorical purpose. Viewers should be able to get the message of your poster within seconds. That means that even if it's more than a one-liner juxtaposed with a clever image, the main message should be instantly discernible.

- Focus on a single, simple message. The target audience should be able to identify and understand your message within a second or two of seeing your poster.
- Use natural, clear language. Write simple and direct sentences—don't use jargon.
- Posters designed to hang in areas where audiences are unlikely to stop walking should not contain body copy (explanation and support of your key message). Rather, include an easy-to-remember URL on the poster where viewers can go to find more information if they want.
- Posters designed to hang in places where target audiences are likely to be lingering (e.g., inside buses and subways, bathroom stall doors, doctors' offices) can include body copy. However, the body copy should also be designed for quick, easy reading. Present key/main points first, then explanation. Use short paragraphs and things like headings, subheadings, and bullet points to establish a clear path for the viewer through the poster.

### Incorporating images in your poster

A public awareness campaign poster doesn't necessarily *need* images—sometimes text on its own can be quite powerful. However, remember the pictorial superiority effect from Chapter 4—viewers are more likely to remember a message when it's attached to an image.

Sometimes a poster can rely almost solely on the image. Consider the example from the World Wildlife Fund in Figure 7.3. The poster only uses four words: "Before it's too late. wwf.org." The image does all the work: It

Source: World Wildlife Fund

**FIGURE 7.3** WWF Public Awareness Campaign Poster

quickly reveals itself as a pair of forest "lungs," a brown "cancer" eating away at the right one. The reason this pun is so clever is that it forces readers to fill in the gaps of meaning and to draw together many different ideas: the idea that forests are the lungs of the planet because they "inhale" carbon dioxide and "exhale" oxygen; the idea that these lungs are being damaged by deforestation; and that deforestation is equivalent to lung cancer. The viewer sees the image first, experiences a moment of surprise as he or she gets the image, then looks to the small text in the lower right-hand corner for an explanation, seeing the Web address and the familiar WWF panda logo. Well played, WWF!

| QUESTIONS TO ASK | **Choosing Images for Your Public Awareness Campaign Posters** |
| --- | --- |

- Images should support your main message. Consider their cultural significations, and make sure they're not somehow undermining the message you want to convey.
- Consider what rhetorical work you want the image to do in the poster:
  - Do you want a straight-up explanatory image (a diagram of how to correctly do something, for instance)?
  - Do you want to appeal to the audience's sense of humor with a light joke? (See the following Reporters without Borders poster.)
  - Do you want to create fear by shocking them? (See the following Meth Project ad.)

- Consider the various visual composition tools in Chapter 14 (e.g., the CRAP principles, color significance) in composing your poster.
- Make sure the image is of high enough resolution and quality for the planned print size of the poster.

**Anti-Censorship Ad by the Reporters Without Borders Organization.**
This is an example of a visual joke that makes a serious argument. You can get the argument (and the joke) by reading the caption in the bottom right corner: "Censorship tells the wrong story."

How does the image and the text work together in this Meth Project ad to create an argument?

# 7e Multimodal Arguments

Multimodal arguments can be among the most powerful because the claims, reasons, and evidence can echo across multiple forms of presentation: via speech, text, image, moving image, and so forth. Multimodal arguments uniquely employ the modality that Chapter 5 defines as haptic, where audiences potentially participate in their own persuasion by interacting physically with the information in some way. Websites explicitly evoke this haptic form of persuasion; many contemporary museum displays similarly draw the reader into a more critical awareness of the topic through creating opportunities for interaction.

**EXAMPLE** The U.S. Holocaust Memorial Museum assigns visitors an individual who experienced the Holocaust to follow through exhibits in the museum. The physical space of the museum was also deliberately designed to prompt visceral reactions and reflections in its visitors.

**EXAMPLE** In another example of how multimodal rhetoric relies on the haptic sense for persuasion, rhetorician and game theorist Ian Bogost makes the case that certain types of "persuasive" video games, which aim to make a point, serve as powerful persuasion devices because players, through following the procedures of such games, implicitly recreate the argumentative logic of the games.

## ASSIGNMENT

### Create an Op-Doc

Though opinionated documentaries are plentiful, the very short version known as an op-doc is specifically a *New York Times* genre. Op-docs, as *The New York Times* Web page describes them, are "short, opinionated documentaries, produced with wide creative latitude and a range of artistic styles, covering current affairs, contemporary life, and historical subjects" (*nytimes.com/op-docs*). There's a special section devoted to op-docs on *The New York Times* website. Op-doc topics cover a very wide range: from a little-girl skateboarding crew to climate change's effects on island life to animal rights.

Op-docs can range from the explanatory to the more overtly persuasive. On the more explanatory end of the spectrum is Elaine McMillion Sheldon's op-doc "The Marijuana Divide," which explores the differences between one town in Colorado that has approved legal sales of marijuana and another close by that has not. The op-doc uses written narrative in black boxes over moving shots of Colorado, interspersed with interviews and voiceovers of people relevant to the issue (including mayors, newspaper editors, marijuana dispensary owners, substance abuse experts, and police). And on the more overtly persuasive side, Brian Knappenberger's short film "A Threat to Internet Freedom" explains the concept of net neutrality and argues for its

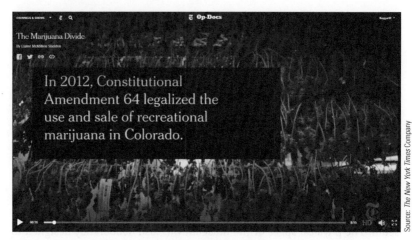

In 2012, Constitutional Amendment 64 legalized the use and sale of recreational marijuana in Colorado.

Source: *The New York Times* Company

Video Still from the Op-Doc "The Marijuana Divide"

importance. It consists of clips of news reporting, interviews with experts explaining and advocating for an open Internet, and animations explaining net neutrality.

While most op-docs are professionally produced by independent film-makers, the editorial board of *The New York Times* will also consider op-docs that "present a clearly articulated argument or viewpoint like a traditional Op-Ed essay and relate to topics in the news," ("How to Submit an Opinion Video"). Thus, you have a potential venue for submitting your op-doc.

### MATERIALS NEEDED

- A video camera. You might find out from your instructor whether these are available for loan through your university; however, in a pinch you could even use the video recording functions on a smart-phone. While the production won't be of professional quality, it will work to at least convey your idea.
- Editing software (available in Microsoft Office for Mac and Windows).

### STEPS TO MAKING AN OP-DOC

See Chapter 15, "Creating Videos and Podcasts," for more explicit instructions.

1. Watch a number of op-docs on *The New York Times* page, paying attention to how they persuade their intended audiences not only through the facts and opinions presented, but also through things like the script, the people included in the film, the "art of the frame" (camera movement, placement of objects within the frame, type of shot), editing, music, etc.

2. Write a one-page, single-spaced proposal or "treatment" for the op-doc that elaborates on
   - the audience, purpose, and message of the op-doc
   - the importance and timeliness of an op-doc on this issue
   - the historical background or context of the issue
   - the people you plan to include
   - the intended style of the op-doc (In terms of shooting the film, will you use voiceover, graphics, direct narration, voiceover narration, direct/indirect interview, location shots, archival footage, montage? In terms of editing, will you use close-ups, reaction shots, "parallel editing," point of view shots, etc.?)
   - format and location
   - a production schedule

3. Schedule interviews, if you're using them.

4. Write the script.

5. Create a list of shots. Consider how your shots will be framed, and the rhetorical effect of each.

6. Shoot individual shots.

7. Edit the film. (This will take the longest, so leave plenty of time.)

---

## FOR REFLECTION

### Transferable Skills and Concepts
Arguments in academic fields and professions often drive the profession forward, generating topics for research and discussion. Understanding these arguments often marks the differences between insiders and out-siders in the profession. Interview one of your professors in your major to find out what argument she or he thinks is the central one for the field, or simply pay attention in your courses to what arguments or disagreements seem to be significant. Then analyze these arguments using the stasis questions. At which stasis does discussion on the issue seem to be stalled? What needs to be understood or agreed upon before the issue can be considered resolved?

# 8

# Explaining

> **LEARNING OBJECTIVES**
>
> *By working through this chapter, you will be able to...*
> - Name the different types of explanations.
> - Understand why explaining is a rhetorical activity.
> - Identify the elements of explanatory discourse.
> - Use the elements of explanatory discourse as building blocks for your own written, visual, or multimodal explanations.

## 8a The Booming Business of Explanations

Here's a sampling of some of the stories recently posted on the popular (leftist) website *Vox's* homepage (January 30, 2017):

- "It looks like Trump's HHS pick didn't tell Congress the truth about a sweetheart stock deal"
- "Why cats love catnip, according to science"
- "9 maps and charts that explain the global refugee crisis"
- "Why Trump's 'Muslim ban' is a moral failure, explained by a political theorist"
- "Who Trump is banning from the US, illustrated"
- "How the war on drugs has made drug traffickers more ruthless and efficient"
- "7 lessons from psychology that explain the irrational fear of outsiders"
- "Loneliness actually hurts us on a cellular level"

The deluge of information in the form of online newspapers, news sites, and gossip sites, along with the ever-growing science and technical industries and the exposure to various sorts of subcultures, has led to a small industry of work whose main purpose is to *explain*, or to *help readers understand something*. But explaining isn't confined to specialized sites: A special category of journalism called "explanatory reporting," consisting of often multipart stories that do in-depth explanations of current issues, has existed as part of the Pulitzer Prizes since 1980 (you can find these by going to the website at *www.pulitzer.org* and searching under "Explanatory Reporting"). Some of the stories in recent years that have won Pulitzer Prizes include *The Washington Post's* explanation of the prevalence of food stamps in post-recession America, *The New York Times'* examination of the dark side of the business practices of technology companies like Apple, and *The Oregonian's* explanation of how Mexican drug cartels infiltrated Oregon and other parts of the country. So, as you can see, explanations can range from relatively focused topics to ones that are more entangled and complex.

What kinds of things need to be explained? While technically *everything* could be subject to explanation, for the purposes of this chapter we'll take the earlier list from *Vox* as a cue and confine our examination to three basic types of explanations:

- **Explanations of current events** (things that have happened or are happening), including news, cultural trends, fads, and memes. Don't know what Benghazi is, what's happening with Kim Jong-Un of North Korea, or why everyone keeps talking about dabbing? You can turn to a number of sites whose primary business is to help readers make sense of what's in the news. The most prominent of these—*FiveThirtyEight*, *Vox*, the *Upshot*, and the more general *HowStuffWorks* and *about.com*—aim to provide historical, geographical, scientific, technical, and cultural context and background to help readers better grasp the significance of current events and stories.

- **Explanations of scientific and technical objects, concepts, or processes.** What is the Higgs Boson particle? How do submarines, SSRIs, cell phones, toilets, Lycra, or light-emitting diodes work? Explanations of such concepts are especially valuable for the lay reader, who typically doesn't have the specialized knowledge required to understand either the process itself or why it's significant or important.

- **Explanations of cultural phenomena.** With the increase in connection among all sorts of people afforded by social media, cultural phenomena that may once have been the interest of confined groups have gained much more prominence; this includes everything from gaming to Islam. In recent years there has also been a growth in what might be thought of as amateur ethnography, where outsiders who serve as participant-observers and insiders from a particular group report on subcultures little known to the public: Star Trek fans, goths, pro-anorexia groups, semi-pro baseball players, and video gamers, to name just a few.

**EXAMPLE**   The writer Susan Orlean has made a career of explaining the worlds of various subcultures, including taxidermy champions, animal actors, orchid poachers, and show dogs, among hundreds of other topics, to the sophisticated readers of the magazine *The New Yorker*.

How can you tell if a piece of communication has explanation as its primary goal? The title or headline should give you the first clue. As the *Vox* headlines suggest, explanatory discourse often has "explain" built into the headline—this makes explanations especially easy to recognize! But even if it's not quite that overt, communication that includes some form of "Here's..."—"Here's what you need to know," "Here's why," "Here's how"—also typically have explanation as their main goal. And as the titles of the sites *HowStuffWorks* and *about.com* suggest, "How X works" and "All about X" both serve as good indicators of discourse that aims to explain.

## FOR DISCUSSION

From a national or international news source (*The New York Times, CNN, The Chicago Tribune, The Guardian, The Washington Post*), choose a current news story about something you find interesting but know little about. Then go to three of the explanation-geared sites listed earlier, and type in some of the key words from the news story. If the sites have explanations of the events featured in or relevant to the news story you chose, print off those explanations and read them, taking notes on what sorts of things each site uses to explain the event. Then answer the following questions:

- How do the explanations differ from site to site? (See the following figure to understand how some sites might be more ideologically liberal or conservative.)
- Why do you think these explanations differed?
- Which explanation was the most helpful, and why?
- Finally, how could you turn the best explanation into a model to use to make explanations about similar events?

**Ideological profile of each source's audience**

Average ideological placement of those who got news from each source in the past week

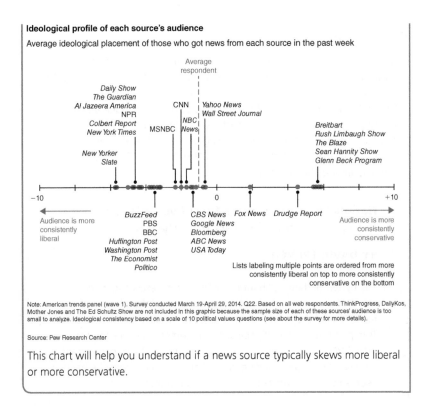

Average respondent

Daily Show
The Guardian
Al Jazeera America
NPR
Colbert Report
New York Times

New Yorker
Slate

CNN
Yahoo News
Wall Street Journal
NBC News
MSNBC

Breitbart
Rush Limbaugh Show
The Blaze
Sean Hannity Show
Glenn Beck Program

−10                    0                    +10

◄───── Audience is more consistently liberal

BuzzFeed
PBS
BBC
Huffington Post
Washington Post
The Economist
Politico

CBS News
Google News
Bloomberg
ABC News
USA Today

Fox News    Drudge Report

Audience is more consistently conservative ─────►

Lists labeling multiple points are ordered from more consistently liberal on top to more consistently conservative on the bottom

Note: American trends panel (wave 1). Survey conducted March 19-April 29, 2014. Q22. Based on all web respondents. ThinkProgress, DailyKos, Mother Jones and The Ed Schultz Show are not included in this graphic because the sample size of each of these sources' audience is too small to analyze. Ideological consistency based on a scale of 10 political values questions (see about the survey for more details).

Source: Pew Research Center

This chart will help you understand if a news source typically skews more liberal or more conservative.

# 8b Explaining as a Rhetorical Activity

Explanations may appear initially to be neutral forms of communication: you're just telling someone how something works, right? But the rhetorical nature of explanations is revealed as soon as one analyzes explanations of the same phenomenon for different audiences. When we consider which sorts of things get explained (and which don't), how they get explained differently according to their audience, and the effects of the means of communication used to create and circulate these explanations, it becomes more obvious why explanation can be considered a rhetorical activity.

As with all communication, then, when you read and compose explanations, you'll need to do so with the elements of rhetoric in mind: communicator, audience, message, purpose, exigence, and means of communication. (See Chapters 1 and 2.)

## FOR DISCUSSION

Read the two following excerpts. Both attempt to explain Donald Trump's January 2017 executive order that banned travelers from seven countries (Iraq, Iran, Somalia, Libya, Sudan, Syria, and Yemen) from entering the United States for 90 days. The ban also stopped all refugee admissions for 120 days and Syrian refugee admissions indefinitely. However, one explanation comes from the right-wing biased *National Review*, and the other comes from the left-wing biased *New Yorker*. After reading the articles, answer the questions that follow.

### National Review: Trump's Executive Order on Refugees – Separating Fact from Hysteria

#### BY DAVID FRENCH

The hysterical rhetoric about President Trump's executive order on refugees is out of control. Let's slow down and take a look at the facts. To read the online commentary, one would think that President Trump just fundamentally corrupted the American character. You would think that the executive order on refugees he signed yesterday betrayed America's Founding ideals. You might even think he banned people from an entire faith from American shores.

. . .

Let's analyze the key provisions, separate the fact from the hysteria, and introduce just a bit of historical perspective.

First, the order temporarily halts refugee admissions for 120 days to improve the vetting process, then caps refugee admissions at 50,000 per year. Outrageous, right? Not so fast. Before 2016, when Obama dramatically ramped up refugee admissions, Trump's 50,000 stands roughly in between a typical year of refugee admissions in George W. Bush's two terms and a typical year in Obama's two terms.

. . .

In 2002, the United States admitted only 27,131 refugees. It admitted fewer than 50,000 in 2003, 2006, and 2007. As for President Obama, he was slightly more generous than President Bush, but his refugee cap from 2013 to 2015 was a mere 70,000, and in 2011 and 2012 he admitted barely more than 50,000 refugees himself.

The bottom line is that Trump is improving security screening and intends to admit refugees at close to the average rate of the 15 years before Obama's dramatic expansion in 2016. Obama's expansion was a departure from recent norms, not Trump's contraction.

Second, the order imposes a temporary, 90-day ban on people entering the U.S. from Iraq, Syria, Iran, Libya, Somalia, Sudan, and Yemen. These are countries either torn apart by jihadist violence or under the control of hostile, jihadist governments.

The ban is in place while the Department of Homeland Security determines the "information needed from any country to adjudicate any visa, admission, or other benefit under the INA (adjudications) in order to determine that the individual seeking the benefit is who the individual claims to be and is not a security or public-safety threat." It could, however, be extended or expanded depending on whether countries are capable of providing the requested information.

The ban, however, contains an important exception: "Secretaries of State and Homeland Security may, on a case-by-case basis, and when in the national interest, issue visas or other immigration benefits to nationals of countries for which visas and benefits are otherwise blocked." In other words, the secretaries can make exceptions — a provision that would, one hopes, fully allow interpreters and other proven allies to enter the U.S. during the 90-day period.

To the extent this ban applies to new immigrant and non-immigrant entry, this temporary halt (with exceptions) is wise. We know that terrorists are trying to infiltrate the ranks of refugees and other visitors. We know that immigrants from Somalia, for example, have launched jihadist attacks here at home and have sought to leave the U.S. to join ISIS.

Indeed, given the terrible recent track record of completed and attempted terror attacks by Muslim immigrants, it's clear that our current approach is inadequate to control the threat. Unless we want to simply accept Muslim immigrant terror as a fact of American life, a short-term ban on entry from problematic countries combined with a systematic review of our security procedures is both reasonable and prudent.

However, there are reports that the ban is being applied even to green-card holders. This is madness. The plain language of the order doesn't apply to legal permanent residents of the U.S., and green-card holders have been through round after round of vetting and security checks. The administration should intervene, immediately, to stop misapplication. If, however, the Trump administration continues to apply the order to legal permanent residents, it should indeed be condemned.

. . .

## *The New Yorker:* A Welcome Setback for Donald Trump

### BY JOHN CASSIDY

"Americans severely misjudged the authoritarians," Umair Haque, a consultant and social-media maven, commented on *Twitter* on Saturday night. "But the authoritarians, it seems, also severely misjudged Americans." Yes, they did, and this weekend's events offered a bit of hope to everybody alarmed by Donald Trump. Saving America from the most unhinged and least qualified figure ever to occupy the Oval Office may well require a long and bitter fight. But a couple of early markers have been put down. The new President is not beyond the law. And many Americans will not stand by quietly as he traduces their country's values, threatens its democracy, and destroys its reputation around the world.

Clearly intent on giving the impression that he is a man of action, Trump spent his first week on the job issuing a stream of Presidential edicts: reining in regulations, approving oil pipelines, undermining the Affordable Care Act, freezing federal hiring, and pledging not to sign any more multilateral treaties. Every day seemed to bring a new display of chauvinism. But it was his executive order suspending entry to the United States for refugees and people from seven predominantly Muslim countries that provoked, for the second weekend in a row, a huge demonstration of opposition to his Presidency and all it stands for.

As news broke of U.S. border agents detaining people—refugees who had worked for the U.S. military in Iraq; Ivy League academics returning to their jobs; other blameless individuals—thousands of people headed out to major airports. Most were going to protest. Others, including immigration lawyers and public defenders, were going to offer their professional services. (My colleague Nathan Heller reported on the scene at J.F.K., in New York City.)

As the number of demonstrators mounted, they received some encouraging news from the Federal District Court in Brooklyn. At about nine on Saturday night, in response to a lawsuit filed by the American Civil Liberties Union, Judge Ann M. Donnelly issued an emergency stay on part of the new policy, ordering that the U.S. government couldn't deport people who had arrived with valid visas or refugee status. Minutes later, at the Federal District Court in Virginia, a second judge issued an order preventing the government from deporting any green-card holders who had been detained at Dulles, and ordering border agents to give immigration lawyers access to them.

On Sunday, the demonstrations expanded to other cities and got larger. At New York's Battery Park and in Boston's Copley Square, tens of thousands gathered to protest against what they regarded as a ban on Muslims. By then, some of Trump's lackeys had given weaselly statements in the press suggesting that some sort of modification was in the works. On Sunday evening, the Department of Homeland Security announced that "absent . . . information indicating a serious threat" legal residents of the United States—i.e., holders of green cards—would be exempted from the bans.

In the scheme of things, it was a small reversal. The indefinite ban on refugees from Syria was still in place, as were the hundred-and-twenty-day ban on refugees from other countries and the ninety-day ban on visitors from Iran, Iraq, Libya, Somalia, Sudan, Syria, and Yemen. All three bans are senseless and arbitrary, and the two that apply to Muslim countries are clearly discriminatory (despite Trump's claim, in a statement on Sunday, that "this is not about religion—this is about terror and keeping our country safe").

For all the awfulness, however, it is worth pausing to consider what has happened. Autocrats subvert democracies by undermining the institutions that sustain them: legislatures; representative local governments; the judiciary; the media and other nongovernmental organizations, such as civil-rights groups; and, of course, an active citizenry. With the Senate and House of Representatives under the control of a Republican Party that has made a Faustian pact with Trump, it was never likely that they would rein him in. In this instance, though, the other institutions of civil society fulfilled their roles.

Civil-rights lawyers sued to block parts of the new policy, and judges ruled against the government. Ordinary citizens demonstrated—to themselves, and to people around the world—that Trump and his bigotry don't represent the United States. Local and national politicians, such as New York City Mayor Bill de Blasio and Senators Chuck Schumer, Kirsten Gillibrand, and Elizabeth Warren, turned out alongside them. (It wasn't just a coastal protest. The mayor of Dallas, Mike Rawlings, issued an apology to people who had been detained at Dallas–Fort Worth International Airport.) On Monday, Barack Obama issued his first statement since leaving office, offering support for the protests and, through a spokesman, saying that "American values are at stake." The media reported what was happening, prompting Trump to go on another online tirade, in which he suggested that someone should buy the *Times* and "run it properly" or close it down.

There were a couple of other encouraging developments. On Sunday, after maintaining a pitiful silence for more than a day, some Republicans distanced themselves from Trump's policy. Senators John McCain and Lindsey Graham said the order "may do more to help terrorist recruitment than improve our security." Of course, McCain and Graham have both criticized Trump in the past. But on this occasion they were joined, for once, by other Republican senators, such as Cory Gardner, of Colorado, who said the Trump order went "too far," and Lamar Alexander, of Tennessee, who said it came close to being a religious test, which is "inconsistent with our American character."

For the first time since Trump's election, prominent business leaders also distanced themselves from him. "We have many employees from the named countries, and we do business all over the region," Jeffrey Immelt, the chief executive of General Electric, said in a memo to the firm's employees. "These employees and customers are critical to our success and they are our friends and our partners. We stand with them." Tim Cook, of Apple, which was founded by the son of a Syrian immigrant, told his employees that the firm "would not exist without immigration, let alone thrive and innovate the way we do." Starbucks announced plans to hire ten thousand refugees in seventy-five countries around the world. In an open letter, Howard Schultz, the coffee-shop chain's C.E.O., said, "We will neither stand by, nor stand silent, as the uncertainty around the new Administration's actions grows with each passing day."

Sergey Brin, the cofounder of Google, who emigrated to the United States from Russia at the age of five, attended a protest at San Francisco International Airport on Saturday. "I am here because I am a refugee," he told a reporter from *Forbes*. And on Monday, Lloyd Blankfein, the chief executive of Goldman Sachs, a number of whose former employees hold senior positions in the Trump Administration, said in an internal memo that was leaked, "This is not a policy we support."

It is far too early to say that corporate America is abandoning Trump and refusing to work with his Administration. But business leaders are indicating that there are limits to what they will go along with. U.S. multinational companies are closely integrated into the global economy. In many cases, they rely on overseas countries for markets, labor, and capital. Trump's effort to turn the United States into a fearful, inward-looking, discriminatory, and isolationist country is potentially disastrous for them. As Immelt put it, "There would be no GE without our smart, dedicated employees from all over the world. . . . We are a very global team, and we will stand together as the global political situation continues to evolve."

Again, this is only a first step in resisting Trump, and nobody should underestimate the challenge ahead. We are dealing with a dangerous singularity—a President who openly acknowledges that he is at war with the press, who endorses torture, who accuses senators who dare to criticize his policies of "looking to start World War III," and who is surrounded by courtiers and advisers who think the United States and other Judeo-Christian countries are engaged in a fight to the death with Islam.

There is no telling how the struggle to rein in Trump, and save America's conception of itself, will play out, or how dark things might get. But the true patriots have raised their colors, and they won't be lowered without a mighty struggle.

**QUESTIONS**

1. What do you think might be the purpose of each of these excerpts, other than to simply explain the event?
2. Despite the fact that they're attempting to explain the same event, what are the differences in the information included and excluded in each explanation? What rhetorical effect does this have?
3. What do we gain by reading both of these excerpts together?

# 8c The Elements of Explanations

Creating good explanations requires that you do several important things.

## Understand Your Audience

To explain something well, you need to understand the following:

- What your audience already knows about the topic
- How your audience feels about the topic
- The audience's primary reason for wanting to understand more about the topic

Thinking carefully about these things will help you tailor your explanation in a way that's usable for your audience. Conversely, if you don't clearly understand your audience, your explanation can go wrong in several ways. You might overestimate their understanding and rely too heavily on technical or jargon-filled language.

Or, even worse than speaking over their heads, you might underestimate your audience's knowledge and appear to speak down to them.

**EXAMPLE** The distaste for patronizing or condescending explanations can be witnessed by the popularity in recent years of the suffix *-splain*, defined by *Dictionary.com* as "to explain or comment on something in a condescending, overconfident, and often inaccurate or oversimplified manner." The suffix "–splain" comes from "mansplaining," a term that arose from the discussion around essayist Rebecca Solnit's 2008 essay "Men Explain Things to Me," and which has evolved to include a host of other "splains": more serious ones like whitesplaining and Mitt[Romney]splaining, along with sillier versions, like kidsplaining and catsplaining. But suffice it to say that the prevalence of "splaining" indicates that people are very cognizant of being condescended to, and they'll react with annoyance to a perceived "splainer."

Avoiding such perceptions requires a clear understanding of what audiences know and why they might need an explanation about a particular topic.

## Have a Specific Purpose for Your Explanation

Explanations may not be traditionally thesis-driven compositions, but they do have an overall focus or point; badly organized information dumps are frustrating and annoying for readers, who won't take the time to wade through them. So before you begin explaining something, take some time to understand for yourself *why* you're explaining it. What do you want your audience to understand, and what do you hope to achieve as a result of explaining?

Following are some common purposes for explanatory discourse:

- *To illuminate the meaning of something*

  **EXAMPLE** After football games, sports analysts will commonly provide explanations about what the results of the game mean for the teams who played, as well as what this means in the larger context of the season and the rankings of all teams.

- *To help readers understand the cause of something*

  **EXAMPLE** An explanation of why acts deemed as police brutality suddenly are much more apparent might focus on the Department of Defense's new program to give military equipment to police departments, for instance.

- *To help readers understand how something works*

  **EXAMPLE** Such purposes are common to explanations of scientific and technical phenomena, but they're important in explaining anything that involves a process. Readers might want to know how something like rugby works or how DSL cameras function.

- *To correct common misunderstandings of something*

  **EXAMPLE** Perhaps people have traditionally misunderstood comics as frivolous and for children, and you want to explain that they've become a serious art form.

- *To help readers accomplish a goal*

  **EXAMPLE** Many of the explanations devoted to the Affordable Health Care Act of 2013 (aka Obamacare) have the goal of helping audiences identify what type of insurance they should get and how they can go about signing up.

## Organize Your Explanation Logically

What's considered logical really depends on what you're explaining. Most formal explanations begin with a hook—a question, an anecdote, or a specific example that demonstrates the significance or interest of the thing being explained. Then, depending on what they aim to explain, they may end up using one of the following schemes.

### Possible scheme for explaining current events

Depending on their scope, explanations of current events may move sequentially through the journalistic questions (who, what, when, where, why, how), or they may focus on one or two of the most important questions for that topic:

- *Who* someone is (including why they're important or significant) or *what* something is or does.

- *When* something happened, perhaps with information about what caused it.

- *Where* something happened, is happening, or will happen, including perhaps the geographical, social, and cultural factors of the region.

- *Why* something happened, is happening, or will happen.

- *How* something happened, is happening, or will happen.

- Most importantly, explanations of current events attempt to answer the question *what does it mean?* (the focus of your explanation).

  **EXAMPLE** Frequently, after elections in which one political party takes a majority of seats in Congress, there will be a spate of news analyses on news sites and blogs that offer explanations of not only why one side lost but also what effects this will be likely to have on future legislation of all sorts, from abortion law to energy policy to financial deregulation.

  **EXAMPLE** Consider an *Upshot* article from November 20, 2014, entitled "Bill Cosby's Sudden Fall, Explained Sociologically." (If you want to read the full text, Google the title or find the article at *The New York Times* website.) This brief article begins with the provocative question "How did Bill Cosby suddenly become radioactive?" As the title suggests, the article relies on the explanation of a sociologist who theorizes that "moral scandals like this one arise when a suspected transgression becomes common knowledge." The article brings up two analogous scandals to explain Bill Cosby's current situation—the 2002 scandal that erupted when former Mississippi Senator Trent Lott made remarks praising a former presidential candidate who ran on a segregationist platform, and radio talk show host Don Imus's 2007 racially offensive comments about the Rutgers women's basketball team, which got Imus fired from CBS radio and dropped from MSNBC.

## Possible scheme for explaining scientific or technical objects, concepts, or processes

Explanations of *scientific or technical objects and processes* aim to help people understand everything from complex, esoteric scientific research (in astrophysics, say) to practical things like what happens when you get a tattoo and the medical value of meditation.

The form of journalism called "science writing" aims to entertain and fascinate readers with its explanations of scientific ideas and natural phenomena. But as Carl Zimmer, a prolific science writer, said in an interview, part of the aim is also to make readers *curious* about the natural world and how science works. Zimmer says, "When I write about slime molds I want readers to become curious so that the next time they're out in the woods they'll stop and take a closer look. I want them thinking about the same questions that the scientists are asking" (Johnson).

Explanations of scientific and technical objects and processes tend to do the following things:

- Situate the object or process in a context that would be familiar to the readers—when, where, or how they may have encountered this object or process already.

- Make a statement about the focus of the explanation.

- Define and describe the basic components (if it's an object) or steps (if it's a process), and show how these are important to the object or process as a whole.

- Provide simpler and more complex examples of the object or process, if these exist (for instance, the article "How Bridges Work," on the *HowStuffWorks* site first walks readers through the "beam bridge," the simplest kind of bridge; then it takes them through the progressively more complicated arch bridge, suspension bridge, and cable-stayed bridge.

- Provide unusual instances or exceptions to the basic elements and components.

See the following sample explanation about fat-free foods. The purpose of the sample explanation about the creation of fat-free foods, for instance, is to help readers understand that contrary to the title, fat is not removed from fat-free foods; rather, the foods are created from the beginning without fat. The marginal comments point out the moves made by the text to engage the audience.

## An Annotated Explanation of a Technical or Scientific Process

The purpose of the following sample explanation about the creation of fat-free foods, for instance, is to help readers understand that contrary to the title, fat is not removed from fat-free foods; rather, the foods are created from the beginning without fat. The marginal comments point out the moves made by the text to engage the audience.

### HowStuffWorks: How Do They Get the Fat Out of Fat-Free Foods?

Wouldn't it be great if we all ate exactly what we wanted and exercised only as much as we genuinely liked, yet still beamed with joy when we stepped on a scale? You know, like if there were some magical machine that just sucked all the fat out of all the foods we like, but still left them tasting delicious?

Alas, until that machine is invented (Nobel Prize 2050?!?), we are left to maintain our weight loss by exercising and actually paying attention to what we eat. For some, that means eating less. For others, maybe it means eating a lot of low-fat or fat-free foods. But given that there is no magical machine, how exactly do these fat-free cookies and cake lose their fat content?

First off, what is fat? We all know what it looks like in our food, but when you zoom in on the chemical structure, you'll find that all fats have in common long chains of carbon atoms, with some oxygen and hydrogen atoms thrown in to keep things interesting (see How Fats Work). The long carbon chains in fat molecules make it really hard for fats to dissolve in water, so generally to get them to dissolve, you need some sort of organic solvent, like chloroform or methylene chloride. You may first think that washing our fatty foods with one of these solvents would do the trick of removing the fat. It's a good thought. After all, that's often how they remove the caffeine from coffee and tea. But fat actually does a lot for our foods, and simply extracting or dissolving away the fat will leave us with foods that don't really resemble their original versions. Fat, of course, adds flavor, but also helps with texture, browning, and even extending shelf life. So before

*Marginal comments:*

Notice the use of "we" in this paragraph, the "hook" for the explanatory piece. The writer uses a familiar form of address to make the reader feel comfortable. The writer clearly sees her audience as part of the idly curious general public – they want to know some things, but only for the purposes of satisfying their curiosity. Had the writer been writing to a fellow chemist, the tone, style, and content would have been markedly different.

Here's the thing that will actually be explained.

The writer continues with the informal tone, using a colloquialism – "first off."

Here's a rhetorical move designed to keep readers engaged – an assumption about what they might think (and an insinuation that they are incorrect). We read on because we want to find out the correct answer.

The "but" here indicates the beginning of the correct answer to how fat is removed.

we just get rid of the fat, we need to think about how to keep all that flavor and texture in the foods so they still taste good.

Dairy products are a good place to start. When we first get milk, it has a good bit of fat in it. For many, that's unwanted fat. How do we get from whole milk down to skim? The process is pretty simple. Manufacturers put the whole milk into a centrifuge that separates out the heavy fat portion into cream and leaves behind skim milk. This skim milk can then be used to make other dairy products like yogurt and sour cream that are either low-fat or nonfat. However, many of these nonfat dairy products that are made simply from skim milk run into the problems we mentioned before: They don't taste good, their textures are funny, and they may not last as long in our refrigerators [source: Millstone]. Dairy products in this category, like fat-free cheese, need to be made the way many diet products are created: not by taking fat out, but by never putting the fat in to begin with.

Instead of making a food product – let's say a cookie – and sucking the fat out (leaving behind something that is no longer anything like a cookie), food scientists need to create that cookie from the start using nonfat-based additives instead of fat to compensate for all that fat brings to the cookie. Let's start with flavor. Fatty cookie ingredients like butter and eggs add a lot of flavor. To make up for the lack of flavor when those items aren't used, manufacturers add in extra spices and a lot more sugar to trick us into not noticing the missing fat. This is why low- and nonfat foods aren't always less caloric, as their "diet" name might imply; they often have a ton of extra sugar added [source: Millstone].

To deal with texture issues, manufacturers will add food binders like gums and starches and also water. However, as a result of adding water, these fat-free products aren't as shelf stable, so surfactants and emulsifiers like mono- and diglycerides (close cousins to fats, which are triglycerides) must also be added.

In the past, food manufacturers have experimented with fat replacements like olestra, but have yet to find much success in their use. The side effects of these materials (let's just leave it at the phrase: anal leakage) resulted in very poor sales [source: Center for Science in the Public Interest].

Long story short: Getting the fat out of fat-free foods, for the most part, actually means never putting the fat in there to begin with. What goes in the place of fat varies, but you'll often end up with a highly processed food product that may be quite different from its fatty counterpart.

**Author's Note:** How they get the fat out of fat-free foods?

As a chemist, I was sure that fat-free foods worked similarly to caffeine-free coffee and tea. The product was washed with an organic solvent to dissolve the unwanted item (caffeine or fat), and then you were left with the final product. But as I stopped to think about it, fat adds a lot to food. It wouldn't be the same and couldn't be marketed as the same food, without the flavor and texture that fat adds. This was confirmed for me by a dietician whom I interviewed for this piece. So the title of this article is actually a bit misleading – they rarely "get the fat out" of fat-free foods, they just formulate them differently to begin with. And honestly, learning about it does not make these foods appealing to eat!

> Note the writer's two ethos moves here: She mentions that she's a chemist (an expert), but also that she didn't know how the process works. This puts her on readers' levels, making us feel that she's not talking down to us.

## Possible scheme for explaining cultural phenomena

The term "cultural phenomena" could encompass a wide variety of things. But here we use the term to mean something that involves people but doesn't necessarily coalesce around a specific event. It could involve cultural trends (the increasing reliance of many Americans on food stamps, the growth of community-supported agriculture, the new molecular gastronomy fad, McMansions), bodily fashions (piercings and tattoos, plastic surgery, CrossFit classes), subcultures (ravers, straight-edge, dumpster divers, jocks), or groups (Greek organizations, Rotary Clubs, Alcoholics Anonymous).

Explanations of cultural phenomena generally require an ethnographic or anthropological approach. That is, to explain things like trends, fashions, subcultures, and groups, you could find materials written about them, but for a credible account, you'd also need to provide primary evidence gathered through observation and interviews.

Your explanations of a cultural phenomenon may contain some or all of the following elements:

- A brief overview of the phenomenon: If it's a cultural trend, your explanation might provide evidence of the thing's prevalence; if it's a subculture or group, it might talk briefly about what kinds of actions or beliefs make the group distinct from other groups.
- A statement about the focus of the explanation: Why is this phenomenon interesting, and what do you want to say about it?
- A profile of who is involved (for example, who participates in the trend, or who are typical members of the group).
- Background or historical context for the group or trend. Where did it come from? How did it start? What forces may have been involved in making it culturally noticeable?

- An explanation of the phenomenon's effects on the larger culture (this should be tied to the focus statement).

For an instance of a visual explanation of a cultural phenomenon, consider the infographic in Figure 8.1, "Shoplifters of the World Unite." Notice that the infographic answers questions like "Who shoplifts the most around the world?" "What are the causes of retail loss around the world?" "What do shoplifters steal?" and "How do retailers try to prevent shoplifting?" all of which reveal an international focus for the explanation.

A different explanation of shoplifting might focus instead on explaining the phenomenon from a psychological perspective. Questions for a more psychological explanation might include: Who shoplifts, and why? How do they shoplift? How many people get caught?

## Decide How to Present Your Explanation

In composing explanations, it's important to consider modality, medium, genre, and circulation. (For explanations of these, see Chapter 2.)

Explanations lend themselves particularly well to a variety of modalities and media. Common genres for explanations include written explanations (like news analyses, which appear in the newspaper), but also visual (infographics, visual essays) and multimodal types (videos or webpages).

**EXAMPLE**   While as a written text, the Bill Cosby explanatory article relies heavily on the verbal modality, it is also multimodal because the article is laden with hyperlinks that take the reader to news stories that provide background and other elements important to the story. The links serve both as evidence of the problem and as further explanation of the events of the Cosby scandal.

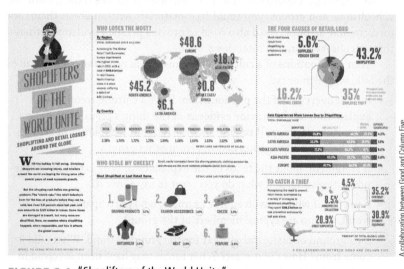

FIGURE 8.1   "Shoplifters of the World Unite"

Here are some of the most common formats for explanations:

- *Articles*. These are by far the most common explanatory format. The length of the article depends on the venue.

- *Listicles*. A combination of "article" and "list," listicles have been long a staple of print magazines but gained enormously in popularity thanks to sites like *Buzzfeed*. Now listicles are a staple of explanatory discourse, mostly because they make it very easy for readers to dip in, get some quick information, and move on.

  **EXAMPLE**  "9 questions about marijuana legalization you were too stoned to ask" (*Vox*).

- *Videos*. Three- to five-minute videos helping readers understand a variety of topics appear alongside other formats on many of the sites mentioned.

  **EXAMPLES**  The news aggregator *Digg* features a video from *Marketplace* with the burning question "Why are sticks of butter long and skinny in the East and short and fat in the West?" *HowStuffWorks* includes a "video" section that includes a number of subcategories of explanation, along with shows (like "Stuff You Should Know," and "Stuff to Blow Your Mind").

- *Podcasts*. First developed in 2004, podcasts are audio or video programs that can be streamed and downloaded to portable media devices like smartphones and tablet computers.

- *Card Stacks*. Unique to *Vox*, these mini-websites are organized around topics and questions. Users can click directly on a specific explanatory question or browse through the whole card stack to get a more thorough explanation of the subject.

- *Infographics*. Though the name "infographic" suggests that the purpose of these compositions is primarily to provide readers with information, most infographics have an explanatory dimension as well—they aim to help readers understand (using visual techniques of presentation) a variety of things.

  **EXAMPLES**  A vast number of infographics are available for browsing at the sites *Visually*, *Piktochart*, *Information Is Beautiful*, and *Cool Infographics*.

## ASSIGNMENTS

## Composing Explanations

### WRITE AN EXPLANATION OF SOMETHING NEW TO THE AUDIENCE

Using what you learned in Section 8c about creating explanations, identify a current event, concept, process, or cultural phenomenon with which you are very familiar. Your goal is to compose a written explanation of this thing for an audience who is unfamiliar with it. You will decide on the audience, purpose, and venue for your explanation.

### EXPLAIN THE SAME THING TO A DIFFERENT AUDIENCE

Once you've written your explanation, explain the same thing for a very different audience. This audience could be in a different class, have different interests, be in a different political party, or have very different beliefs from your first audience.

Write a reflective memo that discusses the difference between the rhetorical choices you made in your two explanations.

### CREATE AN INFOGRAPHIC

Create an infographic that explains a scientific concept or process for an audience. You'll need to decide why this particular audience needs to understand this concept and what understanding it will help them to do.

See Section 14c for a more detailed explanation of how to create an infographic.

### DEVELOP A CONCEPT FOR A VIDEO SERIES

Working in teams or individually, create a concept for a series of explanatory videos to be placed on their own *YouTube* channel. The videos should have a common topic or theme; you should also use Section 8c above to identify the audience, purpose, and organization scheme for your video series.

1. Write a pitch for your video series. A pitch is aimed at potential funders or sponsors for your series. The elements of a good pitch include the following:

   a. A pitch summary. You can use the following formula: "My video series is called (title), and focuses on explaining (topic) to (whom) for the purposes of (explanation of series' purpose)."

   b. A detailed explanation of the topic of the series and why this topic is interesting and relevant.

   c. A detailed explanation of the target audience for the series.

   d. A detailed explanation of the purpose of the series.

   e. A description of the pilot video for the series and three or four other videos.

2. Working with your team, create the pilot video for your series. To create the video, you might use the appropriately named app *Explain Everything*. See Section 15a for a more detailed explanation of how to shoot and edit video.

## FOR REFLECTION

**Transferable Skills and Concepts**

Think about a recent instance in which someone has explained something to you, either in person or in some other format. Write down the situation in a journal entry, then answer the following questions:

- Did you understand the thing better after the person explained it to you? Why or why not?
- If you did understand it, did you resist their explanation? If so, why? If not, why not?

# 9

# Defining

*By working through this chapter, you will be able to...*
- Explain why definitions are rhetorical.
- Understand how the act of defining applies to both concrete things and abstract concepts.
- Understand how and why arguments of definition begin.
- Understand the difference between definition arguments of genus and definition arguments of classification.
- Make your own definition argument.
- Compose definition arguments for different audiences, purposes, and by different means of communication (modality, medium, and genre).

## 9a Definitions within Communities

At first glance, it may not be obvious why definitions have anything to do with rhetoric. "Well, this is a no-brainer," you might be thinking. "Once we figure out what something is, we put it in the dictionary and it's a done deal, right?"

Well... not exactly. A dictionary definition can tell us something about how a term is currently used by a community, but it doesn't *fix* its meaning. And how something is defined depends a great deal on how a community relates to it.

**EXAMPLE** We might all in principle agree with Merriam-Webster's definition of a forest as "a dense growth of trees and underbrush covering a large tract." However, depending on a variety of social factors, a community's definition of a forest's *purpose* might differ (Figure 9.1). A community that relies upon logging as its main economy might define the forest as a natural resource; a community of urbanites who wants to get out of the city for the weekend might view it as a recreational area; and a community of environmentalists might view it as pristine wilderness. When the purposes of these communities conflict (as, for instance, when legislation is proposed to sell off areas designated as wilderness

**FIGURE 9.1** How do you define a forest?

Taina Sohlman/Shutterstock.com

irina02/Shutterstock.com

AustralianCamera/Shutterstock.com

to timber companies), these definitions might come to the forefront as communities attempt to persuade each other of the "correct" definition of a forest.

You probably recognize the difficulties inherent in defining *abstract terms* like justice or love; because these things typically can't be pinned down to specific experiences, it's clear how differences in their definitions might arise. However, it may be more surprising to you that *concrete terms* (things that can be experienced sensually, such as forests) also are subject to arguments of definition.

The most important thing to realize is that something is always *at stake* in definitions; that is, there are always very real consequences for how something is defined. If you can persuasively define a forest as a place that should be untouched by humans rather than as an area to be managed, or a human fetus as a *child*, not a *choice* (as the anti-abortionist slogan goes), or users of drugs as *victims of an illness* rather than as *criminals*, then very different things will happen as a result. Thus, often arguments must be made to persuade others to accept a particular definition of a thing, process, concept, or term.

MindTap®
Student Maker
Video 3: Defining a
Canon

## FOR DISCUSSION

1. Choose one of the following *concrete* things or events, and search on "how has X changed over time?" Read a few of the results to get a sense of the different understandings of the thing. How has the definition changed over time? What factors have influenced these different understandings and definitions?

   a. College
   b. Marriage

c. Social Security
d. September 11
e. Immigrants
f. Athletes
g. Photography
h. Travel

2. Choose one of the following *abstract* terms, and search on "how has X changed over time?" Read a few of the results to get a sense of the different understandings of the thing. How has the definition changed over time? What factors have influenced these different understandings and definitions?

a. Family
b. Friendship
c. Freedom
d. Love
e. Justice
f. Truth
g. Art

3. As a class, brainstorm two different lists of things that currently have contested definitions; make one list for concrete terms and one list for abstract terms, as described in 1 and 2. Choose a few of the most interesting ones to discuss as a class. What are the competing definitions? What prompted the need for redefinition? What are the real, tangible effects of defining the thing in one way rather than another? (This could be a handy way to organize a class debate.)

## 9b Making Arguments of Definition

MindTap·
View Tiny
Lecture Video 8:
Understanding
When a Thing or
Concept Is Ripe for
Redefinition

As Chapter 7 explained, questions about definition are one of the first points of stasis, and as such are common types of arguments. Definition arguments can be similar to explanations when their purpose is to correct a misconception or a misunderstanding. But they are different from explanations in their explicitly argumentative structure. That is, as we'll talk about later in the chapter, definition arguments always include a claim about how something *should* be defined, along with reasons and evidence that the thing should be defined this way.

You make an argument of definition when something is disputed, or, as rhetorical scholar Edward Schiappa puts it, when there is a "definitional rupture" (9).

**EXAMPLE**   In the 1980s, there was an uproar about the definition of a vegetable when the USDA Food and Nutrition Service regulations allowed certain condiments, like pickle relish, to count as vegetables. This meant that schools could meet the nutritional requirements for school lunches by substituting

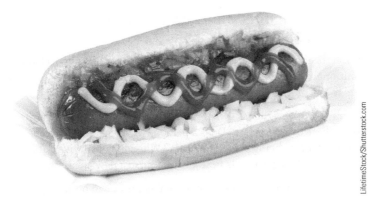

FIGURE 9.2  Would you define this as a vegetable?

condiments for vegetables (so, in essence, under the new regulations, a hot dog with ketchup and relish could be defined as a vegetable). The dispute led to arguments about what actually counted as a vegetable (Figure 9.2).

People can settle some disputes over definition just by clarifying amongst themselves how a term is being used.

**EXAMPLE** To take one sad but common example, maybe you discover over time that your definition of "friendship" differs from that of someone you consider yourself friends with. You define friendship as "loyalty through thick and thin," and they define it as "something convenient and fun." So if a circumstance arises that challenges one of these definitions (they stop calling when you go through a rough patch, for instance), the definition might need to be clarified. If you're good communicators, perhaps you can recognize the difference in your definitions of friendship and resolve them. But if not, perhaps it's time to find a friend that better fits your definition.

However, in some cases, circumstances have changed enough (and there's enough at stake) that one group will reject the common definition of the term. This opens up the opportunity to argue for a different definition of the term. As Schiappa argues, arguments of definition always involve an implicit or explicit argument for how we *should* think about or define the thing in question.

We can break down definition arguments into two basic types: arguments of *genus* and arguments of *classification*. Definition arguments about genus start from the basic question "How should the thing be defined?" Definition arguments about classification start from the basic question "Should the thing be categorized in this way or another way?"

### TWO TYPES OF DEFINITION ARGUMENTS

Genus: How should the thing be defined?
Classification: Should the thing be defined this way (Y) or that way (Z)?

## Arguments about Genus: How Should the Thing Be Defined?

Arguments about genus are the broadest and most philosophical kinds of definitional arguments. While it sounds a bit technical, the term "genus" refers to the most basic ways in which we understand things.

**EXAMPLE**   We might ask "what is a person?" This question is at the center of the debate over abortion. Does a person (with legal rights) come into being when it starts being able to feel pain? When it can survive outside of the womb? When two germ cells first join and form a new entity?

Since questions of genus are open-ended, they can be among the most difficult to answer. They are also most commonly associated with the legal domain.

**EXAMPLE**   The "what is a person?" question was used as the basis of the 1973 *Roe v. Wade* Supreme Court decision that legalized abortion. In this case, the court decided that a fetus was not defined as a person, and was thus not protected under the law.  Many of the legal cases intended to overturn *Roe v. Wade* have focused on defining the fetus as a person.

**EXAMPLES**   The "what is a person?" question also applies in interesting ways to corporations. Since the 1800s, in many ways courts had already treated corporations as persons—to prevent perceived unfair taxation, for example. However, in 2010 the Supreme Court made a landmark decision in the case of *Citizens United v. Federal Election Commission* to define corporations as entities that have freedom of speech under the First Amendment (which thus allowed corporations to spend money to support political candidates). Another landmark decision in *Burwell v. Hobby Lobby* allowed corporations to exercise their religious freedom by not covering contraceptives for employees (as mandated by the Affordable Care Act, better known as Obamacare). Since both of these legal freedoms—freedom of speech and freedom to exercise religion—are extended to persons under the First Amendment of the U.S. Constitution, it stands to reason that corporations have now essentially been legally defined as persons.

### FOR DISCUSSION

1. As a class, choose one of the genus questions below and come up with as many different answers as possible. These answers will serve as your definitional claims. Then take two of these claims and generate as many reasons to support them as you can. Take a poll of the class: Which definitional claims did you find to be most persuasive, and why?

   a. What is a wetland?
   b. What constitutes global warming?
   c. What is wilderness?
   d. What is an endangered species?
   e. What is love?

f. What is a person?

g. What is institutionalized racism?

h. What is a terrorist?

2. Read the following genus argument about the definition of marriage, written by Rev. Tyrone Queen. Then answer the following questions:

a. What is the exigence for Queen's argument? (For the definition of "exigence," see Section 2b.)

b. What is his definition of marriage?

c. What reasons does he provide for this definition?

d. Who do you think Queen sees as his audience? Who is he trying to convince?

e. What are the assumptions in Queen's definition of marriage that Queen likely shares with his audience?

f. Do you agree with these assumptions? If you disagree, how would your definition of marriage differ from Queen's?

## God's Definition of Marriage

### BY REV. TYRONE QUEEN, PASTOR, OAKLAND BAPTIST CHURCH, ALEXANDRIA, VIRGINIA

As the pastor of a Christian church, I am greatly saddened that other ministers have chosen to distort what the Bible says about one of the most fundamental relationships in all of humanity – the relationship of marriage.

As an African-American, I know the importance and necessity of civil rights and civil liberties and I am deeply troubled by their use of those as an argument for altering God's definition of marriage to fit the sexual desires of those who choose to ignore His word.

The God of the Bible is a gracious God, showing goodness and kindness to all of His creation without merit. As Americans, we count on God's graciousness when we repeat that phrase in the Pledge of Allegiance to our flag: "one nation, under God … with liberty and justice for all." Our being one nation under God is the precise reason it is possible to provide liberty and justice for all. Because of God's graciousness, we affirm we have been given "certain inalienable rights" and that among these rights are "life, liberty, and the pursuit of happiness."

But do we understand that enjoyment of God's benefits is linked to heeding His standards? People sometimes mistake God's graciousness to mean He has no standards for right and wrong, and for promoting what is good for the human family.

Our nation underwent the horror of a civil war because we forgot He created all people – and all races – as equal. And, according to the

Bible we are either actively serving God, and can expect His approval, or we are actively disobeying God and can expect His disapproval.

The Bible frankly commends sexual expression between a woman and a man in marriage, while consistently condemning homosexual behavior in both the Old and New Testaments (see Gen. 2:22-24; Lev. 18:22; Rom. 1:26-28).

Our country is involved in a debate as to whether there should be a federal marriage amendment defining marriage as a union between one woman and one man.

It must be recognized that God designed traditional marriage. God's design for marriage is good for all of mankind, and has been since the beginning of the human race. To change God's standard for the family is to put the very future and good of our country in jeopardy.

The issue is not complex – it is easy to see God's design for marriage is also the best design for the human race and promotes the common good of every nation.

Traditional marriage has always been the core unit of the family. It has created an arena for a woman and man to express femininity and masculinity in a complementary and cooperative manner. Additionally, children reared by a mother and father have the advantage of closely observing human sexuality in its male and female forms. This is vital to the sexual identity of children reared in the home environment.

Boys need to see masculinity modeled, and girls need to see feminin-ity modeled. The marriage of a mother to a mother cannot meet a child's need to see healthy maleness modeled. Similarly, a marriage of a father to another father cannot meet a child's need to see healthy femaleness modeled. But the marriage of one man to one woman has done this very well.

The standard of marriage defined as a union of a man and a woman has benefited human development by encouraging male and female cooperation, and by providing vital models of male and female sexu-ality to children nurtured in the home.

These are a few reasons why traditional marriage should be protected from the current attempts to promote same-sex "marriages." While the benefits of traditional marriage and family have contributed to the health and strength of our country, same-sex "marriage" advo-cates have not proven it will not harm the traditionally family unit.

The Bible reminds us that God is especially gracious to those who pursue a life and relationship with Him. He does not stop loving us when we fall short of keeping the standard, and, contrary to what some pastors preach, he does not stop loving us because we sin. He is gracious, forgiving, and Holy. But he loves us enough to hold us accountable to standards, which benefit us, while fulfilling His creative purposes.

The definition of marriage as a union between one man and one woman is one of those standards. We must trust God, and His standard for marriage.

3. The following argument offers a different definition of marriage (as a civil right). Read it, and answer the following questions:

   a. How does Lampo define marriage here, especially as it relates to gay people wishing to get married?
   b. What reasons and support does he provide for this definition?
   c. Who do you think Lampo sees as his audience? What assumptions about marriage does he share (or not share) with his audience?
   d. Map out the differences in the definition of marriage between Queen's and Lampo's articles. Where are these definitions at stasis? (That is, where are they "stuck"?)

## Why Gay Rights Are Civil Rights – and Simply Right

**BY DAVID LAMPO, *THE AMERICAN CONSERVATIVE***

There are many ways to define government oppression of its citizens, and certainly many examples of it in U.S. history. And no doubt some government impositions on individual freedom have been broader than others or have had more widespread and deadlier consequences. Perhaps that was the point that James Antle intended to make in his recent article "Why Conservatives Say No" when he derided the comparison of the black civil rights struggle of the 20th century with the gay civil rights struggle of the 21st. "For liberals, every social issue is Selma," he wrote. "If you disagree with whatever social cause the liberal champions," he continued, "you are the new Hitler, or at least the new Bull Connor."

The widespread misconception today of gay people as mostly smug, well-off whites with fat bank accounts and comfortable (and, we're told, chosen) lifestyles, however, does not negate the undeniable history of often brutal treatment of gays and lesbians and their lack of basic human rights in the eyes of government for most of this nation's history.

The gay rights movement has made enormous strides over the past few decades, and the recent surge in public support for the once unthinkable concept of same-sex marriage reflects this quite radical shift in American culture. Homosexuality and support for the rights of gay and lesbian Americans are now widely accepted, even among Republicans, and a large majority of Americans say they know someone who is gay. But America was not always so accepting.

It was a very different story in the '50s and '60s, when gays and lesbians were still relatively invisible in American society. Many gays lived in ghettos of their own in major cities, and most lived their lives in the closet, concealing their sexual orientation to keep their jobs or prevent eviction. Few commercial establishments served openly gay customers, and many that catered to gay clientele, such as bars and restaurants, were owned or operated by organized crime, required to pay off police in order to operate what were often illegal establishments.

Police were rarely sympathetic to gay victims of assault and other violent crimes, and police themselves were often the perpetrators, raiding gay bars to close them or shake them down. Sodomy laws were on the books in every state except Illinois (after 1961), and some convicted of the crime were sentenced to long prison terms. The American Psychiatric Association (APA) listed homosexuality as a sociopathic personality disorder in 1951, and gays were routinely characterized in the media by crude stereotypes.

Because of the APA designation, 29 states had laws that allowed gays to be detained by the police simply on the suspicion they were gay. According to historian David Carter, sex offenders in California and Pennsylvania could be confined to mental institutes, and in seven states they could be castrated. Electroshock therapy and lobotomies were sometimes used to "cure" homosexuals in the '50s and '60s, and "in almost all states, professional licenses could be revoked or denied on the basis of homosexuality, so that professionals could lose their livelihoods," Carter writes in *Stonewall: The Riots That Sparked the Gay Revolution*.

Known gays and lesbians were forbidden from working for the federal government, and President Dwight Eisenhower formalized this policy of discrimination with an executive order in 1953. Those were the days of the Red Scare and fear of communist infiltration of the U.S. government, so the U.S. Senate and other official bodies routinely held hearings to investigate how many "sex perverts" worked for the feds since they were considered security threats. Between 1947 and 1950 alone, 1,700 federal job applicants were rejected, over 4,300 members of the armed forces were discharged, and 420 were fired from their government jobs simply for being gay or on the suspicion that they were gay.

The FBI and many police departments maintained lists of known and suspected homosexuals, and the U.S. Post Office actually kept track of addresses to which gay-related material was mailed. It was not until 1958 that the U.S. Supreme Court affirmed the right to send such material through the mail, ending the federal watchlist of such addresses.

In today's culture it's hard to believe such a time existed, but it was in that context of routine and widespread persecution of gay people that the modern gay civil rights movement was born in 1969 amid riots set off by police raids at a New York City gay bar called the Stonewall Inn. Not until the late 1970s and 1980s was routine police prosecution of gay people in most large cities ended. Only with the Supreme Court's *Lawrence v. Texas* decision in 2003 were state sodomy laws finally declared unconstitutional, and in spite of that decision some of those laws are still on the books, if rarely enforced. The prohibition against openly gay members serving in our armed forces ended less than three years ago with the repeal of Don't Ask, Don't Tell, and it will take years for that change to be fully implemented and accepted in military culture.

While gay and lesbian legal equality has vastly improved—the overturning of DOMA by the Supreme Court is just the latest example—workplace discrimination on the basis of sexual orientation is still widespread, and many state and local governments are not legally barred from practicing such discrimination. Most states prohibit not just marriage equality but any legal recognition of gay couples, and adoption by gay couples is illegal in most states. The legacy of virulent homophobia and legal inequality still looms large in many parts of this country, and will for many years to come.

Critics of gay marriage would be wise to learn the history of institutional homophobia in America and how it helps drive today's gay rights movement, just as institutional racism inspired and drove the civil rights movement. As I argue in my book, *A Fundamental Freedom: Why Republicans, Conservatives, and Libertarians Should Support Gay Rights*, there is a fundamentally conservative and libertarian case for gay rights, including same-sex marriage, that is entirely consistent with the right's core principles of limited government and individual rights. Gay rights aren't just for liberals anymore: Polls consistently show that even a majority of rank and file Republicans support most of the so-called "gay rights agenda"—as it's derisively called by its opponents—including some form of legal recognition for gay couples.

Conservatives will continue to debate the issues of gay rights and same-sex marriage for years, and many of them will come to understand the fundamental injustice of subjecting gay and lesbian Americans to their own form of Jim Crow rather than sharing in equal rights for all. But one thing that should be clear to all is the demonstrable history of homophobia in this country and why it continues to inspire today's movement for gay and lesbian equality.

David Lampo is the author of *A Fundamental Freedom: Why Republicans, Conservatives, and Libertarians Should Support Gay Rights* and serves on the national board of Log Cabin Republicans.

## Arguments about Classification: Should the Thing Be Defined as Y or Z?

Because they ask whether something should be defined in terms of an already given or developed category, questions of classification are a bit more bounded than questions of genus (see Figure 9.3).

**EXAMPLES**

- Is this soggy area of land a wetland or a swamp?
- Is gun violence a public health crisis or a normal part of a free society?
- Were the *Charlie Hebdo* editorial board and cartoonists (murdered in a surprise attack by Islamic gunmen, presumably in response to the cartoons of Muhammad that were published by the magazine) heroic defenders of free speech or racists?
- Is cheerleading a sport or a display?
- Is pedophilia a disorder or a crime?
- Are termites pests or "soil engineers"?
- Is this scratch on the rental car ordinary wear and tear or damage?
- Are corporations organizations or people?
- Is ketchup a condiment or a vegetable?

stockphoto mania/Shutterstock.com

**FIGURE 9.3** Is this vandalism or art?

Read the following example of a classification definition argument. As you read, answer the following questions:

1. What is the prevailing definition of college, according to the author?
2. What evidence does he provide to show that this is the prevailing definition?
3. What are the author's reasons for disagreeing with the prevailing definition of college?
4. How does he think college should be defined instead?
5. What are his reasons for defining it this way instead?
6. Which definition of college do you find more persuasive?

## Higher Education Needs Soul

### BILL MAXWELL, PITTSBURGH POST-GAZETTE

A former classmate from the University of Chicago telephoned several months ago and asked if I would teach an online journalism course for the university in Illinois where he has taught for the last 15 years.

I declined the offer. But before doing so, I reminisced about the great face-to-face lectures and discussions we had in Chicago's Classics Building, our debates on the lawn in the quads, how our late afternoon classes moved to Woodlawn Tap, and how a group of us regularly studied together in Regenstein Library on the third floor.

My classmate pointed out that such nostalgia wouldn't do anything to help the nation's tens of thousands of students being shut out of our colleges and universities because there is not enough space and professors for them.

He said that MOOCs, short for massive open online courses, are the answer. I said that higher education today is about budget cuts and body counts. It is not about nurturing the whole student.

"Today's education doesn't have any essence or soul," I said. As I expected, my friend countered that "essence and soul don't pay the mortgage."

Since that conversation, MOOCs have been making headlines. These are courses taught online to large numbers of students, with most professors having little involvement with their students. Students usually watch video lectures and do assignments that are graded either by other students or by a machine.

Currently, no colleges or universities offer credit or accept transfer credit for these mega-classes, which are typically taught by outside groups that include unaccredited for-profit outfits. And there is a distinction to be made between these offerings and classes that leverage new technology to maintain direct faculty-to-student interaction despite distance.

But a movement in California has educators everywhere paying attention to MOOCs. Last week, Democratic state Sen. Darrell Steinberg introduced a bill that would require California's 145 public colleges and universities to grant credit for low-cost online courses offered by outside groups. The bill has a good chance to pass.

I wanted to hear from someone whose opinions I trust on such matters, so I spoke with Donald Eastman, president of Eckerd College, a private school in St. Petersburg. He said that online courses have a useful place in higher education. So far, that place has been in courses for adults who, for various reasons, have limited options to attend regular classes.

"Much more importantly, a string of courses—online or not—does not add up to a real college experience, even if these courses do add up, at some places, to a degree," he said. "As the Wizard of Oz says to the scarecrow, 'I cannot give you a brain, but I can give you a diploma.'"

Mr. Eastman argues that the real value of a college education comes through face-to-face debate and discussion with teachers and students before, during, and particularly after class.

He said he takes a lesson about the status of undergraduate education from what the president of the Chautauqua Institute told him about the legal profession over the last generation.

"He said the legal profession used to be about relationships, but now it's about transactions," Mr. Eastman said. "That is exactly what politicians with their insistence on 'no child left behind' and their advocacy of excessive and unremitting testing of students at virtually every grade level are doing: reducing education from a holistic experience to a series of discrete and often meaningless transactions."

It is nonsense, Mr. Eastman said, for public or private universities to pretend that online courses for young undergraduates provide quality education.

Like Mr. Eastman, Robert J. Zimmer, president of the University of Chicago, sees essential value in the campus experience. In a recent article for the *Atlantic* magazine, Mr. Zimmer wrote that college "provides young adults with the intellectual capital to succeed and the social capital to help them make connections, build networks, and establish lifelong relationships.

> "It provides them with skills in analysis and reasoning combined with confidence that will lead them boldly to articulate and embrace new ideas. It transforms their perspectives, opening them up to different cultures, different world views, and different ways of seeing—and solving—some of the world's most complex problems."
>
> MOOCs may be the future in this budget-slashing era, but the intrinsic value of higher education will diminish, and the nation will suffer in unforeseen ways if we continue on this path.

# 9c Formulating Definition Arguments

Both types of definitional arguments (genus and classification) start from the same set of questions:

1. What, exactly, are you (re)defining? (This could be either a concrete thing or an abstract concept.)

2. How has what you're defining been misunderstood? (So, why do you need to make an argument?)

3. What is your definition?

4. Why is your redefinition better?

    A basic template for an argument might look something like this: I'm defining _____ as _____, because I think it's been largely misunderstood by _____ as _____.

    To look at how a (written) argument of definition might shape up, let's start with an example that straddles the abstract and the concrete. In the following essay that classifies technology as a lens, not a prosthetic, I've highlighted the rhetorical moves I made. While of course every argument of definition will shape up differently, remember that they all still rely on the basic components of argument described in Chapter 7: an exigence, an audience, and a claim plus reasons and evidence.

## An Annotated Written Definition Argument

### Technology Is a Lens, Not a Prosthetic

Our commonsense ways of talking tend to carry with them the assumption that technology is under human control. Consider Charlton Heston's famous line (still a favorite among opponents of gun control), for instance: "Guns don't kill people; people kill

> The title states the argument of the piece up front: Note that this is a definition argument of classification (Should the thing be defined as Y or Z?).

> This establishes the typical definition of technology, using a well-known example of this kind of thinking.

people." On the surface, it's hard to argue with Heston's point: In the absence of sci-fi movie machine sentience, of course guns as a technology don't have their own agency or free will—they need to be operated by a person in order to do the job of killing. From a commonsense perspective, then, people do decide to kill people, and they can use a gun as a tool to carry out their will. In that sense, technology here would seem to be defined as a *pros-thesis*, or an extension of our human bodies: A gun here is just a much more lethal extension of our hand. By this logic, it's possible to think of cars, bikes, pencils, smartphones, *Facebook*, sewing machines, and filing cabinets as simple extensions of the human body, things that make it easier to carry out human purposes.

However, a definition of technology as a simple prosthesis or extension of our bodies ignores something very important; that is, the role that habit plays in our everyday lives, and how habits contribute to an embodied understanding of the world around us. If we take the role of habit into account, then it's more accurate to think of technology as a kind of *lens* that influences how we see (and behave) toward the world.

Let's use the gun again as an example. First, the unique function and structure of guns create specific kinds of potential actions that other kinds of technology don't have. For instance, the incredible projectile speed allows a gun to hit something at a distance with great speed, whether that be tin cans on a fence, targets, the tires of retreating vehicles, animals, or people. Its projectile speed also makes it an especially effective and fast way to penetrate flesh and bone.

And while most people could probably figure out how to fire a gun, being able to use a gun in stressful conditions requires a deep habituation that goes beyond a simple understanding of how a gun works. For instance, as an article on the blog "The Well-Armed Woman" points out, for a gun to actually be useful in self-defense, the user would need to be carrying it at all times: "It will become a part of your body. You need to know it, really know it." At the moment that the user needs her gun, the article says, "You will be relying on your instincts, will be forced to make decisions under ex-treme stress and you will not have the time to get acquainted with your gun! This is why practicing with your gun on an ongoing basis is critical." In other words, habituating oneself to the gun means both practicing with it so much that one doesn't need to think about the physicality of how to use it; but it also means habituating oneself to the idea of having a gun with one at all times.

The importance of habituation to a technology can be shown by another famous aphorism: Abraham Maslow's statement that "I suppose it is tempting, if the only tool you have is a hammer, to treat everything as if it were a nail." As Maslow suggests, our interaction with specific technologies creates habits of action and thought that literally reshape our bodies and minds. If we can extend Maslow's point about the hammer, we might say "If you have a gun, everything looks like a target." In other words, the gun introduces a way of responding to problems that would not have been possible without the combination of the gun's specific technological capacities and the human habituation.

To take a less loaded example (pun intended), we might think of regular *Facebook* users. By regularly checking their feed, responding to posts, and posting their own photos or updates, these people have accustomed themselves to social media and the idea that they are at most times a moment away from connection with a large network of people part of their lives. So it wouldn't be surprising if users, so habituated, began to see their experiences in terms of their potential as *Facebook* posts. That striking sky, that funny experience with the customer-service representative, that perfectly framed shot of your dog on the beach: All have the potential to be posted, shared, and responded to by others.

So if we consider technology in terms of the habits it requires us to create, then it seems more accurate to define technology as a *lens* through which we see the world rather than a mere prosthetic, or extension of our bodies. As we see something, so we act toward it, the wisdom goes; and so the technologies that we rely upon literally help to shape how we act toward the world.

## FOR DISCUSSION

1. The previous written piece on technology is written primarily for an academic audience (namely, you) as an example of a definition argument of classification. It is meant to appear as a written essay in a textbook. What other audiences might be interested in such a redefinition of technology? What other forms (i.e., modalities, mediums, genres, and forms of circulation) might it take? Brainstorm a list of possible revisions of this piece.
2. Read one of the three definition arguments reprinted in this chapter ("God's Definition of Marriage," "Why Gay Rights Are Civil Rights – And Simply Right," or "Higher Education Needs Soul"). Then do one of the following things:

   a. Copy and paste the argument into a Word or Google document (or photocopy it). Then annotate the argumentative and rhetorical moves like I did in "Technology Is a Lens, Not a Prosthetic."
   b. Map out the argumentative moves made in the essay. How do they differ from the ones in the earlier essay on technology, and why do you think they are different? Do you prefer one arrangement over the other? You can use the map you created to make your own argument of definition.

## ASSIGNMENTS

## Composing Definitions

### WRITE A DEFINITION ARGUMENT

Write your own definition essay, using the earlier template and sample essay as a model or inspiration. You can choose either a definition argument of genre (How should we define X?) or a definition argument of classification (Should we define X as Y or Z?). The audience for this essay should be your classmates and your teacher.

### TRANSFORMATION: MAKE IT VISUAL OR MULTIMODAL

Then, take the argument you made in your essay and recompose it for a different audience and purpose, using different means of communication. You might recreate it as a comparative infographic, for instance, or a short video or visual essay.

---

### FOR REFLECTION

**Transferable Skills and Concepts**
Can you think of an instance where someone has defined you (or something that you participate in and/or care about) unfairly? Write a journal entry describing this instance and why you thought the definition was unfair. Then answer these questions:

- What was his or her aim in creating this definition?
- What did he or she stand to gain or lose?
- What did *you* stand to lose?

# Evaluating

*By working through this chapter, you will be able to...*
- See how evaluation is part of your everyday life.
- Define and classify the basic types of criteria.
- Defend your criteria for evaluation to an audience.
- Use criteria to evaluate consumer products and policies.

## 10a Everyday Evaluations

Like analysis, evaluation is something we do constantly, something that is the basis of a great many of our decisions.

**EXAMPLES** You decide if that pair of jeans looks good or not. You spend a long time debating with your friends about whether the new Final Fantasy game is as good as the previous version. You gossip about one friend's particularly annoying Instagram posts. You give your meal at T.G.I. Friday's a big greasy thumbs down.

**EXAMPLES** You're also likely very familiar with academic forms of evaluation: In English class, for instance, you may be asked to evaluate your classmate's work, based on a given rubric of evaluation criteria. Evaluating others' creative work is the foundation of almost all creative writing workshops. Design critiques are part of the normal process for art and architecture students. As an advanced undergraduate or graduate student in any number of disciplines, you may be asked to critique a journal article as a way of helping you understand the language and engage with the discourse of that community. And, of course, via the grading process, your work is on the receiving end of evaluation arguments in every course you take.

The things you're good at evaluating are likely things that you encounter frequently, and in which you feel you have something at stake.

**EXAMPLE**   Take jeans, for instance—what's at stake for you in wearing jeans is your appearance, which means different things for different people (Figure 10.1). One person's reasons for buying a pair of jeans might include how they make his/her butt look (not flat, not square, say), the color (no whiskering or faded patches), the stretchiness, and whether they're tapered enough to wear under a pair of boots. Someone else will have a totally different set of criteria for evaluating jeans: for example, do they make me look hipster enough?

Other kinds of evaluations are more complex, particularly those that involve difficult decisions or ideas. When faced with the need to evaluate these more complex things (like when deciding who to vote for, for example), most humans are subject to not especially well-thought-out judgments. Like many, you have probably found yourself saying, "[Insert any politician's name/legislative

Africa Studio/Shutterstock.com

Kamenetskiy Konstantin/Shutterstock

Nick Starichenko/Shutterstock

**FIGURE 10.1**  Three Styles of Jeans

decision/idea here] is the worst." When pressed about why they think this, most people could come up with some reasons for their evaluation. But generally, these knee-jerk evaluations follow a "gut first, logic later" principle. The wrinkle is that so-called gut feelings are actually just crystallized thoughts, ideas, and reasons that have become so naturalized and familiar as to be almost invisible. So the goal for this chapter is to bring these habituated criteria and judgment processes to light—to make them more explicit, to examine them critically, and ultimately to make more careful evaluations.

MindTap®
Student Maker
Video 4: Reviewing
a Video

When you choose criteria to evaluate something (X), you are making an argument for *what makes a good X*.  Good, thoughtful evaluation relies on two basic steps:

1. Establish, rank, and defend criteria for evaluating X.

2. Provide evidence to show that X does or does not meet the established criteria and draw conclusions about X.

While sometimes (as when buying a pair of jeans or deciding who to vote for), WE are the audience for the evaluation, often we are also trying to persuade others that our judgment is correct. Thus, evaluation can be a deeply rhetorical process.

## 10b Establishing and Ranking Criteria: The Heart of an Evaluation

MindTap®
View Tiny Lecture
Video 9: Identifying
and Rating Criteria
for Evaluation

Central to any evaluation or critique are **criteria**. Criteria are the yardsticks by which you measure the value of a thing, whether that thing is a decision (your town's decision to allow a Super Walmart to be built), a person, an event (a movie, a concert, an art show), a book, a place (a restaurant, a college or university), or a consumer object (a smartphone, a car). And *ranking* criteria simply means deciding which are the most important to making the decision.

Criteria fall into several well-established categories, as Table 10.1 shows.

If you're judging a thing that matters only to yourself, you don't really need to defend your reasons for choosing these criteria.

**EXAMPLE**  If for you looking good (aesthetic criteria) outweighs economic considerations, you may not think twice about buying that $197 pair of perfectly fitted True Religion jeans.

But evaluations that involve persuading an audience require you to not only make your criteria explicit, but (depending on whom you're arguing to), may also require you to explicitly defend why those criteria are the most important ones to consider when making the decision.

**EXAMPLE**  While evaluating jeans is typically a process that involves only you, if you wanted to leave a useful review of a pair of jeans on Gap's website, you would have to make explicit to future jeans buyers the criteria by

**TABLE 10.1** Well-Established Categories of Criteria.

| | |
|---|---|
| **Aesthetic criteria** | Have to do with the sensory and emotional aspects of a thing—how it makes someone feel, its beauty, its pleasantness. |
| **Safety criteria** | Involve the risk of mental or bodily harm. |
| **Economic criteria** | Have to do with money—the literal cost of things. |
| **Efficiency criteria** | Related to economic criteria, but they have to do with the "cost" of time or effort involved in enacting the thing. You can think about efficiency and economic criteria in terms of the cost-benefit ratio—does the cost of doing something (in terms of actual money, time, or effort) outweigh the benefits? |
| **Process criteria** | Involve elements specific to a thing. For instance, if you were evaluating a car, you'd need to consider specific things like speed, the quality of its electrical system, safety, and gas mileage along with other types of criteria like aesthetics, economics, and efficiency. |
| **Moral criteria** | Involve the philosophical and ethical aspects of a thing or decision. |

which you judged your pair of jeans. You probably already made your judgment about the jeans before you started making your argument to the audience, but you will still need to walk them through the process by which you established criteria, ranked them, and ultimately arrived at this judgment.

Arguments about which criteria are most important for evaluating something become especially contentious when it comes to questions about whether or not a particular policy should get implemented. For instance, say your university is planning to remake a current roadway into a pedestrian zone (Figure 10.2). What criteria might go into making this judgment? To make it easier, we can put the criteria in terms of what "should" make a good campus:

- Safety: Campuses *should* be safe for students walking.
- Campus aesthetics: Campuses *should* be pleasant places to be.
  But we also need to consider . . .
- Efficiency of movement: It *should* be easy for motorists to get from one area of campus to another.
- Convenience: It *should* be easy to park on campus.
- Economics: Businesses in or near this vehicle-free zone *should* not be affected by the decisions of the university.

The university and the community in which it's situated will have to negotiate these criteria and ultimately decide which are most important in implementing this change (or not).

Before you read the following sample review (of the Disney animated film *Frozen*), pause to think about what makes a good animated film in your own mind. What are your criteria for evaluating animated films? Are they similar to those of the author of the review below, and would you rank them the same as she does?

**FIGURE 10.2 Evaluating a policy decision.** Is it a good idea to convert a roadway to a pedestrian zone?

## An Annotated Example of Identifying Criteria

### *Frozen* an Icy Blast of Fun from the First Snowflake

**BY BETSY SHARKEY, LOS ANGELES TIMES FILM CRITIC**

Walt Disney Pictures has its animation mojo back. Finally.

With a cool, contemporary spin on a fairy-tale classic, a dramatic Nordic landscape animated in splendid storybook style and Broadway vets belting out power ballads, "Frozen" is an icy blast of fun from the very first flake. A certain scene-stealing snowman named Olaf is chief among them.

Directors Chris Buck and Jennifer Lee create a magical 3-D winter wonderland in "Frozen." A sisterhood saga loosely based on Hans Christian Andersen's "The Snow Queen," it is filled with heart and heart-stopping action.

It is a much-needed thaw after a very long winter for Disney's legendary cartoon brand.

Last year's "Wreck-It Ralph" was a hoot — the video-arcade battle between good and evil very current in story and style. But "Ralph" never felt like it belonged to the same family as Disney's modern-day classics such as "The Little Mermaid," "Beauty and the Beast," "Aladdin," and "The Lion King."

The in-between years have been marked by a lot of nice, but not especially noteworthy movies. Meanwhile Pixar stepped in and

The reviewer has laid out most of her criteria for this animated Disney film in these first few paragraphs. According to her review, her criteria for what makes a good animated fairy-tale film are as follows:

- Provides a cool, contemporary spin on fairy tale classics
- Has notable singers performing power ballads
- Has splendid animation
- Has "heart" (emotional resonance)
- Has good action sequences
- Has few "slips or stumbles"

stole the company's animated show with "Up," "Cars," "Toy Story," and "Wall-E," to name a few.

But "Frozen" is fabulous. Its thrills and chills are brought to life by an excellent ensemble of voices led by Kristen Bell and Idina Menzel. As Anna and Elsa, respectively, they are sisters and the princesses of the mythical Scandinavian kingdom of Arendelle where the story is set.

The film represents a fusion of old and new both on-screen and behind it. Lee, who co-wrote "Wreck-It Ralph" (with Phil Johnston) and has sole credit for "Frozen," is also the first female to sit in a Disney animation directing chair. She's done a bang-up job wearing both hats. For Buck, who's been in Disney's animation trenches since 1981's "The Fox and the Hound," "Frozen" is his third feature — and his best — as a director. Despite the blizzard conditions, there is nary a slip or stumble from start to finish.

> Another important criterion: Good animated films must have a good score.

As with the best of Disney musicals, "Frozen's" songs soar. The original pieces come from Kristen Anderson-Lopez and Robert Lopez, who has a couple of Tonys on his shelf for co-writing "Avenue Q" and "The Book of Mormon," the latter with those "South Park" renegades, Trey Parker and Matt Stone. Which makes you wonder whether "Frozen" might be Broadway bound. You'd expect Menzel, who earned a Tony for making Elphaba so deliciously "Wicked," to crush all those soaring notes. But Bell is the stunner.

"Frozen" begins when the princesses are young and wishing for the season's first snowfall. Elsa makes it happen, conjuring up a blizzard — indoors — with magical powers she's just discovering. But the fun soon ends when a slip and a fall puts Anna's life in jeopardy.

Though Anna recovers, Elsa doesn't. Fear of hurting her little sister with her powers sends the princess behind closed doors, separating the girls the entire time they are growing up and presenting the perfect opportunity for one of the film's show-stoppers. A very catchy number called "Love Is an Open Door," it is among the most memorable, in part for the delightful door-slamming antics that accompany it.

The action really gets underway when Elsa comes of age and comes out of seclusion for her coronation. Love is in the air. Anna's already swooning over Prince Hans (Santino Fontana), and a number of suitors are vying for Elsa's hand — glove-covered always to keep her secret secret. Her powers make for some of the film's most stunning animation as snow and ice fly and form into incredible shapes, from lethal shards to towering ice castles.

At the heart of the film is the battle between love and fear. Resolution becomes a long journey when Elsa flees Arendelle, leaving the kingdom locked in winter's fierce grip and Anna searching for her. This is also where the film develops its very playful sense of humor.

> Another important criterion for what makes a good animated Disney film: humor.

Anna's something of a tomboy, forever getting into scrapes, which Bell's comic timing makes absolutely charming. But the entire film is populated by characters who spend a great deal of time teasing and pranking. There is the handsome, reclusive mountain man Kristoff (Jonathan Groff) and his reindeer buddy Sven. By turns captivated and incensed by the headstrong Anna, he's soon enlisted in the search. There are rock trolls rolled out to help decipher questions of magic led by Pabbie (Ciarán Hinds). One of the main villains is the scheming Duke of Weselton (Alan Tudyk), a name that always gets a laugh.

And then there is Olaf. The snowman is an animation marvel, designed to keep coming apart and bouncing back together. His broad smile, buck teeth and wide eyes are the very embodiment of innocence and adoration. Josh Gad, who voices Olaf, is so endearing you really do want to just hug him — knowing Disney, I'm sure there's a plush toy in the works. Gad's been building an impressive career for a while with a Tony nomination in 2011 for his star-turn in "The Book of Mormon." And he was the only reason to watch NBC's short-lived 2013 White House comedy "1600 Penn."

Fortunately, he is far from the only reason to go see "Frozen." In fact, there are so many good ones, I can't begin to count them all — kind of like snowflakes, a flurry of them.

## FOR DISCUSSION

1. As a class, decide on one or several of the things in the following list (or brainstorm your own things to evaluate). Individually, identify and rank the top three criteria that you would use to evaluate each thing. Then, as a class, compare your criteria and rankings. If they are different, discuss the differences: Why are certain criteria more important to some people than others?

   a. A romantic comedy (or, decide on some other film genre)
   b. A snack
   c. A coffee shop
   d. A car
   e. A pen
   f. A history class (or choose some other kind of class)
   g. A vacation
   h. A place to go on a date

2. Using the criteria you generated for the things in the list of above, what would be your example for the *best* one of these? What specific instance of the thing best meets your criteria and rankings?

# 10c Using Evidence in Evaluation Arguments to Draw Conclusions about X

Once you've identified and ranked your criteria for evaluating a thing, you'll need to take the next step to show evidence that the thing does or doesn't meet these criteria.

**EXAMPLE**   To go back to our jeans example, if your most important criterion for evaluating jeans was comfort, you would show how a specific pair of jeans was or wasn't comfortable by demonstrating the stretchiness of material (or lack thereof), where they sit at your waist, and other factors that determine whether or not the jeans meet your specifications of comfort.

For more complex evaluations, you'll need to gather evidence more carefully, from multiple sources. For instance, let's go back to our evaluation of the university's proposal to convert a current roadway into a pedestrian-only zone (Section 10b). If we decided that our top criterion for evaluating the proposal was pedestrian safety, it would be important to provide evidence to the stakeholders in this issue that the current situation (i.e., the road) presented a significant risk to pedestrian safety. We might gather the following as evidence:

- Data on the number of cars that drive on the road per hour, versus the number of students who cross the road between classes.
- Using the above data, we could statistically calculate the relative risk to pedestrians that results from these numbers.
- Data on the numbers of pedestrian accidents on that roadway over the past ten years.
- Data from universities or other institutions that have implemented similar policies to show how the risk to pedestrians has gone down since the implementation of the policy.
- Results from a survey of campus and town to gauge whether there is support for the proposed change.

## FOR DISCUSSION

1. Take one of the other criteria that could be considered in evaluating the university proposal to convert a roadway to a pedestrian zone (e.g., campus aesthetics, efficiency of movement, convenience, and economic impact) and decide what evidence would need to be collected to effectively evaluate the decision.
2. Read the following article and respond to these questions:
   a. What criteria does Florez use to evaluate student loan debt (i.e., what should debt *not* do)?

b. What evidence does she use to support her argument that student loan debt is bad?

c. Do you agree with her criteria, rankings, and overall evaluation?

d. What other criteria and/or evidence might you bring in to either support or contradict her argument?

## Student Loan Debt: A Problem for All

**BY JULIE FLOREZ, TELEGRAPH - HERALD (DUBUQUE)**

As a business community, we need to get ahead of this.

The effects of student loan debt are not somebody else's problem. Our businesses, our community, and our families are all going to be either directly or indirectly affected. Many believe that unless it is addressed, student loan debt could generate the next economic bubble – and when it bursts, it will affect our local economy, as well as the national economy.

Since 2004, the amount of student loan debt has quadrupled, estimated at $1.3 trillion. To put this into perspective, the total amount budgeted for federal government spending in the current fiscal year is just less than $4 trillion, while the entire accumulated national debt is $14 trillion. The amount of student loan debt will impact the economy.

Dollars spent paying student loans means fewer dollars spent buying cars, homes, or electronics, which, in turn, undermines jobs and economic growth. It most likely will impact the startup of small businesses, which create new jobs and services that drive the economy.

We have been fortunate during recent economic downturns compared to many other areas in the country. The Dubuque area has weathered downturns fairly well because it is diversified, thanks to the efforts of local economic development officials.

But student loan debt is pervasive. How many of us have a family member or friend who is facing the burden of trying to get a start in life while they are saddled with tens of thousands of dollars in additional debt?

The average student leaves college with $29,000 in college loan debt. This will impact an entire generation of wage earners. In the decades ahead, consumer spending will be hit harder as more of these debt-ridden former students become a larger and larger part of the buying public – which will be buying less.

There are many factors contributing to the increased level of student debt. It certainly is not an easy issue to address and yes, it is drawing more attention nationally from business and government leaders. We have begun to see more options to assist in this area and there are many resources to help young adults navigate through the beginning years of debt. But it still needs to be part of our everyday discussions.

We have to make sure our community and government leaders know that we take this economic threat seriously. Solutions start with a single idea, but they will never be put into play without that first conversation. Some of those conversations need to happen with the ones most affected – our young people – before they sign their name on their first loan.

At the very least, we need to do more to promote financial literacy to our young people, whether in our schools, at home or with the young workers in our businesses. We have to find positive ways to connect with them and to communicate the seriousness of this whole issue. During the course of four years they might sign their name to loans that could potentially take decades to pay off. On a personal level, they will be paying a serious price because of decisions they made in the early years of adult life.

These are difficult things to understand at a young age, especially for someone who has never balanced a checkbook, created a simple budget or paid off a credit card. The effects of accrued interest can be overwhelming when the time comes to start paying their debts and they realize what it adds to the balance of the loans.

Young people, before they even get to college, need to understand the basics of a checking account, types of loans, budgeting, credit history, credit scores as well as simple and accrued interest. They also need to understand the differences in student loans – public versus private – and what it means to default on student loans. There can be serious ramifications.

These are tough areas to discuss but it is better to be proactive to prevent inadvertent or uniformed decisions that can negatively affect their credit score for years to come. A bad credit score not only affects a young person's ability to take out a loan or the rate they get on a credit card, it can affect their ability to get a job. Some businesses check credit scores during the hiring process.

College student loan debt is not somebody else's problem. It's a problem for all of us, and we should all take it personally. What can each of us do to help educate our young people in this area?

# 10d Evaluating Consumer Products

The need for effective evaluation has become increasingly pressing in the public realm. The number of consumer goods and services available (especially combined with the limitations on time faced by most people) can make decisions about how to spend one's money and time overwhelming. So people have increasingly been relying on the opinions of others like them to help them make decisions about what to buy, where to eat, what movies to see, and so forth—so much so, in fact, that recent research has shown that traditional marketing techniques are losing effectiveness. Many websites have been explicitly designed to allow ordinary people to review a variety of things (Figure 10.3). The compiled evaluations of large numbers of people serve to provide useful information for consumers.

---

**WEBSITES BY CATEGORY THAT ALLOW CUSTOMER REVIEWS**

**Consumer Products:** Almost every site that sells products, such as *Consumer Reports* and *Angie's List*, now provides a place for customers to review their purchases.
**Restaurants:** *Yelp, UrbanSpoon, TripAdvisor*
**Movies:** *rottentomatoes.com, Netflix, IMDB*
**Books:** *Goodreads, Amazon, AbeBooks, Powells*, other sites that sell books online.

---

When you're writing a consumer review, it's necessary to choose criteria that are appropriate for the specific category of thing that you're evaluating.

**EXAMPLE** It's not fair (and in fact, it's rather meaningless) to evaluate a fast-food restaurant using criteria for fine-dining restaurants. You or your

Source: Yelp, Inc.

Source: Angie's List

Source: Consumer Reports

**FIGURE 10.3** Examples of Websites That Allow Customer Reviews

readers wouldn't learn very much if you were to conclude that White Tower Burgers wasn't a good place to take a visiting dignitary because it was full of drunk college students, had florescent lighting rather than candles, and had a limited menu with food that came wrapped in paper instead of being beautifully presented on china. Rather, you judge White Tower by the same criteria that you'd use to judge other fast-food burger joints, and you'd make those criteria explicit.

## FOR DISCUSSION

Find a group of nonprofessionally written reviews for the same restaurant—you can easily find these on apps like *Yelp* or *UrbanSpoon*. With a small group or as a class, identify all the criteria that various people are using to judge the restaurant. Do you agree with their criteria and their rankings? Which reviews do you think are the best or most valuable, and why? Which are the least helpful, and why?

## ASSIGNMENT

### Write a Review of a Local Business, Event, or Attraction

Write a review of something at your college or in your town; this can be anything from a new business to a local concert to an area attraction (like a hiking area or museum). First establish a set of criteria that you'll use to review the thing; rank your criteria; then write the review based on those criteria. Give the review a headline that sums up your evaluation, and make sure to include several good photos in your review. This might also be a class project—you might review a number of local venues and attractions and publish it as a guide for new students, for instance.

# 10e Composing Multimodal Consumer Reviews

Forbes says that video reviews of products are on the rise, for several reasons. First of all, they have more authenticity; they're produced by everyday consumers, and unlike written texts, viewers can judge the trustworthiness of the reviewer by their appearance, body language, and gestures. Second, because the reviewer is holding and interacting with the product, viewers can get a much better sense of the product than with the typical static images that accompany traditional written reviews. For these reasons, it's ostensibly also harder to produce a fraudulent video review.

As with written product reviews, *Amazon.com* and other sites are allowing reviewers to post their own review videos. The site *reelSEO.com* gives some tips for creating good product reviews (i.e., those that an audience will actually watch):

1. The more concise, the better—your video shouldn't exceed three minutes.
2. Focus on the product (not on impressing viewers with how clever you are), and be fair in your treatment of the product.
3. Concentrate on the product's primary features; don't create an exhaustive, boring list.
4. Don't read your script—have talking points, and improvise from there. Otherwise it will sound canned.
5. Edit so that each shot is no longer than 3 seconds.

See Section 15a for more specific tips on shooting good video.

## ASSIGNMENT

### Create a Video Review of a Consumer Product

1. Choose a consumer product. Ideally, it should be something you've recently purchased but that you're fairly familiar with and have an opinion about.

2. Create a loose script that you'll use for the video. In the script, first tell the reader exactly what you're evaluating, when you bought it, and how often and in what way you use the product. Then write your evaluation: Use three to five criteria, rank them in order of most to least important, and walk the audience through each criterion, showing how the product does or doesn't meet it. In the end of the script, summarize your evaluation and make a recommendation for whether or not the viewer should buy the product (with necessary qualifiers).

    For instance, here's an example script that I might create for reviewing the coat I'm currently wearing:

    *Today I'm reviewing this short quilted [Company X] jacket in black with a maroon lining. I bought this jacket to wear for work through fall and early winter.*

    *The first reason I like this jacket is that it's warm, but not too heavy. Because I walk to work, I find that I tend to overheat quickly; this jacket keeps me warm but not too warm, at least while the temperature is above 20 degrees.*

    *The second thing I like about the jacket is how it looks. It's about hip length and unlike many quilted coats, it's tailored and not too puffy, so it looks more professional for work than a ski jacket would, for instance.*

*I also find the black color and the pattern of the quilting to be unique and stylish, and have gotten a fair number of compliments on it.*

*Finally, I've found this jacket to be very durable. I've had it for five years, and it still looks new. The quality of the fabric, seaming, and construction is good, and from other [Company X] reviews I've read, I think the same is true of all [Company X] jackets.*

*Overall, based on the warmth, looks, and durability, I would highly recommend this jacket or other [Company X] products.*

3. Film your video, using the tips provided for shooting good video in the brief list from *reelSEO.com* (earlier) and in Section 15a.

4. After you get feedback from your students and instructor, post the review to *Amazon* or another site that accepts consumer review videos.

---

## ASSIGNMENT

### Review a Film for Common Sense Media

Go to Common Sense Media's site (*www.commonsensemedia.org*). Watch a few of the site's movie reviews (which are aimed at parents to help them decide whether a particular movie is appropriate for children). Determine which criteria the reviewers are using to review the films. Then use these criteria to create your own film review. Create a video of your review with voiceover and clips of the film (see section 15a "How to Create Videos" for an explanation of how to use editing software and create audio components for your review).

---

# 10f Evaluating a Person's Accomplishments

People, like everything else we encounter, are subject to evaluation.

**EXAMPLE** For instance, let's say you've noticed a pattern in which when the boss is around, one of your coworkers is good at looking very busy, but when it's just you and him, this coworker constantly plays on his phone, leaving it to you to do all the work. Naturally, you might get resentful, and think "what a jerk this guy is" (a negative evaluation).

While you may not have been fully aware of it, you arrived at a judgment of your coworker using the same sort of evaluation process we've been discussing here. Your criteria for judgment here is moral—stated as a "should," it would be something like "coworkers should participate equally in work."

Evaluations of people can be very informal, as in the case of your lazy coworker, where most likely you just mutter about him under your breath or gossip about him with other coworkers. Evaluations of people can be more formal, as when you are making a toast about someone's accomplishments, writing a eulogy, or otherwise praising or blaming the individual—this actually is a special form of rhetorical activity called an *encomium*. The most formal sorts of person evaluations (at least, the ones with the most at stake) might be performance evaluations of employees.

Just as with consumer reviews, you must be clear about your criteria for evaluating a person. Specifically, make sure that your criteria are appropriate to their role.

**EXAMPLE**  For instance, most of us have had an experience where a person can be excellent in one role and less-than-excellent in another (think of your football coach who was also your history teacher, for instance, or your boss who was a nice lady but pretty ineffectual at managing employees).

It's important to identify the criteria relevant to the specific role you are evaluating, and be sure to evaluate the person on those criteria. Criteria for evaluating a supervisor at a coffee shop might include the following:

A good supervisor should . . .

- Communicate effectively with employees.
- Treat employees fairly and make sure they feel valued.
- Make sure adequate supplies are always on hand.
- Make it clear what procedures need to be followed and how they should be followed.
- Be able to address problems quickly and effectively.

## FOR DISCUSSION

1. Brainstorm a number of roles (e.g., friend, parent, mentor). Choose several of these roles and individually come up with at least five criteria that you might use to evaluate someone in that role. Then compare your criteria as a class. Does everyone have the same criteria for judging people in that role? If not, how do you account for the discrepancies?
2. Think of someone you've made a judgment about recently. What was your evaluation of that person, and what criteria did you use to judge them? If you were to think more consciously about it and develop more criteria appropriate to the role on which you were evaluating them, would your judgment of them change?

## ASSIGNMENT

### Appreciation or Critique

Compose an appreciation or a critique of a public figure. It could be someone local—the pastor at your church, for instance—or it can be someone more widely known. Your appreciation or critique must include the following:

- An obvious reason for critiquing or praising this person at this moment (aka an *exigence*; see Chapter 2).
- Criteria for judging this person, which you may need to defend to your audience.
- Evidence about how the person meets or doesn't meet the criteria.
- A clear statement of judgment about this person.

Your critique or appreciation can take one of the following forms:

**Written:** An opinion essay, destined for publication in a specific place that you designate (the opinion section of your local paper, an online magazine devoted to the subject that the person is known for, etc.).

**Visual:** An infographic (perhaps organized around a photo of the person).

**Multimodal:** A short (1.5–2 minute) video that uses images, snippets of other video clips, music, and text (whether spoken or written) to create a statement praising or blaming the person (note: this would probably only work if the person was relatively well known).

# 10g Evaluating Policies

Policies are decisions made by governing or legislative bodies that direct people's conduct and behavior. They are at least "the law of the land," if not the actual law. While policy evaluations are used especially in the disciplines of environmental science and political science, they are also very useful tools for thinking through the implications and impacts of policies and decisions of all kinds.

MindTap®
View How to
Video 5: How to
Evaluate a Policy

Evaluating
a Policy

**EXAMPLES**  Policies can be everything from national dictates about how to treat foreign nationals who have been arrested, to a homeowner's association policy about what color drapes residents are allowed to display, to university policies prohibiting sorority houses on campus.

But policies are not once-and-for-all things; because of ever-changing circumstances, policies continually need to be revisited, and perhaps revised. Some organizations make it a priority to continually review policy; others only do so after a problem with the old policy is revealed.

**EXAMPLE** As an instance of the latter kind of approach, the University of Idaho recently decided to change the process of student course evaluations. Previously, course evaluations were available for any student to see, but only available in paper format. Students would have to physically walk to a campus office to look at them (not many students did so). Then the university announced that it would make these evaluations available online. Suddenly, the means by which courses were evaluated (via a simple two-number system) seemed like it wouldn't provide meaningful enough information about the courses, so a university committee was directed to evaluate the policies of the review process and suggest possible changes.

When you write policy evaluations, your audience can be either the creators of the policy or those who will be affected by it. Your purpose for policy evaluations might be to critique or praise a policy that is already in place, or to prevent or champion for a proposed policy. But either way, your policy evaluation should be fair, should acknowledge counterarguments or other points of view, and should be grounded in evidence.

## FOR DISCUSSION

1. Brainstorm a list of policies that are currently being discussed or debated in your school, town, state, and country right now. As a class, choose one or two to discuss in more detail. Do you agree with these policies? Can you see potential problems that might arise as a result of them?
2. Read the following editorial on Florida's proposed campus carry law. Then answer the following questions:
   a. What is the author's opinion about campus carry (i.e., how does he evaluate it)?
   b. What criteria does he use to make his evaluation?
   c. Does he introduce any concessions or counterarguments?
   d. Do you agree with his evaluation?

   ### On-Campus "Carry" Bill

   Last year, state Rep. Greg Steube's bill to arm school personnel failed—fortunately. It would have allowed designated school employees, once trained, to carry concealed weapons on campus. The risks outweighed the potential value of protecting students and school personnel from a would-be attacker.

   This year Steube, R-Sarasota, has reworked the bill and will reintroduce it in the coming legislative session. The legislation this time will be more measured and comprehensive. It deserves careful consideration, but also cautious scrutiny.

There's no doubt that the threat of a school shooting, especially in light of the 2012 massacre in Newtown, Conn., has become all too real for students, parents and school personnel.

Yet any proposal to allow anyone but a law enforcement officer to carry a gun on school grounds should be viewed with extreme skepticism.

That said, Steube's new bill is an improvement over last year's. Among other provisions, it would:

- Require that any armed personnel—whether school employees or volunteer security guards—have a law enforcement or military background. School principals would decide whether to allow armed personnel and whom they would be.

- Require extensive weapons training recommended by the Florida Department of Law Enforcement, and annual retraining.

- Prescribe schoolwide drills to prepare for a potential shooter on campus.

- Require that school construction plans be reviewed by law enforcement to ensure that security measures are incorporated.

## BEYOND THE BACKGROUND

Drills and law enforcement reviews are reasonable and warranted. Many schools and districts, including those in Sarasota and Manatee counties, already include "lockdown" drills and security reviews in their safety plans. Any districts or private schools that have not taken such steps should be required to do so.

As was the case last year, Steube's provisions for arming personnel at schools are the most controversial.

The requirement of a law enforcement or military background is a distinct improvement over the previous legislation, which would have permitted anyone from teachers to cafeteria workers to carry guns.

Yet even expertise in handling weapons is no guarantee that armed individuals can be trusted to have weapons on school campuses, let alone fire them in a tension-filled situation. The record of individual and mass shootings, unfortunately, is replete with military veterans and former law enforcement officers.

Curtis Reeves, the man charged in the recent fatal shooting at Pasco County movie theater, is both a former Tampa police officer and a Navy veteran. Last year, a former Bradenton police officer was convicted of murder in the shooting death of his wife. The shooter in last year's horrific massacre at the Washington Navy Yard, in which 12 people were killed, was a Navy veteran.

## UNDERSTANDABLE CONCERNS

Before the Legislature allows anyone other than a current law enforcement officer to carry a weapon on a campus, it must ensure—by requiring thorough background checks, psychological tests, or other means—that those designated to protect students and school personnel will not themselves pose a threat.

Steube's concerns are understandable. While school resource officers are posted at many high schools and middle schools, they are not normally stationed at elementary schools. To place officers at every school would be hugely expensive. As Steube has noted, in the event of a shooter's attack, law enforcement might be unable to reach suburban or rural schools in time to avert or at least minimize a tragedy.

The Legislature's best response to the threat of a school shooting would be to provide the funding necessary to post an active law enforcement officer in each public school. Short of that, lawmakers must ensure that any proposed solution does not compromise school safety.

## ASSIGNMENT

# Write an Evaluation of a Policy or Decision

1. Identify a specific policy or decision (one that's either already in place or proposed) that you want to review. You might focus on policies or decisions of your state, town, university or college, or an organization you belong to. Mind the scope of the policy, and your own ethos in regards to it; unless this is a long-term assignment, it's unlikely that you'll have enough time to come up something meaningful to say regarding policies about national health care or immigration, for instance (unless, maybe, you're talking about its application to a more local level).

2. Read at least ten different articles on the subject—these can be a mix of opinion pieces and news articles (for instructions on how to find sources, see Chapter 11). Using the list of criteria types in Table 10.1, identify what criteria are being discussed as considerations in making

the decision. Which criteria seem most important to people who want to implement this policy? Which criteria seem most important to people who don't want the policy implemented?

3. Research the origins of the policy, using the 5 Ws:
   - What is it? Summarize the policy. What and who, specifically, does it govern?
   - Who was responsible for implementing it?
   - When was it implemented?
   - Where does it apply? What is its scope?
   - Why was it implemented? Why at that time? What problem was it put in place to address?

4. Identify a list of criteria (three to five) for evaluating the policy. These will probably be based on what the policy should be doing, as well as some basic criteria like the effectiveness or impact of the policy, efficiency (the cost-benefit ratio), sustainability of the policy, and community acceptance.

5. Research the effectiveness and effects of the policy. You might also summarize or clarify what it should be doing (the ideal state of things that it's supposed to govern or dictate).

6. Evaluate the policy using the criteria you established for step 3.

7. The structure of the paper is rather straightforward:
   - An introduction that identifies and explains the policy you're planning to evaluate, and explains *why* the policy needs to be evaluated at this time.
   - Identification, explanation, and justification of the criteria you're using to evaluate the policy.
   - An explanation of how the policy as currently implemented fulfills the criteria you've identified in step 2.
   - A conclusion that presents your recommendations about the policy.

For more on the writing process, see Chapter 13, "Creating Written Compositions."

---

FOR REFLECTION

**Transferable Skills and Concepts**
Think of an evaluation with which you strongly disagree. Write a journal entry describing the evaluation and the criteria being used to judge the thing. Do you think that the wrong criteria are being used? Why would the evaluator use those instead of others?

# Proposing

**11**

*By working through this chapter, you will be able to ...*

- Understand the purpose and different types of proposal arguments.
- Explain the difference between a practical and a policy proposal.
- Use the elements of rhetoric to clarify the scope of a proposal argument.
- Compose your own proposal arguments using the five components of a proposal.

## 11a The Gold Standard of Persuasion: Action

Proposals are organized around the stasis question "Should we do X?" In some ways, proposal arguments are the clearest form of persuasive communication because they aim to get people to take *action*. Action is the gold standard of persuasion: If you can convince people to DO something, you know they've been persuaded—they believe in an idea strongly enough to actually risk time, money, or reputation in the completion of an action.

You are already very familiar with proposal arguments (as with most arguments) because you make them all the time. Proposal arguments come in many forms:

- Informal, everyday proposal arguments, like the kind you make with your friends: "Can we see [a comedy] instead of Saw 11? It's supposed to be hilarious, and I'm not in the mood for a horror film."
- Advertisements, whose fundamental persuasive message is "You should buy this!" or (in the case of public advocacy ads or PSAs), "You should do (or not do) this!"

- Newspaper editorials that aim to get readers or others to take some sort of action.
- Bills, which are drafts of laws proposed to legislative bodies by federal, state, and local governments.
- Internal proposals at companies aimed at identifying and solving an organizational problem.
- Academic conference proposals.
- Grant proposals seeking funding to address some need.

# 11b Components of Proposal Arguments

Whether they are explicitly articulated or implied, all effective proposals have the following components:

- An articulation of an audience's *problem or need* to which the proposal will respond.
- A strong and clear *proposal claim* (what X or Y should do; what should happen).
- *Supporting arguments and evidence* for why this solution is feasible and beneficial, and better than other options.
- An *acknowledgement of potential problems* with adopting the course of action you propose.
- A *demonstration* of how the proposal addresses the need or problem.

The elements of proposals are fairly straightforward; the difficult part is matching a proposal claim to an audience, something we might call the *scope* of a proposal. Proposals vary wildly in scope: They can be as specific as a city councilor's proposal to city council that a restroom get built downtown, or they can be as big as proposals about changes to immigration policy made to the American public in the opinion section of a newspaper. We might also think of a proposal's scope in terms of whether it's intended to address an *event-based problem* or an *everyday problem* (see Chapter 6).

How do you decide on a proposal's scope? For this, you need to consult Chapters 1 and 2 about the elements of the rhetorical situation, including your ethos and agency in the situation, the exigence and kairos of the issue, and the means of communication that are appropriate and available to you. It really depends on what level the issue is "hot" right now. For instance, we could take immigration. This issue suddenly took center stage after President Donald Trump issued a series of statements and executive orders during his first month in office. Proposals responding to the issue emerged at national, state, and local levels. Table 11.1 provides a glimpse of the scope and types of proposals made around this issue:

**TABLE 11.1** The Scope of Proposals Responding to Executive Orders on Immigration, Early 2017

| SCALE | PROPOSER → | PROPOSED ACTION → | AUDIENCE |
|---|---|---|---|
| NATIONAL | Political activists and members of the U.S. public | Calling congressional representatives to voice support or opposition to immigration policy. | U.S. public |
| | Right-leaning newspaper editorial | Calling for Trump's lawyers to "do over" the immigration order with greater care so that it's less likely to be challenged in court. | Newspaper readers |
| | Newspaper opinion piece written by a Republican senator | Calling to make U.S. immigration policy more like Canada's and Australia's, which focus on admitting highly skilled immigrants. | Newspaper readers |
| STATE | State legislator | Bill that forces cities and municipalities in the state to comply with ICE agents and that will withhold state funds from those who don't comply. | State legislature |
| LOCAL | City mayor | Making the city a sanctuary city, in which law enforcement officials and municipal employees cannot enquire about a resident's immigration status. | City council |
| | University faculty senate | Passing a resolution that formalizes as policy current university practices that protect noncitizen students, staff, and faculty. | Upper-level university administration |
| | Local community activist groups | Holding a rally in town and town hall meetings to show (respectively) support for immigrants and opposition to immigration proposals. | Town residents |

## 11c Persuasively Describing a Problem or Need

Problems (or, if you prefer, you can think of them as needs) are the basis of all proposals. Even advertisements must concisely and persuasively define a problem or need for the audience, as the ad for Tile in Figure 11.1 demonstrates.

If your audience doesn't realize they have a problem or doesn't understand the extent of it, a proposal to help solve the problem won't be very effective. For example, I remember seeing an ad a few years ago for a women's depilatory (hair removal) product that featured a distressed-looking woman in a bathtub who seemed to be having trouble holding onto a can of shaving cream. I remember thinking "This is not a thing—shaving cream cans aren't that slippery." The ad's proposal (you should buy this because it's hard to shave!) failed because it didn't make evident enough the need for the product it was selling.

Any proposal you make first requires that you accurately identify the reasons that a problem is occurring. Of course, Chapter 6 extensively discusses how to articulate a problem and give it presence for the audience (see Section 6c), and so as part of the process for creating your proposal you may want to write a problem analysis statement, as explained in Section 6d.

Source: Tile, Inc.

**FIGURE 11.1** This simple ad quickly highlights a common problem that can be solved by buying this product.

Answering the questions that follow will also help you more clearly pinpoint the problem for which you want to propose a solution.

---

| QUESTIONS TO ASK | **Defining Problems** |
|---|---|

- What is the problem or need, exactly?
- What are the manifestations of the problem?
- Why is the problem occurring?
- How does the problem affect your audience?
- What will happen if the problem isn't solved (or the need is unmet)?

---

**EXAMPLE** To take a mundane example, I notice that when it snows here, the steep concrete staircase that goes down to my building in the university often goes unshoveled. This means that the steps eventually get icy and treacherous (Figure 11.2). Anyone who walks down those stairs would probably agree that a problem exists, but in order to propose the best solution to the problem we need to understand more about WHY the problem exists. Is it because the Facilities office doesn't employ enough people to clear the snow? Is the office poorly run, so that there's not a clear enough plan of action for snow removal? Or does Facilities just think some parts of campus are more important to clear than others?

To find out what exactly the problem is, we'd need to do some research, in this case, simply calling Facilities to let them know about the problem and listening to their explanation.

Dariush M./Shutterstock

**FIGURE 11.2** Proposals can arise from everyday problems or practical circumstances.

---

## FOR DISCUSSION

1. Look through your campus and/or local newspaper, and make a list of all the needs or problems that you see. Which of these already have proposal arguments associated with them?
2. Read the following example of a proposal argument, and answer these questions:
   - What is the problem or need that the article describes?
   - Are you convinced by the description of the problem? What would make it more compelling?

- What attempts to persuade the audience of the problem has the article made?
- How does the proposed solution address this problem or need?

## Teaching Handwriting in Early Childhood: Brain Science Shows Why We Should Rescue This Fading Skill

### BY LAURA DINEHARD, ASSOCIATE PROFESSOR OF EARLY CHILDHOOD EDUCATION AT FLORIDA INTERNATIONAL UNIVERSITY

Relegating handwriting to the back burner of early childhood education ignores the close relationship between fine motor skill development and early success in math and reading. Technology isn't the enemy, but jumping to keyboards and calculators before mastering pencil and paper may not be developmentally appropriate for young learners.

Manuscript handwriting does make a cameo appearance in the Common Core for kindergarten through third grade, but the standards have abandoned cursive handwriting completely.

Handwriting is the direct precursor skill to note-taking, writing, and sketching out ideas and plans. We can document practical benefits for students who master legible handwriting, including

- Better grades for neatly written work
- A tighter focus on content and ideas, not the mechanics of letter drawing
- Better motivation and confidence — with less frustration about handwriting

Education technology and blended learning advocates recommend teaching basic computing skills before the age of 5 or 6, and the Common Core standards' computer-based testing is pushing down typing and computer skills from middle school to kindergarten.

### MOTOR SKILLS

As we assess these dissonant signals, the research-based study of childhood development should play a larger role. Digital keyboards don't deliver the same fine motor skill benefits as putting pencil to paper.

Here's why:

When we print the letter A, there is something essentially different happening than when we print the letters B or C. When we first learn how to form these letters, we go back and forth, looking at an A, B, or C and the letters we draw ourselves.

On the other hand, we can press the A, B, or C key on a keyboard without thinking of their differences. The result is perfectly formed letters. We don't get the benefit of following the letters' shapes in detail, and we don't have to struggle with our fingers. As a result, research shows, young students in a school environment dominated by keyboards and touch screens don't recognize as many letters as those who learn to write by hand.

Enter brain science from radiological imaging: Letters are symbols, maps, geometric shapes, and directional arrows, and the brain creates a special pathway for each one as we absorb those shapes and draw them.

We decode letters using the visual cortex, but actually writing them stimulates the brain's prefrontal cortex, a region responsible for re-straining bad behavior, sustaining attention, and avoiding bad habits. These mental processes are essential for success in learning.

In a 2011 study (*http://DAmag.me/handwriting*), our team examined the academic success of 1,000 second-grade students in Miami-Dade County Public Schools. We found a strong connection between their grades and academic scores, on the one hand, and the fine motor skills when they were in pre-K classes.

**IMPROVED GRADES**

Students who received good grades on fine motor writing tasks in pre-K had an average GPA of 3.02 in math and 2.84 in reading—B averages. Those who did poorly had an average GPA of 2.30 in math and 2.12 in reading—C averages. Moreover, those who excelled at fine motor writing tasks in pre-K out-scored those who did poorly in both the reading Stanford Achievement Test (59th percentile vs. 38th) and the math SAT (62nd vs. 37th) in second grade.

We concluded that early writing difficulties can alert us to potentially global learning difficulties for young children, and that positive early writing experiences reinforce impulse control.

Clearly, developmentally appropriate fine motor skills and handwriting readiness deserve more space in the early childhood curriculum, and the benefit of more documentation and research. We can learn much more from these developmental experiences of these early learners.

# 11d Making a Compelling Proposal Claim

Once you've successfully persuaded your audience that they have a problem, you need to propose an action that will solve it. All proposal claims follow this basic template:

"We should do X [solution] to address Y [a problem or need] because of [reasons that X is a good solution]."

Your proposed solution needs to have several characteristics:

- It needs to persuade the audience that it will actually solve the problem or address the unmet need.
- It needs to convincingly show that it's the best possible solution (or at least better than the other options available for addressing the problem).
- It needs to convince the audience that it's something they can conceivably do, and that the benefit of implementing your proposal outweighs the costs (in expense, effort, or difficulty).

**EXAMPLE**   A story came out recently in the local paper about how the university had euthanized a number of "nuisance animals," including feral cats that lived in the bushes outside of some of the buildings on campus and starlings that were eating the Agriculture Department's dairy cows' feed. The story prompted an uproar over the treatment of the animals, including a *Change.org* petition calling for an investigation that collected over 10,000 signatures. The main problems articulated by animal lovers in town and on campus were that the university's own campus veterinarian had euthanized the animals rather than taking them to the Humane Society, and that the method used to euthanize them was not approved by the American Veterinary Society (though this was later proven to be false). This, of course, created a public relations problem for the university, and so it wisely responded by convening a task force to study the issue and reassure the public.

The task force proposed several things: that the university should no longer try to handle the problem of "nuisance animals" on its own, that if it deemed an animal a threat to health or safety it would get an outside agency to come and remove the animal, and that euthanasia would only be used as a last resort. After the university announced its findings and new policy, the local paper ran an approving story about the plan. So clearly, the university's proposed solution succeeded in persuading its audience that it had adequately addressed the problem.

## FOR DISCUSSION

As a class, brainstorm a list of local problems (perhaps the one you came up with for the For Discussion prompt in Section 11c). Choose one, and in small groups, come up with a list of all the proposals you can think of that would address the problem (remember to think about all the different audiences who might be able to address the problem). Then discuss which of those solutions would be the most viable in terms of how well it addresses the problem and if it's something that could conceivably be done.

# 11e Providing Support for Your Proposal

Your proposal claim will only be effective if you can convince the audience that the proposed action

- Is doable.
- Can be done without an unreasonable or impossible amount of effort.
- Will have desirable results.
- Will have a minimum of negative consequences.

To convince your audience of your proposal claim, you need to provide *evidence* that supports your proposal. The kind of evidence you need depends entirely on your audience and the nature of your proposal.

If it's a proposal addressing a practical problem for a specific audience, the evidence required will be fairly straightforward.

**EXAMPLE** If you're proposing to your municipality that they replace the yellow streetlights with more energy-efficient, brighter blue ones, the support for your proposal claim might look like this:

- Evidence about why the yellow bulbs are a problem (perhaps by interviewing or polling current residents).
- Evidence showing why the blue bulbs are better than the yellow ones. Since this is an evaluation argument, you can use the types of criteria for evaluation discussed in Section 10b in Chapter 10 to generate reasons and evidence.

**EXAMPLE** Because they involve persuading someone to give you money, grant proposals have to make very convincing proposal arguments in a somewhat formulaic way. A group of students in a writing class here at the University of Idaho wrote a grant proposal on behalf of a local nursing home asking for money to fund a machine called a blanket warmer. I confess to being initially dubious about the necessity of such a thing, but in their proposal the students used research from journals of nursing to prove that warm blankets make a significant difference in the mental state and care of dementia patients. The granting agency was obviously convinced by their research too, because they awarded the group $4,000 for the purchase of the blanket warmer.

But if you're making a proposal claim to convince an audience of something bigger and more complex—like, say, that we as a society should invest in renewable energy sources such as solar power—the support for your arguments will need to be much deeper and wide ranging, and the audience may be more general. We might call this type of argument a "policy proposal" to distinguish it from the more specific "practical proposal."

Let's consider the issue of plastic shopping bag bans to consider how one published policy proposal argument uses reasons and evidence to support its claim.

## An Annotated Policy Proposal

### How Should We Deal with Plastic Bags?

#### BY JAMES MACDONALD

> Note that the author doesn't begin with a proposal claim; rather, he starts with a description of a current problem (city residents are annoyed that the plastic bag litter problem remains unaddressed), and then brings up questions.

Just recently, New York State's governor blocked a bill that would have charged a 5-cent fee for every disposable shopping bag in New York City. The governor's objections centered around certain financial provisions, but many city residents are annoyed that the plastic litter problem remains unaddressed. How bad is the problem? And what is the best way to get rid of the ubiquitous bags?

> In this paragraph, he brings up the generally acknowledged problems with plastic bags (note that in the original article, posted online, there are hyperlinks to stories that support his claims).

Disposable bags remain in the environment for years, and plastic bags in particular have been blamed for causing damaging floods when they clog up storm drains. Like all plastic products, bags are made from fossil fuel derivatives and some of the greatest environmental impact stems from their manufacture (although of course paper bags also require energy and materials to make).

> Here he acknowledges that in the grand scheme of things, plastic bags aren't the worst environmental hazard.

While plastic bags unquestionably harm marine life, however, the danger of bags in particular compared with other plastic debris is uncertain. And by all accounts, bags themselves account for a small (around 2%) percentage of waste. So why focus on plastic bags?

> He provides evidence from case studies that addressing the plastic bags issue can have rippling effects.

In some views, the real problem with plastic bags is how they symbolize unsustainable, throwaway culture. There is some evidence that tackling bags can impact general attitudes. Following a campaign of persuasion and education, merchants in Modbury, in Devon, England, completely stopped providing disposable plastic bags. Soon, other merchants and individuals began taking steps to reduce their individual environmental footprints, for example investing in better energy efficiency and using other types of sustainable packing materials. Then again, these efforts may have resulted as much from the personal persuasion campaign that led to the ban as from the ban itself.

For a larger municipality that wants to reduce bag use, what is the most effective approach? One method is to mandate bag strength; some countries ban flimsy bags that are less likely to be reused. Some countries have completely banned bags. The most common approach is, like New York City's aborted attempt, a fee. The Republic of Ireland introduced a 0.15 Euro tax per disposable bag and use declined by more than 90%.

Formal studies show that fees are much more effective than incentives; a 5-cent fee in Maryland resulted in far more dramatic declines in bag use than a 5-cent payment to customers who brought their own bag. It's not clear why incentives don't work, but fees are especially effective when framed as a tax. Americans in particular seem to be highly motivated to avoid taxes.

> In this paragraph, he presents evidence (again, from case studies) that fees are the most effective way to eliminate plastic bag use.

Authorities looking to reduce waste should take heed of these results. Waste disposal is a large expense, and discouraging waste through fees seems to provoke less wasteful behavior.

> Here, finally, is his proposal claim: Municipalities should seek to reduce plastic bag waste by implementing fees.

## WORKS CITED

Homonoff, Tatiana A. "Can Small Incentives Have Large Effects? The Impact of Taxes versus Bonuses on Disposable Bag Use." *Proceedings of the Annual Conference on Taxation and Minutes of the Annual Meeting of the National Tax Association,* 105, November 15–17, 2012, pp. 64–90.

Carrigan, Marylyn, et al. "Fostering Responsible Communities: A Community Social Marketing Approach to Sustainable Living." *Journal of Business Ethics,* vol. 100, no. 3, May 2011, pp. 515–534.

## FOR DISCUSSION

Look at the following bumper stickers, which are miniature proposal arguments. Choose one, and see if you can develop its proposal claims further by providing reasons, evidence, and support for why the proposal would be effective.

DON'T BELIEVE
EVERYTHING YOU THINK

Don't spread my WEALTH,
spread my WORK ETHIC!

## 11f Acknowledging Potential Problems with Your Proposal

As with all arguments, it helps your ethos to acknowledge that your proposal (like all argumentative claims) isn't 100 percent infallible. Acknowledging circumstances where your proposed solution may be ineffective shows that you have thought deeply about your proposal and aren't just trying to stubbornly get it passed by any means necessary. It also serves as a cautionary note to potential adopters of your proposal about the potential downfalls.

### FOR DISCUSSION

Choose one of the proposal arguments generated by the class in the previous For Discussion activity. As a class, try to poke as many holes as possible in it. What could go wrong? What are all the ways in which it could fail or cause unintended problems?

# 11g Showing That Your Proposal Will Fix the Problem

In formal proposal arguments like grant proposals, writers are expected to explain how they know their proposed solution will work and how they will measure the success of their proposal. So part of your thinking process about proposals should include answers to the following questions:

- What constitutes success?
- How will I know that my proposal was successful?
- How can I measure its success?

**EXAMPLE** If you claim that implementing stricter campus drinking laws will curb sexual assaults at fraternities, you would need first to provide support that your solution *could* work (as described earlier); perhaps you could base your case on campuses that have applied similar measures with good results. And then you also need to be prepared to show that your proposed solution did, in fact, work. In this case, you would probably want to collect several years' worth of data on sexual assaults at fraternities and then prepare to do the same thing in a year from now. If there were fewer sexual assaults, then your proposal was successful.

**EXAMPLE** Say you wrote a grant proposal for funds to restore the landscape around a polluted creek, a project called "riparian restoration." You would need to show the problems caused by the polluted creek, as well as the benefits that would occur from restoration. While you could use comparative studies, your proposal would need to include data on current measures of problems caused by creek pollution and a plan to measure these problems again in a year's time to show that the riparian restoration was successful in mitigating the problems.

## ASSIGNMENTS

## Composing Proposals

### WRITE A PROPOSAL TO ADDRESS A LOCAL PROBLEM

Write a proposal to address a local problem, whether it's at the university or in your town. Decide whether you want to write a more practical proposal, like one that would be aimed at the city council or the appropriate university administrative offices, or a policy proposal, like one that might appear in the campus or town newspaper.

### WRITE A RESEARCH PROPOSAL

Research proposals draw on some of the skills described in Section 11f. The aim of a research proposal is not only to announce what you plan to work on for an extended, significant project, but also to convince your audience that it's worth focusing on and that you have the wherewithal to accomplish the task. Research proposals are structured in the following way:

1. They introduce the research question and explain why it is significant and interesting.
2. They contain a literature review of the work that's already been done on the question. Literature reviews ultimately identify gaps in the research, which your project can help to fill.
3. They explain the means by which you propose to investigate this question.
4. They explain how/why you are qualified to investigate the question.

For this assignment, you will write a research proposal on a subject that you're interested in understanding better. If you've been keeping a research portfolio (Chapter 6), you might write your research proposal on that topic.

## CREATE A PROPOSAL USING A NONPRINT MODALITY

Use a means of communication (modality, medium, genre, circulation; see Chapter 2) other than a written proposal to propose a solution to a local (campus or town) issue. Depending on your audience and circumstance, it might be a public advocacy ad, bumper sticker, billboard, 30-second public service announcement, or some other form of communication. To figure out which would be best, you need to consider what would be most appropriate for your specific situation; for instance, if your town has a no-billboards policy, you wouldn't want to create a billboard. If your campus uses a lot of changing electronic display signs, you may want to create a display for it. You might do this assignment as a remediation of your earlier written proposal.

## CREATE A JOB APPLICATION VIDEO

While it may seem funny to think of job applications as proposal arguments, what job application packets ultimately say is "You should hire me, and here's why." The newest genre of job application materials is the job application video, or video CV. While not all employers will accept them (because it's possible that they can be used to discriminate against you), these one- to three-minute-long videos supplement your traditional print job application materials by allowing potential employers to see and hear you, which gives a sense of your personality and can breathe life into your application materials.

For this assignment, you can either choose a specific job or internship that you want to apply for, or focus more generally on what kind of job you want and what skills you can bring to it. This might be something that you can post in an online professional portfolio.

For the job application video, DO

- Plan before you film.
- Keep it short: 1–3 minutes.

- Plot the main points of what you want to say, but don't read from a script.
- Introduce yourself and summarize quickly why you're the right person for the job. Then elaborate on the experiences (whether actual jobs, internships, volunteer experiences, course projects, or other sorts of experiences) that make you qualified.
- Maintain eye contact with the camera, and keep a positive, happy disposition.
- Dress as you would for a job interview.
- Imagine the filming as if in you're a face-to-face job interview.

But DON'T

- Film in a messy environment.
- Fidget.
- Mumble or say "uh" a lot.

If you want to see good examples, it's best to Google "good video resumes." And see Chapter 15 for tips on how to effectively film and edit videos.

---

FOR REFLECTION

**Transferable Skills and Concepts**
Skills in proposing actions also work in areas of your life outside of college and public life, of course. For this reflection, describe an instance in your journal where you made a proposal (whether informal or formal, big or small in scope) that *failed*. Then answer the following questions:

- Why do you think it failed?
- What were the differences and similarities to the process of making proposal arguments described in this chapter?
- What might you have done differently?

# PART 4

## Tools for Composing

# 12

# Research: Composing with Multiple Sources

In his book *Philosophy of Literary Form*, the twentieth-century rhetorician and philosopher Kenneth Burke likened all of human discourse (by whatever means it takes place: textually, visually, or multimodally) to an "unending conversation." He wrote,

> Imagine that you enter a parlor. You come late. When you arrive, others have long preceded you, and they are engaged in a heated discussion, a discussion too heated for them to pause and tell you exactly what it is about. In fact, the discussion had already begun long before any of them got there, so that no one present is qualified to retrace for you all the steps that had gone before. You listen for a while, until you decide that you have caught the tenor of the argument; then you put in your oar. Someone answers; you answer him; another comes to your defense; another aligns himself against you, to either the embarrassment or gratification of your opponent, depending upon the quality of your ally's assistance. However, the discussion is interminable. The hour grows late, you must depart. And you do depart, with the discussion still vigorously in progress. (110-11)

Burke's "conversational parlor" provides an excellent metaphor for the work of research that needs to be done when defining and responding to rhetorical problems. Following this metaphor, we might think of the composing process as having three basic steps:

1. Identify the conversation. (See Chapter 6 to learn how to formulate rhetorical problems.)

2. "Listen" to the conversation for a while; that is, conduct extensive research on the rhetorical problem, and pay close attention to the content (i.e., the topics and various lines of argument; see section 7b for identifying stasis questions), the rhetorical stakeholders, and the genre, medium, and mode(s) by which the conversation takes place.

3. Put in your "oar"; that is, join the conversation by responding to one or more of those who have been there before you.

This chapter focuses on the nitty-gritty of step 2: learning how to actively listen to the conversation (otherwise known as research), and how to make decisions about when and how to incorporate that research into your response to the conversation. This involves multiple activities (see Figure 12.1):

- Formulating initial research questions.
- Generating initial keywords for research.
- Identifying initial sources to help clarify your own position.
- Establishing a system to keep track of your sources.

FIGURE 12.1 The Multiple Activities of the Research Process

- Evaluating the validity and relative rhetorical significance of sources.
- Generating more specific keywords as your position on the issue becomes clearer.

Along with this recursive research process, you'll learn to write what we might call a "zero draft" to quickly collect your thoughts. You'll also learn to appropriately incorporate sources into your compositions, both to bolster your ethos and to signal the conversation(s) in which you're taking part.

# 12a The Recursive Steps of the Research Process

Composers do research for two equally important reasons: to *discover the conversation* and to *clarify their position*. While many beginning composers treat research as a "one and done" linear procedure, experienced researchers know that research and composing is a continuous, recursive process involving multiple steps.

## Formulating Initial Research Questions

Effective research starts from sincere questioning; that is, you shouldn't already know what you want to argue before you begin the research process. Too often, beginning composers fall into the trap of only looking for sources that support what they already believe. This is a dishonest approach, since it avoids a true process of inquiry. As philosopher Friedrich Nietzsche said in his essay "On Truth and Lying in an Extra-Moral Sense," "If someone hides an object behind a bush, then seeks and finds it there, that seeking and finding is not very laudable" (251). In other words, trying to find only what you think or know is already there won't help anyone very much.

**EXAMPLE**  Instead of, say, looking for sources that can give you "quotes" to support your already-formed position on wolf population management, you might approach it by asking questions that you don't already know the answer to: maybe "What are different theories about the benefits of wolf reintroduction?" or "What are the costs and benefits of wolf reintroduction to various populations in the West?"

Even if you do have strong opinions about a topic, it's best to approach the research process with a sincere, open mind that seeks to really understand an issue or topic. Initial research questions are best if they're simple and open-ended. Once you start generating and reading through sources, your question will become more refined and specific.

**EXAMPLE**  Let's say that for a video editorial assignment you want to investigate the differences between online and face-to-face education. The president of your university has just announced that she wants to increase enrollment by 25 percent, and with limited physical facilities, most campus administrators and faculty agree that the most logical way to achieve this goal is to increase the number of online courses and degrees. Though you've taken a few online courses (with mixed results), you're uneasy about the implications of this move by the university and want to understand more about the effectiveness of online learning before weighing in on the issue.

Some initial questions about online education generated with the stasis questions (see section 7b) might look something like this:

- What are the trends in online learning? What percentage of all college and university courses are offered online, and is this number growing, shrinking, or has it leveled off? What kinds of courses are offered online? How have online courses changed? Are students with online degrees able to get jobs at the same rates as students who have gotten traditional degrees? (stasis of fact/definition)

- What are some of the reasons that online learning has become more prevalent, if that's indeed the case? Why do universities want to include more online courses? (That is, are they more cost-effective, and if so, why?) What are the implications for the university as a whole? (stasis of cause)

- What do experts say about the quality of online courses versus face-to-face courses? Are some kinds of online courses more effective than others? (stasis of evaluation)

- Given the answers to the questions above, should your university move to more online courses and degrees? If so, why, how, and what kind of courses and degrees? (stasis of policy)

## Generating Initial Keywords to Help You Conduct a Search

Using your research questions, come up with some basic keywords that might help you answer those questions. It's best to search with specifically worded phrases rather than whole questions. Search engines ignore little words (of, in, and, but), so you can also leave those out of your search phrases.

**EXAMPLE** Some good phrases with which to start for our questions about online learning might be "online learning trends," "prevalence online learning," and "effectiveness online learning." Once you've come up with some initial keywords, consider coming up with synonyms to help catch sources that you may have missed:

| ONLINE LEARNING EFFECTIVENESS | |
|---|---|
| distance education | quality |
| online education | success |
| e-learning | value |
| virtual classroom | |
| Web-based courses | |

Searches related to online education value

| | |
|---|---|
| **soundness** of online education | **impact** of online education **articles** |
| **impact** of online education | **quality** of online education |
| value of online **learning** | value of online **courses** |
| **impact** of online **learning** | **benefits** of online education |

Searches related to distance education quality

**issue that impacts distance-education learning**

**challenges** of distance **learning**

distance **learning problems and solutions**

**current issues** in distance education

quality **assurance** in distance education

distance education **issues and challenges**

**trends and issues** in distance education

quality **issues in** distance **learning**

**FIGURE 12.2  Google Searches**

## Identifying Initial Sources to Help You Clarify Your Own Position

It's a good idea to *begin* your search with Google (though not a good idea to *end* there, for reasons discussed below). For one thing, Google can sometimes help you with the search by recommending search terms based on what you type into the search bar. These results—the top search queries—can give you a better sense for how others are thinking about the issue and lead you to more refined keywords, as Figure 12.2 shows.

A Google search on the keywords "trends online education" brings up some potentially useful results but from sites that need to be more thoroughly vetted (see the next step) before they can be used as reliable sources.

Since you're a college student, you also have access through your university library to databases of sources. Some of these, like Lexis-Nexis and Academic Search Premier, will be devoted almost exclusively to popular and academic articles. These periodical databases typically have more thoroughly vetted and trustworthy sources. However, searching on them isn't foolproof: You'll still need a fair amount of practice with keyword searching in order to find relevant information.

**EXAMPLE**  Doing a search on Lexis-Nexis for the terms "trends online education," like my Google search, also produced a number of irrelevant results (though one result did provide a new term that could serve as another search term: "e-learning;" see yellow arrow in Figure 12.4). Lexis-Nexis makes it possible to refine the search results, so I clicked on "Colleges and Universities" and got more relevant results.

While often Lexis-Nexis and other subscription academic databases like it provide more reliable results than general Web search engines, it's important to conduct your initial search across a number of different sites and to continue to follow up on them. (See Figures 12.3, 12.4, and 12.5.)

## Establishing a System to Help You Keep Track of Your Sources

Having some method to keep track of the information in your sources is necessary for several reasons:

- It helps you maintain your sanity. It keeps you from being overwhelmed by the amount of information you find, and it allows you to easily locate sources.

- A system (like tagging or adding keywords to sources) helps you begin seeing topical and argumentative patterns in sources. This will help you *synthesize* the information you find.

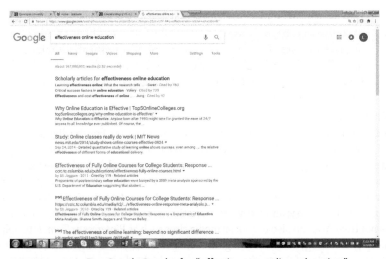

FIGURE 12.3 Top Google Results for "effectiveness online education"

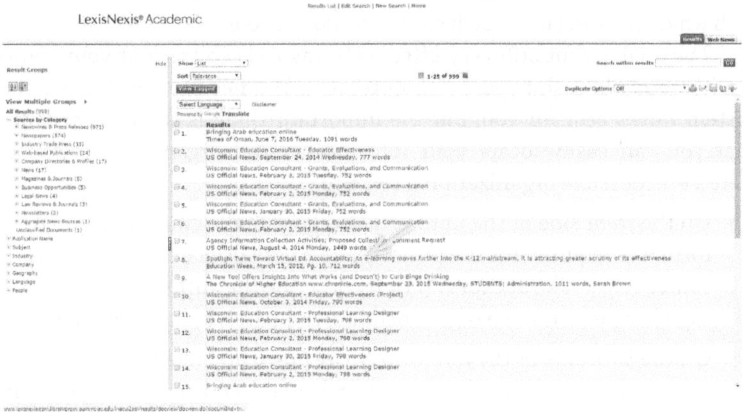

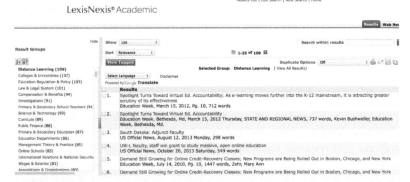

FIGURE 12.4 Top Lexis-Nexis results for "effectiveness online education"; since they were of mixed usefulness, the search could be refined using the categories at the left

FIGURE 12.5 Refined Lexis-Nexis Results for "effectiveness online education," with the "Distance Learning" Filter Applied

- It helps you avoid unintentional plagiarism. Not keeping good track of sources has been the cause of a number of recent high-profile plagiarism cases. To avoid embarrassment, be careful about taking notes (especially when you're writing down direct quotations from the source), and true paraphrasing. See Section 12b for more on how to paraphrase and quote sources.

Chapter 6 discusses how to create a digital or analog research scrapbook. Having such a tool will help you keep all of your sources together. For the digital version of source management, you would use a tool that allows you to create multiple items and to tag them (i.e., mark them with keywords). Such tools include blogs (you can make one post per source), the free online note-keeping system Evernote (you can make one note per source), free online citation software like *Zotero* and *Mendeley*; and commercial citation software like *Endnote* (though this is not free). You can also use social media sites such as *Pinterest* or *Tumblr* to help keep sources together. These digital tools will allow you create citations, write brief summaries of the sources, mark down or highlight key quotes, and indicate how the source will be useful to you; they also allow you to add keywords or tags with which you can later search your collection of sources.

The analog (but still very effective!) way to keep track of your sources is with good old-fashioned 3 × 5 notecards. You need to develop whatever system works best for you, but the important thing is to be consistent so that you can easily locate your information and organize your sources. Here's one possible organizational system:

- On the *front* side of the notecard, you'll write the citation (in whatever format is required for the project) and a very brief summary of the source (e.g., "The author X [briefly describe the author's relation to the topic] argues/summarizes/concludes/compares/[whatever] that . . .").
- On the *back* side of the notecard, write down any relevant direct quotations (keep these as short as possible), and a quick note to yourself about how the source might be useful to you.

After you've created all your notecards, go back through, reread them, and add **keywords** to the front of the notecard. You can develop your own system of keywords based on topic, theme, approach, position, or anything else you decide—the point is that adding the same keyword to multiple cards will reveal links between them. By doing so, you've already begun organizing your ideas about the research question at hand.

## Evaluating the Validity and Relative Rhetorical Significance of Your Sources

Research is a skill and an art, not a science. That is, while it would be great if there were hard and fast rules about what counts as a "good" source ("You can only use peer-reviewed scholarly articles!") and what should be avoided at all costs ("Never use *Wikipedia*!"), a more rhetorical view of research says, "It depends." What it depends on are things like the rhetorical aim of your project, what you're trying to show and prove, and to whom.

Generally speaking, we can distinguish two main types of sources: *primary* sources and *secondary* sources.

- **Primary sources** provide direct, first-hand knowledge about an event. Primary sources might include diaries, interviews, historical and legal documents, speeches, eyewitness accounts, creative writing, and more.

- **Secondary sources** include materials that discuss, analyze, interpret, or comment on primary sources. Secondary sources typically include reviews, newspaper articles, and scholarly articles and books.

Tables 12.1 and 12.2, respectively, explain when you would want to use primary sources and when you'd want to use secondary sources.

**TABLE 12.1** Primary Sources to Use for Different Purposes

| IF YOU WANT TO . . . | → | THEN USE |
|---|---|---|
| Get in-depth, individual perspectives on an issue . . . | → | Interviews, oral histories, first-person accounts, memoirs. |
| Find out what a broad swath of the population (perhaps organized by specific beliefs or demographics) feels or thinks about a topic . . . | → | Surveys, polls. |
| • Reconstruct an original history of a specific idea, topic, or event;<br>• Reconstruct an era through its popular culture;<br>• Show the continuity or change in thinking about a given topic or idea . . . | → | Archival documents (letters, maps, photographs, oral histories), old periodicals. |
| Explain the etymology of a word . . . | → | Dictionary (especially the *Oxford English Dictionary*, available online through most university libraries). |

**TABLE 12.2** Secondary Sources to Use for Different Purposes

| IF YOU WANT TO . . . | → | THEN USE |
|---|---|---|
| • Establish the timeline of a series of events;<br>• Find reliable facts;<br>• Give an overview, comparison, or rhetorical analysis of how the media responded to an event . . . | → | Newspaper articles. |
| • Create a catalog of different points of view or "takes" on a topic;<br>• Find anecdotes or quotes from people affected by an event . . . | → | Magazine feature articles. |

*(continued on next page)*

| IF YOU WANT TO . . . | → | THEN USE |
|---|---|---|
| • Get partisan takes on issues or ideas;<br>• Establish a sense of the range of opinions on a topic;<br>• Find out how nonexperts discuss a topic or idea . . . | → | Blogs. |
| • Read up on the background or get a general overview of a topic, concept, or process;<br>• Gain a sense of the established or common knowledge about a topic . . . | → | *Wikipedia* or encyclopedia articles. |
| • Gain specialized knowledge of a topic and understand the sorts of questions at issue in a topic;<br>• Provide an authoritative take on a topic or issue;<br>• Cite original research on a topic . . . | → | Scholarly (peer reviewed) articles. |
| • Find the history or background of an idea, process, or event;<br>• Provide an in-depth understanding of a debate . . . | → | Biographies, histories (books). |
|  | → | Scholarly books and articles. These are the result of high-level debates as well, so keep in mind that these aren't a neutral source—there may be competing interpretations of a position. |

Your initial research question (and the more refined versions that come after you begin searching for and reading sources to answer that question) will help you decide which of these sources would be appropriate and credible for the audience.

**EXAMPLE**  While you wouldn't want to cite *Joe Blow's Big Website of Guns* as an authoritative source on gun control policy, it could be great as a way to show how nonexperts or everyday gun enthusiasts talk about guns.

In short, *think rhetorically* about the sources you find and how they might be seen by your intended audience. For each source, apply each of the following considerations (based on the journalistic questions: who, what, when, where, how):

**QUESTIONS TO ASK**  **Thinking Rhetorically about a Research Source**

- ***The creator of the source.*** Who created the source? What is their background, and how are they credentialed to speak about the source? What is at stake for them in the topic; that is, what do they stand to gain or lose in the way they talk about the topic? How might these investments or biases mesh with how your audience might see the subject? Again, if the source has a clear bias, this doesn't mean you shouldn't use the source in your composition, only that you'll need to introduce it by pointing out the bias so that your audience knows that *you* understand the position of the source's creator.

- ***The purpose of the source.*** What is the source about? What does it aim to accomplish?
- ***The age of the source.*** When was the source created? If timeliness is important to your topic, was the source created recently enough to be relevant?

   **EXAMPLE** If you're discussing the history of online education, then it's fine to talk about a source from 1999; but if you're making a point about the most recent trends in online education, then even a source from 2007 would be of questionable relevance.

- ***The venue of the source.*** Where did the source appear? Refer to Table 12.1 to figure out how the type of publication dictates the source's purpose and content.
- ***The relevance of the source.*** How is the source relevant to your own topic, purpose, and audience?

---

Table 12.3 demonstrates how each of the previous questions can be applied to a specific source: namely, the following editorial from *The Hindustan Times*.

### E-Learning: India's Education System Needs to Get Online

India, Aug. 31—India's education system—be it primary, secondary, or higher levels—is fraught with quality and quantity challenges: There is a shortage of quality teachers, an enabling environment for students, and infrastructure, just to point out a few.

These hurdles are not going to go away soon even though there is a surge in the number of students at all levels and an increasing demand for quality education. There is also a corresponding demand from industry for skilled human resources.

But this thirst and demand for quality education and trained personnel will not be easy to quench because it takes time, funds, and quality human resources to set up good institutions.

Then there is the rule book: Starting a school or a college in India needs magical levels of energy and perseverance.

In such a scenario, online education could be a boon for those who do not have access to quality education or are keen to reskill.

The e-learning market in India is estimated to be around $3 billion and it is growing. Take, for example, the massive open online course (MOOC) provider Coursera.

With one million users, India ties with China as its biggest source of online learners after its home base, the US. That the market expectations from this business model are robust can be gauged from the fact that the firm has raised $49.5 million, coinciding with the US-based firm's plans to tap the Indian market to increase its user base.

The UTV Group is in talks with top institutions such as IIMs, IITs and even globally to start these courses. A few months ago, IIT-Bombay launched three MOOCs. The world of online learning is attractive not only because learning is no longer tethered to a classroom and timetables but also because software programs can "seamlessly integrate social media, making it possible to create online communities that are course specific."

Along with the traditional textbooks, blogs, tweets, podcasts, webcasts, online chats, discussion boards, virtual study jams ensure that learning becomes multidimensional. Online courses can also help all those who are already in jobs to reskill and remain competitive without taking time off from their careers.

There is evidence that a majority of those registering for these courses have an undergraduate degree or higher and the courses are not being accessed by those who could benefit from education – women, the less educated, and the poor.

India's challenge, say experts, will be to make these facilities reach these social groups. India truly cannot afford to miss this bus.

**TABLE 12.3** Evaluating Sources Rhetorically: "E-Learning: India's Education System Needs to Get Online"

| | |
|---|---|
| The creator of the source | The *Hindustan Times* is a national newspaper, somewhat akin to *USA Today* in the United States. Like *USA Today*, it has broad appeal and interest to Indian citizens. |
| The purpose of the source | The article makes an argument for the value and cost-effectiveness of online education for Indian citizens; it specifically wants Indian schools and companies to begin creating these online courses. |
| The age of the source | The source is from 2015, so it's fairly recent. This makes it especially interesting, since the article is talking about India's lack of an online education system, which the United States has had for almost two decades. |
| The venue of the source | I found this online through *Gale Academic OneFile* in a search for "online education trends." Because of the phrase "needs to" and the proposal argument being made in the article, I'm assuming it's an editorial. |
| The relevance of the source | The source is relevant to my project because it's written from the perspective of a country that doesn't yet have a fully developed system of online education. This helps me to understand how people think about the value of online education. |

## Finding Better Sources and Generating Better Keywords as Your Position on the Issue Becomes Clearer

This is where research gets recursive: Finding, reading, and taking notes on your initial results will help you understand more clearly what you're looking for.

For instance, if you find a good scholarly article on the topic, you can use its bibliography to lead you to more sources, which will further help you clarify your emerging argument. In turn, you'll be able to search with better terms since you understand more clearly what you're trying to find out. You'll have a second (and probably a third) round of research using more refined search terms, and this process will continue throughout your research and composing process.

**EXAMPLE** I may have started with "trends online education," but through a lot of reading and hard work, I discovered that really what I'm trying to ask about is the student experience of online courses, specifically how online courses might allow students to interact with each other in better and worse ways. So my new search terms might be something like "student interaction online courses."

### Writing "Zero Drafts" to Clarify Your Thinking

A "zero draft" (sometimes called a "thinking draft") is a low-stakes draft in which you try to answer your initial research question after you've done the hard work of finding, logging, and thinking about all your sources. The purpose of zero drafts is to clarify what you think and know about a topic.

To write a zero draft, clear your desk of everything but a notepad and a pen, and write your research question at the top of the page. Set a timer for 20 to 30 minutes. Start the timer, begin writing, and continue writing until the timer goes off. Don't edit yourself or cross anything out, but stay focused on answering your research question.

By the end of your quick writing session, you should have a clearer grasp of the conversation about your topic or question, and (hopefully) a better sense of what you want to say about it. Note that this is purely a thought-gathering and clarification exercise. You will likely not use any writing from your zero draft in your actual composition—it's designed only to help you come to an understanding of what you now think about your research question. If the zero draft works, though, you might just have written your way into a thesis or main point!

# 12b Incorporating Sources into Your Compositions

Any type of composition—textual, visual, or multimodal—that is in conversation with outside sources needs to have established a clear and consistent way to signal (a) *that* it is participating in a conversation, and (b) *how* it is participating in a conversation. Ways to do this will differ according to the conventions of various genres and disciplines, but one thing is for certain: being able to signal your participation in a given conversation in a smooth, knowledgeable way is a sure way to bolster your ethos with your audience. So while you may find issues of formatting like summarizing, paraphrasing, quoting, and citing insufferably dull, it may help you to know that paying careful attention to these details helps ensure that your message is actually taken seriously by your audience.

There are two related activities involved in incorporating sources. The first is incorporating the content of the sources into the body of your composition (summarizing, paraphrasing, and directly quoting). The second is following the conventions of a citation style in order to provide your audience with the information they need to find that source themselves.

## Summarizing, Paraphrasing, and Quoting to Incorporate Texts and Avoid Plagiarism

The idea that you should avoid copying or "stealing" other's intellectual work is a particularly Western idea. In many other cultures, using other's words without attribution is actually considered to do honor to the audience because it assumes that they are a cultured person who shares the same repository of knowledge as the composer and would thus recognize the source. However, because this is an American textbook and we're in an American context, we need to discuss how NOT to plagiarize.

Most student problems with plagiarism come from clumsy or incomplete paraphrasing, summarizing, and quoting, so practicing with these and developing good, careful habits of handling sources will likely reduce your likelihood of plagiarism.

So when is it more appropriate to summarize, paraphrase (put the content of someone else's ideas into your own language), or directly quote someone's words as they said/wrote them? The basic rule of thumb is to think about what point you're making, and whether it's best illustrated or supported with an explanation, or whether it matters how someone has said something.

**Use summary when . . .**

- You are responding to a specific piece: for instance, you would need to summarize when you're doing a review, or when you're writing a letter to the editor or composing something in response to some other composition. (See Chapter 3 for a more extensive explanation of how to summarize.)

**Use paraphrase when . . .**

- The content you want to incorporate into your composition is more factual or data based (you don't need to directly quote someone else's presentation of statistics, for instance).

- You want to maintain the flow of your own piece. Too many "undigested" quotes makes a piece feel choppy. Plus, if the communicator uses too many direct quotes, it creates the impression of laziness, as if they were implicitly saying, "Well, I'll just let someone else go ahead and say this."
- You want to incorporate only information that's relevant to the topic of your composition (you can also mix paraphrase and quoting).

**Use direct quotations when . . .**

- It's important that you capture how someone has said something—if you're introducing a contentious idea, for instance.

    **EXAMPLE**  But Professor Smedley argues that trees are not actually a species separate from humans. "It's time for us to open our eyes and embrace our green leafy brothers," he said in a recent press release.

- Someone phrases an idea in a really interesting or unique way.

    **EXAMPLE**  "A foolish consistency," as Ralph Waldo Emerson memorably said in his essay "Self-Reliance," "is the hobgoblin of little minds."

- It's a difficult concept, and you're planning to analyze it immediately following.

    **EXAMPLE**  But one of the most central concepts in Heidegger's thinking is that of *Zuhandenheit*, or "ready-to-hand."

- You want to introduce a unique or important word or phrase.

    **EXAMPLE**  Wolverines, or what the Blackfeet Indians called "skunk bears," live in several states across the northwestern United States.

Often, incorporating sources involves a mix of summarizing, quoting, and paraphrasing: For instance, you might quote a somewhat complicated or difficult passage, and then explain it "in other words." Or you can paraphrase part of what the author is saying and quote only the important bits.

    **EXAMPLE**  Dr. John Bonbon, the curator of the new exhibit "Kangaroos in Glass," first conceived of the idea when he realized that the world associated kangaroos with dirty creatures who bound across the Outback or get into "kangaroo boxing matches," which are filmed and uploaded to *YouTube* by curious bystanders. It was his intention to highlight kangaroos' more elegant characteristics. "These animals are really quite graceful, even delicate," he explains in the exhibit brochure. "I wanted to show that they're more than just silly, goofy creatures with pouches and big tails." The exhibit features life-sized sculptures of kangaroos composed in transparent materials from glass to glycerin.

Remember that you don't need to quote entire paragraphs or even sentences; in fact, in general you should aim to quote as little of the text as possible in order to convey your point. In other words, for most compositions, you have a responsibility to your readers/viewers/listeners to control the flow of the piece, so your voice should be dominant.

### Indicating use of sources

Also remember that when you incorporate summary, paraphrase, or direct quotes, you can't just plop them in your composition willy-nilly. The audience is using your voice (or in the case of videos, your whole persona) as a guide through the composition. So if suddenly someone else starts talking or just shows up without an introduction by you, it can be abrupt and rather jarring (not to mention confusing: the reader will ask "Who's talking here?" or "Who is that who suddenly appeared on the screen?"). Thus, to smoothly incorporate outside sources, you must establish a consistent way of indicating that you're using them. In writing or in podcasts, you might use phrases like these:

- In her article "...," X [argues] that... "[this can be followed by either a direct quote or a paraphrase]."
- According to X, "..."
- X [articulates the issue as] "..."
- "...," writes X.
- As X has [noted], "..."

The verbs inside the brackets can be replaced by any of the verbs listed in Figure 12.6.

| VERBS INDICATING ACTIVE ARGUMENT | VERBS INDICATING A NEUTRAL STANCE |
|---|---|
| advocates for | adds |
| argues | comments |
| asserts | explains |
| believes | illustrates |
| claims | notes |
| confirms | observes |
| denies | points out |
| disputes | remarks |
| endorses | reports |
| insists | suggests |
| pleads | thinks |
| refutes | writes |

FIGURE 12.6 Verbs Commonly Used to Indicate Incorporation of Sources

In videos, of course, you have the option to simply show the person and let them talk; but you'll still need to introduce them and explain their relevance, by introducing them directly and/or through the use of title graphics at the bottom of the screen.

## FOR DISCUSSION

Read the following passages. Then use them to practice paraphrasing and quoting:

### PASSAGE A

A new study published in *Frontiers in Aging Neuroscience* has found that social dancing is a powerful antidote to brain degeneration caused by aging. As our brains age, there is a degeneration of the white matter, the stuff that basically serves as the wiring of the brain. White matter consists of specialized cells that pass messages from one part of the brain to the other. The study took 174 people in their 60s and 70s and assigned them to different physical activities: One group was assigned to walk briskly for an hour three times a week, another was assigned to do a supervised gentle stretching and balance program three times a week, and the third group was assigned to learn country line-dancing. The researchers scanned the volunteers' brains before the study began and after six months, and found that the brains of the dancing group showed less degeneration of the white matter. Researchers don't know the exact reason for the difference; but they guess that social dancing, unlike other activities that are more self-driven, requires the ability to process instructions and execute them all while moving and responding to other people. So if you want to maintain a young, healthy brain, dancing might be the key.

—"Dancing to Help an Aging Brain" by Geoff Jorgensen, *The Washington Times* (newspaper article)

### PASSAGE B

While they may not have the bourgeois bohemian caché of quinoa, acai berries, or other super-health-foods du jour, good old-fashioned steel-cut oats are just what athletes need to pack a punch of slow-releasing energy in the morning. Since they are high in B vitamins and fiber, a breakfast of steel-cut oats will keep you full well past the 10:00 snack hour. Though it takes a bit of forethought, they're also supremely easy to make: Mix ½ cup oats into a cup and a half of water with some chia seeds and let them sit overnight. Then in the

> morning, microwave and add almonds or other nuts, a handful of
> dried cranberries or fresh apples and a drizzle of honey, and voila!
> You have a healthy, tasty breakfast treat that will fuel your muscles
> through the morning.
>
> —"Steel Cut Oats, a Non-Fancy Superfood" by Janily
> Wellspring, *FitnessHealthBlog* (blog post)

1. Read each passage, then put them away. On a separate sheet of
   paper, write down a brief paraphrase of the main point of each
   passage. Compare these with others in your class and decide whose
   paraphrase was best, and why.
2. Imagine that you're writing a research paper critiquing ideas such
   as those contained in either Passage A or Passage B. Write a single
   paragraph doing this, using a mix of summary, paraphrase, and direct quote. (You can make up any position you like—the important
   thing is to practice using the source.)
3. Using the signal phrases in the earlier "Indicating Use of Sources"
   section, make up four sentences that incorporate partial direct
   quotes. (Again, you can use the quotes to support any kind of
   sentence you like.)

## Citing Sources with Different Citation Styles

For many who are new to academic discourse, formal systems of citation like
those of the Modern Language Association (MLA), the American Psychological Association (APA), the Institute of Electrical and Electronics Engineers
(IEEE), and others might seem like a persnickety exercise in dealing with
frustrating minutiae. As you pore through books and websites trying to figure out how to cite a source using MLA format, you might well be thinking,
"Who *cares* whether the comma goes inside or outside the parenthesis? Who
lives or dies by this stuff?"

So it's worth pausing to think about *why* scholars use these citation
systems, as well as the reasoning behind the practices.

Generally speaking, scholars use citation systems for the following
reasons:

- To situate the concept, method, framework, or approach used by the
  authors within a wider disciplinary context.
- To signal belonging to an academic community (insider knowledge).
- To signal the validity of the ideas.
- To provide readers with the ability to read further into the topic if
  they want.
- To generate a scholarly conversation about an issue or to encourage
  the production of more knowledge.

These functions (and therefore the citation formats) differ according to how the discipline creates knowledge. The following sections give a brief overview of how to cite sources using two very common academic citation systems: the Modern Language Association (MLA), used in many humanities disciplines, and the American Psychological Association (APA), used frequently in social sciences disciplines and business.

## MLA Style

Humanities disciplines like English literature typically focus on textual interpretation. Thus, the predominant citation format for this discipline—MLA—uses parentheses with the author's name and the page number after the quotation, like this: (Nicotra 52). This allows readers the ability to track down the edition being cited and to do their own interpretation of the work in question if they desire. Other scholarly citation conventions, like footnotes, allow a parallel conversation to happen alongside the text; in fact, some academic texts are so rife with footnotes that they threaten to overwhelm the main text.

MLA style emphasizes citing traits shared across sources and formatting these traits in consistent ways. These are the nine core elements to consider when creating entries for your list of works cited; every source contains some combination—but not necessarily all—of them:

### The core elements of a works-cited entry

| 1. Author. | Who created the source—or whose work on the source you choose to emphasize first and foremost. |
|---|---|
| 2. Title of source. | The title of the *specific* source you are citing. This could be a whole book or a short poem within it, if your focus is on that poem. |
| 3. Title of container, | The title of a larger source containing the source you are citing. When a source stands alone (like a whole film or novel), there is no container. When an essay (source) is published in a journal (larger source), then that journal is called a *container*. |
| 4. Other contributors, | Noteworthy contributors to the work, such as editors, translators, or performers. |
| 5. Version, | Description of a source that appears in more than one version, such as a book in revised editions. |
| 6. Number, | Number indicating the source's place in a sequence, such as volume and issue numbers for journals, or season and episode numbers for television shows. |
| 7. Publisher, | Organization that produces or sponsors the source, delivering it to readers. |
| 8. Publication date, | When the source was made available to the public. This might be a year, a month, a specific date, or even a specific time. |
| 9. Location. | Where to find a specific source. This could be page numbers for print sources, a URL or DOI for online sources, or the location of a lecture or performance. |

## The elements of an in-text citation

Within the body of your paper, provide brief citations to any sources that you quote, paraphrase, or summarize. Each citation points readers to a more detailed entry in your list of works cited. The citation may be introduced with a signal phrase, contained in parentheses, or both.

| | |
|---|---|
| **SIGNAL PHRASE** | Critic Judith Thurman argues, "Ma Ke's couture dignifies the harshness of proletarian life" (54). Note how a direct quotation is punctuated. |
| **NO SIGNAL PHRASE** | In that political climate, attention to fashion was considered unpatriotic (Thurman 54). Note how a paraphrase is punctuated. |

**Long quotations.** When citing a direct quotation that is four lines or longer, indent the quotation a half inch from the left margin. Do not use quotation marks, and place the period before the parenthetical citation: ...and peace is here. (319)

## Formatting the core elements in a works-cited entry

| 1. Author. | Examples |
|---|---|
| *One author.* Invert the author's name. For online sources, pseudonyms and handles may be used; provide the author's real name (if provided) in parentheses. Corporations can also be authors. | Jacob, Mira. King, Martin Luther, Jr. @pronounced_ing (Celeste Ng). Environmental Protection Agency. |
| *Two authors.* Invert the first author's name, but put the second name in traditional order. Separate them with a comma. | Pratchett, Terry, and Neil Gaiman. |
| *Three or more authors.* Name only the first author, followed by et al. | Raabe, William A., et al. |
| *Beyond writers.* The primary contributor could be an editor, a director, a composer, a performer, etc. Spell out roles after names. | Dunham, Lena, performer. Lamar, Kendrick, composer. Mayer, Richard E., editor. |
| **2. Title of source.** | **Examples** |
| *Longer works.* For books, Web sites, films, and other standalone works, italicize the title. | *Design for How People Learn.* *The Martian.* |
| *Shorter works.* For essays, poems, Web pages, and television episodes, place the title in quotation marks. | "The Yellow Wallpaper." "The One with Phoebe's Wedding." |
| *Sections of a work (untitled).* | Introduction.        Afterword. |
| **3. Title of container,** | **Examples** |
| Italicize most containers. When citing a standalone source, element 3 is not needed. When citing an essay *within* a book or an episode *of* a television show, the container is the book or show. | *The New Yorker,* *African American Review,* *Serial,* *The Unbreakable Kimmy Schmidt,* *The River Reader,* |
| **4. Other contributors,** | **Examples** |
| Introduce each name (or names) with a description of the role. If listed after element 2, capitalize the description; if listed after element 3, do not. If there are multiple roles you wish to emphasize, separate them with commas. | , translated by David McLoghlin, <br><br> , adapted by Anne Carson, <br><br> . Directed by Mira Nair, performance by Vijay Raaz, |

| 5. Version, | Examples |
|---|---|
| Use abbreviations *ed.* (edition) and *rev.* (revised); spell out other words. Use numerals for numbered editions. | rev. ed.,<br>3rd ed.,<br>updated ed.,<br>version 2.1, |

| 6. Number, | Examples |
|---|---|
| Use abbreviations *vol.* (volume) and *no.* (issue), but spell out other descriptors, such as *episode*. | vol. 7, no. 11,<br>season 1, episode 5, |

| 7. Publisher, | Examples |
|---|---|
| List publishers for books, films, television shows, and sites that have sponsors that differ from their title and author. Separate multiple publishers with a slash (/). | Vintage Books,<br><br>University of Virginia Library / Museum of Design, |
| Spell out most names, but omit initial articles and any corporate words (*Inc.*). Do use abbreviations for university presses (UP). | Melville House,<br>Free Press,<br>Rutgers UP,<br>U of Michigan P, |

**NOTE:** *Do not* list publishers for periodicals, sites for which titles and publishers are similar, or sites that do not produce the works they house. Do not include cities of publication.

| 8. Publication date, | Examples |
|---|---|
| This could mean the date a work was published, republished, released, broadcast, or performed. | 2016,<br>Jan.-Feb. 2014,<br>10 May 2015, 9:30 p.m., |

**NOTE:** *Access dates* should only be included when a source is unstable or likely to change. Place these at the end of your citation, after the location.

| 9. Location. | Examples |
|---|---|
| For sources with page numbers, use the prefix *p.* or *pp.* | p. 9.          pp. 1065-89.<br>pp. 185-89. |
| For sources accessed online, provide DOIs when given. If a DOI is not available, use a direct URL, ideally a permalink. Do not use angle brackets or any *http://* prefixes. | doi:10.1002/cplx.21590.<br><br>milkdelivers.org/about-milkpep/.<br><br>www.refinery29.com/fitness. |

**Containers within containers.** Sometimes you will access sources in containers within larger containers. This means that if you cite an article from a journal (container #1) that you accessed through a database like *EBSCOhost* (container #2), then you should include relevant information about the larger container (such as its title and the source's location within it) to help readers retrace your steps. Place any information about container #2 after all information about the source itself and container #1, separated by a period. See examples of how to cite sources with two containers in Sample Works Cited Sections F, G, and I.

**Format.** Indent the second and all subsequent lines of a works-cited entry a half inch from the left margin.

## Sample works-cited entries: Books

### A. Book
PRINT

Oyeyimi, Helen. *Mr. Fox: A Novel*. Riverhead Books, 2012.

ONLINE DATABASE                                        original pub. date (follows title)

Wells, H. G. *The Invisible Man: A Grotesque Romance*. 1897. *Bartleby.com*, 2000,
bartleby.com/1003/.                                        date published online

E-READER (APP OR ON DEVICE)            translator

Cadhain, Máirtín Ó. *The Dirty Dust*. Translated by Alan Titley, Kindle ed., Yale UP, 2015.

### B. Book with an author and an editor

Woolf, Virginia. *A Writer's Diary*. Edited by Leonard Woolf, Harcourt, 1954.

### C. Revised book

Chaucer, Geoffrey. *The Canterbury Tales: Fifteen Tales and the General Prologue*. Edited by V. A.
Kolve and Glending Olson, 2nd ed., W. W. Norton, 2005.

### D. Selection from an anthology or textbook

Díaz, Junot. "Aurora." *The Ecco Anthology of Contemporary American Short Fiction*, edited by
Joyce Carol Oates and Christopher R. Beha, Harper Perennial, 2008, pp. 213-26.

### E. Book in a multivolume work

Kennedy, David M., and Lizabeth Cohen. *The American Pageant: Since 1865*, 15th ed., vol. 2,
Wadsworth, 2012.

## Sample works-cited entries: Periodicals

### F. Journal article
PRINT

Parikka, Jussi. "Earth Forces: Contemporary Land Arts, Technology, and New Materialist
Aesthetics." *Cultural Studies Review*, vol. 21, no. 2, 2015, pp. 47-75.

ONLINE DATABASE

Pavlovic, R. Y., and A. M. Pavlovic. "Dostoevsky and            container #1
Psychoanalysis: Psychiatry in 19th-Century Literature." *The British
Journal of Psychiatry*, vol. 200, no. 3, 2012, p. 181. *PsycINFO*,
doi:10.1192/bjp.bp.111.093823.            container #2

### G. Magazine or newspaper article
PRINT

Brennan, William. "TV's Fake-Language Master." *The Atlantic*, Apr. 2016, pp. 16-18.

Simon, Lizzie. "The Art of Obsession." *The Wall Street Journal*, 19 Mar. 2012,
pp. A24+.  A plus sign stands in for nonsequential pages.

ONLINE

Chen, Brian X. "Virtual Reality Is Here. Is Oculus Rift Worth It?" *The New York Times*, 28 Mar.
2016, nyti.ms/1XYcowB.  permalink

ONLINE DATABASE

When there is no listed author, begin with the title.

"Outsider Candidates Generating Buzz." *The Toronto Star,* 19 Mar. 2016, p. A16. *LexisNexis*
  *Academic,* www.lexisnexis.com.proxy.wexler.hunter.cuny.edu/lnacui2api/api/version1
  /getDocCui?lni=5JBB-WWG1-DY91-K4PR&csi=237924&hl=t&hv=t&hnsd=f&hns
  =t&hgn=t&oc=00240&perma=true.

## Sample works-cited entries: Other source types

### H. Recording (music, film)

Beyoncé. "Flawless." *Beyoncé,* performance by Chimamanda Ngozi Adichie, Columbia
  Records, 12 Aug. 2014.

### I. Episode or program (app, streaming service)

"Cops Redesign." *Portlandia,* directed by Jonathan Krisel, performances by Fred Armisen and
  Carrie Brownstein, season 2, episode 5, IFC, 3 Feb. 2012. *Netflix,* www.netflix.com
  /watch/70236274.

### J. Podcast or video podcast (online)

Kine, Starlee, narrator. "Belt Buckle." *The Mystery Show,* episode 3, Gimlet, 18 June 2015,
  gimletmedia.com/episode/case-3-belt-buckle/.

### K. Page on a Web site or blog post

Wise, Hannah. "An American Mystery: Who or What Is Killing All These Bald Eagles?" *The
  Scoop Blog,* Dallas Morning News, 28 Mar. 2016, 4:31 p.m., thescoopblog.dallasnews.
  com/2016/03/an-american-mystery-who-or-what-is-killing-bald-eagles.html/.

### L. Map or chart

*West Virginia State Map.* Folded ed. Rand McNally, 2011.

### M. Work of art  *Place the date of creation immediately after the title. Treat the physical location (museum, city) of the artwork as its location.*

                                                                location

Vermeer, Johannes. *The Astronomer.* 1668. Louvre Museum, Paris.

### N. Advertisement       description

"Apple Watch – Dance." Advertisement. *YouTube,* 21 Oct. 2015,
  www.youtube.com/user/Apple?v=fHE5WDO5l5Y.

### O. Public speech or live performance

                   description of speech, which is untitled

Rankine, Claudia. Keynote Address. 2016 AWP Conference and Bookfair, 31 Mar. 2016, Los
  Angeles Convention Center.
            location

### P. Personal interview

  interview subject

Jackson, Sha-Mena. Personal Interview. 7 July 2015.

## APA Style

The style guide for the American Psychological Association (APA) is used most frequently in the social sciences, including psychology, sociology, linguistics, anthropology, economics, and criminology; it is also used in business and nursing.

APA style is geared especially toward scientific reports, which typically have a more prescribed format than humanities articles. In such a format, the use of first-person ("I") is discouraged, transitions between sections may be less important (since they're at least to some extent prescribed), and the dates of articles are much more important, since they indicate how recently the research of the article being cited was conducted.

APA style also includes guidelines for bias-free language. By using these guidelines, writers can help ensure that their treatment of groups and individuals is fair. Essentially, the guidelines require writers to avoid use of any language that demeans or discriminates and to strive to use accurate, inclusive language at all times. This can be done in part by describing people and groups with an appropriate level of specificity and by being sensitive to labels. For details, see https://apastyle.apa.org/style-grammar-guidelines/bias-free-language.

A typical in-text citation in APA style looks like this:

**EXAMPLE  A Typical In-Text Citation**

Hoadley (2012) briefly describes the theoretical assumptions and key processes that begin and maintain communities of practice.

The core elements of a References entry in APA format are similar to those of MLA Works Cited format: Author, title, page numbers, and so on. APA format also requires the inclusion of an element called a Digital Object Identifier, or DOI, if it is available. A DOI is a unique sequence of letters and numbers assigned to digital content by the publisher, and it's used to provide a permanent identity to digital sources. The DOI is typically located with the copyright information on journal articles and books and can also be found with the database landing page for the article. Not all digital content has a DOI, but if it does, your APA References entry must include it (see Figure 12.7).

### The elements of in-text citations in APA format

Summary and paraphrase are used much more frequently in APA style than direct quotation. When you summarize, use the basic author–year citation. If you are paraphrasing, it's a good idea to include a page number as well.

When quoting in APA style, you must provide the author, year, and specific page citation if the source has page numbers. And, as with MLA format, for each in-text citation you must include a complete reference in the References list. If a quotation you're using is fewer than forty words, you should enclose it in quotation marks, cite the source in parentheses immediately

**A framework to understand depression among older persons:
Depression among older persons** in a Chinese context
by Zeng, Wen; North, Nicola; Kent, Bridie

Journal of Clinical Nursing, 09/2012, Volume 21, Issue 17-18

Article/Essay: Full Text Online

Preview ▴

      Permanent Link

| | |
|---|---|
| **Publication Title:** | Journal of Clinical Nursing |
| **Volume:** | 21 |
| **Issue:** | 17-18 |
| **Pages:** | 2399 - 2409 |
| **Date :** | 09/2012 |
| **ISSN:** | 0962-1067 |
| **EISSN:** | 1365-2702 |
| **DOI:** | 10.1111/j.1365-2702.2011.04049.x |
| **Language:** | English |
| **Altmetrics:** | |

FIGURE 12.7 Source from Library Database Showing DOI Number

after the final quotation mark, and continue the sentence. As in the following example, the date, in parentheses, often directly follows the author.

**EXAMPLE** **A Quotation in the Middle of a Sentence**

Blikstein (2013) discusses Freire's "culturally meaningful curriculum construction" (p. 4) as well as Papert's advocacy of digital technologies.

**EXAMPLES** **Quotations at the End of a Sentence**

- As with quotations in the middle of a sentence, you can note the author and date within the sentence itself and place only the page number after the quotation.

  The data provided by Jemehoochie et al. (2018) suggests that children who watch television "display tendencies toward agitation and hyperactivity, especially when a period of physical inactivity is accompanied by an intake of sucrose" (p. 32).

- If the quotation appears at the end of a sentence and you haven't previously introduced the author, include the author, date, and page number at the end of the sentence:

  Alternatively, it's possible to consider a situation in which participants volunteer to be immersed in isolation tanks, whereby "cutting off exposure to typical sensory experience can produce the Ganzfield effect, which devotees typically describe as relaxing and meditative" (Chizzlefield & Jacobs, 2010, p. 132).

- If you are quoting material without page numbers (such as material that's online), find the closest thing that would help readers track down the source if they want to find it. You could use the abbreviation *para.* (if the publication contains paragraph numbers), or the heading, if that's available. (You can shorten overly long headings where necessary.)

Quotations that are longer than forty words should appear as a block quotation. Block quotations are indented the same amount as a new paragraph, and do not include quotation marks around them. The in-text citation (Author, Year, p. 100) should be included after the final punctuation mark, but if you've already introduced the author and date before the block quotation, only the page number(s) would be needed here.

## Sample references entries: Periodicals

> **General reference form for periodicals:**
> Author, A. A., Author, B. B., & Author, C. C. (year). Title of article: Subtitle of article. *Title of Periodical, xx,* pp–pp. https://doi.org/xx.xxxxxxxxxx

Include the DOI if one is assigned. If no DOI is assigned to online content, include the URL instead.

### A. Journal article with DOI

Pavlovic, R. Y., & Pavlovic, A. M. (2012). Dostoevsky and psychoanalysis: Psychiatry in 19th-century literature. *The British Journal of Psychiatry, 200,* 181. https://doi.org/10.1192/bjp.bp.111.092823

### B. Journal article when DOI is not available (print journal)

Parikka, J. (2015). Earth forces: Contemporary land arts, technology, and new materialist aesthetics. *Cultural Studies Review, 21*(2), 47–75.

### C. Magazine article

Wong, A. (2016, December). Why kids need recess. *The Atlantic Monthly,* 22.

### D. Newspaper article

Pells, E. (2017, April 1). Gut-wrenching end for Gonzaga. *Moscow-Pullman Daily News,* B1.

### E. Online newspaper article

Sonne, P., & Ostroukh, A. (2013, September 6). Putin vows continued aid to Assad: Russian president blames Syrian rebels for gas attack. *The Wall Street Journal.* https://www.wsj.com/articles/SB10001424127887323623304579058923844385820

**F. Editorial without signature**

Michigan is forced to do right by Flint, finally. [Editorial]. (2017, April 3). *The New York Times.* https://www.nytimes.com/2017/04/03/opinion/michigan-is-forced-to-do-right-by-flint-finally.html

## Sample references entries: Books and book chapters

**G. Print book**

Barnett, S., & Boyle, C. A. (Eds.). (2016). *Rhetoric, through everyday things.* University of Alabama Press.

**H. Online book**

Benkler, Y. (2008). *Wealth of networks: How social production transforms markets and freedom.* http://www.benkler.org/Benkler_Wealth_Of_Networks.pdf

**I. Edited book**

Charlow, N., & Chrisman, C. (Eds.). (2016). *Deontic modality.* Oxford University Press.

**J. Entry in reference book**

Edwards, P. (1967). Dialectic. In *The encyclopedia of philosophy* (Vol. 2, pp. 387–388). Macmillan.

**K. Chapter in an edited book**

Mackenzie, A. (2015). Machine learning and genomic dimensionality: From features to landscapes. In S. Richardson & H. Stevens (Eds.), *Postgenomics: Perspectives on biology after the genome* (pp. 73–102). Duke University Press.

**L. Chapter in an edited book with DOI**

Phillips, B. F., Chubb, C. F., & Melville-Smith, R. (2000). The status of Australia's rock lobster fisheries. In B. F. Phillips & J. Kittaka (Eds.), *Spiny lobsters: Fisheries and culture* (2nd ed., pp. 43–77). Fishing News Books. Wiley Online Library. https://doi.org/10.1002/9780470698808

## Sample references entries: Other source types

**M. Motion picture**

Reitman, I., & Pascal, A. (Producers), & Feig, P. (Director). (2016). *Ghostbusters* [Film]. Columbia Pictures.

**N. TV episode**

Morgan, P. (Writer), & Daldry, S. (Director). (2016). Wolferton splash [TV series episode]. In P. Morgan (Executive Producer), *The Crown.* Left Bank Pictures and Sony Pictures Television for Netflix.

**O. Podcast**

Reed, B. (Host). (2017). *S-Town* [Audio podcast]. Serial Productions. https://stownpodcast.org

**P. Page on a website or blog post**

Glabau, D. (2016, January 14). Why does everyone hate Martin Shkreli? http://somatosphere.net/2016/01/why-does-everyone-hate-martin-shkreli.html/

## Informal Citation in Written, Visual, and Multimodal Compositions

Many compositions aimed at the general public (i.e., a nonacademic audience) rely on *informal citation*; that is, they provide enough information that readers, if they wanted to follow up on the topic or check the veracity of the story, could locate the source reasonably easily (in the case of Web-based compositions, simply by clicking on the provided links).

### Informal citation in print texts

While it's generally more important to keep the flow of the writing than to document source information in nonacademic texts, as a matter of ethos and of situating your points, you should provide some information. Typically, giving the author name and a title is enough (in informal citation, you almost never get as specific as page numbers). And, of course, in nonacademic writing, you should not include a Works Cited or References page.

**EXAMPLES**

- Yet, others have found different pleasures in knitting. In her article "Knit Outside," Ellen Kitterling recommends yarn-bombing as a way to beautify towns.
- ...things get muddled quickly, as film director Terrence Malick explains in an interview.
- Another researcher writing in *The Journal of American Psychiatry* pointed out that...
- Governor Badger declared that...
- Moscow gardener Karen Thompson calls daffodils "the true harbingers of springtime."

### Informal citation in Web texts (linking)

The most effective way to lead readers to sources on the Web is by one of the Web's most basic functions, hypertext. That is, a writer can "cite" a source on the Web simply by linking to it. In the *Wikipedia* page (Figure 12.8), you can probably guess that the blue links in the entry are definitions of the terms; in fact, all of them link up to *other Wikipedia* pages, which themselves are full of links. The "Blogging and Intellectual Property Law" blog post (on the site *legalzoom*) (Figure 12.9) uses the link for more traditional citation purposes—the author is quoting from the United States Copyright Office and includes a link to the page from which she's quoting.

### Informal citation in infographics

Because they can be extended vertically, infographics conventionally include citations of the sources used to create the infographic, typically at the very bottom of the page. Depending on the infographic creator

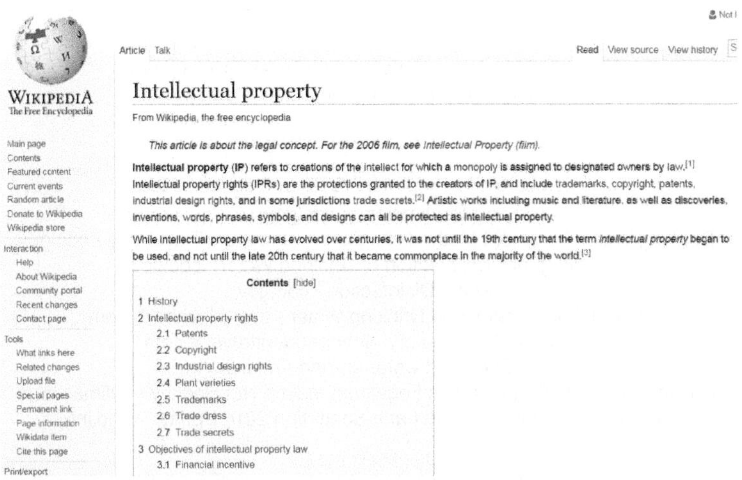

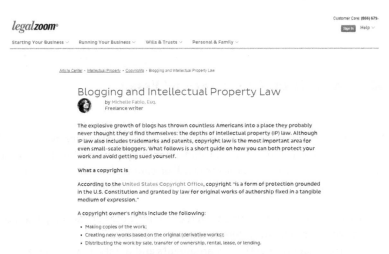

FIGURE 12.8 "Brachiosaurus" *Wikipedia* Page Showing Links Used as Informal Citations

FIGURE 12.9 Link Used as Citation of Source in a *Legalzoom* Post

and the audience and purpose of the infographic, these can be more or less formal (i.e., in a specific citation format); infographics aimed at an audience of scientists might have more of an imperative to cite formally, whereas infographics meant to entertain or instruct the general public might use less formal citations, as the "A Traveller's Guide to Tap Water" infographic source list, shown in Figure 12.10. The list, which appears at the very bottom of the infographic, includes brief identifying phrases and a link to the related site.

You can't live without water, but the wise traveller knows how to drink safe and make the most of their journey.

### SOURCES

Destinations - cdc.gov
Drinking Water Treatment Methods for Backcountry and Travel Use - cdc.gov
Emergency Disinfection of Drinking Water - cdc.gov
Water Disinfection - cdc.gov
International Travel and Drinking Water - everydayhealth.com
Drinking Water Safety - independenttraveler.com
Food and water abroad - nhs.uk
Millions Drink Tap Water That Is Legal, but Maybe Not Healthy - nytimes.com
Progress on Drinking Water and Sanitation 2014 Update - who.int

PRESENTED BY

**NeoMam Studios**

Source: "A Travellers's Guide to Tap Water"

**FIGURE 12.10** Informal Citation in an Infographic

## ASSIGNMENT

## Write a "Critical Conversation" Essay

### TASK

Using at least 20 sources, write an essay on your topic that summarizes and synthesizes the current variety of understanding, uses, and feelings about your topic. The audience for the essay will be your instructor and classmates.

### ASSIGNMENT GOALS

- To gain facility in interacting with (i.e., taking notes on, keeping track of, and organizing) many different sources on a topic.
- To practice identifying the key arguments and points of written texts.
- To gain a much deeper understanding of the public dimensions of your topic: why and how it's significant to people other than yourself.
- To practice logically organizing ideas, using topic sentences and smooth transitions.

### PREPARATORY STEPS

1. See Section 12a to help you generate initial research questions and keywords, and to keep track of the sources you find.

2. Begin grouping your sources into different lines of thinking about your topic. You might use these questions to help you do this:

What is the basic history or background on the topic?
Who talks about this thing, and who is it important to?
What are the common themes that characterize discussions of the topic?
What sorts of arguments have been made about it?
What is at stake in the topic; that is, how do people understand its cultural significance?
Why/how is it important?

## WRITING THE ESSAY

Each exploratory essay will shape up a little differently depending on the topic, but just keep in mind that you're developing for yourself, in a formal way, an understanding of the scope of this topic beyond your own personal interest in it. So a typical writing structure might look something like this:

1. The introduction will set the context and hook the reader by introducing your topic, making a case for why this topic is worth exploring, and stating your research question(s) (i.e., what you wanted to discover as a result of doing the research and why you are interested in the topic—a good research question for this paper would be "What is the broader cultural significance of X topic, and what are some typical themes and arguments that characterize discussions of it?"). Your introduction should also help forecast what's in the paper: You can provide an overview of the types of sources you cite in the body of the paper, and outline the structure of your paper.

2. The body of the paper will answer your research questions. It logically leads the reader through the previous questions (though perhaps not in that particular order). Though you'll be citing a great many sources, the body of your paper won't be organized by individual source but by patterns of theme and/or question (use the earlier questions as a guide).

3. The conclusion will situate your own personal feelings on the topic within the broader context that you established in your paper.

---

### FOR REFLECTION

**Transferable Skills and Concepts**
Think about a recent situation in which a course (other than a course in writing) required you to do research for an assignment. How did the instructor and assignment talk about the research process? How was it different and/or similar to the way the research process is discussed in this chapter?

# 13

# Creating Written Compositions

## LEARNING OBJECTIVES

*By working through this chapter, you will be able to...*

- Understand composing as a continuous, recursive, messy process.
- Use freewriting, mind-mapping, questioning, and other invention activities to generate material for composition.
- Learn to "re-see" your paper through reverse outlining and other techniques in order to identify opportunities for revision at the global and local levels.
- Understand the academic essay as a genre with its own set of conventions.

**ANALYZE**
**and CREATE**

**Chapter 3**
Analyzing Textual
Rhetoric

**Chapter 13**
Creating Written
Compositions

As Chapter 2 explains, each modality, medium, and genre (what we refer to collectively as the *means of communication*) has certain advantages and disadvantages when it comes to effectiveness of communication. To be a rhetorically effective communicator, you need to think carefully and make good decisions about what means of communication you're using in a given situation.

While we already examined the rhetorical effects of written communication in Chapter 3, it's worth pausing to consider what distinguishes writing as a form of communication:

- It can convey a potentially infinite amount of complex information, limited only by the amount of paper and ink or computer memory available.

- It conveys information linearly (but also visually and simultaneously). For readers to fully understand everything the writer has communicated, they need to read linearly, from top to bottom, left to right; but they can also skim and scan the page or screen to find what they want.

- It's the predominant form of composition taught in schools today, so readers are habituated to using it as a form of communication.
- It can be copied and transmitted to audiences other than the intended one.
- Because it is experienced as uniform words on a page or screen, readers need to imagine the voice behind the words.

This chapter assumes that you've already weighed your communication possibilities and decided that a written form of communication would be most rhetorically effective given the particulars of the situation in which you're communicating. It covers topics and concerns that are specific to writing: the writing process (invention, drafting, revising) and writing in academic and public genres, the two areas that you'll probably focus on most in this course.

---

## FOR DISCUSSION

1. Choose one of the areas of your life—college, work, family, friends, public life—and write a list of the forms of communication you typically use for it. When do situations seem to call for writing and when do they call for other forms of communication? Why do you think this is?
2. Have you ever used (or been witness to someone using) a form of communication that turned out to be wrong for that particular situation? What happened? How did you know it was the wrong form of communication?

---

# 13a Embracing the Messiness of the Writing Process

Depending on the complexity of what you're writing and how familiar you are with the topic, sometimes you can sit down and write something that's reasonably complete and polished, or at least that's good enough for the audience and situation. But for other writing tasks—if you're writing in an unfamiliar genre or about unfamiliar ideas, for instance—it may take you several attempts to clarify what you're trying to say and to polish it so that you'll best convey it to your audience. These attempts comprise the writing process.

The writing process sometimes gets inaccurately portrayed as a rigid step-by-step process:

1. Generate ideas (invention).
2. Write them out (drafting).
3. Consider them critically.
4. Revise them (revision).

While sometimes writing may happen like this, it's more likely that the "process" will actually be somewhat fluid and recursive, or looping back on itself. For instance, writing through your ideas (drafting) may actually help you understand what you were trying to say (invention), and in the process of revising your work, you might realize that you have written it to the wrong audience, and that it needs to be totally rewritten for a different purpose and audience (revision).

**EXAMPLE**  You want to email your boss describing an incident that took place at work last night, just for the record (employees are expected to report such incidents). However, in the course of writing the email, you realize that this problem is really an instance of a larger pattern to which you want to call her attention. So you revise your email to fit the pattern "as I was discovering X, I also discovered Y." You begin by describing the specific incident, then explain that you think the larger issue needs to be addressed.

## FOR DISCUSSION

Think of one nonacademic and one academic example of writing you've done recently. In as much detail as you can, write down your writing process for each of these. Are they different? If so, how and why?

## Invention: Generating Ideas

"Invention" technically means coming up with ideas, which can happen at any point during the composing process, not just at the beginning. Sometimes you might spend a lot of time thinking about what you want to write and how you want to write it before you commit anything to paper; and sometimes you may find that you can't really think your ideas through until you write them down.

In his book *Writing with Power*, composition theorist Peter Elbow points out that writing calls on two different brain functions: creativity and critical thinking. These two functions are actually at odds with one another; that is, when you are trying to be *creative* and generate ideas, material, and so forth (aka invention), the worst thing you or someone else can do is *critique* those ideas because the flow of ideas will quickly dry up. So Elbow and other experts on writing recommend that writers keep these processes separate. When you're trying to generate ideas, send your inner editor (who may or may not have the voice of your junior-high grammar teacher) away for a bit. The editor is invited to come back after you have something down on paper.

Plan for your process of idea generation to be messy and wasteful. Sometimes in order to find out what you think, you need to write a lot that you won't actually use. This is OK, but as you can imagine, it does take time. So the most important thing is to deliberately set aside time to generate ideas. Your best ideas might not actually happen during the time that you've set aside to brainstorm (mine tend to happen when I'm out running, in the shower, or walking to school, all times that I don't have writing implements handy). However, in deliberately setting aside time to brainstorm ideas, you signal to your brain that you are trying to solve a problem—and it will keep working on that problem even after you've put away your writing materials.

There are multiple strategies for generating ideas, and they don't all work for everyone. Some people simply like to make lists; others, being more visual learners, might draw out confusing tangles of ideas on paper so that they can see what they're writing about in a different way. So, what follows are a few suggestions for generating ideas. Try several and see which works best. Also keep in mind that invention can happen at any stage of the writing process, including drafting and revision.

### Considering purpose, audience, and the means of communication

As Chapters 1 and 2 discuss, the foundational elements of rhetoric will helpfully constrain your possibilities for the invention process. Once you've established *why you're writing* (the exigence and the purpose of your communication), *who you're writing to* (the audience), and *by what means you'll be presenting your message* (the means of communication), you'll have a good sense of what sorts of information you need to include. Sometimes these things are already given, but sometimes coming up with them forms part of your invention process.

**EXAMPLE** You've been assigned to write a review of an activity or event that's popular among locals. The review will be published on an "unofficial" online university student magazine, which is read mainly by students at the university. The editors specify that the review should be no more than 600 words and that it should include several images.

Here, obviously, much in the rhetorical situation has already been given to you. In this case, your invention process will involve deciding what kind of local place, activity, or event would be surprising and interesting to your audience of college students. Then you would apply the evaluation process to the thing you chose in order to write the review. So your invention process may look something like this:

- You write down a list of local places, activities, or events that might be of interest to college students.

- You choose the one that seems the quirkiest or most interesting; in this case, a building on campus that is supposedly haunted.

- You go to the building during normal working hours and then again at night with a friend and jot down your impressions (paying special attention to any potential otherworldly events).

- Once you get home, you map out some sensory impressions and descriptions of the place. Once these are written down, you use them to come up with your overall evaluation of the place.

### Freewriting

This is an exercise most famously articulated by Peter Elbow in his book *Writing with Power*. In freewriting, you force yourself to write without stopping for a certain amount of time (typically 10 minutes or so). There are three rules in freewriting:

1. Keep writing for the designated amount of time. Though you can write a question or subject on top of the page to keep yourself focused, ultimately it doesn't matter *what* you write, just *that* you're writing.

2. Keep your pencil/pen on the page. (You should do freewriting the analog way, with pencil/pen and paper—you'll be less tempted to erase and edit that way.)

3. Don't erase or cross out. If you don't feel like completing a thought, just begin another one. Nobody will see this freewriting but you.

The goal of freewriting is not to produce good writing but to put *words on paper*. As Elbow puts it, "Freewriting makes writing easier by helping you with the root psychological or existential difficulty in writing: finding words in your head and putting them down on a blank piece of paper" (14). Freewriting helps to get the mechanical process of writing started. And, if you do it every morning, as is recommended in Julia Cameron's book *The Artist's Way*, you'll ideally have created the *habit* of writing, which is about 85 percent of the battle. Elbow also recommends freewriting as a way of clearing the "junk" from your head before you start on something that you have to write. So if you're feeling bummed about, say, the fact that your team just lost the NCAA championship, it might help to consciously devote some time to putting those feelings on paper before you begin composing your letter to the editor about the dangers of the intersection in town that doesn't have a stoplight.

### Mind mapping

Like freewriting, mind mapping is a way to get thoughts down on paper, but it's less linearly organized, and it's more focused than freewriting (because you do begin mind-mapping with a specific topic or question). Some will find mind mapping to be a more intuitive process because it mimics the associative qualities of our brains—rather than writing down thoughts one after the other, as in freewriting, you arrange them in clusters. These clusters can then lead to other clustered ideas, which can actually help us generate more thoughts. If you're a visual learner, you may also appreciate the visual connections between ideas that mind maps create. Some forms of mind mapping also involve drawing pictures or being creative with color and text, which is another form of visual learning.

Free mind-mapping software exists (it's useful if you have a big or long-term project and plan to keep adding and adding to your mind map); however, to create a mind map for a project you only need paper and pencil.

- Begin by posing a question or putting a topic in the middle of the page.
- Then let your mind free associate about the topic or question, generating as many categories and associations as you can.
- You can take that mind map and redraw it in a more organized way if it gets too messy or if you see another potential area for exploration that you hadn't counted on.

Remember that the mind map is a means to an end; it helps show you what you know and gives you the geography of a particular issue or project. It's a handy way to generate ideas for a project. It also helps you find deeper meaning in your topic and to figure out what you're missing or what questions still need to be answered (see Figure 13.1).

## Questioning

Questions are excellent idea generators because action is already built into questions—they inherently prompt one to look for answers. For this invention activity, you basically write down all the questions you can possibly imagine about your idea. Some of these can be artificial questions (i.e., ones you already know the answer to), but the act of questioning will naturally lead you to unknown (or less well-known) territory. Not only will you have natural places to start researching your topic, but you might discover a genuine question that you don't know the answer to, which could serve as a great research question.

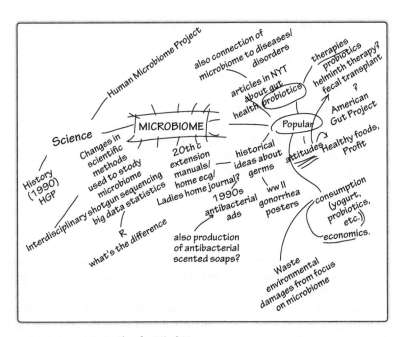

FIGURE 13.1 Example of a Mind Map

**EXAMPLE** Here are some questions about the microbiome in the popular imagination that could be explored:

- Why is the public so interested now in stories about the microbiome?
- When did this interest start?
- How did they think about bacteria/microbes before this, and what changed?
- Is microbiome science changing the way that the public thinks about health and disease?
- What therapies are available now? How "legitimate" are these considered to be?
- How do economic concerns shape what forms of therapies are available?

## FOR DISCUSSION

1. Consider the following two situations. What might the invention process look like for each of them?

   a. Your history professor has given you a take-home test in which you need to write an essay that defines the meaning of the word "civilization" using ten words from a list of thirty that she's discussed in lecture over the past month and applying them to a specific historical example of a civilization. How would you start?

   b. The state legislator from your district has publicly denied the existence of climate change and has proposed a bill that eliminates mention of climate change from your state science education standards. He is also sending extremely hostile responses to anyone who writes to him expressing concern about the issue. What are some ways in which you as a citizen might address this situation?

2. Try out each of the above invention activities for a project you're working on. Then discuss: Which one did you find the most effective, and why? Which was least effective?

3. What are some other ways of generating ideas or deepening your understanding of the topic?

## Drafting

Maybe you're the kind of person who needs to have a fully finished introduction and a detailed outline before you start. Maybe you would prefer to just start writing from the thing you know best or are most interested in—even if it's in the middle—and work out from there. Either way, drafting is about just getting the words down. You'll likely find even if you thought you knew what you were trying to say, the act of actually articulating it will show you ideas and connections you didn't know were there. So drafting can be an invention process too.

In *Bird by Bird*, her well-known book about writing, Anne Lamott advocates for writing "shitty first drafts." No writer, she points out, starts off writing beautiful, polished prose à la Mozart, who supposedly got his musical compositions straight from God. Rather, to overcome the horrible anxiety and sense of dumbness that accompanies most initial writing attempts, Lamott recommends just forcing your fingers to the keyboard and allowing yourself to write several pages of trash (in this way, "shitty first drafts" are somewhat akin to freewriting). Following a writer friend's description, she calls this the "down draft"—it's when you get things down on paper. The down draft can be full of terribly stilted or overblown prose, overly lengthy descriptions, a long-winded introduction, and it can be totally out of order. But it doesn't matter because in writing through your ideas, you have given yourself some material to work with. You can let your down draft sit, and then the next day, you can work on creating the "up draft" (i.e., cleaning it up).

What often happens in the drafting process (in the process of creating the "down draft") is that you'll write your way into a main idea or thesis. So often when I read student papers, I'll find the thesis statement at the end of the essay, where it unfortunately remains, undeveloped. To be clear, writing your way into a main point or thesis isn't the problem—but after you do that, you need to take it and reframe the piece around that. This is what we call *revision*.

## Revising

Revising your work can be painful, but only if you see the words and ideas in your draft as precious flowers that mustn't be uprooted, rather than as dirt that has to be pushed around in order to find the potatoes (or diamonds, if gardening isn't your thing). In trying to understand the differences between the revision strategies of novice and expert writers, composition scholar Nancy Sommers noticed that novice writers typically characterize their revision process as a matter of scratching out and replacing words, while leaving the (often inadequate) substance of the work untouched. Expert writers, on the other hand, treat revision as a way to *find* the argument or message. As one of her expert subjects put it, "My first draft is usually very scattered. In rewriting, I find the line of argument. After the argument is resolved, I am much more interested in word choice and phrasing" (384).

Note that "revision" literally means "seeing again": now that you've done the hard work of writing through your initial ideas, you can look with fresh eyes to see not only your best and most cogent ideas but also how to present those ideas in a way that is most appropriate for your intended audience and purpose. This might mean that you use only one sentence from your first draft and start building again from there; it might mean that you need to find new evidence, new reasons, new sources (and maybe even a new audience and purpose).

We might think of two different levels of revision: the **global level** and the **local level**. Global-level revisions relate back to the purpose, message, and audience of the piece: What are you trying to do for this purpose and this audience? You might even recognize in the course of revising globally that your composition is in the wrong medium—you thought a letter to the editor was the best idea, when preparing a speech and delivering it to a recorded town hall meeting with your representative would actually be more effective. Local revisions are more about how you've said something: Whether there are adequate transitions, or if the syntax sounds off, or whether, indeed a better word could be used.

The question that works the best for revising at both the global level and the local level is, *"What am I trying to say here?"* At the global level, the question forces you to make big decisions about what point you're trying to make and whether it's appropriate to your purpose and audience. At the local level, the question can help cut through the confusion that sometimes results when you want to say something in a certain way (perhaps a way that sounds "academic," depending on who you're writing for). If you ask, "What am I trying to say in this sentence?" and can say it out loud, you can often just write down what you said and it'll be clearer than if you get lost in gobbledygook.

### Reverse outlining

If you're having trouble "re-seeing" your work, one helpful tactic is called reverse outlining. Reverse outlining is just what it sounds like. Using what you've already written, you outline the main points of the piece (typically the thesis statement and the topic sentences of paragraphs), stripping away all the supporting evidence. The point of reverse outlining is to make your work seem a little foreign, and to read a highly condensed version of what you wrote. Then decide if your ideas make sense in that order, if you need to add or subtract points, and if the paper meets its goals. **Note:** If you can't find your thesis statement or topic sentences, that's probably a good indication of a problem with the paper.

Following is an earlier draft of an essay that appears in Section 7c, with comments from Martha Mendez's instructor. Martha created a reverse outline from this draft, which appears after the draft.

## Annotated First Draft

Great title for suggesting the gist of the argument, but it should also indicate the PURPOSE of the paper.

Ha. I love the personality here, but "damn" in the first paragraph of an academic essay probably isn't genre-appropriate. Also, there are too many ideas here—break it up so that you develop ONE idea per paragraph.

### You Better Teach Your Boys to Cry

"Sugar and spice and everything nice." "Tough it up and be a man." Excuse me, but no. I'm a 5'4" woman who has a lot more than just sugar in my personality. If you want sugar, go bake some damn cookies. I've got things that make my blood boil; one of those things being gender stereotypes. Do you want to know one of my least favorites? "Real men don't cry." Say that to me and I can almost guarantee you will have lost my respect. The boy down the street has been told his whole life not to cry, and although he may try to hold back tears, he should not have this pressure placed on him. Men are men, and women are women, but both are human. Chitra Ramaswamy posted an article earlier this year titled, *"How a Sexist T-Shirt Harms Us All."* Her article demonstrated how gender stereotypes are both common and harmful to everyone. While I support her conclusion, her article failed to adequately explain the effects that stereotypes have. Therefore, in order to do this topic justice, I would like to extend her argument by taking the time to examine the effects that one specific gender stereotype has had on men specifically. Before I begin to extend my own argument, however, allow me to first recap the original article and analyze how Ramaswamy made her article speak to her audience.

Ramaswamy began her article by summarizing a Gap advertisement in which a girl is displayed as social butterfly while a boy is portrayed as a future genius. She later notes how even shapes have been reserved to specific genders. Girls get polka dots and boys get stripes. Next, she makes an appeal to logos, by providing evidence of a company, Marks & Spencer, that brought out a clothing line for boys only, and therefore, like Gap, is guilty of gender discrimination. By recognizing the stereotypes in both advertisements, Ramaswamy proved that gender stereotypes are a prevalent issue in our society. Moreover, she took time to recognize that there are other companies, like Hamleys and Sainsbury, that, unlike Marks & Spencer and Gap, are making appropriate accommodations to avoid gender discrimination. She shared how Sainsbury has stopped labeling costumes for a specific gender. She also states how Hamleys is leaving behind its pink and blue signs. To further support Ramaswamy's argument on gender discrimination, she recalled a specific experience where her son was judged against because of his gender. She had gone to the store to buy a little stroller for her son, as a tool to help him learn to walk. The saleswoman commented that she had never seen a boy with a stroller before. Although Ramaswamy shared her frustration with this situation, which appealed to pathos, she also acknowledged that everyday individuals living everyday lives are guilty of discriminating based off gender as well. Furthermore, she confessed that she too, is guilty of victimizing her son through gender stereotypes. By admitting this, she again applied pathos to her argument, because she displayed the shame she had for imposing gender stereotypes upon her own flesh and blood. Her reference to situations where her son was judged because of his gender, in addition to the confession of her own participation in gender stereotyping, caused an emotional uproar within my heart. How could we, as a society, be so naive as to

> This last part explains the purpose and your thesis—could you condense it to get to your point more quickly?

> When you have a new idea (or are going to make a big move like summarizing), start a new paragraph.

> Review the "writing summaries" section in Chapter 3—start by stating Ramaswamy's main point rather than working chronologically through what the article says.

> Condense your summary—it's a little hard to find Ramaswamy's main points here.

fail to recognize that this little boy was first a human? What were we telling our young men? And how do the things we tell them, shape them as individuals? And how could Chitra Ramaswamy, acknowledging that gender stereotypes were real, not provide more details, outside of the last two paragraphs, about how gender stereotypes affect our world? Therefore, although I believe her article proved that gender stereotypes are a real issue in our society, I stand by my original claim: She does not give this issue an adequate explanation. Consequently, as both a witness and guilty participant to these gender stereotypes myself, I have a moral obligation to relay to you the poisons that gender stereotypes have breed.

> *Here is really the beginning of your response to Ramaswamy, so give it more oomph by starting a new paragraph with it.*

Andrew Reiner, author of "Teaching Men to Be Emotionally Honest," began his article by recalling how a student of his "showed a video clip she had found online of a toddler getting what appeared to be his first vaccinations" (Reiner). He continued by explaining how, in the video, the young boy begins to cry and the father responds by telling his son, "Don't cry!...Aw, big boy! High five, high five! Say you're a man. 'I'm a man!'" (Reiner). After watching this video, the author acknowledged, "how boys are taught, sometimes with the best of intentions, to mutate their emotional suffering into anger" (Reiner). Reiner concluded by stating that when we mislead boys into believing that they must block out their emotions, there are unfortunate repercussions that follow.

> *Use the topic sentence of your paragraph to state a claim of your own—it should be more immediately clear why you're bringing up the Reiner article.*
>
> *This is a good summary of his article!*

Lena Aburdene Derhally, a psychotherapist, wrote an article titled, "Here's how (and why) to help boys feel all the feels." In this article, Derhally shares how she has seen this specific stereotype cause a lot of damage in her own patients. "What stands out to me when counseling men is that much of their struggle with anxiety, depression, and relational trouble has a connection to the inability to understand and process their feelings. This is largely to do with the messages that start in childhood, not only from the family but often from peers and the community. Issues of rage, anxiety, depression, and unhealthy coping mechanisms like heavy drinking often manifest when men don't understand their feelings or don't give themselves permission to have them" (Derhally). The argument that stereotypes are harmful to our society is reinforced when Derhally shares that, "suicide rates are four times higher in men than in women" (Derhally). How absolutely devastating is that? Our men are killing themselves because we, as a society, have burned the stereotype, that men are not supposed to be emotional, into their skin. I cannot speak on behalf of the whole world, but, in my eyes, this is absolutely disgusting. By telling our boys that they cannot cry, we are teaching them that we would rather have them kill themselves and bleed blood than show their emotions.

> *Make a stronger connection in this topic sentence between Derhally and Reiner. Use transition words like "Likewise" or "Similarly" to signal this transition to readers.*

> *Good interpretation of Derhally's article that links back to your main point.*

Chitra Ramaswamy was correct in her original argument: Gender stereotypes are prevalent today and the stereotypes hurt all genders. However, she failed to unmask just how deeply rooted these gender discriminations are, and how severely they affect people. The truth is this: When we tell men they cannot cry, we restrict their outlets for emotions. Without this outlet, their coping mechanisms are limited to unhealthy drinking habits or suicide, as Derhally mentioned. Therefore, if we want our boys to live, we need to tell our boys to cry.

> Beautiful, ringing last sentence, and great conclusion overall!

**WORKS CITED**

Derhally, Lena Aburdene. "Here's How (and Why) to Help Boys Feel All the Feels." *The Washington Post*, 1 Oct. 2015, *www.washingtonpost.com*. Accessed 26 Oct. 2016.
Ramaswamy, Chitra. "How a Sexist T-shirt Harms Us All." *The Guardian*, 2 Aug. 2016, *www.theguardian.com*. Accessed 17 Oct. 2016.
Reiner, Andrew. "Teaching Men to Be Emotionally Honest." *The New York Times*, 4 Apr. 2016, *www.nytimes.com*. Accessed 26 Oct. 2016.

If you read the teacher's comments on the original version of the essay, you'll notice that while the content and substance of the essay (a coherent response to Chita Ramaswamy's article "How a Sexist T-shirt Harms Us All") were there, the arrangement and transitions of the essay needed some work to bring out Martha's points and make them more powerful. To make her points clearer and more obvious, Martha also needed to condense her summaries and revise her paragraphs so that they made only one point and had strong topic sentences. You can read her revised version in Chapter 7.

## Reverse Outline, "You Better Teach Your Boys to Cry"

| PARAGRAPH | WHAT DOES THE PARAGRAPH DO AND SAY? | THOUGHTS FOR REVISION |
|---|---|---|
| 1 | Introduces common gender stereotype clichés for men and women, says what I think about them, talks about how harmful male stereotypes are specifically. Talks about Ramaswamy's article, and my basic response (thesis) to her article. | Too much going on! Maybe split this into two or three paragraphs. |

*(continued on next page)*

| PARAGRAPH | WHAT DOES THE PARA-GRAPH DO AND SAY? | THOUGHTS FOR REVISION |
|---|---|---|
| 2 | Summarizes Ramaswamy's article by starting with the beginning and working toward the end. Ends by questioning Ramaswamy's points and restating my thesis. | Too much happening here too (summary + the beginning of my response)—split into two paragraphs. Also, the summary does seem to ramble, and now that I re-read it, the point that I want to respond to doesn't come out very well. Revise it to begin with the overall point of the article, then show her supporting points. |
| 3 | Summarizes Reiner's article. | It does need a transition—I just kind of start talking about it without explaining why it's important to my point. |
| 4 | Summarizes Derhally's article, has my thoughts in support of what she's saying after the summary. | Same thing—needs a better connection to Reiner and to my main point. |
| 5 | Conclusion reiterates Ramaswamy's point and my main response to her. | Maybe mention Derhally and Reiner once more for a clear connection back to those points. I like my conclusion otherwise. |

## FOR DISCUSSION

Take something you wrote (perhaps the last assignment you did for this course), and make a reverse outline of it. What did you learn from doing this?

# 13b Writing in Academic Genres

Academic or college writing is a genre unto itself, with its own set of conventions. Some scholars argue that academic writing is actually its own language, which students need to learn before they can speak it like an insider. Now, if you think academics (aka professors) are a bunch of nerds who are interested in arcane subjects and write in hopelessly jargon-filled, bad prose, you might wonder exactly why you *should* want to learn to speak like them. It's true that certain aspects of academia seem rather silly (and people delight in making fun of academic research—just Google "shrimp on a treadmill"). However, defenders of academic writing maintain that becoming versed in it is helpful for developing one's ability to critically assess arguments, weigh evidence, and spot lies and contradictions; it also conveys the ability to mobilize written arguments and use evidence effectively.

---

## FOR DISCUSSION

Think about the last academic essay you wrote, and break it down according to the elements of rhetoric:

1. Who was the audience?
2. What was the context?
3. What was the exigence?
4. What ethos did you as a communicator try to generate?
5. What was the purpose?
6. What were the means of communication (i.e., modality, medium, genre, and circulation)?

Now answer the same questions about the last nonacademic thing you wrote (this could be anything). What are some of the major differences between the academic and nonacademic writing situations?

---

## Anatomy of Academic Essays

Academic essays frequently get reduced to a formal exercise à la the infamous five-paragraph essay (an intro with a thesis, three body paragraphs, and a conclusion) of your high-school English class. While there's nothing particularly *wrong* with the five-paragraph essay, it often feels like a contextless assignment, a rote activity designed to show your teacher that you in fact did read *Hamlet* and analyze its Freudian elements (or, a bit closer to home, that you did understand the rhetorical moves of that Nike ad).

It might be better to think rhetorically about the academic essay (like you would all communication) as a genre with its own audience, purpose, and conventions. To be sure, the audience for academic essays is most typically your professor and classmates; but by engaging in academic writing, you're also engaging in scholarly conversations about this topic and thus participating in a community of knowledge makers. Successfully employing the conventions of academic writing is a way to signal your belonging to this community.

So what are the conventions of academic essays and their rhetorical function?

- Titles (frequently with a colon) that convey the purpose of the essay and the gist of the argument to readers, helping them decide if the essay contains information or an argument that would be useful to them.

- An introduction that introduces the topic/issue, lays out the stakes, presents the argument in the form of a thesis statement, and forecasts the rest of the paper. Introductions help the reader decide with more confidence whether the paper will be of use to them.
- Body paragraphs that develop each assertion using sufficient evidence. Paragraphs employ topic sentences and summary, paraphrase, and quoting. Also known as "signposting," things like topic sentences and indicator phrases help guide the reader through the moves of your argument.
- A conclusion that might do one of the following things: explain why considering this issue is important, resolve the problem or question that the paper started with, or make a forward-looking point about what researchers might focus on in the future.
- The use of academic citation formats like MLA and APA.
- Sometimes very specialized language (jargon) that's specific to that particular academic community. This and the use of citation format signal that the writer belongs to a specific community, and they are thus a form of ethos.

Each of these is discussed in turn in the following sections.

### Titles

**EXAMPLES** Here are a few recent titles from academic journals in various disciplines:

- "Man Interrupted: Mental Illness Narrative as a Rhetoric of Proximity" (*Rhetoric Society Quarterly*)
- "Efficient Removal of Antimony (III,V) from Contaminated Water by Amino Modification of a Zirconium Metal-Organic Framework with Mechanism Study" (*Journal of Chemical & Engineering Data*)
- "Gender Role Attitudes, Relationship Efficacy, and Self-Disclosure in Intimate Relationships" (*Journal of Social Psychology*)
- "'We Can't Grow Food on All This Concrete': The Land Question, Agrarianism, and Black Nationalist Thought in the Late 1960s and 1970s" (*Journal of American History*)
- "Cholinergic, but Not Dopaminergic or Noradrenergic, Enhancement Sharpens Visual Spatial Perception in Humans" (*Journal of Neuroscience*)

Upon first read, these titles may seem forbidding and in some cases even unreadable. But if you patiently work through the titles, you'll see that contained within the obtuse language are clues about what arguments the article will contain. For instance, let's take the article from the *Journal of Neuroscience*: "Cholinergic, but Not Dopaminergic or Noradrenergic, Enhancement Sharpens Visual Spatial Perception in Humans." While I don't know three of the words in the title, if I ignore those for the time being, I notice that the title basically says "A, but not B or C, sharpens visual spatial perception in humans." So the title tells me, basically, that *something more* than other things causes people to perceive better. That's all I know without reading the article, but I can guess that the authors of the article are responding to prior research on human spatial perception—either that they didn't know what caused perception to be better, or they thought it was one or both of the two other factors. (The curious get a gold star for defining "cholinergic," "dopaminergic," and "noradrenergic.")

> This part of the title provides the gist of the argument made in my essay: that Kristof compares the Arab Spring of 2011 to the American Revolution.

So, the title of your academic essay likewise needs to contain an indication of your *subject* and *argument*. For instance, take the title for a sample rhetorical analysis essay I wrote several years ago:

> The use of a colon is common in academic titles.

"Echoes of 1776 in 2011: A Rhetorical Analysis of Nicholas Kristof's "Watching Protesters Risk It All""

> This part of the title indicates the purpose of this piece of writing: It's a rhetorical analysis of an article.

## FOR DISCUSSION

Choose one of the other titles of the previously listed academic journal articles and see if you can dissect it in order to figure out the purpose and argument of the article.

### Introductions

Introductions of academic essays are meant to intrigue the reader in the question that drives the essay and to give a sense of the issue's scope. Often, introductions will also signal what stance the writer is taking on the issue. Thus, introductions typically have some or all of the following components:

**A "hook."** By "hook," I mean something that's meant to intrigue readers. A hook might present an intriguing or contradictory question, or a puzzling situation (perhaps in the form of an anecdote) that directly relates to the argument that's about to be made. The introduction could also begin with an epigraph (a quote from someone that's positioned between the title and the text), which the introduction will then explain.

**A sense of the stakes of your argument.** Your introduction might also explain why what you'll be arguing in the essay is significant to the audience. For instance, will your argument change a common perception or understanding? Will it make a surprising connection? Focus on finding an element of surprise or intrigue, a sense that this is important to your readers.

**A thesis statement.** As Chapter 12 explains, thesis statements are the product of a process of inquiry—they will be the answer to your refined research question that has come from a great deal of thought, research, and initial drafting. Unless you already know your topic very, very well (and much of the time not even then), you should not begin an academic essay with an already-formulated thesis statement.

As a condensed version of the argument you wish to make, thesis statements serve in an academic essay like the coiled spring that helps propel your argument forward (think of them as the plunger on an old-fashioned pinball game). If you have a weak thesis statement, you won't be able to create enough intellectual momentum to keep a reader involved in your essay. To be considered strong, a thesis statement should have three main qualities:

- It should be *debatable*.
- It should be *focused*.
- It should be *positioned properly in the essay*.

First, a thesis statement must be *debatable*; that is, it must state a claim with which reasonable people could disagree. Chapter 7 explains what a claim is and how to make one. You might consider how you could frame your thesis statement in terms of the points of stasis (fact, definition, cause/effect, evaluation, and policy).

Put negatively, the thesis statement should not be a statement of fact. For instance, if you were to say, "People who work in cities frequently use public transportation" nobody would argue this point—it is objectively true. But more importantly, it's not clear from this statement what is at stake, or why this observation is significant. (A reader could reasonably ask, "So what? Why are you telling me this?")

The thesis statement also should not be stated as a matter of personal opinion, because that's also not debatable. If you say, "I believe the children are our future," nobody can argue with you, because what you think is what you think.

But suppose you were to rephrase these statements as. . .

"Owing to the vulnerable state of the American auto industry, people who work in cities shouldn't use public transportation."

and

"The generation currently about to enter school is the future workforce of a country that currently can't keep pace with the demand for high-tech laborers; thus, there should be a greater focus on STEM education in elementary schools."

These revisions show thesis statements that are actually debatable. And note that both of these arguments will need to be supported with reasons and evidence (as discussed in Chapter 7).

Second, thesis statements need to be *focused*. You may think that making a broader argument will help you because you'll be able to find more sources to support your points, but you'll find yourself (a) quickly overwhelmed with managing information and (b) really bored with what suddenly has become a somewhat meaningless exercise in arguing for an overly general point. Having a broad or unfocused thesis statement commonly happens when writers begin their essay with a thesis statement in mind rather than discovering their thesis through the process of inquiry described in Chapter 12.

Finally, thesis statements should be *positioned appropriately* in the essay. Because of the Western habits of reading from top to bottom and left to right in any form of writing, the beginnings and ends—of sentences, paragraphs, sections, and whole essays—are the most powerful and obvious positions from the perspective of placing important information. Typically, a straightforward academic essay will have a thesis statement toward the end of the introduction. If you wanted to be bold, you could put it in the very beginning of your paper; this is best when you're pretty sure your audience will buy your argument.

It's also possible to write an essay in which the thesis statement comes at the end, a method called Rogerian argument (named after Carl Rogers, a mid-twentieth-century psychologist). Typically, writers who use this technique are writing on a highly contentious, charged topic. A Rogerian essay begins with a presentation of the issue and a question; the writer works to build trust with readers by focusing on commonalities and presenting in the issue in a neutral way. Writers of Rogerian essays thus slowly build toward their point so as not to alienate readers early on, and the thesis statement comes at the end of the essay.

The only thing you should NOT do is bury your thesis statement somewhere in the middle of a paragraph.

**Forecasting**. Typically, introductions of academic essays tell readers what they can expect to find in the essay.

**EXAMPLE** A forecasting statement is fairly straightforward. It might look something like this: "[**Thesis statement.**] In this essay, I first [provide background on X]; then I explain the limitations of typical views of [the subject]; and then explain why [X position] is a more effective way to think about it."

The length of the introduction depends on the length of the paper: if it's longer than five pages, the introduction could be several paragraphs long; if the paper is short (one to three pages), typically the introduction would be only one, at most two, paragraphs.

## FOR DISCUSSION

Look at the following thesis statements. Which are weak, and which are strong? Why? How would you rewrite the weak ones to make them stronger? (You can make things up.) Tip: Ask "And so. . .?" of each statement; if you get a reasonable answer, it's probably a strong thesis. Also ask "What would I need to do to research and develop this idea?" If the answer to that is clear, it's probably a strong thesis.

- The 2016 election showed that fake news is a problem.
- Though coffee is said to be detrimental to bone health in certain cases, the positive effects it has on memory and energy make it an important beverage for senior citizens.

- The Sharpie company is wonderful, but it could do better at regulating the intense smell of its pens.
- With Congress's March 2017 passage of the Investigatory Powers Bill, your Internet search history can now be sold to the highest bidder.
- The United States entered the war on Iraq for many reasons, some of which were legitimate, and some of which were not legitimate.
- To address the increase in crime in downtown Chicago, the city should not respond by increasing the police force and/or criminal penalties; rather, it should follow the examples of LA and other large urban areas by fostering a community policing program.
- Since the statements made by the current head of the Environmental Protection Agency are not believable, we need to turn to an alternate source for news about the environment.

### Paragraphing with PIE (Point, Illustration, Explanation)

Paragraphs in academic essays frequently serve as mini-essays in themselves: They begin with a topic sentence that makes a clear claim, they develop that idea, and then they end by asserting what readers should take away from the paragraph. A handy (and tasty!) acronym to remember when composing paragraphs in academic writing, PIE stands for point, illustration (or information), explanation. (See Figure 13.2.)

- The *point* of the paragraph is the main point or focus of the paragraph (there should be only one of these per paragraph in academic writing). Traditionally, the point is made in the topic sentence.

- The *illustration/information* of the paragraph is the evidence you provide to support or develop the point. What type of illustration you make depends, of course, on what claim is being developed in the paragraph.

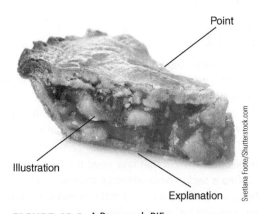

Point

Illustration

Explanation

Svetlana Foote/Shutterstock.com

**FIGURE 13.2**  A Paragraph PIE

- And finally, the *explanation* of the paragraph is a statement of your own interpretation or analysis of the point and evidence. What was your purpose in bringing up the evidence in relation to the main point? What do you want your audience to take away from it?

As an example of PIE, let's look at the paragraph below, taken from my rhetorical analysis of Kristof's 2011 *New York Times* op-ed piece.

---

### Mapping a Paragraph Using PIE

Like many opinion columnists, Kristof writes for an audience who is already likely to buy into his opinion about Bahrain. *New York Times* readers in general tend to be well educated (the newspaper is written on a twelfth-grade level, far above national newspapers like *USA Today* and more local papers like *The New York Post*, both of which are written on a sixth-grade level). *Times* readers also tend to be fairly liberal—the *Times* is known for having a liberal bias, something that can be seen just by perusing the other regular op-ed columnists: Maureen Dowd, Paul Krugman, Thomas Friedman, and Bob Herbert are known for espousing liberal points of view. And in addition to being well educated and liberal, readers of Kristof's columns typically are interested in international affairs. Kristof is famous for writing about the genocides in Rwanda and Sudan, human trafficking in Vietnam and Thailand, and the need for foreign aid in Africa. Thus, typical readers of Kristof's article would have a good sense of at least Kristof's basic worldview before they even read his article.

> Point of the paragraph, expressed as a topic sentence.

> Illustration 1: NYT readers are well educated.

> Illustration 2: NYT readers are fairly liberal (followed by evidence about typical columnists).

> Illustration 3: NYT readers are interested in international affairs.

> Explanation: Note that it's called out with "thus," followed by a statement about what I wanted readers of my paragraph to understand about the evidence I presented.

---

Paragraphs in academic essays (and really, in most types of expository or argumentative writing) also need to be *cohesive* and *coherent*. Cohesiveness has to do with the internal consistency of the paragraph: whether the sentences follow logically from one another. Coherence has to do with whether all the sentences refer back to the main purpose of the paragraph. Say a paragraph started off with this sentence:

> **Certainly the Pacific Northwest had more than its fair share of rain this year.**

What would you expect to follow from that sentence? Probably an explanation of unusual weather conditions—something like this:

> Washington got 130 inches of rain, about 146% of normal, and Oregon had 153% of its average yearly amount of rainfall. While this may not be exactly Noah's ark conditions (yet), the seemingly

> "This" refers back to the conditions caused by the unusual amount of rain described in the previous sentence.

never-ending precipitation did have its effects: not only on the mood of PNW residents, who reported an above-average level of seasonal depression but also on agriculture. Researchers recently discovered a strange variety of mold on the grape vines in the Willamette Valley vineyards, and many farmers in Washington reported severe erosion to their wheat fields from mini-mudslides due to rain.

> The above-average amount of precipitation caused effects on agriculture: The highlighted phrases in the next sentence show the connection.

As the annotations describe, each sentence in the paragraph carries over ideas from the sentence that came before it, and each sentence helps to explain the topic sentence of the paragraph.

But what if what came after the topic sentence was something like this?

> **Certainly the Pacific Northwest had more than its fair share of rain this year.** The Olympic Peninsula in Washington State has one of the only North American rainforests, and so it has a lot of interesting creatures like the Cope's giant salamander and banana slugs. Seattle, Eugene, and Portland architecture has been shaped by the amount of rain that the region gets: Homes use a lot of cedar and other hardwoods that resist rot, and typically have a lot of windows to let in light even when it's gloomy. While one would think that umbrellas are the best defense against the rain; it's considered "uncool" by those who live in the Pacific Northwest to actually use one. If you do, you're marked as an outsider or just not very tough.

It probably drove you a little crazy because while each sentence is nominally about rain in the Pacific Northwest, the individual sentences don't relate to one another. The paragraph has coherence, but lacks *cohesion*, in other words.

OR, what if what followed the topic sentence was this?

> **Certainly the Pacific Northwest had more than its fair share of rain this year.** Areas with rainy climates prove to be very good for those who tend to have dry skin. When you scratch someone with dry skin, it leaves behind white lines. White lines on skin aren't very attractive and can be made to disappear with lotion. The best kind of lotion, I think, is EO Products Everyone Lotion in coconut-lemon scent (product placement!). EO is a California-based company that uses all organic ingredients and essential oils in its products, so it's a favorite among hippies and Whole Foods shoppers. Whole Foods is really overpriced.

Reading this *also* probably drove you crazy, because it reads like the results of the parlor game Exquisite Corpse, where each player writes a sentence based only on the sentence that the previous player has written. That is, while each sentence in this paragraph relates to the topic of the one prior to it, it doesn't relate to the topic sentence of the paragraph. The paragraph has cohesion, but lacks *coherence*.

FOR DISCUSSION

Find two paragraphs: one from any academic publication and one from a feature story in a popular magazine or newspaper. Dissect each paragraph, identifying how it creates cohesion and coherence. Can you identify any differences between the paragraphs in the academic and the popular sources?

## Conclusions

Conclusions are tricky. Since (if the essay is read from beginning to end) the conclusion will be the last thing readers read, it's your last chance to make a final push for your argument. Ideally, a conclusion will leave readers with a clear answer to the "so?" questions of good writing: "So what's the big deal?" "So why have I spent my time reading this?" "So what have I learned that I didn't know before?" A really excellent conclusion also has an emotional resonance with readers (aka pathos); it moves them and perhaps it makes them think more deeply about the issue or the topic and leaves them thinking about it for days afterward. So while the standard high school writing advice is to summarize your main point and restate the main idea, this formula (while it's not the worst thing you could do) doesn't make for the most resonant, powerful conclusions.

**QUESTIONS TO ASK**   **Drafting a Conclusion**

To write a conclusion, first let your draft sit for a few days while you chew on these questions:

- What do you want readers to feel or understand once they set your essay down?
- Why does what you say really matter, and to whom? What will be lost if what you argue for in this essay doesn't happen?
- Looking forward, where do we go from here?
- Is there something you came across in the course of researching and thinking about your essay—an anecdote, an insight, a quote, an idea— that really captures what you feel about your argument? (Note that the conclusion isn't the place to include random or tangential information. New information should only be included if it doesn't bring up more questions and if it directly relates to the "so?")

Then try drafting your conclusion. Remember that while you want to aim for emotionally resonant or powerful, the conclusion still needs to be written in the style of the academic essay of which it's a part. Be careful not to go off on a Miss America-style speech about how resolving your issue will lead to world peace and the end of sadness.

## An Annotated Academic Essay

As discussed previously, the title indicates the gist of the argument and the type of paper it is (a rhetorical analysis).

### Echoes of 1776 in 2011: A Rhetorical Analysis of Nicholas Kristof's "Watching Protesters Risk It All"

The initial paragraph provides context and background for Kristof's article by explaining the events of the so-called Arab Spring.

The beginning of 2011 witnessed what most had considered unimaginable: spontaneous pro-democracy revolutions in several traditionally authoritarian Middle Eastern countries. Sparked by anger from citizens who were fed up with poor living conditions and the lack of political freedom, protests in both Tunisia and Egypt led to the ousting of dictators who had held power for almost three decades. The success of the revolutions in Tunisia and Egypt emboldened citizens of the nearby, equally authoritarian country of Bahrain to begin its own agitations for revolution. But despite their initial enthusiasm, Bahraini protesters met with far more resistance than did the Tunisians and Egyptians: Brutal crackdowns from the Bahraini government threatened to squash the revolution before it even got off the ground.

Astonishing or not, historic or not, the events in Bahrain at first received only uneasy, half-hearted attention from the United States government. In his *New York Times* op-ed article "Watching Protesters Risk It All," Nicholas Kristof suggests that perhaps this is because the United States had for years "[turned] a blind eye to torture in repression" in Bahrain so long as U.S. economic interests (like maintaining an uninterrupted oil supply) were protected. In part this was because the United States feared that the "democratic rabble" might turn against it: At least with authoritarian regimes, one only has to deal with a small group of crackpots. But in his article, published February 20, 2011, Kristof argues that the time has come to change this way of thinking. Claiming that "Far too often, we were both myopic and just plain on the wrong side," Kristof argues that this time, we should make sure we're on the right side: Americans should support the Bahrainis in their quest for democracy. By drawing a comparison between the events in Bahrain to a revolution near and dear to American hearts—i.e., the American Revolution of 1776—Kristof delivers a powerful rhetorical appeal for Americans to stand behind the pro-democratic enthusiasm of the Bahrainis.

We start to see what's at stake in Kristof's article: a change in U.S. treatment of Bahrain.

Here is the thesis statement; note that it makes a case for how Kristof's article appeals rhetorically to readers.

Like many opinion columnists, Kristof writes for an audience who is already likely to buy into his opinion about Bahrain. *New York Times* readers in general tend to be well educated (the newspaper is written on a twelfth-grade level, far above national newspapers like *USA Today* and more local papers like *The New York Post*, both of which are written on a sixth-grade level). *Times* readers also tend to be fairly liberal—the *Times* is known for having a liberal bias, something that can be seen just by perusing the other regular op-ed columnists: Maureen Dowd, Paul Krugman, Thomas Friedman, and Bob Herbert are known for espousing liberal points of view. And in addition to being well educated and liberal, readers of Kristof's columns typically are interested in international affairs. Kristof is famous for writing about the genocides in Rwanda and Sudan, human trafficking in Vietnam and Thailand, and the need for foreign aid in Africa. Thus, typical readers of Kristof's article would have a good sense of at least Kristof's basic worldview before they even read his article.

At the center of Kristof's argument to support the Bahrainis is an explicit analogy between the American and the Bahraini revolutions. "To me, this feels like the Arab version of 1776," he writes. Kristof compares one severely wounded young Bahraini determined to continue protesting to Americans who showed "a similar kind of grit" in the U.S. revolution against Britain. Simply by suggesting this analogy, Kristof sets off a chain of logical dominos in readers' minds. America is a democratic society, so democracy is good; therefore countries like Bahrain who are protesting for democracy must by extension be good. Likewise, just as Americans showed determination and fought against the injustice of a repressive government several hundred years ago, the Bahrainis are fighting back against their own repressive government. And finally, if Americans hadn't had the support of outside countries like France, we would have lost the Revolutionary War; thus, by analogy, it's important for us to support Bahrain in its quest for democracy.

> The topic sentence makes a claim/point about Kristof's central thesis, then goes on to explain it.

Kristof repeats "democracy," "democratic," and "freedom" throughout the article, as if to remind Americans not to dismiss the events in Bahrain as a regular old revolt, something that seems to be happening all the time in those countries "over there." Rather, as Kristof writes in the first paragraph, these Bahraini men, women, and teenagers "risk torture, beatings, and even death because they want freedoms that we take for granted"—again, creating an explicit analogy between Americans and Bahrainis. Even though the situations of America in 1776 and that of Bahrain in 2011 are vastly different, simply suggesting this similarity is likely to foster agreement in Kristof's target audience.

To persuade his readers of the importance and rightness of supporting the Bahraini cause, Kristof relies heavily on emotional appeals to awe at the human spirit, to a sense of justice, and to hope. Along with the example of the young man above, for instance, Kristof also mentions a paraplegic who "had been hit by two rubber bullets and was planning to return to the democracy protests for more." Examples of such clear determination and drive for democracy are designed to inspire awe in readers of Kristof's article. If these people are willing to wait "until democracy arrived, or die trying" (just like we did 300 years ago!), shouldn't we at least support them in their cause?

In fact, to *not* support Bahrainis in their quest for democracy, Kristof suggests, would put his *New York Times* readers on the side of a government that perpetuates systematic injustice. Because the king and the government are Sunni and the majority of the Bahraini people are Shia, injustice is built into the currently existing Bahraini system. As Kristof writes, the United States has up until now "been in bed with a minority Sunni elite...that is also steeped in corruption, repression, and profound discrimination toward the Shia population." This discrimination manifests itself in multiple ways: The majority Shiites have poor living situations and are excluded from finding jobs in the public sector or in the armed forces, which are dominated by Sunnis. By including examples of anti-Shiite prejudice by the Bahraini government, Kristof appeals to the sense of fairness that's deeply engrained in his liberal readers and makes his case for supporting the Bahraini pro-democracy revolution more urgent.

Finally, Kristof shows that despite the depressing situation that Bahrainis have faced until now, there is real hope for change. He begins his article with a harrowing situation. He, along with other journalists are watching as pro-democracy protesters march toward the "spiritual center" of the protests and their possible deaths by pro-government forces. He writes, "I flinched and braced myself to watch them die." However, miraculously the protesters didn't die—and we find out later that it was because President Obama had called the Bahranian king after he had started shooting protesters and the shooting subsequently stopped. As Kristof describes it, "The protesters fell on the ground of the roundabout and kissed the soil. They embraced each other. They screamed. They danced. Some wept." Including such moving scenes is designed to create a sense of relief and hope among Kristof's readers. It also gives readers the idea that if they support the Bahrainis, they will be on the winning side. And who doesn't want to be on the winning side—the side of justice, of freedom, and of democracy?

> The conclusion is emotionally resonant, though it's appropriate to the tone of the rest of the piece, and relates back to the ideas in the introduction.

## WORK CITED

> I include a Work Cited page and an entry in proper MLA citation format.

Kristof, Nicholas. "Watching Protesters Risk It All." *The New York Times*, 20 Feb. 2011, www.nytimes.com/2011/02/21/opinion/21kristof.html

# 13c Writing for Civic Participation

Thanks to the age of social media, you have more opportunities than ever to have your ideas heard, at least by those in your circle of influence, and potentially by many more than that.

## Letters to Legislators

The 2016 presidential election produced a renewed surge of interest in political action, and so a great deal of discussion focused on the most effective ways to reach and persuade elected officials. Of the various options (petitions like those shared by *Change.org* and *MoveOn.org*, emails, letters, calls, and office visits), face-to-face visits were deemed to be the most effective, followed by phone calls, then letters, and then electronic forms of communication like emails, social media comments, and petitions.

Letters to legislators are probably most helpful as part of a multi-pronged effort. If you are concerned about proposed legislation or any other issue at the local, state, or national level, you may want to try calling your legislator (where you'll likely talk to staffers, who will record your opinion and report it to the legislator). The second step would be to write a letter to the legislator in which you more fully develop your opinion on the issue; and the third step would be to make your letter public by publishing it as a letter to the editor, an open letter, or a blog post. In this way, you maximize the results of your efforts—the legislator knows your opinion on the issue (in two different ways, via a phone call and a letter), and you've made the conversation public.

Tips for writing letters to your legislator:

- Keep letters to one page. Focus on only one issue per letter.
- Letters should be in traditional business letter format (see Figures 13.3 and 13.4 for visual examples of how to address your letter). Letters should conclude with "Sincerely" and your signature.
- Introduce yourself and state your purpose writing (e.g., "I am a college student at the University of South Carolina, and I'm writing to express my concern about the proposed legislation [be as specific as you can—if you're writing about a bill, use the number] to cut state funding for higher education.")
- Provide a concise explanation of why you support or oppose the proposed legislation. Why is this a good/bad idea?
- Explain specifically why this issue will be detrimental or beneficial for the legislator's constituents. The more specific and relevant the information is to local issues, the better. Anecdotes are appropriate as well.
- Always be polite and respectful; whether you agree with the legislator's positions or not, being rude won't get you anywhere (this is a matter of ethos).
- Ask for follow-up ("I'm interested to hear what you think about my points, and would appreciate a reply. You can contact me at . . .").

```
953 E. 23rd St.
Moscow, ID 83843


The Honorable Mike Crapo
United States Senate
Washington, DC 20510


April 1, 2017


Dear Senator Crapo,
```

FIGURE 13.3  Addressing Written Correspondence to a U.S. Senator

```
953 E. 23rd St.
Moscow, ID 83843


The Honorable Mike Simpson
U.S. House of Representatives
Washington, DC 20515


April 1, 2017


Dear Representative Simpson,
```

FIGURE 13.4  Addressing Written Correspondence to a Member of the U.S. House of Representatives

## Opinion Pieces (Newspaper Op-Eds, Opinion-Based Web Content)

Opinion pieces are one step more involved than letters to the editor or to legislators. They offer an opportunity to write potentially longer, more in-depth pieces to a general audience. Nonprofessional writers have plenty of opportunities to write publicly, thanks to both good old-fashioned blogs and platforms like *Medium*, which has been described as "*YouTube* for prose."

Blogging platforms like *WordPress* assign unique URLs to blogs, and so building readership can be a challenge. You need to be committed to it, and you'll need to promote it by using social media and community building—linking back and commenting on similar blogs by other authors. *Medium* is a publishing platform that is connected to *Twitter*; anyone can publish on it, and indeed politicians and other professionals use it, along with amateur writers. *Medium* organizes content into "collections."

You also have the opportunity to write opinion pieces in print format. Depending on the size of your local newspaper, there may be opportunities for community members to write regular opinion columns; for instance, my local paper, which serves two towns and a combined 60,000 residents, has a regular "Town Crier" column that makes calls for new writers every fall and asks them to commit to a certain number of columns over the year. Often the writers achieve a certain level of fame (or infamy) in the community, and sometimes running dialogues will develop between the Letters to the Editor section and the Town Crier columns as members of the community parry back and forth.

The advantage of local newspaper columns is that they already have an established readership. However, they also are limited to that readership; that is, because it would be very difficult to grow the numbers of readers of the paper, response to your column is likewise limited. The topics you write about also should be relevant to a more local audience. While they might take the angle of dealing with national or international politics from a local perspective, typically the most relevant and interesting community opinion columns have to do with local issues and perspectives.

Print-based community opinion columns and opinion-based blog posts have other differences that arise from the means of communication. Web content is obviously less constrained by space, so these pieces can be longer (which is not necessarily better, as I'll discuss shortly). They can also contain links as a means of citation, images, gifs, video, and other multimodal elements.

In terms of content and style, though, print-based community opinion columns and opinion-based blogs are fairly similar.

Tips for writing opinion pieces:

- Begin with the exigence for writing. The exigence could be what Chapter 6 describes as an event-based problem (e.g., "[This week's events] have made clearer than ever the need for X"). Or you might identify an everyday problem, perhaps by describing a scenario that encapsulates the issue.

- Make the significance of the issue clear.

- Clearly state your opinion on the issue, and make your strongest point first.

- Use information or make connections that the audience doesn't already know. This could include a personal anecdote or an angle that they hadn't thought of (see the following annotated opinion piece, "Their View: Why Health Insurance Isn't a Rolls Royce or a Beater," for instance; the writers include personal information about their family's experience with health care).

- Write opinion columns and blogs in a friendlier, more personal tone and style.

- Keep print-based writing short: between 400 and 700 words is typical for op-ed columns. You have more latitude with platforms like *Medium*, which offers a category called Long Form, but consider carefully how much you need to say to get your point across.

## An Annotated Opinion Column

### Their View: Why Health Insurance Isn't a Rolls Royce or a Beater

BY CHRISTOPHER DRUMMOND AND JESSICA BEARMAN

Note that the writers immediately establish the exigence for the column.

With great interest, our family watched the Republicans in Congress over the past few weeks as they grappled with replacing the Affordable Care Act in the name of improving "access" to health care.

Here's some new information—an unexpected metaphor for health care. Pay attention to how they carry this metaphor through the column.

The Republicans seemed to mean "access" in the same sense that you might have "access" to a Rolls Royce. Sure, they are available on the salesroom floor in Bellevue, Wash. The only catch is that you need the money to pay for it.

On the one hand, we had "Ryan Republicans" who wanted to offer large tax credits to people who already have enough money to pay for that Rolls Royce, with the caveat the dealership could charge older people far more than they charge younger people, while a majority of the less wealthy would get a small rebate for something they couldn't afford to purchase in the first place.

On the other hand, we had "Freedom Caucus Republicans" like Idaho Rep. Raul Labrador, who believed the dealership should just charge whatever it wanted for a Rolls Royce. This would give a whole lot of people the "freedom" to buy a broken down car that requires payments each month, but could only be used in catastrophic circumstances after spending thousands of dollars to keep it running.

Here's their opinion. Notice that they don't state it up front, but first explain the problem with the other positions.

The fallacy of both positions is that health care is not like purchasing a Rolls Royce on the free market. If you are sick or injured, there is no freedom in not having coverage. The Republicans talk a good game about access to health care. But reading between the lines, it seemed their only plan was to abolish any reasonable government guidance and let American citizens purchase whatever they can afford, if they can afford it at all.

Nobody is looking to buy the proverbial Rolls Royce. Personally, we would be satisfied with a decent family sedan that starts up in the morning and makes it home in the evening. As it is, our country is moving toward an economy characterized by short-term employment, part-time positions without benefits and individual entrepreneurship. Consistent access to employer-sponsored health insurance is becoming less the norm.

As parents and small business owners who have purchased individual health insurance since before the ACA, we hope our legislators remember how a relatively unregulated insurance market worked for many residents of Idaho. Hunting each year to find a new plan that would accept us. Arbitrary limits on coverage for services, hidden behind confusing language that made comparison shopping meaningless. Accelerating rates decoupled from services provided. High deductibles and exclusions that covered comparatively little routine care.

> Note that the writers ground their argument in personal experience.

Under the Your Health Idaho state-run exchange (created in response to the ACA), individuals have been able to compare plans and purchase insurance with baseline coverage guarantees that could not be refused or revoked annually. More importantly, many lower income families have been able to obtain coverage they could not otherwise afford. According to the state of Idaho, over 100,000 residents enrolled in the state-run exchange for 2017, representing the second highest per capita rate in the nation. Of those, nearly 85 percent receive some form of assistance to defray costs.

The ACA and Your Health Idaho have room for improvement. As rates continue to increase, coverage takes a larger slice of income (we currently pay more than $12,000 a year on the individual market for a family of four), and others are priced out entirely due to the coverage gap between state Medicaid eligibility and ACA subsidies. Now that they have abandoned their ill-advised attempt at "repeal and replace" (at least for now), Republicans in Congress should drop their political posturing and return to the business at hand: providing affordable health care for the citizens of this country.

> Here's their final plea—the idea that they want readers to take away.

## Fact Sheets

While "fact" in the title may make it sound like fact sheets are an a-rhetorical genre ("just the facts, ma'am"), fact sheets are used for three definitively rhetorical purposes: to call attention to something, to provide information about that thing, and to present a point of view on it. Fact sheets can be written on almost any subject imaginable, from diseases to public issues to organizations. They are commonly used for government purposes and in university extension departments, both of which aim to educate the public (see Figure 13.5). Fact sheets are also commonly used in marketing and PR and are frequently written for reporters, legislators, and other stakeholders in a given issue.

Characteristics of fact sheets:

- The title typically contains the terms "Fact Sheet" and/or "Information."
- They are typically no longer than a page, in 10- to 14-point font.

- They focus on only one thing or one aspect of an overall topic. You would not create a fact sheet on the Affordable Care Act, for instance (though perhaps you could create one about how it affects the citizens of a specific place, say, Philadelphia).

- They are *concise* and written in lay terms.

- The first paragraph explains the purpose and main message of the fact sheet, as well as what action readers are being asked to take.

- They are carefully designed and uphold the CRAP principles (see Chapter 14).

- They use clear, easy-to-see graphics and charts, and incorporate text boxes.

- They provide references that direct readers to more information.

---

The title contains the word "information," indicating that this is a fact sheet.

The title clearly indicates the audience (the "your" here clearly refers to a parent; the introduction clarifies that it's pregnant women).

The colored, highlighted boxes are phrased as simple commands, followed by explanatory text.

The other headings are phrased as questions that the fact-sheet creator assumes the audience will have (or should have).

The fact-sheet creator gives the audience several places to go if they have more questions or want more information.

**USDA** United States Department of Agriculture

## Food Safety Information

### Protect Your Baby and Yourself from Listeriosis

*Pregnant women are at higher risk of getting sick from Listeria monocytogenes, a harmful bacterium found in many foods. Listeria can cause a disease called Listeriosis that can result in miscarriage, premature delivery, serious sickness, or the death of a newborn baby. If you are pregnant, you need to know what foods are safe to eat.*

**Clean**
- Clean up spills in your refrigerator right away, especially juices from raw meat and poultry.
- Clean the inside walls and shelves of your refrigerator with hot water and liquid soap.
- Wash your hands for 20 seconds with soap and water after touching hot dogs, raw meat, poultry or seafood.

**Separate**
Keep raw meat, fish and poultry away from ready-to-eat foods.

**Cook**
Cook food to a safe minimum internal temperature. Check with a food thermometer and heat lunch meats until steaming.

**Chill**
*Listeria* can grow in the refrigerator. The refrigerator should be set to 40°F or lower and the freezer to

0°F or lower. Use a refrigerator thermometer to check the inside temperature.

**How do I know if I have Listeriosis?**

- Symptoms can include fever, fatigue, chills, headache, backache, general aches, upset stomach, abdominal pain and diarrhea.
- Gastrointestinal symptoms may appear within a few hours to two to three days, and disease may appear two to six weeks after ingestion. The duration is variable.
- Pregnant women are at higher risk and may develop problems with pregnancy that include miscarriage, fetal death or severe illness or death in newborns.
- Every year an estimated 1,600 Americans become sick and 260 people die from Listeriosis.

**What should I do if I think I have Listeriosis?**

Call your doctor, nurse or health clinic if you have any of these

signs. If you have Listeriosis, your doctor can treat you.

**What foods are associated with Listeriosis?**

- Hot dogs, luncheon meats, bologna, or other deli meats unless they are reheated until steaming hot.
- Refrigerated pâté, meat spreads from a meat counter, or smoked seafood found in the refrigerated section of the store. Foods that do not need refrigeration, like canned meat spreads, are okay to eat. Remember to refrigerate after opening.
- Raw (unpasteurized) milk and foods that have unpasteurized milk in them.
- Salads made in the store such as ham salad, chicken salad, egg salad, tuna salad or seafood salad.
- Soft cheeses such as Feta, queso blanco, queso fresco, Brie, Camembert, blue-veined cheeses, and Panela unless it is labeled as "MADE WITH PASTEURIZED MILK."

**Food Safety Questions?**
Call the **USDA Meat & Poultry Hotline** toll free at **1-888-MPHotline (1-888-674-6854)** The hotline is open year-round and can be reached from 10 a.m. to 4 p.m. (Eastern Time) Monday through Friday. Available in English and Spanish.

Send E-mail questions to MPHotline@usda.gov
Consumers with food safety questions can also "Ask Karen," the FSIS virtual representative. Available 24/7 at AskKaren.gov.

@USDAFoodSafety  @FoodSafety.gov  Check Your Steps

USDA is an equal opportunity provider, employer, and lender.
Food Safety and Inspection Service
June 2017

Source: USDA

**FIGURE 13.5** An Annotated USDA Fact Sheet on Listeriosis and Pregnancy

# 14

# Creating Visual Compositions

*By working through this chapter, you will be able to...*
- Identify when to use visual compositions for rhetorical purposes.
- Use the basic principles of visual design to create visual compositions.

Here's a powerful example of the rhetorical effect of visual compositions:

In the 1980s, John Gotti, the infamous Mafia don, was arrested in an FBI crackdown on crime syndicates. In a remarkable turn of events, Gotti was acquitted on all charges and released. A *New York Times* news analysis of the time attributed Gotti's acquittal in part to a chart created by Gotti's defense that visually documented the criminal acts of all the witnesses for the prosecution. The chart (Figure 14.1) implied that the witnesses brought against Gotti were unreliable, their cooperation likely having been bought or traded with the FBI in exchange for favors or leniency.

The chart isn't visually beautiful or particularly snazzy. But, as Edward Tufte explains in his book *Envisioning Information*, several clever visual moves make it rhetorically effective. First, it uses the power of repetition and contrast in the form of the heavy black Xs that are lined up prominently below the names of each witness for the prosecution. Some of the witnesses, like Polisi, have an X in almost every box, creating a black vertical line that draws the viewer's eye. Second, the chart's creator used the left, top, and bottom—for Western viewers, the most important positions in a document—to highlight the worst crimes (murder, attempted murder, and, near the bottom, pistol-whipping a priest). As Tufte says, graphics used strategically in the courtroom can overcome the "one-dimensional sequencing of talk talk talk" (31) that typically characterizes courtroom proceedings, allowing the jury to absorb the information at their own pace and thus giving that information more weight.

| CRIMINAL ACTIVITY OF GOVERNMENT INFORMANTS | | | | | | | |
| --- | --- | --- | --- | --- | --- | --- | --- |
| CIME | CARDINALE | LOFARO | MALONEY | POLISI | SENATORE | FORONJY | CURRO |
| MURDER | X | X | | | | | |
| ATTEMPTED MURDER | | X | X | | | | |
| HEROIN POSSESSION AND SALE | X | X | | X | | | X |
| COCAINE POSSESSION AND SALE | X | | X | X | | | |
| MARIJUANA POSSESSION AND SALE | | | | | | | X |
| GAMBLING BUSINESS | | X | | X | | X | |
| ARMED ROBBERIES | X | | X | X | X | | X |
| LOANSHARKING | | X | | X | | | |
| KIDNAPPING | | | X | X | | | |
| EXTORTION | | | X | X | | | |
| ASSAULT | X | | X | X | | | X |
| POSSESSION OF DANGEROUS WEAPONS | X | X | X | X | X | | X |
| PERJURY | | X | | | | X | |
| COUNTERFEITING | | | | | X | X | |
| BANK ROBBERY | | | X | X | | | |
| ARMED HIJACKING | | | | X | X | | |
| STOLEN FINANCIAL DOCUMENTS | | | X | X | X | | |
| TAX EVASION | | | | X | | X | |
| BURGLARIES | X | X | | X | X | | |
| BRIBERY | | X | | X | | | |
| THEFT: AUTO, MONEY, OTHER | | | X | X | X | X | X |
| BAIL JUMPING AND ESCAPE | | | X | X | | | |
| INSURANCE FRAUDS | | | | | X | X | |
| FORGERIES | | | | X | X | | |
| PISTOL WHIPPING A PRIEST | X | | | | | | |
| SEXUAL ASSAULT ON MINOR | | | | | | | X |
| RECKLESS ENDANGERMENT | | | | | | | X |

FIGURE 14.1  Gotti's Defense Chart

ANALYZE
and CREATE

**Chapter 4**
Analyzing
Visual Rhetoric

**Chapter 14**
Creating Visual
Rhetoric

In Chapter 4, you learned how to analyze the rhetorical impact of ads, photos, illustrated news and magazines stories, and other images to understand why and how they might move a viewer to do, think, or feel something. But while this critical ability is important, *only* being able to analyze images would put you into the passive role of mere consumer of images. To be an effective communicator, you also need to be able to *produce* rhetorically powerful images of your own. This chapter aims to help you do that.

# 14a When to Use Visual Compositions for Rhetorical Purposes

So, how do you know when to address a rhetorical problem (as defined in Chapter 1) with images, rather than with some other mode?

The short answer is that you *don't* know. Except in rare instances, public communication doesn't give you any hard and fast rules that define when and how to address rhetorical problems. But that doesn't mean you can't think strategically about how and when images would be the most powerful and effective means of response.

Rhetorically effective images are likely to work in the following situations:

- **When you want to memorably draw an audience's attention to a problem.** Remember the "pictorial superiority effect" discussed in Chapter 4? Incorporating images with text to help viewers remember a message is a strategy used almost universally among marketers and political campaigners. You, too, can effectively use the pictorial superiority effect to make viewers aware that a given rhetorical problem exists.

- **When you have only a short amount of time to capture an audience's attention.** The reason that ads, posters, and other visual messages are frequently posted in public places is that they're likely to be seen by people as they circulate. These images need to draw people's attention and convey a clear message that can be quickly absorbed. They are also understood to be relatively "disposable"—think of these visually based messages as part of a longer-running and broader series of efforts to address a rhetorical problem.

- **When you want to combat images about a subject that are already circulating.** In a recent article, rhetorical scholar David Sheridan discusses the rhetorical damage done to the city of Detroit by the images that tend to dominate media coverage of the city's problems. Sheridan characterizes these images—which portray the city as abandoned, decrepit, a haven of crime and desperation—as "ruin porn." These images of Detroit, he argues, are deceptive because they don't show the whole picture, including parts of Detroit that are in fact thriving. Sheridan points out a project called "The People of Detroit," which combats the ruin porn with much more positive images of Detroit. While it might also be effective to address the ruin porn by way of texts (blog posts, letters to the editor, etc.), circulating the positive images of Detroit means that the images are fighting on their own turf, so to speak.

To create rhetorically effective visual compositions, first you need to assess the situation, thinking carefully about whether or not the rhetorical problem would be best addressed (at least in part) with images.

## Using Visuals to Address Rhetorical Problems

The following questions can help you to strategize about when, where, and how to use visual rhetoric:

- What message do you want to convey?
- To whom do you want to convey this message?
- What are this group's movements, agendas, modes of getting around, and so forth? Why might a visual composition be effective for this group?
- Where would this visual composition appear? How would it be circulated or distributed?
- What would be the ultimate purpose of this visual composition?

Also remember that any rhetorical intervention isn't a once-and-for-all action. So it's best to think of any visual compositions you might create in response to a rhetorical problem as part of a series of responses, or a larger, longer-running campaign. Visual interventions can serve to point viewers in the direction of more extensive resources. A visual in the form of a poster, public advocacy ad, t-shirt, or infographic, for instance, can direct interested viewers to text that appears elsewhere—on a blog, in an article, a pamphlet, or similar text. It's most effective to think of whatever you produce to address a rhetorical problem as one piece in a multipronged series of interventions.

The first half of this chapter discusses the fundamentals of all visual design: contrast, repetition, alignment, and proximity. The second half provides tutorials on specific kinds of visual compositions, namely infographics, presentation slides, posters, and brochures.

## 14b Good Visual Design: Basic Building Blocks

Whether you're designing for print (e.g., posters, flyers, public advocacy ads, brochures, business cards) or for the Web, there are some fundamentals that underlie all visual design. Put simply, you have to think about what you want your intended viewers to take away from looking at your piece; then you have to design it in a way that directs them to this information clearly and unambiguously.

Good design creates a **visual hierarchy of information**. The hierarchy of information refers to how clearly a visual composition portrays the relative importance of different pieces of information. A clear hierarchy of information creates a visual path through a document, allowing viewers to intuitively and quickly grasp the important information. For instance, as a designer, you can create clear, distinct headings and subheadings to help viewers see the major divisions in your composition. Compositions with an unclear hierarchy of information leave a reader confused about how to navigate the information, as well as what information is important.

You don't want to force viewers to do extra work to figure out your message—because, quite simply, they won't. Attention is in short supply these days, and if you want your message to come across, you'll need to make it easy for an audience to see it. Luckily, there are tried and true methods for designing visual information to create a clear hierarchy.

In her excellent book *The Non-Designer's Design Book*, design theorist Robin Williams has boiled design principles down to four fundamental things to consider while designing for print and the Web. These form an unfortunate but memorable acronym:

- **C**ontrast
- **R**epetition

- **A**lignment
- **P**roximity

Each of these fundamental elements of visual design is discussed below.

## Contrast: Boldness Creates a Hierarchy of Information

A psychological theory of perception called Gestalt theory argues that one of the most fundamental aspects of human vision is figure/ground separation. Figure/ground separation refers to the ability to distinguish the important subject of an image from the background. Poor separation of figure and ground can mean that viewers have trouble distinguishing the important information in an image. While poor figure-ground separation can make for interesting optical illusions (i.e., the famous vase/two faces example), in information design it can create confusion, frustration, or annoyance on the part of viewers, as the example in Figure 14.3 shows.

FIGURE 14.2  Remember the CRAP principles of visual design.

Poor figure/ground separation frequently results from a lack of **contrast** on the page. The first image in Figure 14.3 is hard to look at because the reader has to squint to make out the text (the figure, in this case) from the image of the trees (the ground).

Creating clear, bold contrasts between the subject and the background of your visual composition makes it easier for viewers to identify important information. The second image lightens the background so that the text stands out more clearly. The main rule of contrast, as Williams puts it, is "don't be a wimp" (84). To effectively draw the viewer's eye and to create clear hierarchies of information, strategically use strong, definitive contrasts. The main ways to create contrast are through **color**, **size**, and **typeface**.

 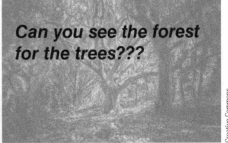

Creative Commons

Creative Commons

FIGURE 14.3  Example of poor and better use of contrast: "Can you see the forest for the trees?"

### Creating contrast with color

Color is a critical tool for designers, and understanding it will help you learn to use it well. Color has three properties that you need to consider when deciding on a palette to use for your visual composition:

1. **Hue** is what we typically think of as "color." You're talking about hue when you refer to the color names—red, orange, yellow, green, blue, purple, and all the variations thereof. Contrasting hues, known as complementary colors, appear opposite each other on the color wheel, as shown in Figure 14.4. Red-green, blue-orange, and purple-yellow are the main complementary pairs. However, as you'll see by looking at Figure 14.7, pairing two complementary hues (like red against green) actually creates quite an obnoxious effect. For a contrast that doesn't hurt viewers' eyes, you also need to consider the next two properties of color: value and saturation.

2. **Value** refers to a color's relative lightness or darkness. If you click on the color wheel in any software program that allows you to change backgrounds or format shapes (like PowerPoint, for instance), it will likely bring up an image like the one shown in Figure 14.5. Along the right-hand side is a gradient that shows different values for a particular color (in this case, red). Mixing a hue with black to make it

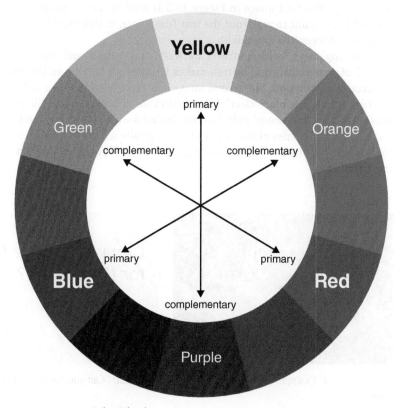

**FIGURE 14.4**  Color Wheel

darker is called *shading*. Mixing a hue with white to make it lighter is called *tinting*.

3. **Saturation** refers to a color's brightness or intensity. The purer the color, the more highly saturated it is and the brighter and more intense it will appear. Desaturated colors are mixed with gray and are duller. Highly saturated colors are considered to be of medium value, in that they're mixed equally with white and black. Figure 14.6 below shows different levels of saturation for the color yellow; the most saturated shades are at the top right.

Pairing colors that are too close in hue (like orange on red), value (dark on dark or light on light, as in the "Weak Contrast" squares in Figure 14.7), or saturation (like in the "Obnoxious Contrast" square in Figure 14.7) makes text difficult to read. In some cases (if a viewer is colorblind, for instance), the text will be totally unreadable—fail!

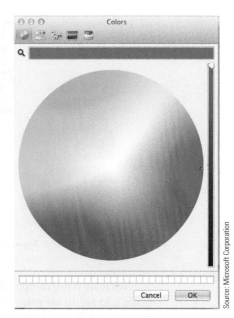

**FIGURE 14.5** PowerPoint Color Value Gradient

Source: Microsoft Corporation

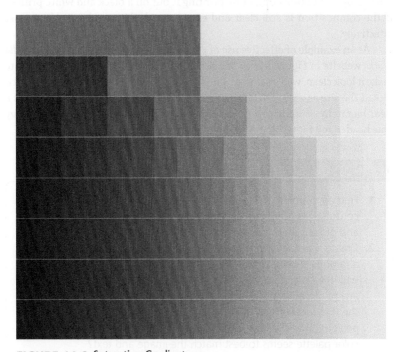

**FIGURE 14.6** Saturation Gradient

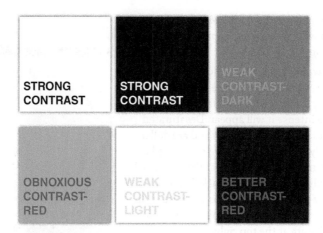

FIGURE 14.7 Types of Color Contrast

To create visual compositions that effectively create contrast with color—which is to say, to use color in a way that (a) positively draws attention to your message and (b) is visually appealing—you'll need to consider all three properties of color. For instance, you might pair a highly saturated color with a darker, duller tone (as in the "Better Contrast – Red" square in Figure 14.7).

You can check to see whether your visual composition effectively uses color contrast or not by converting it to grayscale (if you're working in Adobe Illustrator and Photoshop), or by printing it out on a black and white printer. If the composition is still clear and easy to read, then you've used contrast effectively.

As an example of effective use of color contrast, consider the *Church Media Works* website in Figure 14.8. The crisp navy and white that dominate the site make it look clean, well organized, and inviting. As the *Web Design Ledger* (which picked the site as a good example of color contrast) explains, the site creates a clear hierarchy of information by posing a white content area against a navy blue header and footer that contain information about navigating the site.

## FOR DISCUSSION

1. Find an example of a print document or a Web page that uses color contrasts well and one that has poor color contrasts. Bring them in and prepare to discuss why they work or don't work.

2. Create a simple composition that uses an image and text (perhaps a famous quote or saying). Now create four different color palettes with it (you can use the "Format Picture" function in MS Word or any photo editing software). Share them with the class, and discuss the rhetorical effects of each color palette. What changes in your perception of the text and image with each color palette? Which color palette seems to best match the image and text?

FIGURE 14.8 Church Media Works Website

## Creating contrast with size

Using text and other items of different sizes is another easy way to create a hierarchy of information. Creating contrast through size is especially useful when you have a limited use of color (say, when a flier you're making will be photocopied in black and white and hung up on telephone poles around town).

As with other elements of contrast, remember Robin Williams' admonishment to not be a wimp. Making different elements too similar in size won't do anything except to confuse the reader by messing up the hierarchy of information. If you're planning to create contrast with size, make the different elements *significantly* different.

Big says "I'm important—look at me first, and I'll help you understand what this site or document is about." Big typefaces should be used for the most important headings. Smaller typefaces should be used for subheadings or body text. The most important thing (as we'll discuss in "Repetition" later in this section) is to be consistent—to use the same visual cues to indicate similar levels of your hierarchy of information.

Figure 14.9 is a good example of how a page (a website, in this case) can use text size to create a clear hierarchy of information. The *Discover*

FIGURE 14.9  Using Text Size to Create Contrast (*Discover Los Angeles*)

*Los Angeles* site features three distinct areas marked by large, bold text: a slideshow at the top featuring specific attractions and areas of LA, a clickable map that invites readers to "Explore the Regions of LA" in large bold text, and a third section, "Listography," with the same bold text. Hence the site's use of text to create unmistakable divisions of information helps to orient viewers and make it easy to understand how to navigate the site.

### Creating contrast with typeface

Typeface (often mistakenly called "font") refers to the design of the text in printed and Web-based documents. While the *look* of the words might seem relatively unimportant compared with their *content*, typeface actually has a powerful rhetorical effect. Perhaps because typeface is something that many people typically look *through* (instead of *at*) as they attempt to absorb a text's content, it is very effective in creating a mood in a visual composition. In other words, the typeface creates a subtle message of its own.

It might seem like an insignificant thing to focus on, but many people with design proclivities are quite passionate about typefaces. You'll find a number of diatribes out there against **Comic Sans**, for instance, which might strike you as a fun, cute font, but which many designers are convinced is the work of the Devil.

Most page design and Web design software (Word, PowerPoint, InDesign, and so on) comes with a huge list of typefaces. This is both a blessing and a curse for good page design. The very abundance of typefaces suggests to some beginning designers that the more, the better. Avoid this mistake—too many typefaces, like too much of anything else, can create a jumbled mess on the page that will make it difficult to read and obscure your message.

There are two basic kinds of typefaces:

**Serif typefaces** have little "hats" and "feet" at the top and bottom of the letters, called (appropriately) "serifs." These hats and feet serve as subtle guides for readers' eyes, pulling them along the line of words. Because of this, serif typefaces are typically used for the body text of documents, where readers are expected to focus for long periods of time. Common serif typefaces include Times New Roman, Palatino, Garamond, and Century Schoolbook.

**Sans-serif typefaces**—which include among others Helvetica, Arial, and Avenir—lack the hats and feet of serif typefaces (*sans* means "without" in French). They have much cleaner lines, and are hence bolder and easier to read from a distance. Hence, sans-serif typefaces are commonly used as headings in printed text, and on things that are designed to be read from a distance, like billboards, signs, and license plates. The exception to the rule of serif typefaces for body text is text that appears on the Web. Sans-serif

Source: American Folk Art Museum

**FIGURE 14.10** Creating Contrast with Typography (Folk Couture Site)

typefaces like Verdana (a commonly used Web typeface) are easier to read on the screen.

> **Design rule of thumb: No more than three typefaces per visual composition!**

You can see the use of typeface contrast in Figure 14.10 for the website of the Folk Couture Museum. The links, the site title, and the dates at the bottom are all done in the same sans-serif font. The viewer's eye is drawn first to the title in the top left-hand corner, then to the brightly colored photo, then to the body text in the middle of the page, which is done in serif font to make it easier to read. Note the good use of color contrast here as well.

### Don't overdo it: Use contrast sparingly

Finally, remember the last rule of thumb: If everything contrasts, then nothing contrasts. Contrast is best when used to highlight the most important things in your visual composition. Thus, you'll need to make some design decisions about what's really most important for viewers to take away from your visual composition. Decide what that is, then design around that purpose.

Consider the following visual example, taken again from Edward Tufte's book *Envisioning Information*. The "before" image (from a manual of airplane marshaling signals) uses *too much* contrast: Heavy black squares compete with the black figures within the squares (Figure 14.11). The important information in the image—the signals—gets lost in all the visual "noise."

FIGURE 14.11 Before Image of "Marshalling Signals"

FIGURE 14.12 Revision of "Marshalling Signals"

Now consider Tufte's revision of the image (Figure 14.12). Removing the heavy black squares calms down the whole composition and allows the eye to focus on the figures. Tufte has reduced the contrast of the figures (who are relatively unimportant compared to the signals being shown) by changing them from black to dark gray. And he's increased the contrast of the signals themselves with a clever use of color: He's made the signal lights yellow, and the directional arrows red. Now the message of this chart is much clearer.

## DESIGN PRO TIP: DOCUMENT AND COLLECT DESIGN INSPIRATIONS

People who design for a living often recommend documenting and keeping things that you find interesting, beautiful, or steal-worthy. Conversely, you can also keep track of things that seem like really bad examples of design. The London-based designer Ben Terrett keeps just such a collection on his blog *Noisy Decent Graphics*. Luckily, in the age of smart phones, photo-sharing sites like *Flickr* and *Instagram*, easy-to-use blog sites like *Tumblr*, and social media "curating" sites like *Pinterest*, documenting and storing your collections is pretty easy.

## Repetition: Create Meaningful Visual Patterns

After contrast, the next important visual design fundamental is the concept of repetition. Our brains naturally seek patterns, and any time we recognize a pattern, we attempt to make some sort of meaning from it. Look again at the "Marshalling Signals" example in Figure 14.12, for instance. Even

without the title, and even if you've never seen the people on airport tar-
macs waving in planes, the repetition of the black figures and red arrows
probably helped you intuit that this was a demonstration of how to do
many different kinds of actions (as opposed to, say, a story about a guy with
two lights).

Repetition creates continuity between experiences; for instance, I understand the basics of how to shop in a grocery store in a foreign country
because I've shopped in so many at home. Conversely, lack of repetition will
leave people struggling to make sense of the world. For instance, imagine if
the color or shape of stop signs differed from town to town. Drivers would
be forced to divert precious attention from the complicated and multifaceted task of driving in order to decode where and when to stop. At the least,
this would be very stressful, and at worst it would increase the number of
traffic accidents.

The same goes with visual compositions. If you use a different size
typeface every time you introduce a subheading in a poster, for instance,
viewers will be confused about the poster's hierarchy of information. As a
designer, you can tap into the brain's love of patterns by repeating certain
elements in visual compositions: color, typography, images, navigation elements, and so forth. That way, the message of your visual composition is
reinforced by the design itself.

Look at the brochure in Figure 14.13. The teal and white color palette,
along with the lines of gray squares, creates visual continuity across the
three panels. It's clear without even reading the content that the white

FIGURE 14.13 Repetition in "Booktalks" Brochure

words above the black text under "Why Booktalks?" are probably subheadings that answer the question posed by the heading. At least, that's our expectation—if they *don't* happen to answer that question, then you've just confounded viewer expectations and hence confused (and subtly annoyed) them.

### . . . But TOO much repetition is boring

Chances are that you've seen (or maybe created) a lot of bad PowerPoint presentations. You know, the kind that use a template with the same color, background, cheesy graphic, and typeface on every single slide. If you're like most people, such presentations make your brain shrivel with boredom.

Just as with contrast, overdoing repetition can have a negative effect. Basically, you can bore the viewer's eye—and when that happens, you've lost their attention. So the trick is to repeat *with a difference*.

Consider the following examples of repetition with a difference. Figure 14.14 shows two Web page ads for Somersby Cider: One, an overview of all the Somersby Cider products, and the other, an ad specifically for the Pear Cider. Both visual compositions contain a palette of warm colors, the Somersby logo, the watermark of a tree, and some blowing leaves. But if you look carefully, these things are not identical in each composition: the Pear Cider page is primarily in greens and yellows, and also has an image of a hot-air balloon (another typical Somersby graphic element). The repetition of similar but not exactly the same elements helps to create a sense of visual continuity that is pleasing, but not boring.

Similarly, the website of the Digital Public Library of America in Figure 14.15 uses repetition of similar, but not identical elements to create a clear hierarchy of information. Note the similarity in typeface, the conjunction with a photo, and the repeating line of the three major divisions on the page ("Exhibitions," "Explore by Place," and "Explore by Date"). The similarities suggest that these three divisions occupy the same level of

Source: Carlsberg Breweries A/S

FIGURE 14.14 Repetition with a Difference in Somersby Cider Promotional Material

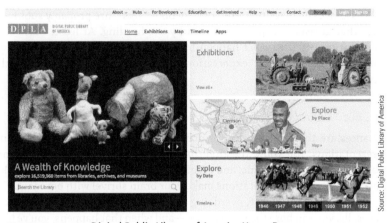

Source: Digital Public Library of America

**FIGURE 14.15** *Digital Public Library of America* Home Page

importance, but the differences in color differentiate them. The repetition of link titles across the top make the yellow box around the "Donate" link stand out that much more.

## Alignment: Strong Lines Guide the Viewer's Eye

Alignment refers to the way various elements are placed on the page. Good alignment helps create a sense of order—it organizes page elements and creates connections between related things. It's invisible, but it helps direct the viewer's eye.

Figure 14.16 shows different kinds of text alignment, along with some notes about when each would be best to use.

The general rule for alignment, as it was for contrast, is "don't be a wimp." Creating bold alignments (and then strategically breaking them for interest) attracts viewers to your visual composition and helps them easily find the information they need. Draw literal or invisible lines, and make sure that your text and images all fall along that line. Don't use centered headings with left-aligned text—that confuses the eye, looks messy, and makes it hard to find information.

### Don't center everything

Because centering text creates an automatic sense of balance, the instinct of the beginning visual designer is to center everything. Centering is safe, but it can be boring. As you can see from the example in Figure 14.17, centering everything can mean that nothing on the page captures the viewer's eye. Centering when you have a lot of text also is hard on the eyes of readers who are trained in reading left-to-right, top-to-bottom, because they have to spend time hunting for the beginning of the next line. So the general rule of thumb is not to use center alignment when you have a lot of content.

**Left alignment** uses a strong line to the left and creates a "ragged" (not aligned) right margin. This is the most typical alignment for body text in cultures that read top to bottom and right to left. It's the default setting on most word processing software.

**Right alignment** uses a strong line to the right, creating a ragged left-hand side. It's much less common in body text.

**Centered alignment** puts the text – you guessed it! – in the center. Centered text is difficult to read because the reader's eye has to search for the beginning of the next line.

**Justified text** lines up evenly on both the left and right sides, except for the last line of paragraphs. It's commonly used in newspaper and magazine columns. It packs more text in per line, and is generally considered more formal and less "friendly" than left-aligned text.

**Forced Justification** can stretch letters and words out so that the left and right sides line up. This can look

w      e      i      r      d      .

FIGURE 14.16  Different Types of Text Alignment

However, of course, this is not to say that you should never center anything—it can create a beautiful effect, as the birthday invitation in Figure 14.17 shows.

The problem with the "invitation" on the left in Figure 14.17 is that nothing about it looks deliberate. There wasn't much thought given to line breaks (e.g., why do "You are" and "invited to" appear on two lines?), much less a heading that would help viewers to understand the document's

*You are invited to what, judging from the lack of design sense of this invitation's creator, will probably be an extremely boring event.*

Western Girl!

Come celebrate Zoe's 5th birthday at the RODEO!

Lewiston Fairgrounds
Saturday, September 23
5 p.m. – 7 p.m.
Cake to follow!

FIGURE 14.17  A Boringly Center-Aligned Page and Good Use of Centering

purpose. The centering here is static, and it makes it difficult to read this chunk of text—the eye isn't drawn to any particular piece of information. By contrast, the "Western Girl" birthday invitation has a strong center line topped with the cowboy hat and anchored at the bottom with the party details. The photo provides a strong visual anchor and lets viewers know how they should direct their attention. The lines above the photo are aligned to the edges of the photo, which guides the eye down the page.

As with all of the other design principles, you need to walk a fine line between not applying the rule and applying it in a stifling way. Too symmetrical a design can feel overly formal or dull, so once you've established strong alignments, you can consciously break them with some elements. This will help add visual interest to the page.

### Design with a grid to ensure alignment

To create strong alignments, most designers begin their visual composition with a grid. Grids are especially critical in the design of websites, which frequently have a huge amount of information for users to navigate, but they're also handy for visual compositions that are meant for print (like brochures and posters).

One very common and useful grid is based on the "rule of thirds." Rule of thirds grids, as the name suggests, divide a page into thirds—vertically, horizontally, or both (see Figure 14.18). Content is then organized within those thirds. You can break the grid by using two-thirds for some chunks of information, or the whole top third for an image. Figure 14.19 shows an example of a flyer designed using the rule of thirds. While the grid is implicit, notice that most of the content falls in the left two-thirds of the page, drawing the viewers' eye to that side and leaving white space in the right third of the page.

Depending on how much information you have to organize, you can use as fine a grid as you want. Grids ensure alignment and balance, and so are a very useful design tool.

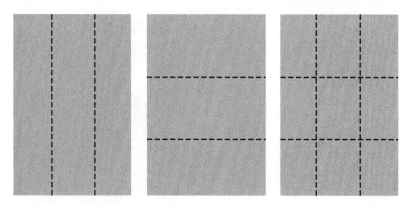

FIGURE 14.18  Rule of Thirds Page Grids

FIGURE 14.19 Flyer Designed Using Rule of Thirds Grid

## Proximity: Keep Related Things Together

A good argument for paying attention to proximity can be seen in Figure 14.20, the front page of the *Brampton Guardian*.

The image is funny because the conjunction of the headline and the photo automatically leads the viewer to assume that Pooh and the Abominable Snowman are the dastardly duo in question. Only squinting at the image caption clarifies that Pooh and the Abominable Snowman were actually victims of other (presumably human) criminals.

FIGURE 14.20  Violent Crime Duo Caught on Video

As this example illustrates, viewers assume that things placed close to one another are related. So the most fundamental rule of proximity might be stated as **"keep related things together."**

As an example of how viewers automatically try to make meaning from a visual hierarchy of information, consider Figure 14.21:

| FRUIT | SPARKLY |
|---|---|
| **Citrus Fruit** | **Hippopotamus** |
| Lemon | Pinecones |
| Lime | Comfortable |
| Orange | Pillow |
| Key Lime | Light |
| Clementine | Tall |
| Tangerine | High-flown |
| Tangelo | Given |
| Blood Orange | The |
| | |
| **Melons** | **Green** |
| Cantaloupe | Word |
| Watermelon | Fascinator |
| Honeydew | Moving van |
| Canary melon | Spying |
| | |
| **Berries** | **Shiver-Me-Timbers** |
| Strawberry | Radiator |
| Raspberry | Handkerchief |
| Blueberry | Wild |
| Blackberry | Shopping |
| Boysenberry | Rapids |
| Gooseberry | Museum of Modern Art |

FIGURE 14.21  Logical and Non-logical Uses of Proximity

Both fulfill our visual expectations for a hierarchy of information, though only one follows through on that expectation in terms of content. In the left-hand image, "fruit," the most general category, is also in the largest font. The three groups that follow the general heading include subheadings with different classifications of fruit, followed by examples of that classification. In the image on the right, a hierarchy is visually indicated; even though it's nonsensical, a viewer's automatic inclination is to try to make some sense of the textual groupings here.

### Use white space deliberately

Resist the urge to fill up all the available space with text, or to spread around your text to evenly fill up the space. In Figure 14.21, the spaces also contain information—here, they physically create separate groupings. The use of "white space" (which doesn't actually have to be white, just free of text) can help guide the viewer's eye to the important information. White space is often said to let the text "breathe." The idea is that if viewers know where to focus their attention (i.e., if there's obvious space between elements), they'll be more relaxed and able to grasp your message.

Consider the following business card (Figure 14.22), for example.

Here, there's no clear hierarchy of information; the elements of the card are evenly distributed (one in each corner and one in the center). The viewer's eye has to skip around to try to make sense of the information being presented. Because of the principle of proximity, for instance, there seems to be a connection between the street address and "Takeout and Delivery," but this connection isn't made clear by the card.

The revision to the card in Figure 14.23 makes better use of proximity. Now, at least, related information is grouped together, so the message is clearer and more understandable. Note the bolder use of contrast, too.

| | |
|---|---|
| **Moe's Pizza** | (812) 354-6783 |
| *It's Delicious!* | |

| | |
|---|---|
| 3542 Cheesy Pie Way | |
| *Takeout and Delivery* | Rafton, NJ 34985 |

FIGURE 14.22 Moe's Pizza Business Card #1

# 14c How-Tos: Tutorials for Specific Visual Compositions

## Designing Infographics

While infographics—short for information graphics—have been around since the 1800s, they've gotten extremely popular with the rise of the Internet. Not only is it easy to

FIGURE 14.23 Moe's Pizza Business Card #2

store and circulate visual images, even ones bigger or different from typical print size, but they also perform a service that's extremely valuable in this information age: They take complex data and stories and represent them in a more digestible, relatable form. As Hal Varian, former Chief Economist at Google explained,

> The ability to take data – to be able to understand it, to process it, to extract value from it, to visualize it, to communicate it [will] be a hugely important skill in the next decades...because now we really do have essentially free and ubiquitous data. So the complimentary scarce factor is the ability to understand that data and extract value from it.

Infographics are a good way to try your hand at visual composition, and there are thousands of examples out there. To see just a few, you might start by browsing popular blogs like *Information Is Beautiful* or *Cool Infographics*.

## Identifying a subject for your infographic

You should aim to visualize data or a story that is substantive, not trivial (something that in an era of information overload, provokes ire, as the title of the saucily titled *Gizmodo* post "Stop Already With the F*cking Infographics" suggests). The data you visualize should help viewers understand the complexity of a problem or issue.

For your infographic, you might choose to focus on representing a particular set of data (sites like *BuzzFeed*, *FiveThirtyEight*, and *Socrata* make their data sets available for visualization, or you can try searching "data sets for visualization"). Or you might identify a question that you want to answer and research until you've found an objective focus (What is happening to bees in North America? What is the life cycle of an LED lightbulb?). Or you might look more broadly at patterns or trends, differences, similarities, or cause/effect relationships that would become more interesting or persuasive by virtue of being visually represented (How many extreme weather events occurred in 2016 compared to the previous twenty-five years?).

Your infographic could

- Tell a story.
- Explain a process or concept.
- Give the history of an idea.
- Compare two competing ideas.
- Inform readers about a new process or finding.

## Identifying an audience for your infographic

Along with finding an idea for what information you want to present, you need to identify the audience for your infographic. What is at stake for them in this data set, question, or relationship? Why would they care?

### Creating your infographic

As the blog *Visual News* points out, the best infographics are created around a cohesive story or point. In a completed piece, every data point, piece of copy, and design element should support the story or point.  So keep the following things in mind when designing your infographic.

Before you begin:

- Come up with a question or identify a data set that you want to visually represent.
- Clarify your objective and find a focus.
- Research the data—make sure it's solid.
- Keep track of your sources and where the graphics come from.
- Identify the type of infographic that best suits that question.

Things to remember:

- Engage the reader with an interesting title and subtitles.
- Provide context for the data.
- Guide the reader through the graphic with visual cues.
- Apply principles of effective design (remember the CRAP principles described earlier!).
- Highlight notable findings/insights.
- Provide a clear call to action that lets your audience know what they're supposed to take away from this information.
- Cite your sources (include a section at the end).

Importantly, don't start by trying to create your infographic on the computer—this will inhibit your invention process and ultimately be frustrating and time-consuming. Instead, work out the components of the infographic by sketching them out on a piece of paper. This will help you find the story or point, and will help you understand what is necessary to get to that point. Then after you have a solid grasp of your story or point and what you want the infographic to look like, you can start committing it to the computer.

There are several good, free tools for creating infographics; while you can do a search on "free tools for infographics," some of the most reliable have been *Piktochart*, *Canva*, and *Easel.ly*.

## Designing Presentation Slides

Some of your deadliest moments as a student (though it doesn't end when you graduate, as many professionals will attest) will be spent in a darkened room, watching a terrible slide presentation. While it has the potential to be a wonderfully effective tool for communication, PowerPoint (as well as other slideware programs, including Apple's Keynote, Slideshare, and other cloud-based programs), is notoriously one of the most misused communication technologies. As such, it's been the object of a fair amount of derision: Look up "PowerPoint Gettysburg Address" for a good example.

While there's plenty to say about all the things that make for bad presentations, here I'll focus specifically on slide design.

The most important thing to remember is that slides are meant to serve as *visual placeholders* for the audience, something that they can focus their attention on while they listen to you talk. Keep in mind that they won't be able to process two sources of information at once (i.e., your speech and the visual information on the slide). So keep the slides simple and graphic. The most effective slides serve as a mini-mystery, engaging the interest and attention of the audience—they will pay closer attention because they want to know how you're going to explain the slide. Figure 14.24 provides an example (taken from a conference presentation I did recently) of an attempt to convey a concept (namely, bacteria as a specific thing that causes disease).

While it's obviously a bit tongue in cheek, the intent here was to create a visual metaphor for a relatively complex idea so that viewers would associate the image with that idea.

What slides should NOT do is serve as the script for your presentation. Some of the worst presentations involve the speaker reading off the slide to the audience. Remember that the audience can read for themselves; they've come to hear a *presentation*, so the slides should be used primarily either to remind them of what you're talking about or to show images and graphics. In fact, some of the more draconian business consultants will recommend that there be no more than six words per slide.

To create engaging, memorable, well-designed slides, first, of course, you have to know the gist of what you're presenting. Thinking about how to best represent those ideas visually to the audience in a way that will interest

FIGURE 14.24  A Slide Showing the Bacteria as an Agent of Disease

them can actually serve as an invention tool. If I get stuck when I'm writing a presentation, I often pause to think about what my ideas will *look* like on a slide, and that can help me generate content for the presentation. As you design your slides, use the following rules of thumb:

- Avoid using templates. While you can have a visual theme, stock templates are overused and generally not all that attractive.
- Use the CRAP principles of design (see Section 14b).
- Think clean: Slides should have a minimum of text (no more than six words, unless it's a chart or table that you're explaining). They shouldn't be too busy.
- Don't overuse bullet points—you should have only one idea per slide.
- Use at least 32-point font, and make sure it's a sans-serif typeface (e.g., Calibri, Arial, Helvetica, Gill Sans).
- Generally speaking, use single images. These will be more powerful than a photo-album approach to slides (unless you're trying to show how something is visualized in differing ways, for instance).
- Use high-resolution graphics, and make sure that images aren't distorted or fuzzy.

For inspiration (because all good designers borrow ideas from others), you might try browsing a site like *Slideshare*, which includes featured and top slideshows on its homepage.

## Designing Posters

Different kinds of posters can serve different rhetorical purposes, but they are united by one important fact: they need to appeal to *people on the move*. For this reason, posters need to be visually interesting and well designed (based on the CRAP principles above). Their message has to be (a) easy to identify and (b) easy to remember. Posters thus present a challenge to designers, but for this reason they can also be really fun to make.

Posters come in several varieties:

- Posters to announce events
- Posters to disseminate information and advocate for certain kinds of behaviors (e.g., awareness campaigns, public health and safety campaigns)
- Posters to present research findings and arguments (used mainly in academic contexts)

### Designing posters to announce events

Despite the fact that we have more venues than ever before to communicate information, the good old-fashioned paper poster (photocopied 8.5 × 11 posters are also known as "flyers") is still considered to be the best and cheapest way to make sure that one's announcement reaches a diverse public audience. After all, not everyone belongs to *Facebook* or listens to NPR, but almost everyone goes to the grocery store or walks around town.

Along with advertising messages, posters announcing events are probably the visual compositions that most dominate your everyday experience. Just walking down the hall of a building on campus or around town exposes you to dozens of posters announcing concerts, meetings, public talks, taco sales, symposiums, plays, movies, restaurant openings, and everything else imaginable. The public announcement boards and the windows of shops whose owners graciously allow groups to put up posters are typically crammed with posters and fliers, sometimes two or three deep. Thus, posters announcing events are competing with hundreds of similar messages at the same time. They need to convey their message quickly and memorably to people on the move.

Before you actually begin designing the poster for an event, you need to consider several factors:

**Audience.** Who are you hoping or expecting will come to the event? Is it truly the general public—whoever wants to come? Or do you have a more specific group in mind? Where are members of this group most likely to see your poster?

**Reproduction.** How do you plan to print and copy your poster? If you're using graphics in a poster, consider how they'll look printed out on the printer you have available (some noncommercial printers won't "bleed" graphics all the way to the edge, for instance, leaving a white border around the paper). If you're planning to create flyers to reproduce on a photocopy machine, you'll need to take that into consideration when you're designing— how will this look as a black and white copy?

Also make sure to consider costs. What's your budget? How many copies of the poster will you need? Compare prices at your local copy centers. Full or partial color posters will be more eye-catching, but they also cost more to print and copy. If you're only making a few copies, this is OK, but maybe not if you need 100 copies.

**Circulation/Distribution.** Where can/should you post your poster or flyer? What rules govern posting in a public space? Make sure you know these so you don't make your organization look bad or run afoul of the law; your municipality may not allow posting on telephone poles, for instance. Consider alternative places you can hang your poster that won't seem obnoxious or invasive.

**Necessary Information.** How much information do you need to communicate in a poster or flyer announcing an event? At the very least, you need to answer questions like what is the event? who is sponsoring it? when is it? and where is it? Beyond that, decide what information really needs to be there, given the constraints of your rhetorical situation. If it's an event that's familiar and self-explanatory (a concert, a free movie, etc.), you don't need much more information than the basics. If it's less familiar—say, for instance, you're trying to get people to come to a meditation class offered by the Buddhist Student Association—then you might consider including a paragraph that briefly explains meditation, and perhaps (depending on the audience) making it clear that it's not weird or scary.

### Remember the CRAP principles!

Look at the two flyers in Figure 14.25, for instance. They contain exactly the same information, announcing an aikido class, but you probably found the one on the left harder to read than the one on the right.

The flyer on the left violates every one of the CRAP principles discussed earlier:

- It tries to make everything stand out, so as a result nothing does (principle of contrast).

- It doesn't repeat size or typeface to create a clear hierarchy of information (principle of repetition).

- The alignments are confused—it uses a grid with two columns, but all the text is aligned in the center (principle of alignment).

- It doesn't use white space effectively to draw the eye; instead, it fills up the space with text. It also boxes in all the information, making it feel even busier (principle of proximity).

Now study the flyer on the right. What changes have been made?

FIGURE 14.25 Aikido Flyers, Before and After

## FOR DISCUSSION

Find a poster (announcing an event) that you find to be particularly compelling and another that you find to be boring or poorly designed, regardless of whether you're interested in the actual event that each is announcing. If you have a smartphone, you can snap a photo of it and bring it to class or post it to your class website; otherwise, you can borrow the poster and bring it with you to class (be sure to put it back where you found it afterward). Talk about what specifically makes the better poster more memorable and interesting than the other poster. For the poorly designed poster, what would you change?

## ASSIGNMENT

### Design a Poster Announcing an Event

If you're in a club or group that has an actual event coming up, you can use this opportunity to do some work for it; otherwise, you can find an event on the "Upcoming Events" page of your university or town website. Remember the basic rhetorical goal of your poster: to entice people to come to the event. Also remember to use the CRAP principles as you're designing the poster. Adobe InDesign and its free, open-source cousin Scribus are both desktop publishing programs that allow for good quality page layout and design. If you don't have easy access to a computer, you can still create a mock-up of your poster using analog technology (i.e., scissors, ruler, etc.).

#### Designing posters for presentations

Typically an academic genre, presentation posters summarize your research, scholarly, or creative project in a way that's visually interesting and memorable. They are used either in lieu of or in addition to a spoken presentation on one's original research to an audience of researchers or people in a similar field. Poster presentations are especially common at scientific conferences, and increasingly common at other sorts of research gatherings. They're valuable because while not everyone will be able to hear your presentation (since conferences typically schedule multiple panels at the same time), everyone can walk around the poster display area and read about your work.

A viewer should be able to read your poster in five minutes or less, and they will be doing so in what one scientist describes as a "hot, loud, congested room with really bad lighting." In other words, nonoptimal conditions for reading long, dense, complicated prose. That means you need to take complex information (extremely so, in the cases of some research), extract the most important bits, and visually format the information to be easily digestible and memorable. See the differences between Figures 14.26 and 14.27.

As scientist Colin Purrington explains on his website, posters for presentations should include the following sections:

**A catchy title.** As with titles of academic essays, this should include a sense of the issue you studied and the results or argument. A person walking slowly past your poster should be able to almost immediately grasp why your project is interesting. The title should be no longer than two lines, and it should be visually situated to be the first thing the viewer notices.

**An introduction that makes a pitch for why this work is interesting.** It should focus primarily on showing why the question that drove the project is interesting and significant, and it should put the question in context of published work in the area. It should also introduce the hypothesis or main thesis. Don't spend too much time on background information. You can include an illustrative image with the introduction (about 200 words).

**Methodology.** What materials, methods, theory, or approach did you use to do the project? If it's a scientific poster, briefly explain the design of the experiment; otherwise, explain what you actually did to answer your research question. For an English literature project, for instance, you might explain the theoretical framework you used to study the texts (about 200 words).

**Results or conclusion.** If it's a scientific poster, first explain if the experiment actually worked. Then describe the general results and present your data analysis. Otherwise, explain your main argument and insight you gained as a result of doing the work (about 200 words).

**Future directions** (optional). Where do you see research going from here? What questions still need to be answered?

**Works Cited.** Follow the citation format of your discipline, and make sure you get it exactly right.

**Acknowledgments.** Make sure to thank all of the people who gave you help on your project: your professor(s), fellow students, lab, classmates, administrators, anyone who provided equipment, advice, or comments (about 40 words).

**Contact information.** Provide your email address or other contact information so that interested observers can followup with questions or comments.

Similar to other posters and projects discussed in this chapter, designing your presentation poster requires you to keep some basic things in mind (Figures 14.25 and 14.26 illustrate how these principles can transform your poster):

- Don't make it too long: At most it should be 800 words. Be concise!
- Remember the CRAP principles: Contrast, repetition, alignment, proximity.
- Maintain a clear visual hierarchy: Viewers should be able to quickly grasp the purpose and main points of the project. Make sure your title and headings are distinct and well ordered.
- Make the font size big enough to read from a distance: Title should be at least 72-point font, headings should be 30- to 60-point font, and body text should be at least 24-point font.

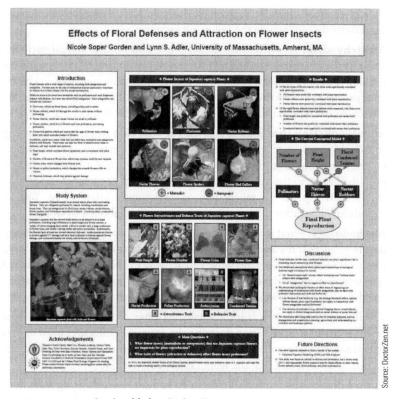

FIGURE 14.26  Serviceable but Boring Poster

- Use a sans-serif font like Helvetica or Arial for the title and headings, and a serif font like Garamond or Times New Roman for the body text (since it's a poster, you can also use a sans-serif font for the body text if you prefer).
- Make sure graphics are clear and undistorted.
- Use a grid for alignment. Remember the rule of thirds described in section 14b.
- Use adequate white space: Provide at least one-inch margins of space around every element on the poster.

## Designing Brochures

Brochures exist somewhere between posters and websites for the amount and depth of information they provide. If a poster or flyer is meant to capture the attention of a potentially unwilling audience and quickly impress an idea or argument upon them, and a website is designed to provide more in-depth information and arguments to those whose interest has already been piqued, brochures are aimed at audiences who have shown some level of

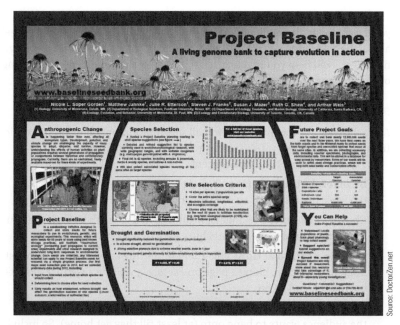

**FIGURE 14.27** Example of Excellent Poster Design

interest in or sympathy to a topic (enough to peruse slightly more in-depth information), but who have not fully committed to exploring it in more detail. Brochures are extremely valuable means of getting more information into an audience's hands and letting them decide, based on it, whether they want to pursue the topic any further. Thus, they straddle interesting rhetorical territory. A good, well-targeted brochure can tip the balance in favor of persuasion.

### Getting started: Using audience to determine a brochure's content and format

Of course, the potential audience shapes the format and content of any composition. For brochures, ask yourself the following two questions:

- **In what circumstances will the audience receive the brochure?** Will it be mailed in response to requests for information? Is it meant to be given away at an exhibition or left in a public area in the hopes of catching someone's attention? Is it one of a series of informational brochures, to be given as a takeaway for educational purposes (for example, one that details different kinds of health conditions that could be given away to patients in a clinic or doctor's office or brochures about different majors at a university)?

- **What is the purpose of the brochure?** Is it meant to answer audience questions about a topic and direct them toward more resources, to sell a product or a service, to briefly argue for an argumentative position?

Understanding these two things, along with the other basic questions that you'd ask about the audience for any composition (how they already feel about the topic of the brochure, what relationship they have with its originator, etc.) will help you to make decisions about the design and the writing of the brochure.

### Brochure content

A brochure is not meant to provide all information possible about a topic. It's a teaser, meant to get the reader to investigate further.

Tips for creating brochure content:

- **Be brief, but interesting**. Include no more than five points about the topic for audiences to remember.
- **Chunk your text.** Use bullets, headings, and so forth to organize your information and make the brochure easy to scan.
- **Include a call to action.** This could be getting an audience to request more information, liking a page on *Facebook*, visiting a website, donating money, and so on.
- **Make it worth keeping**. A good brochure should be something that the audience wants to hang onto (at least till they get home). So include more than just fluff; for example, visitors to a dentist's office would be more inclined to hang onto a brochure that included instructions about how to floss than one that only extolled the virtues of flossing. People will also be inclined to keep a brochure that includes things like directions, URLs, physical addresses, and contact information.

### Brochure format

When you see the word "brochure," chances are you think of the most common kind: a tri-fold, printed on either 8.5 × 11 or 8.5 × 14 paper. However, there are a number of possibilities for formats, so don't confine yourself to one particular design until you more thoroughly consider the range of design possibilities. Figure 14.28 shows a range of possible brochure folds.

If the purpose of your brochure is to educate or provide information, then the trifold, Z-fold, or accordion fold typically works well. If the purpose of the brochure is to highlight or sell a product or service, customers may overlook or be put off by a typical brochure format; it would behoove the organization to use a more unique format and snazzier printing (full color and glossy). Think about what the audience will expect.

Of course, all of the design fundamentals (contrast, repetition, alignment, proximity) apply to brochures. But here are some reminders and design tips specific to brochures:

- Design with a grid. The grid, of course, will be based on how you're planning on physically folding the brochure. Remember to start with the grid, but then be playful with it so that the brochure doesn't feel too boxy or stifling.

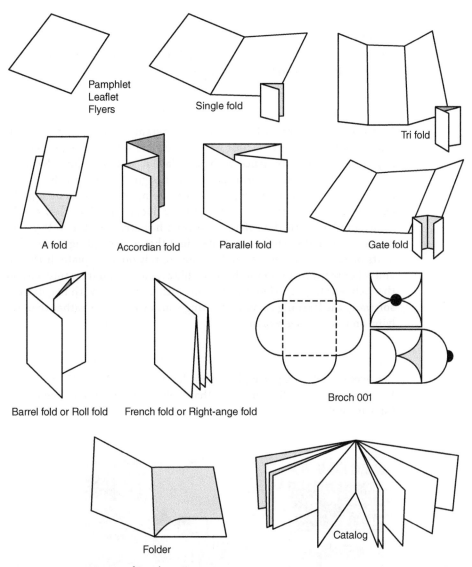

**FIGURE 14.28** Range of Brochure Formats

- Justify text, and make sure that you don't leave "orphans" or "widows"—short lines left dangling from paragraphs that fall at the top or bottom of a column.

- Don't run the text into the folds of the brochure; make sure to leave a healthy cushion of white space around your columns of text. Use print bleed in your settings to make sure images go to the edges of the brochure. Don't put boxes around your text.

- Use only meaningful graphics and images. Avoid visual clichés and stock photo images—better to use no graphics at all than to use cheesy clip art.

- If you use graphics, make sure they're of a resolution appropriate for printing.
- Make an interesting cover—it should grab an audience's attention and make it immediately clear what it is.

### A word about templates

Microsoft Word and other software programs come equipped with templates for brochures. These aren't a terrible way to start, especially if you have little experience with page layout software. But like most templates, they lock you into particular design choices, which may be contrary to your own impulses and ideas. Templates also create a problem if you're attempting to create a unique document; since they clearly come standard with the software, anyone has access to them. If you're designing something for a corporate client that is attempting to set itself or its products apart, you wouldn't want to rely on a template. InDesign and other software programs have readily available (and free) tutorials on the Web. For the experience you'll gain with design and with negotiating software, the learning curve in creating your own designs rather than relying on templates is worth it.

### A good example: "The Chicken Dance Trail" brochure

Consider the following example of a brochure in Figure 14.29. "The Chicken Dance Trail" is a birding brochure that makes excellent use of the design fundamentals.

**FIGURE 14.29**  Example of a Good Brochure: "The Chicken Dance Trail"

The Chicken Dance Trail, Holdrege, NE. Bulldog Graphics, Greeley, CO.

Note first the visual theme that unifies the brochure through the principle of repetition: the coordinated color palette of warm rusts and yellows, along with the photo of the sun shining through grasses, used as a backdrop for both sides of the brochure.

Though it's designed as a three-column grid, the brochure breaks the grid enough (with the photos of birds that spill across two columns, for instance) to provide visual interest. The text has plenty of white space and the typefaces used for the headings (as well as the repetition in the form of size and color) makes the purpose of the information included apparent via a quick scan.

The back of the brochure contains a large, easy-to-read map of the trail, along with descriptions at the bottom of the various birding adventures, which correspond with different areas on the map. The map, along with the photos and identifying information of various birds that might be spotted along the trail, ensure that the brochure would be a useful tool for people who want to explore the trail to have in hand.

# 15

# Creating Multimodal Compositions

**ANALYZE
and CREATE**

**Chapter 5**
Analyzing
Multimodal
Rhetoric

**Chapter 15**
Creating
Multimodal
Rhetoric

As Chapter 5 explains, technically all compositions are multimodal. Even reading or writing text on a screen involves the verbal modality (words), the visual modality (the look of the document), the auditory modality (the sound of keys tapping and mouse clicking), and the haptic modality (the sense of your body in space in front of the computer).

While most people who refer to multimodal compositions are talking about digital compositions such as videos, Web pages, and podcasts, it's important to keep in mind that, as in the example above, "multimodal" means attending to all the different sensory means by which information is being conveyed. Rhetorically effective composers can maintain awareness of the multiple registers on which their compositions may be affecting the audience.

We've considered in Chapter 5 how multimodal compositions affect their audiences. In this chapter, we'll mobilize that understanding in order to create multimodal composition for our own purposes. To discern whether a multimodal composition is appropriate for your purpose and audience, you first need to answer the following questions, building on concepts introduced in Chapters 1, 2, and 5:

---

**QUESTIONS TO ASK** **Creating Multimodal Compositions**

- What is my purpose in creating this composition?
- Given the context and habits of my audience, what type of composition would reach them most effectively?
- Which modalities and media do I have available to create compositions?
- What material things (budget, technical skills, availability of materials) do I need to create this composition?
- How will this composition be distributed (circulation)?

---

**EXAMPLE** Say I've just created a new course and to run it needs a certain number of students. I need to somehow advertise it both to faculty advisers (who can encourage their advisees to enroll) and directly to students. What kind of composition would be most appropriate for that? After answering the questions above, I can better discern what sort of composition I need:

- I need to convey to students and advisers that this course will not only be interesting and worth their while but will fulfill specific requirements.

- I know that students aren't good about checking their email regularly, so I don't trust that sending an email out to the entire campus about the course would work (plus, I'm not allowed to do that anyway, given the rules of the university email system). I do know that faculty check their email, but the same constraints about emailing all faculty apply.

- So I need a multipronged approach. First, to reach students, I will create an attractive, colorful flyer describing what students can expect to get out of the course and what requirements it fulfills. I can get these printed in color and hang them around campus, especially in common areas and in buildings where students are likely to get credit for the course. Second, I will write an email explaining what the course is and what requirements it fulfills, attach the flyer, and send it to the director of advising, who can then send out an email to advisers if she chooses (she does have the power and ability to email faculty). And finally, I will ask the campus radio station if they can do a brief announcement about the course, since this is something they do fairly regularly. So I've reached people via multiple modalities and attended to the specific means of circulation in my context.

Multimodal compositions, then, encompass more than digital compositions like videos, podcasts, and Web pages. However, these types of compositions tend to be the ones that students and instructors have the least experience with. Therefore, this chapter focuses on explaining how to create these sorts of compositions. However, it doesn't simply offer a catalogue and explanation of various new apps and software programs that will allow you to create these sorts of multimodal compositions, since they'd probably be outdated within six months. Rather, it aims to help you think about the general factors—rhetorical and technical—involved in creating videos, podcasts, and Web sites.

# 15a How to Create Videos

Whether it's a how-to video, an interview, a job application video, a video editorial, or even a video of your grandparents' fiftieth anniversary party, there are three basic steps in creating good, watchable, interesting video: PLAN, GET FOOTAGE, EDIT. Each of these steps is discussed in more detail in the following sections.

## FOR DISCUSSION

Choose ten videos from *YouTube* or your *Facebook* feed: A mix of amateur and professional would be best. For each video, note exactly when you stopped being interested in the video and write that down. Choose one of the videos that kept you interested the whole time and dissect it—what made it entertaining? Choose another video that you stopped watching a short time into it. What turned you off? Write down your responses and present them briefly in groups or to the class as a whole. As a class, see if you can discern some patterns for what makes videos interesting and watchable, and, conversely, what makes them bad or boring. Compile this into a list of "Dos and Don'ts" for making videos.

## Planning the Video

The best way to ensure that nobody will watch your video is to create it without a plan. Nobody wants to waste time watching a video without a clear purpose (unless, perhaps, it involves baby goats or is less than ten seconds long). Planning has multiple levels: You need to plan your basic concept and story, and then break that concept and story down into a series of shots.

### 1. Answer the basic rhetorical questions.

- Who is your audience? Use the questions for analyzing audience in Section 1c.
- What is the specific purpose of your video? What, exactly, are you trying to convey to your viewers? See Section 2c.

- What is the genre of your video? (An instructional video, a video that explains, a music video, a video editorial, or something else?) See Chapter 2, "The Expanded Rhetorical Situation."

## 2. Pitch your idea in a "treatment."

A treatment is a short document used to sell the idea of a film. Treatments are typically designed to help a third party (usually someone whom you want to convince to fund or produce your video) visualize the end product. But they are also excellent for nailing down the purpose, visual approach, and story of your video.

---

**QUESTIONS TO ASK**   **The Elements of a Treatment**

A. **Overview:** The overview consists of your working title and your core idea/purpose for the project. You are selling this concept to a third party. If you like, you can use this basic template:

> "In [title of your video], I want to [show/explain/persuade /argue/etc.] [what you want to show]. The purpose will be to make viewers [understand/feel/do] X. Presenting this film is important NOW because [establish the exigence or need for the video]."

B. **Editorial Approach:** What is your point of view or attitude toward the topic?  What tone will your video take?

C. **Story:** Who are the characters and what do the viewers see them doing? What is the beginning, middle, and end of the video? Use vivid details to help viewers imagine what will be happening on screen, and speak in the present tense (as if the video is already made).

D. **Visual Approach:** Help the reader visualize your film.  What kind of style will help you tell your story and make your point?

E. **Conclusion:** What is your personal investment in this idea? Why does it matter to you?

---

A bit more on the usefulness of story for video: No matter the genre of your video, you can try thinking about it in terms of telling a very basic story—something that has a protagonist with whom the audience can relate (maybe even a villain!), and a beginning, middle, and end.

**EXAMPLE**  Say you're creating an instructional video for how to apply eye makeup correctly. Instead of thinking of applying makeup as a (boring) series of steps, think of a basic story that might underlie a viewer's desire to learn to apply eye makeup: perhaps the protagonist is an older woman who wants to know if wearing different makeup might help her look younger. You might begin the video not with "Hi, here's my video on applying makeup," but with your character looking at herself in a mirror and sighing. This serves to get the viewer interested in the problem of the protagonist, an interest that is then satisfied by instructions on how to apply makeup to older eyes, concluding with the protagonist looking expertly made up and happy. It's not Shakespeare, but it gives viewers a better hook than "first you do this, then this, then this . . . "

### 3. Write a script.

At the very least your script should indicate who's talking and about what. In some cases you'll want to write out every word and memorize them; but often, it's enough to script some of your video and leave some to chance. As with all public speaking, the improvised parts should contain a minimum of meaningless interjections ("uh," "um," "like," "you know"). If the actors in the video (including you) can't seem to control it, you can always edit out some of the more irrelevant parts.

### 4. Plan your shots (brainstorming, sequencing, and storyboarding).

Not every "shot" in a video has to be something you've recorded yourself. "B roll" or found footage from videos posted on *YouTube* can be included here as well (as long as they fall within the boundaries of fair use, described later).

One important rule of thumb for creating videos is that each "shot" or bit of film should contain a new piece of information. As soon as the viewers have had enough time to absorb that information (no more than five seconds), the shot should change. Bad videographers just turn on the camera, point it in the direction of the action, and let the camera run. The well-meaning friend of my father who recorded my college graduation party, for instance, captured a good three minutes of me going through the buffet line and putting food on my plate—not most people's idea of gripping video. By contrast, a typical shot sequence for a professionally shot music video might look something like this: shot 1: close-up of singer's face; shot 2: looking up at the band playing on a stage; shot 3: brief pan over audience dancing in the front row; shot 4: close-up of fingers on a guitar; shot 5: band doing something quirky in a secondary location; and so on.

So to develop a good plan for your video, it helps to think in shots. Since you might get overwhelmed by planning a video that's longer than, say, 30 seconds, it helps to first to generate as big a list of potential shots as possible after you've created your general concept. Think not just about what kinds of action you want to capture, but *how* you want to capture that.

- Brainstorm a list of shots (including types of things you might get from videos that already exist). Don't discount or throw out any idea—just try to write down as many as you can. Be specific about what kind of shots would be best to capture specific types of action and create different kinds of effects. Think about how you can use each shot to convey information, and don't be redundant—if you can convey an idea visually, you don't need to also talk about it.

- Once you have a list, select the ones that will help you best convey your purpose and arrange them into a sequence that supports the story idea you've come up with (for your treatment).

### 5. Create a storyboard.

Storyboarding your video is the final process in planning. Storyboards can actually be graphic images. Figure 15.1 shows an example of a storyboard with quite crude images—I downloaded and printed a free template from a site called *StudioBinder* to make this one. Or storyboards can simply be descriptions of what will be happening in the shot, along with descriptions of the visual and audio elements. You don't always need to storyboard (since it can be quite time-consuming), but it's vital if you want to have a clear sense of what your final product will look like. See the following "How to" box for a sample graphic organizer that will help you with storyboarding.

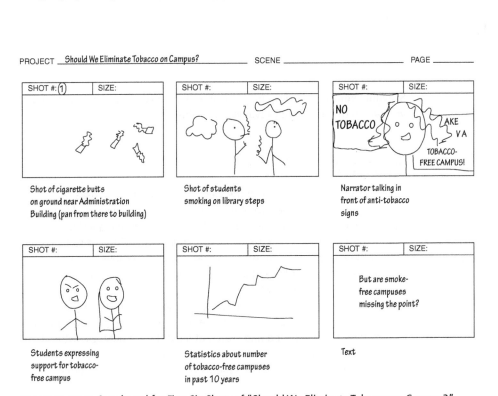

PROJECT __Should We Eliminate Tobacco on Campus?__          SCENE _____          PAGE _____

| SHOT #: (1) | SIZE: |
| SHOT #: | SIZE: |
| SHOT #: | SIZE: |

Shot of cigarette butts on ground near Administration Building (pan from there to building)

Shot of students smoking on library steps

Narrator talking in front of anti-tobacco signs

Students expressing support for tobacco-free campus

Statistics about number of tobacco-free campuses in past 10 years

Text

**FIGURE 15.1** Storyboard for First Six Shots of "Should We Eliminate Tobacco on Campus?"

## HOW TO...
### Plan the Sequence of Your Video

Create a table like the one below to plan the specific sequence of your video. Use one row for each individual "shot" or element of the video.

### Storyboard Graphic Organizer

|  | NOTES | VISUAL | AUDIO |
|---|---|---|---|
| Shot 1 | Description of what will happen in this shot | Description of what the viewer will see on screen | Description of what the viewer will be listening to (music, sound, speech, and so on) |
| Shot 2 | | | |
| Shot 3 | | | |
| Shot 4 | | | |
| etc. | | | |

### 6. Schedule as necessary.

Schedule your interviews, any special location visits, or other elements of your video that may need advance scheduling.

## FOR HOMEWORK AND DISCUSSION

1. Go to *YouTube* and look at the week's top ten videos. In pairs or small groups, choose one of these and "reverse engineer" it: Identify the audience and purpose, write a treatment using the questions in "Questions to Ask: The Elements of a Treatment." Create a storyboard of the first six to ten shots of the video using the graphic organizer above. From all of these things, decide on the specific elements that made the video successful.

2. Choose a video genre to focus on; for example, profile, explanatory, how-to, op-doc, news (different groups in the class could take different genres). Find and watch at least three examples of these videos, and make note while you watch about the features. Then compare them. Are there elements that they all include? What

distinguishes them as a genre? Write a brief "genre guide" that other video creators could use to make a video in this particular genre.

3. Using the list of elements in a treatment in "Questions to Ask," write a treatment for the video you're proposing. Once your instructor gives you feedback on and approves your treatment, brainstorm a list of shots and storyboard your video.

## Getting Footage for the Video

There are two ways to get footage for a video: You can gather it from the Internet (always keeping fair use in mind; see "Copyright and Fair Use" discussed later), or you can shoot it yourself. Most videos are a combination of both.

### "Found footage," B-roll, and other elements

Rhetorically, found footage (including clips of other videos, still images, voiceover, animation, music, and text) can function as a way to establish a mood, as visual evidence for a point you're making, to show a historical scene, or as a way to direct or control the narrative. Depending on your subject, the entire video can consist of spliced-together video that someone else has already made.

To gather found footage, first you need to follow the steps outlined earlier to have a clearly articulated purpose and plan for the video. Your storyboard will serve as a guide for the kinds of video footage you need. Once you decide on the clip, you'll need to do searches on sites like *YouTube* and *Vimeo* to find videos that have what you want. Then you can use a free online tool like Clip Converter to download and convert *YouTube* URLs to other formats. You can then upload these into your project library on your movie editing software and splice them together with other footage, and add music and voiceover narration (see the section on editing).

### Shooting your own video

In shooting video, you don't just blindly execute the shots in your storyboard. For each shot, you need to maintain your focus on the ultimate purpose for creating your video. In shooting video, you need to pay attention to two aspects at once: the *rhetorical* aspect (the focus of your shots) and the *technical* aspect (everything having to do with your equipment).

### Rhetorical considerations for shooting video

Here are some basic things to keep in mind while filming subjects:

**Focus on the right things.** To give viewers information about where they should be putting their attention and to create a sense of story (with protagonist, beginning, middle, and end), make sure that your protagonist is the focus of each shot. This can look different based on the effect that you want to create. If the protagonist of your video (or of just one scene in your video) is a wheat farmer, for instance, you might shoot an establishing shot through the ripening wheat of him walking toward a barn. When he's interacting with other farmers, or with his grandchildren, make sure that the camera is focused on *him* rather than the scene as a whole, or on the other actors. This will remind viewers of whose story it is.

**Make sure you can clearly see the subjects' eyes.** Humans get a huge amount of information, as well as a sense of the emotional impact of an event from other people's faces, especially their eyes. When you shoot video so that it's difficult to read the facial expressions or eye movements of the subject, you'll drain your shot of emotional impact. While not *every* shot needs to be focused on people, make sure your camera is positioned close enough to allow this to happen.

**Create or find establishing shots (but keep in mind how they'll look on a small screen).** Help to orient viewers (and get them out of the narrow cage of the camera lens) by first giving them a sense of where they are via an establishing shot. If you're in your university student union building, for instance, you might take some quick shots of some distinguishing, easily recognizable features: the name of the building is one obvious one, or a well-known statue or fountain in the building. If you have multiple shots set in the building, you can edit in a different establishing shot before each shot or scene to remind readers where you are and to create a sense of place.

You can also use your establishing shots to create a mood. Say you're filming a scene in a skate park, for instance. You might hold the camera still over the top of the half-pipe as skaters pop their boards up over the top and go back down. You might have some close-ups of young kids smoking or looking sullen (or goofy), depending on what understanding you want your viewers to have of your subject.

Taking shots of wide, empty spaces, though, won't translate well to the tiny screens that many people now watch videos on. If you're in the desert, you can find some distinguishing desert features (cactuses, say) to provide a sense of place without needing to waste film and viewing time on shots that viewers won't really be able to see or appreciate.

**Don't center everything.** Remember the rule of thirds? (See Section 14b, "Design with a Grid to Ensure Alignment.") The same thing applies to video. While it's tempting to continually frame subjects in the center of the shot, too much centered composition gets rather dull. Following the rule of thirds, you might try positioning interview subjects in the thirds to the right or left of center.

### Conducting interviews

Interviews are an important part of many videos, and the best interviews not only provide interesting, in-depth information but they also make for good viewing—they get viewers emotionally involved in the topic matter through the person being interviewed. Getting good interviews is an art. Of course, all of the earlier rules for filming in general apply (find a good place to conduct the interview, create good three-point lighting, use an external mic, focus on the subject's face, and don't center the subject in the camera). But there are a few other techniques that will help you get good interviews:

- *Let your interviewee know you won't use everything they say.* The more comfortable they are, the more they'll talk (and the less likely they'll be to sound stiff and uncomfortable). Most people are uncomfortable talking on camera because they become hyper-aware of every answer they give. You can help with this by letting them know that you'll be editing the film, and that you probably won't use most of the material they give you.

- *Follow up on things that interest you, even if it takes you off-script, or away from your intended line of questioning.*

- *Establish eye contact.* If they talk to you, an actual human, your subject will be more comfortable and more likely to talk than if they have to talk to the camera. Set the camera up so that it's slightly off to the side (but not so much that the subject is in full profile).

## FOR DISCUSSION

Watch clips of some films in different genres: an activist documentary, a "chick flick," an action-adventure film, a music video. Note, for each genre, how frequently the camera shows somebody's face clearly enough for you to see their expression and their eyes. How often and at what points in the scene are faces/eyes shown for each genre? You might even keep an actual count and compare these. What do you think accounts for the differences between genres? What different effects are created?

### Technical considerations for shooting video

The good news is that it doesn't matter what kind of equipment you use to film. You can shoot pretty good videos with a smartphone or cheap flip camera, or really bad videos with a $10,000 professional camera. What matters most is good planning, awareness of the rhetorical effects of different types of shots, and some (very) basic technical knowledge. With these things, you can create videos that people will want to actually watch (which is the most fundamental goal of video creation).

On the technical side, here are some basic rules of thumb to keep in mind as you set up and film the shots in your shot list:

**Don't keep the camera running as you shoot.** As discussed earlier, bad videographers tend to turn on the camera and let it run as they walk around the action, leading to not only shaky shots, but also a lot of useless filler (and boring video). This method of filming also makes the editing process more onerous than it needs to be.

Instead, treat the video camera as if it were a still camera. For each shot, point the camera at the action and stay still as you record. Then, after you've captured the relevant action from that angle, turn the camera off, move to a different location, point it at the action, and stay still as you record again. Steve Stockman, in his aptly titled *How to Shoot Video that Doesn't Suck*, calls this "Move, Point, Shoot" (12).

**Avoid the camera's built-in zoom function.** Most (nonprofessional) cameras blow up the image without simultaneously focusing the image, so the resultant film looks grainy and terrible. If you want to create a zooming effect, walk toward the action while holding the camera. However, keep in mind that walking normally with a camera will create a jiggling effect. An article from videomaker.com suggests holding the camera "as if it were a flimsy foam cup excessively full of scalding coffee," and to walk in a "partial squat, with . . . knees flexed" so that your head stays level. Yes, you'll probably look silly doing this, but the shot will be better.

**Pay attention to the light.** Your viewers shouldn't have to squint to figure out what's happening in the shot, and even slightly less-than-ideal lighting conditions will produce grainy, dim video (see Figure 15.2). So make sure there's plenty of (ideally, natural) light on your subject. Filming outdoors and in brightly sunlit rooms is the best way to ensure that you have enough light. But if you're filming indoors without natural light, or at night, plan to use extra lighting.

A standard technique for creating adequate lighting is three-point lighting, three light sources arranged around the subject in a triangle (see Figure 15.3 for an example of a subject lit with three-point lighting):

- The *key light*, a 300- to 500-watt light placed in front of the subject, sheds the most light (if you're shooting outdoors, your key light is

Jack Swift

**FIGURE 15.2** Inadequate lighting produces poor video quality.

FIGURE 15.3 A Standard Three-Point Lighting Scheme and a Subject Lit with Three-Point Lighting

the sun). Ideally you want a bright, diffuse light for your key light. If you don't have access to professional lights, you could substitute a bright halogen lamp diffused with a clear shower curtain, or a bright Japanese lantern with a white shade.

- The *fill light* is placed below the key light and to the side of the subject. Its role is to soften harsh shadows and "fill in" some of the light that the key light misses. The fill light doesn't have to be an actual light: you could use a piece of white posterboard to reflect some of the key light, or even strategically place the action near a white wall.

- The *back light* shines on subjects from behind (albeit to the side) in order to clearly separate them from the background. The back light should be about half as bright as the key light.

As with still photography, the light should be *behind* you as you're filming, unless you want to create a silhouette effect, as Figure 15.4 shows.

**Use an external microphone.** While the quality of the images is important, if viewers can't hear what's going on, or if the sound is tinny or muffled, it can ruin the video. So it's important to make sure that you have a microphone in addition to the one on the camcorder itself. If you have access to a clip-on mic (also called a *lavalier*), you can discreetly improve the sound on interviews. But if you don't, you can do a lot of things with a regular old handheld (*cardioid*) microphone (see Figure 15.5). For interviews, the subject can hold it just out of view of the camera, and that will improve the sound quality. For other sorts of scenes, you can create a homemade boom

**FIGURE 15.4** Make sure the light is behind you while filming, unless you want to create a silhouette.

**FIGURE 15.5** Ordinary Cardioid Microphone

mic by taping a handheld mic to a long dowel rod and having someone hold it above the subjects' heads, out of sight of the camera.

## Editing Video

The first step of video production (planning) gives you a direction, and the second (shooting, gathering footage) gives you raw material. The third step is what makes the video, though—you organize the raw material according to the audience, purpose, and story, and maybe even in the process refine your ideas about audience, purpose, and story. A well-edited video will engage and intrigue the audience—it will keep them watching till the end.

While editing will likely be the most time-consuming part of the video creation process, the actual process is fairly straightforward: Make a back-up of your original files, import your footage (found and created) into your editing software, cut and splice, arrange/sequence, and add sound. Each step is described in the following list.

1.  *Make a back-up of your original file.* It may be tempting just to get moving on the editing, but don't skip this step—it will save you time and heartache if something should happen to your raw video files. These files will be quite large, so if you shot on your phone, move them to your computer and potentially to a separate flash drive.

2.  *Import footage into your editing software.* This is the easiest part of the process. Luckily, much of the best free editing software out there comes with most basic computer software packages: MovieMaker for Windows and iMovie for Mac. While each editing program will be slightly different, they are all designed for nonexperts, and so (at least in theory) are fairly intuitive and easy to use. For most editing programs, you create a project (give it a distinctive name: Engl102_Tobacco-Free-Video, for instance); then you upload your footage. You'll also have the option to upload or even create music or sound effects, though frequently these programs come with a small library of transitional music and sounds.

3. *Cut and splice the footage.* Less is more when it comes to editing. Humans receive an extraordinary amount of information visually (recall the "picture superiority effect" discussed in Chapter 4), so the key is to use that to make your video as rich in information as possible. The most general rule of thumb for editing videos is *err on the side of cutting.* This rule is the multimedia version of Ernest Hemingway's writing dictum "kill your little darlings." Be brutal: If it's repetitive, badly focused, poorly lit, grainy, or shaky, cut it (and consider that you may need to re-shoot some segments). If it's interesting but doesn't fit with the overall purpose and focus of your video, cut it.

4. *Arrange the footage into a sequence.* Most video editing programs will allow you to simply drag and drop your clips into order. (To determine what this order is, you should refer to your original treatment and/or storyboard.)

5. *Add transitions, sound effects, and background music.* Err on the side of simplicity: though movie editing programs have many bells and whistles (novelty transition effects like swirling down a drain, flickering, etc.), don't be tempted. Using these looks amateur and creates a cheesy effect. Many experts recommend giving a little breathing room between shots to allow the audience time to process information. Don't cut from one interview immediately to the next, for instance; rather, include a couple seconds of B-roll or shots of surroundings between the two speakers. To complete the effect of a transition, you might add in a few seconds of music, then turn it down again as the next interviewee begins talking.

## FOR HOMEWORK

This exercise aims to help you become familiar with both the technical and rhetorical aspects of video editing.

1. You'll need some raw footage to edit. Everyone in the class should work from the same footage. The footage could be literally anything, though it will work best if it's a film of an actual event. If you're in a face-to-face class, someone in the class could be assigned to film part of a single class session, for instance (again, using the principles outlined earlier). The resultant footage could be uploaded onto *YouTube* and distributed to everyone in the class. While you can use any amount of footage for this project, probably somewhere between ten and twenty minutes of footage would be most manageable.

2. Using the raw footage and whatever editing software you like (iMovie comes free with Mac, and MovieMaker comes free with Windows), you will create three different stories. These stories will

take different forms depending on the footage you have. It's your job as an editor to find the elements of each story (protagonist, beginning, middle, end). The stories should be 45 seconds each.

3. Select members of the class can show their edited stories in class (or otherwise make them available for others to see). As a class, discuss the differences in the stories created by different editors. Argue for which are the most compelling, and discuss what considerations different editors used in creating their stories.

## Copyright and Fair Use

As with written copyrighted material, you can't just use multimodal copyrighted material however you want. (You probably have encountered a "This material has been removed because of copyright concerns" message on *YouTube*.) However, according to the Center for Media and Social Impact's "Code of Best Practices in Fair Use for Online Video," there are six situations where using copyrighted material is acceptable; therefore it is not necessary to pay the owners of the copyright. These are called instances of "fair use" of copyrighted material.

1. *When you are commenting on or critiquing copyrighted material.* For instance, you might be reviewing a film or making a point about the way a certain character is portrayed in the film. The CMSI also mentions "fan tributes" as an instance where this exception applies. However, similar to quoting in written work, you should provide only as much of the original (copyrighted) material as is necessary to make your point. CMSI points out that "the new use should not become a market substitute for the work."

2. *When you are using copyrighted material as an illustration or example.* Again, this practice is a kind of quoting, though not for the purpose of commenting on or critiquing the work itself. For example, if you wanted to show how reality shows unrealistically portray certain aspects of celebrity life, you might use clips from multiple shows that demonstrate what you're saying.

3. *If you capture copyrighted material incidentally or accidentally.* The examples of this provided by the CMSI include filming something at home while a copyrighted song plays incidentally in the background, or filming something with copyrighted posters on the wall, or filming someone wearing a licensed T-shirt. The copyrighted material in question is there more or less by accident and is unstaged. But the line between when copyrighted material is captured incidentally and when it constitutes a central part of the new material can be rather blurry.

**EXAMPLE** A few years ago, a viral video circulated showing a baby waking up suddenly and doing a frantic car dance to Psy's "Gangnam

Style" while her sister laughs hysterically. The video was temporarily removed when the copyright owner argued that the song was a critical part of the video. It was reinstated after commenters protested that the copyright holder was being a bit Grinchy; however, removing the material would have been entirely within their rights under current copyright law.

4. *Reproducing, reposting, or quoting in order to memorialize a cultural event, experience, or phenomenon.* You can document and post a rock performance you attended; you can post or repost a notorious moment like a speech or television performance; and you can revive something that's been taken out of circulation. However, the use should not compete with or impair the market for the original work. If the content is already readily available from authorized sources, your posting of it may be a violation of copyright.

5. *Copying, restoring, and recirculating material in order to create a discussion.* This rule applies if, for example, you found something (a commercial, a speech, an ad, a performance, etc.) offensive or annoying and want to get others' takes on it, or perhaps if you disagree with how others see it and want to redirect the discussion. It's legitimate to post it, but you must be sure that your purpose for reposting it (i.e., to launch a discussion) is clear; otherwise, it may not be considered fair use.

6. *Remixing or mash-up.* Certainly pastiche or collage can be done with analog materials (collage was central to the work of twentieth-century artists like writer William S. Burroughs and sculptor Joseph Cornell, for instance). However, digital media lends itself especially well to this activity, with the added bonus that it can be easily circulated. In the past twenty years, "remix" or "mash-up" has been an important form of commentary and is protected in many cases under fair use.

   **EXAMPLE** Musical artists like Girl Talk and DJ Danger Mouse rely almost exclusively on mash-up and remix (though the Recording Industry Association of America has pursued lawsuits against both). More successful have been video remixes that make political commentary, like the Black Lantern's "George Bush Don't Like Black People," a 2005 commentary on the response to Hurricane Katrina, featuring a sequence of images of Katrina set to Kanye West's "Gold Digger" (which in turn samples Ray Charles's "I Got a Woman"). Googling "subversive and political remix videos" will bring up more results.

The important thing to keep in mind, and the general principle behind fair use of copyrighted material, is to make sure that you're using copyrighted material for something other than its original purpose (or a very similar one). As the CMSI puts it, you should be attempting to "create new value" from the original works.

# 15b How to Create Podcasts

Podcasts, a portmanteau (combined word) of "iPod broadcasts," are digital audio productions that can be listened to on smartphones and other mobile devices. While videos or written compositions can stand alone or be part of a larger series, podcasts almost always appear in *series* composed of *episodes*. Listeners can subscribe to a podcast series: When new episodes appear, they can be automatically sent to the listener's mobile device.

Podcasts have become much more popular in recent years, mostly thanks to the growth of mobile devices like smartphones and tablets. Now there are podcasts on every conceivable subject, in a wide variety of formats. Some, like *Radiolab* and *This American Life*, are thirty minutes to an hour long and provide in-depth coverage of a specific topic, incorporating interviews from multiple people. But podcasts can also be as short as five minutes; they might aim to quickly explain a single topic, for instance, or give tips or advice to people on various topics (career, investment, exercise, etc.).

As with blogs and videos, you don't need to be a professional to create a podcast. However, there are certain measures you can take to make it more professional. As with creating videos and other multimodal compositions, *planning* is the key.

---

### FOR DISCUSSION

What makes a podcast good? Listen to part of a popular podcast (*Radiolab, This American Life, Serial*, or *Welcome to Night Vale*, for instance) in class or for homework. As you listen, write down what you notice about the podcast's audio elements, how it presents its material, the format, and the language. How does the podcast attempt to engage listeners and keep their attention? As a class, compile the list into a "how to" list of tips for creating podcasts.

---

## Basic Steps for Creating a Podcast

1. *Decide on an audience, purpose, and genre/format for your podcast.* See Chapters 1 and 2 to help work through questions of whom you'd want to subscribe to your podcast and its overarching purpose. Wrapped up with questions of audience and purpose are questions of podcast genre. What form do you imagine this taking? Is it a talk show podcast (e.g., *The Brain Candy Podcast*, *LGBTQ&A*), an educational podcast (e.g., *Grammar Girl's Quick and Dirty Tips for Better Writing* or *Stuff You Missed in History Class*), a scripted (fictional) podcast (*Welcome to Night Vale*), or an advice podcast (*The Hilarious World of Depression*)?

2. *Decide on a topic or overarching theme for your podcast and come up with a series title.* Brainstorm a list of potential episodes that your podcast

might include. You might come up with a series idea as a class, and each member of the class could develop individual episodes.

3. *Choose one particular episode to focus on, and research the topic.* See Chapter 12 for instructions on how to do effective research.

4. *Decide on the structure for your podcast.* Even if it's very short, your podcast will likely have some predictable elements. A sample structure for a talk show podcast, for instance, might look something like this:

   a. Intro music
   b. Intro to the theme of the show
   c. Welcome, introduction of host
   d. Announcements
   e. Interview with guest
   f. Final comments
   g. Outro music

   Your structure, of course, can evolve as the podcast matures.

5. *Write the script and interview guests.* Depending both on the format for your podcast and on how comfortable you are speaking off the cuff, your script can be entirely written out or it might be much looser. If you're doing one or more interviews, for instance, you would bring several broad, open-ended questions for guests in order to stimulate conversation, and then ask follow-up questions as needed. Then you'll listen to the interviews as you create your podcast and incorporate only the most interesting and relevant things they say into your podcast. Remember that, while guests are important for providing evidence and another voice for added interest, you're still primarily responsible for controlling the overall direction of the podcast. Thus, you should plan to summarize or paraphrase a significant part of the discussion and only include your interviewee's voice for short snippets.

6. *Record the podcast.* As with creating videos, you don't need much equipment to make a good podcast, though you do need some basics:

   • Something to record with. Ideally this would be a microphone, with a cable for linking to a computer (see Figure 15.6); however, you can use the software that comes with your computer. (GarageBand for Mac will let you record as well as edit; with Sound Recorder for Windows, you can record, but you'll need to convert the file to an MP3 and upload your recording elsewhere in order to edit it.) You can use a digital recorder; smartphones also have built-in microphones, and you can download free or cheap apps that will let you record and often even edit right on the phone. Search under "best apps for recording interviews" to find a list.

   • A quiet space to record. If you're on a university campus, there may be a media room designed specifically for this purpose. If you're recording at home, choose the quietest room in the house—nothing

FIGURE 15.6 Basic Podcasting Setup: Microphone, Cable, Computer

says "amateur podcast" like the (unplanned) sound of a flushing toilet or slamming door in the background.

- Editing software. Several reputable "freemium" sites online will let you do this. Audacity and Acoustica (Basic) are typically recommended as the best free software for creating and editing podcasts.

- If it's available, podcasters recommend a pop filter for the microphone. This will soften your "plosives," those letters like p, b, and d that can make a popping sound.

7. *Edit the podcast*. As with videos, editing is where the podcast is really created. You have raw material, which might include your own recorded voice, interviews, music, and other sound effects. Now you need to shape this into a show that is interesting, compelling, and engaging for listeners.

8. *Keep narrative control of the podcast*. As with all compositions, the purpose and intent of a finished podcast should be clear. This will be the biggest challenge of editing. Especially if you're using interviews and other elements, you need to make sure that the podcast is still under what we might call "narrative control." The show should be edited to have a clear structure. In professionally produced podcasts like *Radiolab*, for instance, the hosts set the tone for the show and serve as guides or emcees to the topic for listeners; they also decide when new ideas or people relevant to the topic will be introduced.

Pay special attention to how *Radiolab* and other podcasts manage the audio footage from interviews. The editors don't simply let whoever they're interviewing talk at length, but incorporate paraphrasing and summary with snippets from the interview. Just as with written compositions, podcast quotes that are too long can detract from the main point and interrupt the smooth flow of the show.

9. *Use sounds and music to establish mood*. Music and other audio effects are important components of podcasts. It's critical to think about the "mood" or feel that you want the overall podcast to have, and to choose music accordingly. In a podcast giving business advice tips, you probably don't want music that's too cool; music that is upbeat but not too distracting is probably more appropriate to a podcast aimed at professionals.

   Free music and sounds are available online (search under "free music and sounds for podcasts"). Typically these are free for personal or educational use, but sites like *Freeplay Music* may charge fees if you're using them for profit. *SoundCloud* (a common podcasting host site) recommends that you only use music and sounds that are royalty-free and "podsafe." If you use tracks or sounds that have a Creative Commons license, you may need to get the creator's permission to use them. Make sure you check the terms of the license.

10. *Publish the podcast*. Numerous free online sites like *Podomatic* and *SoundCloud* host podcasts. To make your podcast more findable by search engines, make sure that you tag the podcast by adding keywords that describe its content and genre.

# 15c How to Create Websites

Chances are you are already do a fair amount of composing in online environments, whether it's texting, instant messaging, emailing, posting on social media sites, or using apps like *Snapchat* or *Instagram*. You may engage with strangers in subreddits or online role-playing games. You may write fan fiction or have your own *YouTube* channel.

As should be no surprise by now, the focus of this section is on learning to compose *rhetorically* in such spaces. Specifically, we'll consider websites because as discussed later, websites tend to be mashups of a number of other online components. Websites have always been multimodal compositions; in fact, they're the multimodal compositions that first called significant attention to the idea of multimodality.

## Rhetorical Considerations for Creating Websites

It used to be in the good old days of the Web (that ancient era of 2009 or so), websites were typically detached, standalone virtual places where people went to learn things, buy things, or be entertained. Website genres more or less mimicked print genres: Media sites took the form of online magazines, and business sites looked an awful lot like marketing brochures or product catalogs.

Of course, these sorts of standalone sites still exist. But increasingly, as Colleen Jones, the author of the book *Clout: The Art and Science of Influential Web Content* observes, "Our websites are becoming all of those things *at once*. And, our websites are becoming connected to social networks. As a result . . . websites are evolving into complex mashups" (110). The expanding connectivity and capabilities of the Web make it possible to imagine a magazine where one could click on the dress a model was wearing as part of a fashion spread and buy it from an external site; or to import all of a user's financial information from various sites into one central app (as, indeed, the site *Mint* does); or read a blog featuring recipes and healthy food choices on a local restaurant's website. Even ordinary personal websites can include *Twitter* and other social media feeds, videos that play when a viewer scrolls over them, and other multimodal, connected components (see Figure 15.7 for an example).

## Nathaniel A. Rivers Ph.D

FIGURE 15.7 The home page of a personal website (e.g., *www.nathanielrivers.org*, created with *Squarespace*) can include multimodal components.

To create a website, whether the purpose is to establish an individual Web presence; to promote a cause, organization, or business; to sell products; or to have an online magazine, you need to first answer the following questions (which I hope are becoming very familiar):

---

**QUESTIONS TO ASK**    **Planning Website Content**

- What is the purpose for your intended website—what are you hoping to achieve or accomplish?
- Is a website the best way to fulfill this purpose?
- Who is the audience (users) for this website?
- What user needs or wants are you trying to fulfill?
- What will be the content of the website?
- What sorts of modalities will the content be in?
- Who will create the content?
- What type of website (genre) will best allow this content to be distributed?

---

It might surprise you to learn that experts in content strategy for the Web almost uniformly recommend having *less* content than you might expect. As Kristina Halvorson and Melissa Rach, the authors of *Content Strategy for the Web* explain, a typical mistake of novice website creators is to overload the site with things that they think might be interesting, useful, or persuasive to their users, without thinking carefully about the reasons their users are coming to the site. They argue that content is "more or less worthless" unless it supports a key objective and/or fulfills users' needs (6).

**EXAMPLE**    They use the example of a user visiting an insurance site and finding that the site simply has every possible type of insurance that they offer on the site (in a way that quickly becomes overwhelming and makes it difficult for users to locate the information they need). By contrast, a different insurance site anticipates user needs appropriately by imagining what they might be coming to the site for and organizing the site around those imagined needs. For instance, instead of including everything they do as a business and letting readers pick through it to (hopefully) find the valuable information, the good site organizes user experience by providing actions for users to take: "Get a Quote," "Contact Us," and "Manage Claims."

The danger of having too much content is that it will become too much to manage and that it will get stale very quickly. The trick with contemporary websites is to keep people coming back, and to do that you need to have links that work and up-to-date, relevant content. This requires some fairly constant attention, so it's best to think of website composition as an ongoing project, not a one-and-done thing.

**Example of a student planning website content**

Say I'm a formerly bad student who learned how to study using fairly unique tactics. I feel like I've figured things out about how to study well that I want to share with others: first, because I enjoy composing, and second, because it seems not only like a fun thing to do, but also potentially a good thing to put on my resume, especially if I end up getting a lot of followers. So, using the earlier questions as a guide, I'll work through what sort of content I need and will create.

- *What is the purpose for your intended website—what are you hoping to achieve or accomplish?*

  I want to show that even bad students can become good ones if they develop a few key skills and learn to enjoy studying. For me, studying is not only fun, but also kind of an art, and I think it would be useful for people to understand it that way.

- *Is a website the best way to fulfill this purpose?*

  Yes, because I have multiple components in various modalities that I want to include (photos, blog posts, videos, content from other sites, etc.), and a website seems like the best way to keep these together.

- *Who is the audience (users) for this website?*

  Students who are worried about their performance in school and who think they could be doing better than they're doing.

- *What user needs or wants are you trying to fulfill?*

  They will want specific tips on study skills, but they want it to be entertaining and interesting, and from the perspective of a student. They also want to be convinced that being a "good" or "bad" student isn't a natural trait—that it's possible to learn and practice how to be a good student. They'll be wondering about the most effective strategies for doing this.

- *What will be the content of the website?*

  Beautiful images of "study scenes" to inspire viewers; explanations and reviews of the latest gadgets and organizing systems; a blog aimed at helping users improve specific aspects of studying that would include posts on using flashcards, revising writing, "deep learning," the latest research on the cognitive skills involved in retaining information, etc.; relevant content from other sites.

- *What sorts of modalities will this content be in?*

  Content will include images, written text with images, some videos.

- *Who will create the content?*

  I will create and manage most of it, but I'll also add guest posts on featured topics that week.

- *What type of website (genre) will best allow this content to be distributed?*

  I imagine it being more in blog format—I could use a *Tumblr* site, since *Tumblr* makes it easy to create posts with images and compile information from other sites. However, *Tumblr* also can make it hard to categorize posts, and I want it to be easy for users to browse through study topics. So I may create the site using *Wix*, which I've used before and found to be reliable.

---

**FOR HOMEWORK**

Answer the questions in the previous list in order to plan the content for your own website.

---

## Technical Considerations for Creating Websites

You may be intimidated by the idea of actually building websites, but thanks to some excellent free tools available on the Web (and everything you've learned about rhetoric and design principles), you don't need to know HTML, Java, or really any code in order to create a pretty snazzy website. In fact, you really only need two things to create a site: a domain name and website-building software, each of which I discuss below.

### A domain name

A domain name is the "friendly" naming system for websites. Domain names hide the technical website identifiers and give users something easy to remember: for example, *nytimes.com*. If you use online website-building software like *Wix*, *Weebly*, or *WordPress* to create your site (which you'll have to do, unless you know code), it helps your ethos to own a domain name. That way, the website builder site won't advertise itself in the Web address, and your site will look more professional and easier for users to find. So, for instance, instead of *https://jnicotra.wixsite.com/rhetoricisawesome/14-325*, a website address with a domain name attached would be *https://www.rhetoricisawesome.com*.

Domain names do cost money, but they are fairly cheap: typically around $10 to $15 per year. You can usually buy them through website-building software (see the next section), or you can buy them separately through a site like *GoDaddy* and hook them up later to your website.

### Website-building software

The most popular and easiest way to build websites is through online website-building software like *WordPress*, *Wix*, *Weebly*, and *Squarespace*. These are known in the industry as WYSIWYG ("what you see is what you get," pronounced "wiz-ee-wig") sites, meaning that they are made up of components that users can typically drag and drop to create a site (see Figure 15.8 for a screenshot for components that you can add to your site on *Wix*).

These sites allow you to choose and modify templates designed for sites with different purposes; for instance, among others you can find templates for an online store, a music site, a restaurant, a portfolio, a photography site, and a blog. Though these templates can make life easier, coincidentally, they are also the limitation of website-building software—by necessity, they end up taking some decision-making power away from the website creator, so you may find yourself running up against the limitations of the template and software. However, most people who consider themselves non-technologically savvy find that such website builders work suitably well for most purposes.

While it may be tempting to overload your site with the many bells and whistles available through website-building software, as with the content of videos, it's important to consider whether these WYSIWYG components will truly help you to support your key objectives and/or fulfill your users' needs. The fact that there's a way to allow music to play on your site automatically is only awesome if it directly supports your objectives and/or fulfills your audience needs.

Source: Wix.com, Inc.

FIGURE 15.8 Users can add a variety of multimodal WYSIWYG components on *Wix*.

# Glossary

**Action** The thing in a narrative that is happening or has happened. [4a]

**Actors** Who or what does the action in an image. [4a]

**Addressed Audiences** The people who actually receive a text and interact with it. [1c]

**Analytical Circle** Linking your observations about the text back to the text's rhetorical effect. [3d]

**Argument** Using a process of inquiry to develop a response to a rhetorical problem. [7a]

**Audience** The intended recipient(s) of an act of communication. Includes addressed audiences and invoked audiences. [1]

**Auditory Modality** A communication modality involving spoken language, song, music, or ambient noise. [2d, 5]

**Campaign Brief** A document that spells out the problem, audience, goals, message, and methods for evaluating a campaign. [6e]

**Campaign Kit** Information that describes in detail the specific campaign materials (typically 4–6 different types) and rhetorical actions that will be a part of a campaign. [6e]

**Campaign Materials** The materials that will serve as the actual substance of the campaign (what the audience will see). [6e]

**Circulation** The physical means by which a message gets distributed. [2]

**Claim** A very condensed version of an overall argument; the basic message. [7b]

**Color** An important design element for creating mood, visual interest, and visual hierarchy. Elements of color include hue, value, and saturation. [14]

**Communicator** The person or entity responsible for the act of communication. [1]

**Context** The circumstances of communication; includes citational, geographical, historical, and sociocultural contexts. [2a]

**Contrast** The use of opposites in design elements to create visual excitement and a clear visual hierarchy. [14]

**Criteria** The factors used to evaluate a thing. [10]

**Ethos** A rhetorical appeal that refers to how messages persuade (or "appeal" to an audience) as a result of the communicator's character. [1]

**Exigence** Whatever prompted a rhetorical action. [2b]

**Formal Layer** The structural features of photographs such as framing, emphasis, camera angle, focus, distance from subject, lighting and contrast, and color. [4a]

**Genre** Somewhat stabilized yet flexible forms of communication that have developed over time and in response to all these other rhetorical factors: purpose, audience, context, exigence, modalities, media, and circulation. [2d]

**Global-Level Revisions** Revisions that relate back to the purpose, message, and audience of the piece. [13a]

**Haptic Modality** A communication modality involving a sense of touch, and where/how the body is positioned in relation to the communication. [2d]

**Hue** What we typically think of as "color." [14]

**Invoked Audiences** Audiences imagined by the author. [1c]

**Keywords** Search terms that capture the essence of a subject or topic. [12a]

**Local Revisions** Revisions dealing with how something is said. [13a]

**Logos** A rhetorical appeal that refers to how the logic (internal consistency of a message) appeals to an audience. [1]

**Medium** The technical means by which communication is disseminated. [2]

**Message** The content or gist of an act of communication. [1b]

**Modality** The basic sensory means by which a message is communicated; includes verbal, auditory, visual, and haptic. [2]

**Multimodal** Communication involving a complex mix of verbal, visual, and auditory composition. [0]

**Narrative** A story of something that is happening or has happened. [4a]

**Pathos** A rhetorical appeal that refers to how messages persuade by arousing the emotions of the audience. [1]

**Primary Evidence** Information gathered directly about a topic through observation, interview, experiment, or questionnaires/surveys. [7b]

**Primary Sources** Sources that provide direct, first-hand knowledge about an event. [12a]

**Public Awareness Campaigns** Campaigns that aim to build awareness in the public for an issue that's unknown or misunderstood, but important. [6e]

**Purpose** What the communicator hopes to achieve with this particular rhetorical action. [2c]

**Reason** An explanation of why an audience should believe an assertion. [7b]

**Rhetoric** The wide array of communicative devices humans have at their disposal to create effects on each other. [0]

**Rhetorical Action** Techniques used to deliberately shape messages for an audience. [0]

**Rhetorical Analysis** The effort to understand how communication (by a variety of means) creates particular effects on people. [0]

**Rhetorical Stakeholders** Everyone who is affected by an issue in some way. [6]

**Sans-Serif Typefaces** Typefaces that lack the hats and feet of serif typefaces (*sans* means "without" in French). [14]

**Saturation** A color's brightness or intensity. [14]

**Secondary Evidence** Interpretations of primary evidence through scholarly articles, newspaper analyses, and op-ed columns. [7b]

**Secondary Sources** Sources that discuss, analyze, interpret, or comment on primary sources. [12a]

**Serif Typefaces** Typefaces with little "hats" and "feet" at the top and bottom of the letters, called "serifs." [14]

**Size** A design element frequently used to create contrast and visual hierarchy. [14]

**Social Layer** The cultural meanings of the images in an image. [4a]

**Stasis Theory** A strategy for helping to clarify which questions are most important to an issue. [7b]

**Transfer of Knowledge** The ability to take understanding, knowledge, skills, or concepts from one field of knowledge and apply it in a different situation. [0]

**Typeface** Often referred to as fonts, typeface refers to different letter designs. The two basic kinds of typeface are serif typefaces (which include guiding lines at the tops and bottoms of letters, used for body text) and sans-serif typefaces (those without guiding lines at the tops and bottoms of letters, used for headings and on the Web). [14]

**Value** A color's relative lightness or darkness. [14]

**Verbal Modality** A communication modality involving words spoken, sung, handwritten, or typed. [2d]

**Visual Hierarchy of Information** How clearly a visual composition portrays the relative importance of different pieces of information. [14]

**Visual Modality** A communication modality involving still and moving images, color, written text, gestures, or facial expressions. [2d]

# Bibliography

Akhondi, Masoumeh, Faramarz Aziz Ma-layeri, and Arshad Abd Samad. "How to Teach Expository Text Structure to Facilitate Reading Comprehension." *The Reading Teacher*, vol. 64, no. 5, Feb. 2011, pp. 368–72.

Alexander, Kathryn. "Writing Up/Writing Down: Literate Practices in a Mental Health Boarding Home." *Literacy & Numeracy Studies,* vol. 10, no. 1-2, 2000, pp. 23–38.

Almowassi, Ali. *An Illustrated Book of Bad Arguments*. The Experiment, 2014.

*American Diabetes Association*. "Healthy Weight Loss." www.diabetes.org.

Aristotle. *On Rhetoric*. Translated by George A. Kennedy, Oxford University Press, 1991.

Barnett, Jenna. "An Open Letter to Recent College Grads Who Are Already Paying Their Own Phone Bills." *McSweeney's*, 1 Oct. 2015, www.mcsweeneys.net /articles/an-open-letter-to-recent-college -grads-who-are-already-paying-their -own-phone-bills. Accessed 20 Jul. 2016.

Bawarshi, Anis and Mary Jo Reiff. *Genre: An Introduction to History, Theory, Research, and Pedagogy*. Parlor Press, 2010. *The WAC Clearinghouse*. wac.colostate.edu/books /bawarshi_reiff/. Accessed 6 Sep. 2016.

Biddle, Pippa. "The Problem with Little White Girls (and Boys): Why I Stopped Being a Voluntourist." pippabiddle.com /2014/02/18/the-problem-with-little -white-girls-and-boys/. Accessed 18 Feb. 2014.

Bogost, Ian. *Persuasive Games*. MIT Press, 2007.

Burke, Kenneth. *Rhetoric of Motives*. California ed., University of California P, 1969.

——. *Philosophy of Literary Form*. California ed., University of California P, 1974.

Burneko, Albert. "Rainbow-Cake Recipe Inspires Comment Apocalypse." *Deadspin*, 18 Jun. 2014, theconcourse.deadspin.com /rainbow-cake-recipe-inspires-comment -apocalypse-1592575661. Accessed 4 Aug. 2014.

"If Women's Roles in Ads Were Played by Men." *YouTube*, uploaded by Buzzfeed Video, 15 Mar. 2014, www.youtube.com /watch?v=2SrpARP_M0o.

Cameron, Julia. *The Artist's Way*. 10th anniversary edition, Jeremy P. Tarcher /Putnam, 2002.

Cassidy, John. "A Welcome Setback for Donald Trump." *New Yorker*, 30 Jan. 2017, www.newyorker.com/news/john-cassidy /a-welcome-setback-for-donald-trump.

Center for Media and Social Impact. "Code of Best Practices in Fair Use for Online Video." 3 Apr. 2016, cmsimpact.org /code/code-best-practices-fair-use -online-video/.

Chaney, Nancy. "That Third Street Bridge." Letter. *Moscow-Pullman Daily News*, 1 Oct. 2016.

"Crying Jordan Afghan Girl." *Know Your Meme*, knowyourmeme.com/photos /1111631-crying-michael-jordan.

"Dear Microsoft." *Slack*, 2 Nov. 2016, slackhq.com/dear-microsoft -8d20965d2849.

Dinehart, Laura. "Teaching Handwriting in Early Childhood: Brain Science Shows Why We Should Rescue this Fading Skill." *District Administration*, vol. 51, no. 6, Jun. 2015, p. 85, www.questia .com/read/1G1-418980272/teaching -handwriting-in-early-childhood-brain -science.

Drummond, Christopher and Jessica Bearman. "Their View: Why Health Insurance Isn't a Rolls Royce or a Beater." *Moscow-Pullman Daily News*, 29 Mar. 2017, dnews.com/opinion/their-view -why-health-insurance-isn-t-a-rolls -royce/article_16089c30-6884-5d32 -bf40-ebba20214937.html.

Dyer, Gillian. *Advertising as Communication*. Routledge, 1982.

Editorial Board. "Readers, Not Censors, Keep Fake News from Spreading." *The St. Louis Post-Dispatch*, 6 Dec. 2017, www.questia.com/read/1P2-40292343 /editorial-readers-not-censors-keep-fake -news-from.

Edwards, Dave. "South Carolina mass murder-suicide leaves 6 dead after 'edgy' gunman calls 911," 30 Oct. 2013, www .rawstory.com/2013/10/south-carolina -mass-murder-suicide-leaves-6-dead -after-edgy-gunman-calls-911/.

Elbow, Peter. *Writing with Power*. Oxford University Press, 1981.

"E-Learning: India's Education System Needs to Get Online." Editorial. *Hindustan Times*, 6 Mar. 2017, www.hindustantimes .com/editorials/e-learning-india-s -education-system-needs-to-get-online /story-GsitwEdCHPZMmBOSjUt49K .html.

Elliott, Chad. "Chad Elliott Trick Shot Quarterback – Better than Alex Tanney

and Johnny Mac." *YouTube*, www.youtube .com/watch?v=QjeIboNgfnk 20 Jun 2012. Accessed 14 Oct. 2013.

Eshna. "The Six Sigma Problem Statement." *simpl;learn*, www.simplilearn.com /six-sigma-problem-statement-article.

Fleming, David. "Rhetoric as a Course of Study." *College English*, vol. 61, no. 2, Nov 1998, pp. 169–91.

Florez, Julie. "Student Loan Debt: A Problem for All." *Telegraph-Herald*, 4 Aug. 2016, www.questia.com/article /1P2-39902440/student-loan-debt -a-problem-for-all.

French, David. "Trump's Executive Order on Refugees – Separating Fact from Hysteria." *National Review*, 28 Jan. 2017, www.nationalreview.com/article/444370 /donald-trump-refugee-executive-order -no-muslim-ban-separating-fact-hysteria.

Fulkerson, Richard. *Teaching the Argument in Writing*. NCTE, 1996.

George, Diana. "From Analysis to Design: Visual Commuication in the Teaching of Writing." *College Composition and Communication*, vol. 54, no. 1 (Sep. 2002), pp 11–39. *JSTOR*.

"Hal Varian on How the Web Challenges Managers." *Mckinsey*, Jan. 2009, www .mckinsey.com/industries/high-tech /our-insights/hal-varian-on-how-the -web-challenges-managers. Accessed 29 Jan. 2016.

Halvorson, Kristina and Melissa Rach. *Content Strategy for the Web*. 2nd ed., New Riders, 2012.

Hudson, Laura. "Why You Should Think Twice Before Shaming Anyone on Social Media." *Wired*, 24 Jul. 2013, www.wired .com/2013/07/ap_argshaming/.

"The Importance of Practicing with Your Gun." *The Well Armed Woman*, thewellarmedwoman.com/the -importance-of-practicing-with-your-gun.

Jensen, Andrew. "An Arms Race We Can't Win." *New York Times*, 26 Jul. 2012, www.nytimes.com/2012/07/26/opinion/an-arms-race-we-cant-win.html.

Johnson, Eric Michael. "Probing the Passions of Science: Carl Zimmer Delves Beneath the Surface of Science Writing." *Scientific American*, 20 Dec. 2011, blogs.scientificamerican.com/primate-diaries/carl-zimmer-part-two/.

Jones, Colleen. *Clout: The Art and Science of Influential Web Content*. New Riders, 2011.

Kress, Gunther, and Theo von Leeuwen. *Reading Images*. Psychology Press, 1996.

Lamott, Anne. *Bird by Bird: Some Instructions on Writing and Life*. Anchor, 1995.

Lampo, David. "Why Gay Rights Are Civil Rights – and Simply Right." *The American Conservative*, 8 Jul. 2013, www.theamericanconservative.com/articles/why-gay-rights-are-civil-rights-and-simply-right/.

Licino, Hal. "5 Tips for Producing Product Review Videos That Wow." *Tubular Insights*, 5 Apr. 2011, www.reelseo.com/five-tips-for-creating-product-review-videos-that-wow/.

Macdonald, James. "How Should We Deal with Plastic Bags?" *JDaily*, 28 Feb. 2017, daily.jstor.org/how-should-we-deal-with-plastic-bags/.

Magid, Joe. "View of Civil Rights Troubling." Letter to George Parry. *Philadelphia Inquirer*, 8 Feb. 2017, www.philly.com/philly/opinion/20170208_Letters__Writer_revealed_his_bias_in_calling_civil_rights_laws__social_engineering_.html.

Maslow, Abraham. *The Psychology of Science: A Reconnaissance*. Gateway Editions, 1969.

Millenson, Elliot. "College Rankings Should Account for Binge Drinking." *The Examiner*, 3 Apr. 2015. *Questia*. Accessed 16 May 2017.

Morrongiello, Gab. "White House Supports Making Women Register for the Draft." *The Examiner*, 1 Dec. 2016. *Questia*.

Nelson, Douglas, Valerie Reed, and John Walling. "Pictorial Superiority Effect." *Journal of Experimental Psychology: Human Learning and Memory*, vol. 2, no. 5, 1976, pp. 523–28.

Nietzsche, Friedrich. "On Truth and Lying in an Extramoral Sense." *Friedrich Nietzsche on Rhetoric and Language*. Edited and translated by Sander L. Gilman, Carole Blair, and David J. Parent. New York; Oxford: Oxford UP, 1989, pp. 246–57.

Nyhan, Brendan. "Bill Cosby's Sudden Fall, Explained Sociologically." *The New York Times*, 20 Nov. 2014, www.nytimes.com/2014/11/21/upshot/bill-cosbys-sudden-fall-explained-sociologically.html.

Parry, George. "With Gorsuch, Don't Judge a Book by Its Cover." *Philadelphia Inquirer*, 5 Feb. 2017, www.philly.com/philly/opinion/20170205_Commentary__With_Gorsuch__don_t_judge_the_book_by_its_cover.html.

Pauwels, Luc. "A Multimodal Framework for Analyzing Websites as Cultural Expressions." *Journal of Computer-Mediated Communication*, vol. 17, 2012, pp. 247–65. doi:10.1111/j.1083-6101.2012.01572.x.

Perelman, Chaïm and L. Olbrechts-Tyteca. *The New Rhetoric: A Treatise on Argumentation*. Trans. John Wilkinson and Purcesll Weaver. Notre Dame UP, 1991.

Queen, Rev. Tyrone. "God's Definition of Marriage." *The Washington Times*, 25 Jul. 2004, www.questia.com/read/1G1-119750374/god-s-definition-of-marriage.

Reporters without Borders. "Censorship Tells the Wrong Story, Obama-Clinton." *Ogilvy*, 26 Jun 2011, adsoftheworld.com

/media/print/reporters_without_borders _censorship_tells_the_wrong_story _obama_clinton.

Schiappa, Edward. *Defining Reality: Definitions and the Politics of Meaning*. Southern Illinois UP, 2003.

Sharkey, Betsy. "*Frozen*, an Icy Blast of Fun from the First Snowflake." *Los Angeles Times*, 21 Nov. 2013, latimes.com /entertainment/movies/moviesnow /la-et-mn-frozen-20131122,0,2982612 .story.

Sheridan, David M. "Digital Detroit and the Frail Particulars of Everyday Life." *Journal of Literacy and Technology* 2.1 (2002), 12 Jan. 2005, www.literacyandtechnology .org/v2nl/sheridan.html.

Sheridan, David M., et al. *The Available Means of Persuasion*. Parlor Press, 2012.

Solnit, Rebecca. "Men Explain Things to Me." *Guernica,* 20 Aug 2012. www.guernicamag .com/rebecca-solnit-men-explain-things -to-me/. Accessed 28 Jun 2017.

Sommers, Nancy. "Revision Strategies of Student Writers and Experienced Adult Writers." *College Composition and Communication*, vol. 31, no. 4, 1980, pp. 378–88.

Sontag, Susan. *On Photography*. Picador-Farrar, Straus, and Giroux, 1977.

Stockman, Steve. *How to Shoot Video That Doesn't Suck: Advice to Make Any Amateur Look Like a Pro*. Workman Publishing Company, 2011.

Tannen, Deborah. *The Argument Culture*. Ballantine-Random House, 1998.

Tanney, Alex. "Alex Tanney Trick Shot Quarterback – Better than Johnny Mac." *YouTube*, 20 Feb. 2011, www.youtube .com/watch?v=SxDJb03a0yo.

Tryon, Tom. "On-Campus 'Carry' Bill." *Sarasota Herald Tribune*, 24 Jan. 2014, www .questia.com/newspaper/1P2-36792745 /on-campus-carry-bill.

Tufte, Edward. *Envisioning Information*. Graphics Press, 1990.

United States Department of Agriculture. "Protect Your Baby and Yourself from Listeriosis." www.fsis.usda.gov/wps /wcm/connect/75e22bf1-8763-4dc8 -a6b7-d16b4151ff90/Protect-Your -Baby-and-Yourself-from-Listeriosis.pdf.

"Waiting for You to Notice." *Shared Hope International*, 3 Nov. 2015, creativity-online .com/work/shared-hope-international -waiting-for-you-to-notice/44092.

Walley, Jonathan. "Lessons of Documentary: Reality, Representation, and Cinematic Expressivity." *American Society for Aesthetics*, 2011, aesthetics-online.org/?page =WalleyDocumentary.

Wayne, Teddy. "An Open Letter to Writers of Open Letters." *The Morning News*, May 2011, www.themorningnews.org/article /an-open-letter-to-writers-of-open -letters.

WebWise Team. "What Are Cookies?" *BBC WebWise*, 10 Oct. 2012, www.bbc.co.uk /webwise/guides/about-cookies.

Williams, Robin. *The Non-Designer's Design Book*. 4th ed., Peachpit Press, 2014.

WWF. "Before It's Too Late (Lungs)." *TBWA*, 1 Apr. 2009, adsoftheworld.com /media/print/wwf_lungs.

Yake, Josh. "Mushroom Discrimination." Letter. *Moscow-Pullman Daily News*, 5 Oct. 2016.

# Credits

### Chapter 1
Page 12, Elliott Millenson, "College Rankings Should Account for Binge Drinking," *Questia,* a part of Gale, Cengage Learning. www.questia.com. Publication information: Article title: College Rankings Should Account for Binge Drinking. Contributors: Contributor, Op-Ed-Author. Newspaper title: *Examiner* (Washington, DC), Publication date: April 3, 2015. Page number: Not available. Reprinted with permission from *The Washington Examiner.*

Page 15, American Diabetes Assoc., "Healthy Weight Loss," found at www.diabetes.org /food-and-fitness/weight-loss/healthy-weight-loss.html.

### Chapter 2
Page 31–32, Letter: Josh, Yake, "Mushroom Discrimination," *Moscow-Pullman (ID) Daily News*, Oct. 5, 2016.

Page 32–33, Letter: Nancy Chaney, "That Third Street Bridge," *Moscow-Pullman (ID) Daily News*, Oct. 1, 2016.

Page 33–34, Gab Morrongiello, "White House Supports Making Women Register for the Draft," Questia, a part of Gale, Cengage Learning. www.questia.com. Publication information: Article title: White House Supports Making Women Register for the Draft. Contributors: Gab Morrongiello-Author. Newspaper title: *Examiner* (Washington, DC), Publication date: December 1, 2016. Page number: Not available. © Clarity Media Group, Inc. Provided by ProQuest LLC. All Rights Reserved.

Page 43, Anis Bawarshi and Mary Jo Reiff, *Genre: An Introduction to History, Theory, Research, and Pedagogy*, adapted from http://wac.colostate.edu/books/bawarshi_reiff /chapter11.pdf.

### Chapter 3
Page 54, Republished with permission of John Wiley and Sons from Akhondi, Masoumeh, Faramarz Aziz Malayeri, and Arshad Abd Samad, "How to Teach Expository Text Structure to Facilitate Reading Comprehension," *The Reading Teacher* 64:5 (Feb 2011), 368–372; permission conveyed through Copyright Clearance Center, Inc.

Page 55–57, Laura Hudson, "Why You Should Think Twice Before Shaming Anyone on Social Media," Laura Hudson/Wired; © Conde Nast.

### Chapter 4
Page 87–88, Adapted from Gillian Dyer's *Advertising as Communication*. Routledge, 1982.

Page 96, Figure 4.19, Based on "A Taxonomy of Trump Tweets," by George Lakoff. First aired January 13, 2017, on WNYC's On the Media. Reprinted with permission from Greg Gibilisco.

## Chapter 6
Page 17–19, Pippa Biddle, "The Problem with Little White Girls (and Boys): Why I Stopped Being a Voluntourist," found at http://pippabiddle.com/2014/02/18/the-problem-with -little-white-girls-and-boys/.

## Chapter 7
Page 164–165, "You Better Teach Your Boys to Cry: A Response to Chitra Ramaswamy," by Martha Mendez, student at University of Idaho. Reprinted with permission from the author.

Page 166–167, Editorial: "Readers, Not Censors, Keep Fake News from Spreading," *The St. Louis Post-Dispatch (MO)*. Found at www.questia.com/read/1P2-40292343/editorial -readers-not-censors-keep-fake-news-from.

Page 169–171, Commentary: "With Gorsuch, Don't Judge the Book by Its Cover," *Philadelphia Inquirer*, February 5, 2017, www.philly.com/philly/opinion/20170205_Commentary__ With_Gorsuch__don_t_judge_the_book_by_its_cover.html. Reprinted with the permission of the author.

Page 171, Letter: "View of Civil Rights Troubling," by Joe Magid, Wynewood, *Philadelphia Inquirer*, February 8, 2017, www.philly.com/philly/opinion/20170208_Letters__Writer_ revealed_his_bias_in_calling_civil_rights_laws__social_engineering_.html. Reprinted with the permission of the author.

Page 173–175, "Dear Microsoft" letter, found at https://slackhq.com/dear-microsoft -8d20965d2849#.gqevhlp7u.

Page 175–176, Jenna Barnett, "An Open Letter to Recent College Grads Who Are Already Paying Their Own Phone Bills," found at www.mcsweeneys.net/articles/an-open-letter -to-recent-college-grads-who-are-already-paying-their-own-phone-bills.

## Chapter 8
Page 190–191, "Trump's Executive Order on Refugees – Separating Fact from Hysteria," Copyright 2017 *National Review*. Used with Permission.

Page 192–195, "A Welcome Setback for Donald Trump," John Cassidy, *The New Yorker*; © Conde Nast.

Page 199–201, From *HowStuffWorks.com*, June 9, 2014 © 2014 *HowStuffWorks.com*. All rights reserved. Used by permission and protected by the Copyright Laws of the United States. The printing, copying, redistribution, or retransmission of this Content without express written permission is prohibited.

## Chapter 9
Page 211–213, "God's Definition of Marriage," Rev. Tyrone Queen, *The Washington Times* (Washington, DC), July 24, 2004, p. B05. Reprinted with permission of the author.

Page 213–216, "Why Gay Rights Are Civil Rights – and Simply Right", *The American Conservative*, www.theamericanconservative.com/articles/why-gay-rights-are-civil-rights -and-simply-right. Reprinted with permission.

Page 217–219, "Higher Education Needs Soul," Bill Maxwell, *Pittsburgh Post-Gazette*, March 2, 2013. Reprinted with permission of the author.

# Index

*AbeBooks*, 233
*About.com*, 187, 188
Abstract terms, 207
Academic conference
   proposals, 244
Academic essays
   anatomy of, 303–314
   annotated example,
      312–314
   arguments in, 305
   conclusions, 311
   introductions, 305–308
   paragraphing with PIE,
      308–310
   titles, 304–305
Academic summary, 59
Accomplishments,
   evaluation of, 236–238
*Acoustica*, 375
Action, 85, 243–244
Actors, 86–88
Addressed audiences, 18–19
Addressing written
   correspondence to
   legislators, 316
Advertisements
   introduction to, 67–68
   persuasion in, 243
   print, 96–98
Aesthetic criteria, 226
*Amazon*, 233, 235
American Diabetes
   Association, 15–16
American Psychological
   Association (APA), 276.
   *See also* APA style
*Angie's List*, 233
Anthropological approach,
   201
Anti-trafficking video,
   109–111

APA style
   for books and book
      chapters, 284–285
   other source types, 285
   overview of, 282
   for periodicals, 284
   in-text citation, 282–284
Apps, multimodal analysis
   of, 118–119
"Argument culture," 147
Arguments, 146–183
   in academic essays, 305
   of classification, 216–219
   of definition, 208–219
   of definition, formulation
      of, 219–221
   of genus, 210–216
   identifying your position,
      155–159
   as inquiry, 147–149
   introduction to, 146–147
   multimodal, 183–185
   as response, 149–161
   statis theory, 151–154
   structuring, 159–161
   visual, 178–182
   written, 161–178
Aristotle, 9, 14, 21
Articles, 203
*The Artist's Way* (Cameron),
   294
Associated Press, 70
Attention economy, 4
*Audacity*, 375
Audience, 18–22
   addressed audiences, 18–19
   appealing to emotions, 21
   appealing to through
      character, 9–13
   appealing to through
      strength of message, 14

defining, 131–133
   for explanations, 195–196
   format, influence on,
      20–21
   intended, 156, 158
   invoked audiences, 19
   opinion of communicator,
      20
   for public awareness
      campaigns, 141–142
   purpose, 19–20
   stakes for, 20
   for websites, 379
   of written compositions,
      293
Auditory modality
   definition of, 100
   of video, 103, 105–106,
      111

Bachmann, Michelle, 92–93
Back light, 367, 368
Background music, 370, 376
Bandanas, 89–90
Barnett, Jenna, 175–176
Basic rhetorical situation
   audience, 18–22
   communicators, 8–13
   message, 14–18
Bearman, Jessica, 318–319
Biddle, Pippa, 137–139
Binge drinking, 12–13
*Bird by Bird* (Lamott), 297
Blogs, 113–114, 316
Body paragraphs, 304
Bono, 10
Book metaphor, 118–119
Books
   APA style for, 284–285
   MLA style for, 280
Booth, Wayne, 2

Brainstorming, 360–361
B-roll footage, 363
Burke, Kenneth, 9, 260–261
*Burwell v. Hobby Lobby*, 210
*Business Insider*, 114
*Buzzfeed*, 203

Cameron, Julia, 294
Campaign brief, 141–143
Campaign kit, 143–144
Campaign materials,
    144–145
Card stacks, 203
Cardioid, 367
Cassidy, John, 192–195
Center for Media and Social
    Impact (CMSI), 371
Character, appealing to
    audience through, 9–13
Circles, 83
Circulation, 44–46
Circulation of images, 90–91
Circumstances of
    communication. *See*
    Context
Citation software, 266
Citation styles, 276, 304
    APA style, 282–285
    informal, 286–288
    MLA style, 277–281
*Citizens United v. Federal
    Election Commission*, 210
Civic participation
    annotated opinion
        column, 318–319
    fact sheets, 319–320
    letters to legislators,
        315–316
    opinion pieces, 316–319
Claim of definition, 159
Claim of fact, 159
Claim of procedure, 159
Claim of quality, 159
Claims, 159
    in proposals, 244,
        249–250
Clarins ad, 83, 85
Classification, arguments of,
    216–219
Click-bait, 91

Clip Converter, 363
*Clout* (Jones), 377
"Code of Best Practices in
    Fair Use for Online
    Video," 371
Coherence, 309–310
Cohesiveness, 309–310
College ranking, 12–13
"College Rankings Should
    Account for Binge
    Drinking" (Millenson),
    12–13
Color, 79–81, 107
Color scheme, 117
Communication
    circulation, 44–46
    genre, 42–44
    means of, 26, 38–46,
        157, 158
    means of for written
        compositions, 293
    medium, 41–42
    modality, 39–40
Communicators
    audience opinion, 20
    ethos, building, 9–13
    examples of, 8–9
Communities
    definitions within,
        206–208
    everyday problems, 128
Comparative ad analysis,
    98–99
Composition, of video, 106
Conclusions, in academic
    essays, 304, 311
Concrete terms, 207
Consumer products,
    evaluation of, 233–234
*Consumer Reports*, 233
Consumer reviews, 233,
    234–236
*Content Strategy for the Web*
    (Halvorson/Rach), 378
Context, 26, 27–28
Contrast, 79
"Conversational parlor,"
    260–261
Copyright, 371–372
Counterarguments, 157–158

Creative Commons license,
    376
Creativity, 292
Creators, of stand-alone
    images, 70–71
Credibility, 142–143
*CrimeReports*, 115
Criteria
    categories of, 226
    definition of, 225
    establishing and ranking,
        225–229
    identification, example of,
        227–229
Critical thinking, 292
"Crying Jordan Afghan Girl"
    meme, 14
Cultural phenomena
    explanations of, 187–188
    organization schemes,
        201–202
Current events
    explanations of, 187
    organization schemes,
        197–198

"Dancing to Help an Aging
    Brain" (Jorgensen), 275
*Deadspin*, 146
"Definitional rupture," 208
Definitions
    annotated argument,
        219–222
    arguments of, 208–219
    assignment, 222
    claim of, 159
    formulation of arguments,
        219–221
    questions of, 152
    within communities,
        206–208
Degree of focus, 77
*Dictionary.com*, 196
Digital Object Identifier
    (DOI), 282, 283
Dinehard, Laura, 248–249
"Dirty Lie" campaign,
    140–141
Distance from subject,
    78–79

Distribution of images, 90–91
Domain names, 380
Dominant shapes,
    significance of, 83
"Don't Believe the Dirty Lie"
    campaign, 140–141
"Down draft," 297
Draft, women registering
    for, 33–34
Drafting written
    composition, 296–297
Drummond, Christopher,
    318–319
Dynamic websites, 113

"Echoes of 1776 in 2011:
    A Rhetorical Analysis
    of Nicholas Kristof's
    'Watching Protestors
    Risk It All'", 312–314
Economic criteria, 226
Editorial judgment, 92
Editorials, 166–167, 244
Efficiency criteria, 226
Einstein, Albert, 122
Elbow, Peter, 292, 294
E-learning, 269–270
Emotions, appealing to, 21
Emphasis, 74–75
Encomium, 237
Endnote, 266
Energy of colors, 80
Essay-writing services,
    131–132
Ethnographic approach, 201
Ethos
    building, 9–13
    defining, 133
    from external sources, 10
    from the message itself,
        10–11
Evaluation
    of consumer products,
        233–234
    criteria, establishing and
        ranking, 225–229
    everyday, 223–225
    evidence in, 230–232
    multimodal consumer
        reviews, 234–236

personal accomplishments,
    236–238
of policies, 238–241
public awareness
    campaigns, 143
Event-based problems,
    123–126, 244
Evernote, 266
Everyday problems, 126–128,
    244
Evidence
    in evaluations, 230–232
    overview of, 160–161
    in proposals, 244,
        251–254
Exigence, 26, 28–34
Expanded rhetorical
    situation
    context, 27–28
    exigence, 26, 28–34
    introduction to, 26–27
    means of communication,
        38–46
    purpose, 34–38
Explanation (in PIE), 309
Explanations
    annotated example,
        199–202
    audience, 195–196
    of cultural phenomena,
        187–188
    of current events, 187
    elements of, 195–203
    organization of, 197–203
    overview of, 186–189
    purpose for, 196–197
    as rhetorical activity,
        189–195
Eye contact, 365

Facebook, 92, 147
Fact sheets, 319–320
Facts
    claim of, 159
    questions of, 152
Fair use, 371–372
Fairy, Shepard, 91
Fake news, 11
"Fear, Sorrow, and Finally,
    Relief: A Rhetorical

Analysis of 'Waiting
    for You to Notice'
    by Shared Hope
    International,'" 109–111
Fill light, 367, 368
FiveThirtyEight, 187
Fleming, David, 2, 4
Florez, Julie, 231–232
Focus
    degree of, 77
    in thesis statements, 306
Footage, video, 363–369
Forecasting, 307
Formal layers
    color, 79–81
    degree of focus, 77
    distance from subject,
        78–79
    emphasis, 74–75
    framing, 75–76
    lighting and contrast, 79
    point of view, 76–77
Format, 20–21, 47
Found footage, 363
Framing, in video, 106–107
Freeplay Music, 376
Freewriting, 294
French, David, 190–191
"Frozen an Ice Blast of
    Fun from the First
    Snowflake" (Sharkey),
    227–229
Fulkerson, Richard, 157

GarageBand, 374
Genre, 42–44
Genus, arguments of,
    210–216
Ghostwriting services/
    websites, 131–132
Global-level revisions,
    297–298
GoDaddy, 380
"God's Definition of
    Marriage" (Queen),
    211–213
Goodreads, 233
Google Maps, 115
Google searches, 264, 265
Grant proposals, 244

Greenpeace, 140–141
Gun control, 219–222,
    239–241

Habit of writing, 294
Halvorson, Kristina, 378
Handwriting, teaching,
    248–249
Haptic modality, 100, 112
Hashtags, 130
Health insurance, 318–319
"Healthy Weight Loss"
    (ADA), 15–16
High key tone, 79
"Higher Education Needs
    Soul" (Maxwell),
    217–219
Highly saturated images, 80
Holder, Eric H., Jr., 77
"Hook," 305
"How a Sexist T-shirt Harms
    Us All" (Ramaswamy),
    164–165, 301
"How Do They Get the Fat
    Out of Fat-Free Foods?"
    199–201
"How Should We Deal
    with Plastic Bags?"
    (MacDonald), 252–254
How To Shoot Video
    that Doesn't Suck
    (Stockman), 366
HowStuffWorks, 187, 188,
    198
Hudson, Laura, 55–57,
    63–65
Huffington Post, 114
Humanities disciplines, and
    MLA style, 277
Hyperlinks, 286

Ideas
    freewriting, 294
    generation of, 292–296
    mind mapping, 294–295
    purpose, audience, means
        of communication,
        considering, 293
    questioning, 295–296
Identification, 9

Ideologies, 85
An Illustrated Book of Bad
    Arguments, 160
Illustration (in PIE), 308
Illustrations
    images used as, 91–96
    technologies used to
        produce, 73
Image maps, 94–96
Images
    illustrations, 91–96
    placement, circulation,
        and distribution of,
        90–91
    on posters, 180–182
    print advertisements,
        96–98
    in texts, 91–99
IMDB, 233
IMovie, 369
"India's Education System
    Needs to Get Online,"
    269–270
Infographics, 203, 286–288
Informal citations, 286–288
Information (in PIE), 308
Instagram, 80, 376
Institute of Electrical and
    Electronics Engineers
    (IEEE), 276
Intended audience, 156,
    158
Internal consistency, 14
Interviews, 364–365, 374
In-text citation
    APA style, 282–284
    MLA style, 278
Introductions, in academic
    essays, 304, 305–308
Invention, 292–296
"Invisible Child: Dasani's
    Homeless Life," 93
Invoked audiences, 19
IPad Calendar app, 118–119

Jargon, 304
Jeans, styles of, 224
Jensen, Andrew, 10
Jones, Colleen, 377
Jorgensen, Geoff, 275

Kerouac, Jack, 89
Key light, 366–367, 368
Keyword searches, 263, 271
Keywords, 266
King, Martin Luther, Jr.,
    172–173
Kress, Gunther, 82
Kristof, Nicholas, 312–314
Kulik, Cassandra, 16–17

Lamott, Anne, 297
Lampo, David, 213–216
Lavalier, 367
Layout, 117
Leeuwen, Theo von, 82
Legalzoom, 286, 287
Legislative bills, 244
Legislators, letters to,
    315–316
"Letter from Birmingham
    Jail," 172–173
Letters
    to the editor, 167–171,
        317
    exigence, 31–32, 32–33t
    to legislators, 315–316
Lexis-Nexis, 264, 265
Life Cycle of the Malaria
    Parasite, 86
Lighting, 79
    in video, 107, 366–367,
        368
Links, 116–117
Listicles, 203
Local scale proposals, 245
Local-level revisions,
    297–298
Logos, 14
Low key tone, 79

MacDonald, James,
    252–254
Magid, Joe, 171
"Mansplaining," 196
Marriage, 211–216
Mash-ups, 372
Maxwell, Bill, 217–219
Maybelline, 70
McDonough, Denis, 79
McSweeney's, 175

Means of communication, 26, 38–46

Media, everyday problems and, 128

Medium, 41–42

*Medium*, 316

"Men Explain Things to Me" (Solnit), 196

*Mendeley*, 266

Message, 14–18, 142

Metaphors, 115–116, 118

Microphones, 367–368, 374, 375

Microsoft, 116, 173–175

Millenson, Elliott, 12–13

Mind mapping, 294–295

"Miranda Parks Visualized Her Way to a Better Body" (Kulik), 16–18

MLA style
for books, 280
humanities disciplines, 277
other source types, 281
overview of, 277
for periodicals, 280–281
in-text citation, 278
works-cited entries, 278–279

Modality, 39–40

Modern Language Association (MLA), 276. *See also* MLA style

Moral criteria, 226

Morrongiello, Gab, 33–34

Motivation, 155, 158

Movement, in video, 107

MovieMaker, 369

Multimodal arguments, 183–185

Multimodal composition, 3
overview of, 356–358
podcasts, 373–376
videos, creation of, 358–372
websites, 376–381

Multimodal consumer reviews, 234–236

Multimodal genres, 143–144

Multimodal rhetoric, analysis of, 100–119
annotated example, 109–111
of apps, 118–119
example of, 109–111
interactions, 101–102
introduction to, 100–101
video, 103–112
of websites, 112–118

Mushroom discrimination letter, 31, 32–33t

Music, in video, 105

Narrative, 85

Narrative control, 375

Narratives, rhetorical effect in images, 83–86

Nation, everyday problems and, 128

National scale proposals, 245

Navigation of websites, 115–116

Net neutrality, 173

*Netflix*, 233

*New York Post*, 76

*New York Times*, 10, 93, 187

*New Yorker*, 92, 188

Nietzsche, Friedrich, 262

Notecards for sources, 266

Obama, Barack
formal layers, examples of, 74–81
photographs, 70–71

Obama, Michelle, 76

Obama "Hope" campaign poster, 91

Objections, to argument position, 157, 158

Objectives, of public awareness campaigns, 142

Objects
rhetorical effects of, 89
social meanings of, 89–90

Olbrechts-Tyteca, L., 134

*On the Road* (Kerouac), 89

"On Truth and Lying in an Extra-Moral Sense" (Nietzsche), 262

"On-Campus 'Carry' Bill," 239–241

Online citation software, 266

Online comments, 177–178

Online learning research example, 262–265, 269–270

Online stores, 113

Op-Ed pieces, 66, 316–319

"An Open Letter to Recent College Grads Who Are Already Paying Their Own Bills" (Barnett), 175–176

Open letters, 172–176

Opinion pieces, 316–319

*The Oregonian*, 187

Organization schemes
for cultural phenomena, 201–202
for current events, 197–198
scientific or technical objects, concepts, or processes, 198–199

Orlean, Susan, 188

Outcomes, 157, 158

Overview effect, 78

Owners, of websites, 114–115

Panda, 86–87

Paragraphing, in academic essays, 308–310

Paraphrase, 272–276

Parry, George, 169–171

Pathos, 21

People, in video, 107

Perelman, Chaïm, 134

Periodical databases, 264

Periodicals
APA style for, 284
MLA style for, 280–281

*Persona*, 115

Personal accomplishments, evaluation of, 236–238

Persuasion. *See* Proposals
*Philadelphia Inquirer*,
    169–171
*Philosophy of Literary Form*
    (Burke), 260
Photographs
    altering, 72
    technologies used to
        produce, 71–72
Photoshop, 72
"Picture superiority effect,"
    68
PIE (point, illustration,
    explanation), 308–310
*Pinterest*, 130, 266
Placement of images, 90–91
Plagiarism, 266, 272–276
Plastic bags, 252–254
Podcasts, 203, 373–376
*Podomatic*, 376
Point (in PIE), 308
Point of view, 76–77
Policies
    evaluation of, 238–241
    example of, 239–241
Political communications, 66
Pollan, Michael, 173
Position, appropriate, 307
Posters, images in, 180–182
*Powells*, 233
Presence, 134–135
Primary evidence, 160
Primary sources, 267
Print advertisements, 96–98
Print texts, informal
    citations in, 286
Problem
    articulation of, 244
    potential problems,
        acknowledging, 244
Problem analysis statement,
    136–137
Problem solutions,
    demonstrating, 244,
    255
"The Problem with Little
    White Girls (and Boys):
    Why I Stopped Being a
    Voluntourist" (Biddle),
    137–139

Procedure, claim of, 159
Procedure, questions of,
    153–154
Process criteria, 226
Proposals
    action, 243–244
    annotated example,
        252–254
    claims, 249–250
    components of, 244–246
    description of problem/
        need, 246–249
    example of, 248–249
    potential problems,
        acknowledging, 254
    problem solution,
        demonstrating, 255
    scope of, 244–245
    support for, 251–254
Public awareness campaigns,
    140–141
    campaign brief, 141–143
    campaign kit, 143–144
    campaign materials,
        144–145
    posters, 180–182
Public responses to
    arguments
    comments to blogs and
        news stories, 177–178
    letters to the editor,
        167–171
    open letters, 172–176
Pulitzer Prizes, 187
Purpose, 26, 34
    for arguments, 156, 158
    determining, 36–37
    for explanations, 196–197
    types of, 35–36
    of written compositions,
        293

Quality
    claims of, 159
    questions of, 153
Queen, Tyrone, 211–213
Questioning, 295–296
Questions of definition,
    152
Questions of fact, 152

Questions of procedure,
    153–154
Questions of quality, 153
Quotations, 272–276

Rach, Melissa, 378
*Radiolab*, 373, 375
Ramaswamy, Chita,
    164–165, 301
*The Raw Story*, 93–94
Reaction papers, 161–167
"Readers, Not Censors,
    Keep Fake News from
    Spreading," 166–167
*Reading Images* (Kress/
    Leeuwen), 82
Reagan, Ronald, 10, 11
Reasons, 159–160
Rectangles, 83
Recursive process, 127
Recursive steps in research
    process, 262–271
*ReelSEO.com*, 235
Relevancy, 160
Remixing, 372
Research
    citing sources with different
        citation styles, 276–277
    to deepen understanding
        of problem, 129–131
    incorporating sources into
        compositions, 271–288
    initial keywords for
        searches, 263
    initial questions, 262–263
    initial sources,
        identifying, 264
    overview of, 260–262
    position, clarifying, 264,
        271
    recursive steps of, 261,
        262–271
    sources, incorporating
        into compositions,
        271–288
    sources, keeping track of,
        264–266
    summarizing,
        paraphrasing, and
        quoting, 272–276

Research (*Continued*)
   validity and rhetorical
      significance of sources,
      266–270
   "zero drafts," 271
Research scrapbook,
   129–130, 134
Response papers, 161–167
Reverse outlining, 298,
   301–302
Revisions
   global and local levels,
      297–298
   reverse outlining, 298,
      301–302
   of written compositions,
      297–302
Rhetoric, 2
Rhetorical action, 5–6
Rhetorical analysis
   annotated essay, 63–65
   importance of, 4–5
   skill development, 6
Rhetorical practice, 6
Rhetorical problem
      statement, 135
   describing problem, 136
   organizing statement,
      136–137
   problem analysis
      statement, 136–137
   providing evidence, 136
Rhetorical problems,
      formulation of, 122
   event-based problems,
      123–126
   everyday problems,
      126–128
   example of, 137–139
   public awareness
      campaigns, 140–141
   rhetorical problem
      statement, 135–140
   tasks for defining, 129–135
Rhetorical purpose, of
   websites, 114–115
Rhetorical self, 22–25
Rhetorical situation.
   *See* Basic rhetorical
      situation; Expanded
      rhetorical situation

Rhetorical training, 3–4
Rhetorical triangle, 9,
   26–27
*Roe v. Wade*, 210
Rogerian argument, 307
Rogers, Carl, 307
Rosie the Riveter, 89
*Rottentomatoes.com*, 233
RSS (Really Simple
   Syndication), 141
Rule of thirds, 364
Russia, 11

Safety criteria, 226
Sagan, Carl, 78
Same-sex marriage, 211–216
Schiappa, Edward, 208
School, everyday problems
   and, 127
"Science writing," 198
Scientific or technical
   objects, concepts, or
   processes
   annotated example,
      199–202
   explanations of, 187
   organization schemes,
      198–199
Scope of proposals, 244–245
Secondary evidence, 160
Secondary sources, 267–268
Sequencing, 360–361
Settings, social meanings of,
   89–90
Shakur, Tupac, 89
"Shaming as Bullying: A
   Rhetorical Analysis of
   Laura Hudson's "Why
   You Should Think Twice
   Before Shaming Anyone
   on Social Media,'"
   63–65
Shapes, 83, 84
Shared Hope International,
   104, 105, 107–108,
   109–111
Sharkey, Betsy, 227–229
*Shutterstock*, 94
*Slack.com*, 173–175
Smith, Lamar, 124
*Snapchat*, 376

Social layers, 73, 82
   actors, 86–88
   dominant shapes,
      significance of, 83
   narratives, rhetorical
      effect of, 83–86
   objects and settings, social
      meanings of, 89–90
Social media sites, 266, 377
Soft focus, 77
Software for website
   building, 380–381
Solnit, Rebecca, 196
Sommers, Nancy, 297
Sontag, Susan, 71
Sound effects in video, 370
Sound Recorder, 374
*SoundCloud*, 376
Sources
   citing with different
      citation styles, 276–277
   evaluation of, 270
   incorporating sources into
      compositions, 271–288
   indicating use of, 274–275
   keeping track of, 264–266
   in-text citation, 278
   validity and rhetorical
      significance of, 266–270
   works-cited entries,
      278–279
Specialized language, 304
Squares, 83
*Squarespace*, 377, 380
*St. Louis Post-Dispatch*,
   166–167
Stakeholders
   identifying, 131–133
   public awareness
      campaigns, 142
Stakes of an argument,
   305
"Stand Up 4 Public Schools"
   campaign, 144–145
Stand-alone images, 69
   creator, 70–71
   formal layers, 73–81
   social layers, 82–90
   social meanings of, 73
   technologies used to
      produce, 71–73

State scale proposals, 245
Static websites, 113
Statis theory, 151–154
"Steel Cut Oats a Non-Fancy Superfood" (Wellspring), 275–276
Stock narratives, 85
Stock photos, 94
Stockman, Steve, 366
Stop Online Piracy Act (SOPA), 124
Storyboarding, 360–362
"Student Loan Debt: A Problem for All" (Florez), 231–232
*StudioBinder*, 361
Subject
    in academic essays, 305
    distance from, 78–79
Sufficiency, 160
Summary, 272–276
Support
    in proposals, 244
    for proposals, 251–254

Tag cloud, 130
Tannen, Deborah, 147
Target audience, 114–115
Tasks for defining rhetorical problems
    describing problem, 133–135
    ethos, defining, 133
    identify stakeholders, 131–133
    research to deepen understanding, 129–131
"Teaching Handwriting in Early Childhood: Brain Science Shows Why We Should Rescue This Fading Skill" (Dinehard), 248–249
*Tech Crunch*, 114
Technology, used to produce images, 71–73
"Technology Is a Lens, Not a Prosthetic," 219–221
*10 Minute Mail*, 115

Textual modality
    public awareness campaigns, 143
    of video, 110
"Their View: Why Health Insurance isn't a Rolls Royce or a Beater" (Drummond/Bearman), 318–319
Thesis statement, 305–307
"Thinking draft," 271
Third Street bridge letter, 31–32, 32–33t
*This American Life*, 373
Timeliness, 155, 158
Titles, in academic essays, 303, 304–305
*TMZ*, 114
Topic sentence, 308
Transfer of knowledge, 6
Transfer of skills, 6–7
Transitions in video, 370
Treatments, 359–360
Triangles, 83
*TripAdvisor*, 233
Trump, Donald, 244
"Trump's Executive Order on Refugees - Separating Fact from Hysteria" (French), 190–191
"Truth effect," 71, 73
*Tumblr*, 266, 380
*Twitter*, 377
Typography, 117

University of Davis pepper-spraying cop, 91
*Upshot*, 187
*UrbanSpoon*, 233
U.S. Bank, 117

Verbal modality
    definition of, 100
    of video, 103–104
Verbs, and incorporating sources into compositions, 274
Video, multimodal analysis of
    auditory modality, 105–106, 111

interactions of modalities, 109
    textual modality, 110
    verbal modality, 103–104
    visual modality, 106–109, 111
Videos
    answering basic rhetorical questions, 358–359
    brainstorming, sequencing, and storyboarding, 360–362
    copyright and fair use, 371–372
    creation of, 358–372
    cut and splice, 370
    editing, 369–370
    editing software, 369
    explanations, 203
    footage for, 363–369
    found footage, 363
    interviews, 364–365
    planning, 358–363
    planning shots, 360–361
    reviews, 234
    rhetorical considerations, 363–364
    scheduling, 362–363
    script, 360
    technical considerations, 365–369
    transitions, sound effects, and background music, 370
    treatments, 359–360
*Vimeo*, 363
Visual arguments, 178–182
Visual evidence, 92
Visual literacy, 82
Visual modality
    definition of, 100
    public awareness campaigns, 143
    of video, 103, 106–109, 111
Visual rhetoric, analysis of
    images in texts, 91–99
    introduction to, 67–69

Visual rhetoric, analysis of
  (Continued)
  placement, circulation,
    and distribution of
    images, 90–91
  stand-alone images, 69–90
Visual semiotics, 82–83
Visualization, 16–17
Voluntourism, 137–139
Vox, 186, 187

"Waiting for You to Notice"
  video, 104, 105,
  107–108
Walley, Jonathan, 108
Washed-out images, 80
Washington Post, 187
"Watching Protestors Risk It
  All" (Kristof), 312–314
Web content, opinion-based,
  316–317
Websites
  basic types, 113–114
  consumer reviews, 233
  content, 115
  example of, 379–380
  ghostwriting, 132
  informal citations in,
    286
  interactions of modalities,
    117–118
  interface, 115–117
  multimodal analysis of,
    112–118
  owner, rhetorical purpose,
    and target audience,
    114–115
  rhetorical considerations,
    376–380

software for building,
  380–381
technical considerations,
  380–381
Weebly, 380
Weight loss, 15–18
"A Welcome Setback for
  Donald Trump"
  (Cassidy), 192–195
Wellspring, Janily, 275–276
"Why Gay Rights Are Civil
  Rights—and Simply
  Right" (Lampo),
  213–216
"Why You Should Think
  Twice Before Shaming
  Anyone on Social
  Media" (Hudson),
  55–57, 59
Wikipedia, 114, 124, 286, 287
Wikis, 114
"With Gorsuch, Don't Judge
  the Book by Its Cover"
  (Parry), 169–171
Wix, 380, 381
Women registering for draft,
  33–34
WordPress, 316, 380
Workplace, everyday
  problems and, 127
Works-cited entries,
  278–279
  books, 280
  MLA style, 278–279
  other source types, 281
  periodicals, 280–281
Worm's-eye view, 76
"Writer revealed his bias in
  calling civil rights laws

'social engineering,'"
  171
Writing process, messiness
  of, 291–302
Writing with Power (Elbow),
  292, 294
Written arguments
  responding to in public,
    167–178
  response/reaction papers,
    161–167
Written compositions,
  creation of, 290
  academic genres,
    302–314
  annotated first draft,
    298–301
  civic participation, writing
    for, 315–320
  drafting, 296–297
  idea generation, 292–296
  revising, 297–302
  writing process, messiness
    of, 291–302
WYSIWYG sites, 380–381

Yale Web Style Guide, 116
Yelp, 233
"You Better Teach Your Boys
  to Cry: A Response to
  Chitra Ramaswamy"
  (Mendez), 164–165,
  298–302
YouTube, 363, 376

"Zero drafts," 271
Zimmer, Carl, 198
Zoom function, 366
Zotero, 266

## ASSIGNMENTS BY MODALITY

### Textual

Uncover Your Rhetorical Self (Chapter 1)

Compare Compositions That Have Similar Purposes but Different Formats (Chapter 2)

Analyze an Op-Ed Piece (Chapter 3)

Analyze Political Communications (Chapter 3)

Write a Comparative Ad Analysis (Chapter 4)

Write a Rhetorical Analysis of a Controversial Website (Chapter 5)

Write a Comparative Analysis of Competing Websites (Chapter 5)

Evaluate the Rhetorical Effectiveness of a Website or App (Chapter 5)

Tune into Event-Based Problems (Chapter 6)

Write an Initial Position Statement on an Issue, Then Question It (Chapter 7)

Write an Academic Response Essay (Chapter 7)

Write a Letter to the Editor (Chapter 7)

Write an Open Letter (Chapter 7)

Write an Explanation of Something New to the Audience (Chapter 8)

Explain the Same Thing to a Different Audience (Chapter 8)

Write a Definition Argument (Chapter 9)

Evaluate a Policy or Decision (Chapter 10)

Write a Review of a Local Business, Event, or Attraction (Chapter 10)

Compose an Appreciation or Critique of a Public Figure (Chapter 10)

Write a Proposal to Address a Local Problem (Chapter 11)

Write a Research Proposal (Chapter 11)

Write a "Critical Conversation" Essay (Chapter 12)